LONDON CLUBLAND

Also by Seth Alexander Thévoz

Club Government: How the Early Victorian World was Ruled from London Clubs (2018)

Behind Closed Doors: The Secret Life of London Private Members' Clubs (2022)

LONDON CLUBLAND

A COMPANION FOR THE CURIOUS

SETH ALEXANDER THÉVOZ

ROBINSON

ROBINSON

First published in Great Britain in 2025 by Robinson

Copyright © Seth Alexander Thévoz, 2025

Cartoon illustrations by Simon Pearsall
Maps by David Andrassy

1 3 5 7 9 10 8 6 4 2

The moral right of the author has been asserted.

All rights reserved.
No part of this publication may be reproduced, stored in a
retrieval system, or transmitted, in any form, or by any means, without
the prior permission in writing of the publisher, nor be otherwise circulated
in any form of binding or cover other than that in which it is published
and without a similar condition including this condition being
imposed on the subsequent purchaser.

A CIP catalogue record for this book
is available from the British Library.

ISBN: 978-1-47214-998-5

Typeset in Garamond by M Rules
Printed and bound in Great Britain by Clays Ltd, Elcograf S.p.A.

Papers used by Robinson are from well-managed forests and
other responsible sources.

Robinson
An imprint of
Little, Brown Book Group
Carmelite House
50 Victoria Embankment
London EC4Y 0DZ

The authorised representative
in the EEA is
Hachette Ireland
8 Castlecourt Centre
Dublin 15, D15 XTP3, Ireland
(email: info@hbgi.ie)

An Hachette UK Company
www.hachette.co.uk

www.littlebrown.co.uk

*To John Timbs (1801–75),
ambler, antiquarian, Athenian, author, and pioneer of
Clubland exploration.*

CONTENTS

Introduction 1

Section 1: Club Directory

PART I: HISTORIC CLUBS

The Aristocratic Clubs 16
    Boodle's — Brooks's — Buck's — Turf Club — White's

The Pall Mall Clubs 25
    The Athenæum — Oxford and Cambridge Club
    Reform Club — Travellers Club

The Military Clubs 31
    Army and Navy Club — Cavalry and Guards Club
    East India Club — Naval and Military Club — Oriental Club
    Special Forces Club — Yeoman Warders Club

The Artistic and Cultural Clubs 42
    Arts Club — Chelsea Arts Club
    The Club for Acts and Actors — Garrick Club — London Sketch Club
    The Magic Circle — Royal Kennel Club — Savage
    Club — Savile Club — University Women's Club

The Dining Clubs 55
    Beefsteak Club — Pratt's

The 'Ex-Pat' Clubs 57
    Caledonian Club — Ognisko Polskie

The Political Clubs 60
    Carlton Club — House of Commons — House of Lords
    National Liberal Club — Winchester House Club

The City Clubs 69
    City of London Club — City University Club
    Guildhall Club — Little Ship Club

The Mass-Membership Clubs 73
    Civil Service Club — Farmers Club — Lansdowne Club
    Royal Air Force Club — Royal Automobile Club
Royal Over-Seas League — Union Jack Club — Victory Services Club

The Sports Clubs 82
    All England Lawn Tennis and Croquet Club — Ham Polo Club
    Hurlingham Club — Marylebone Cricket Club — Queen's Club
    Roehampton Club — Royal Ocean Racing Club
    Royal Thames Yacht Club

PART II: MODERN CLUBS

The Soho Drinking Clubs 94
    Academy Club — BBC Club — Gerry's — New Evaristo Club
    Phoenix Arts Club

The Mark Birley Clubs 99
    Annabel's — Bath and Racquets Club — George — Harry's Bar
    Mark's Club — Walbrook Club

The Robin Birley Clubs 105
    5 Hertford Street — Oswald's

The Soho House Empire 107
    40 Greek Street — 76 Dean Street — 180 House — Electric House
    High Road House — Little House, Balham — Little House, Mayfair

Ned's Club — Shoreditch House — Soho Mews House
White City House

The Home House Chain 117
    Home House — Home Grown

The Casino Clubs 119
    Les Ambassadeurs — Aspinall's

The Maslow's Clubs 122
    1 Warwick — Mortimer House

The Creative Clubs 124
    Academicians' Room — BAFTA — Brydges Place Club
    Century — The Conduit — The Dally — Frontline Club
    Groucho Club — Shoreditch Arts Club — Union Club
    Upstairs at the Department Store — Vout-O-Reenee's

The Gastronomic Clubs 135
    67 Pall Mall — Le Beaujolais Club — Ivy Club
    Mosimann's — Quo Vadis — Snail Club — UnHerd Club

The Hotel Clubs 143
    Admiralty Arch Club — Cambridge House — Dartmouth House
    The Other House — St James's Club — Sloane Club
    Ten Trinity Square — The Twenty Two

The Business Networking Clubs 151
    12 Hay Hill — Albert's — Arboretum — CEO Club London
    The Clubhouse — Eight — The Ministry
    Pasley Tyler — Pavilion Club

The Nightclub Clubs 159
    The House of KOKO — Maison Estelle
    The Roof Gardens — Tramp

The Family Clubs 163
    Cloud Twelve — Little Houses — NEXUS Club — Purple Dragon

The Club Bars 167
    Apollo's Muse — Keystone Crescent — Nikita

Country Clubhouses of London Clubs 170
    Babington House — Bretton Hall
    Emblehope and Burngrange Estate — Estelle Manor
    Soho Farmhouse — Stoneleigh Park — Woodcote Park

Section 2: Club Culture

Joining a Club: A Step-by-Step Guide 178
Visiting the Club 189
The Good, the Bad and the Ugly 193
Club Personality Types: The Members 198
Club Personality Types: The Staff 210
Subscriptions Explained 216
Clubland Founders 219
Clubhouse Types: A Bluffer's Guide 229
Listed Clubhouses 238
Freeholds 240
Club Mottos 242
Clubs with Sobriquets for their Members 244
Club Songs 245
Associations of Associations 250
Complaints 253
Feuds 256
Glossary of Clubland Slang 258
Etymological Roots 261
Something for the Weekend 262
Events of 'The Season' 263
Selected Betting Book Entries 268
Games Played Inside Clubhouses 275
Games Played Outside Clubhouses 285
Clubs That Stephen Fry Has Apologised To for Taking Drugs In 286

Taxes Past and Present That Have Been Paid by Clubs	287
Reciprocation	289
Club Anniversaries	293
The Committee	294
The Battle of the Sexes	296
The Clubs of UK Prime Ministers	298
Percentage of a Club's Members Listing Their Club Membership in an Entry in the Latest (2024) Edition of *Who's Who*	302
Some Animals Are More Equal Than Others	304
Where Clubs Are Found Today: The London Districts with Most Clubs	306
Dress Codes: A Short History and Guide	308
Mergers and Acquisitions	322
Clubs Within Clubs	324
Wartime Lodgings, Due to Bombings	326
Clubland Bombings by the IRA	328
Lost Property	329
Home Improvements	330
Club Crashers: Why They Fail	331
Global Club Statistics	339
World of Superlatives	340
City of Superlatives	341
Select Film Appearances of London Clubs	343
Conversations That Bore Me	347
Reading List	349
Resignations	352

Section 3: Food and Drink

Background	358
Beverages in Clubs	360
Club Cocktails	362
Wine	367
Ordering in Clubs	371

Beefsteak Surprise 372
Club Signature Dishes 373
Hunting Open Seasons 385
Toasting 386
Weighty Matters 388
Hangover Cures 389

Section 4: London Clubs, Past and Present

Maps of London Clubland 393
Index of Clubland Addresses, Past and Present 405

Rules of Engagement 421
Declarations 424
Acknowledgements 426
Index 430

Introduction

'The Club would prefer not to be included in the proposed publication', an internationally known, venerable old London club wrote to me, when I was preparing this book. So how did the tome you are holding come about?

It began with a simple challenge: 'It's all very well and good, Seth, telling us about the history of these old clubs. But what I *really* want to know is what these clubs are like today.' This was the most common response to my previous book, *Behind Closed Doors: The Secret Life of London Private Members' Clubs* (2022), a romp through three hundred years of Clubland history, which tried to explain how and why these singular institutions have evolved into the shape they occupy today. And so, dear reader, I have listened. (Or tried to.) Having spent the last couple of decades keeping a watchful eye on London's evolving Clubland, old and new, and maintaining extensive private notes on the topic, I felt it was high time that readers were offered a proper up-to-date guide to this world.

Why?

The first reason, quite simply, is to engage in a spot of myth busting. There is no shortage of confidently asserted 'facts' on Clubland, which are easily disproved by the simple collation of verifiable facts. And that can be fun. For instance, 'No one builds new clubs any more, except for 5 Hertford Street and Soho House', is something I hear a great deal of. As readers will find here, that is simply not true: London is in the middle of a club 'boom', with dozens of establishments having popped up in the last thirty years.

Secondly, however you so wish to engage with the clubs, I am all too mindful that there is no single, convenient entry point for navigating this unusual world. It is not the case that a prospective club member, having carefully weighed up all the factors, and compiled a spreadsheet of dozens of possible clubs, makes an objective and informed decision based upon hundreds of variables. Instead, you would typically join the first club you have heard of, or the first one where you have enough friends to get you in. This is akin to buying the first laptop you see in a showroom. And so regret often slowly sets in, and you spend the next few years shilly-shallying over the matter of resignation, and whether you might try your luck somewhere else that is more to your liking. A club is not just a building. People are often unaware that in joining a club, they are joining a tribe, with a certain culture and traditions, and that not all clubs are alike – they can feel *very* different from one another. This book hopes to shed some light on that, so that people considering membership have an idea of what they may be getting themselves into, and whether it suits them or not. But this book is equally suited to the curious, who have no intention of joining such odd gatherings, and would just like to know where all these clubs are, and might be surprised to learn that there are three of them within gargling distance of their office.

I was very much motivated by the number of people who complained to me that they didn't think there was any up-to-date guide. It was not always that way. During the Victorian heyday of London clubs, when they numbered some four hundred, there was a litany of published guidebooks; and every reference work worth its salt, from *Whittaker's Almanac* to *Dod's Parliamentary Companion*, included an appendix offering readers a comprehensive, up-to-date listing of clubs, including their contact details and short descriptions. During the years of Clubland decline in the twentieth century, as scores of these institutions closed down, the Clubland sections of those guidebooks died a death. Even until recently, the clubs were an essential part of 'The

Introduction

Knowledge' drilled into every taxi driver in London; but the last time I tried asking a cab driver for 'The Reform Club, please', I was met with a blank stare. This remains the case, even though clubs have been doing a roaring trade for much of the last forty years, meaning they are now more widespread than at any time since the 1920s, while their mystique has never been greater.

London Clubland: A Companion for the Curious aims to be a convenient, at-a-glance guide to the state of Clubland today. Yet I didn't think it fair to just cobble together a bland catalogue. What was needed was a fuller handbook to shine some light on club culture. Plenty of people *visit* a club. But one of the most common complaints, whether a club intends this to be the case or not, is that visitors can feel ill at ease on their first call. Clubs have their own traditions, mannerisms and slang; so that even people steeped in one club can be at a loss in another. This book hopes to empower the reader, showing you that you have nothing to fear.

It is a book of two halves. The first is a simple, club-by-club overview of each and every establishment today that has drawn my eye. There is no attempt at a value judgement, or anything so gauche as a 'review'. Reviews are for others to write. Each overview sets out to establish the particulars, and to give you an idea of each club's vital statistics, history, aims and culture, though there may be some more tongue-in-cheek observations along the way. It is possible – likely, even – that some clubs have so far escaped my attention. But after twenty years of roaming Clubland, and fifteen years of professionally analysing clubs worldwide as an academic historian, economist and consultant, I have done my best to try to give as complete a portrait as possible.

The second half of the book (encompassing Sections 2, 3 and 4) is entirely geared towards club culture; a literary potpourri, offering up some insight into the customs, rules, routines, traditions and even recipes that make up many of these clubs. There are no rituals – clubs are not (usually) Masonic establishments, although a few have been known to take private hires from all manner of groups, including Freemasons – but there are some mildly amusing songs. It also gives some sense of the full scale of these clubs, and how many have been scattered across the city that became (and still is) the global capital of clubs. Any Londoner walking through the city centre will doubtless pass scores of ex-clubhouses, possibly without ever realising it. You may choose to read the book from cover to cover, but it is also designed to be dipped into at a leisurely pace; a reference work to make you chuckle.

Outsiders look on clubs with some bafflement. Given the aloof image projected by so many of them, this is completely understandable. Yet they are an obvious reflection of the human condition. Not only have 'the 1 per cent' of many cities worldwide built emulations of the British clubs (some on an even more opulent scale); and not only have the British built a range of popular institutions spinning off from the model of a private members' club, including subscription libraries, cricket clubs, football clubs, working men's clubs and private gyms; but the appeal of clubs is more fundamental than that. Humans are inherently social creatures, and in cultures the world over, people who have never heard of Pall Mall have nonetheless built remarkably club-like establishments in all manner of cafés, bars and restaurants frequented by regular visitors who might pay a bit extra for some shared facility between them – whether it's the hire fee for the use of a back room for a weekly card game in New Orleans, or an extra levy for the ingredients of a particularly sumptuous communal meal in Pamplona. And so to 'club together' is innately human. The curious way the British have institutionalised this – taking what was originally a North American and Italian idea, and then placing it on the organised footing of a club – tells us much about how the British socialise. And they do love the bureaucracy of a committee.*

As the first sentence of this Introduction makes clear, the clubs themselves have not endorsed this project in any way. The book was researched and written entirely independently of them – albeit with wide-ranging support from scores of members, and building on extensive archival

---

* I say 'They'; I've actually been a UK citizen since 2012. But being Swiss-born, and a lover of all things Portuguese, I will never be entirely British, however frightfully English I may sound.

Introduction

research into Clubland history and practices. However, today's clubs were all contacted late in the day with an initial draft of their respective entries, inviting comment or correction; and well over half of them did respond (about two-thirds of the historic ones, and about one-fifth of the modern ones), the vast majority quite favourably. One initially wrote, 'we must respectfully request that you refrain from including any details about us in your publication' (before later backtracking). Most, however, were overwhelmingly constructive, offering factual corrections and additional insights. Particularly enjoyable were the meetings. When clubs asked for a face-to-face meeting with the club secretary about my text, I imagined I was being dragged up to the headmaster's study for a dressing down. Far from it. They generally chuckled amiably through the copy, murmuring, 'Fair comment.' Bless them.

The single question I get most often, the world over, is 'What is the best club?' I hate it. It's a tedious and unanswerable query. Type 'best London clubs' into Google, and you will be assaulted by a torrent of paid-for advertorials offering their pick of 'the top' 5, 8, 10, 12, 24, 37, or however many clubs the writer was themselves able to Google. Few, if any, give a particularly accurate or representative picture of Clubland as a whole.*

Why do I hate this question so much? Clubs come in all shapes and sizes, and all themes and memberships. There is simply no one-size-fits-all answer to this question; one person's idea of paradise is likely to send someone else running a million miles. In his old age, Andrew Cavendish, 11th Duke of Devonshire, looked back on his life, including a somewhat louche youth, and said, 'When I was young, I used to like casinos, fast women and God knows what. Now my idea of Heaven, apart from being at Chatsworth [House], is to sit in the hall of Brooks's, having tea.'† Some people reading this might quite like casinos, fast women (or, indeed, fast men), and God knows what. There is no shame

---

* I'm setting myself up for a fall here. The standard response from club members to my last book was, 'What you wrote about my club was a travesty and a disgrace. You were spot-on about all the others, though.'
† 'Obituary: The Duke of Devonshire', *Daily Telegraph*, 5 May 2004.

in that, and there are clubs which cater to that. Others might prefer a cup of tea. If this book serves one purpose, it is hoped to give readers a firmer idea about the lay of the land, and whether any of these places might suit their own needs and interests – and to paint as full a picture as possible, including the quieter places that do not always draw attention to themselves.

Far more interesting are the questions I cannot easily answer. Why do people even join clubs? Which prime ministers have belonged to which clubs? (A particularly never-ending topic, given how promiscuous the likes of Wellington, Churchill and Macmillan could be with their memberships.) Which clubs have been bombed over the years? I have had a stab at tackling all of these.

In writing this book, two sets of work have been particularly influential. The first is in the guides of John Timbs, Victorian journalist and antiquary – to whom this book is dedicated. He was a tireless chronicler of the mid-Victorian clubs. Between 1853 and 1872, several permutations of his *Clubs and Club Life of London* shone light on the full range of this side of the city, in many cases sharing them for the first time with a mass audience. The second was Charles Graves, whose 1963 guide *Leather Armchairs: The Chivas Regal Book of London Clubs* remains a perceptive guide to the clubs that were left by the early 1960s.

I did consider covering the whole of the United Kingdom – or even Europe – in this book, for there is a rich club tradition more broadly. But such a project would only have been possible as a multi-volume set, which would set many bookcases creaking, and that would have ended my ambition of an up-to-date, browsable, at-a-glance guide.

To those of you asking, 'Why hasn't [X Club] been included?', or 'How dare you include [Club Y]?', I would gently direct you to the 'Rules of Engagement' at the back of the book. There is a method to my madness – though I may have also made some genuine omissions, for which I can only apologise in advance.

I have not accepted any inducements or bribes to speak well or badly of any particular establishments. I could have made a mint if I had.

Introduction

This is not the result of any idealism or integrity on my part; I'm just a spectacularly poor businessman.

It often confuses people that my ragbag of interests seems to be in such a disparate series of fields: academic, teacher, researcher, historian, investigative journalist, traveller, and writer about clubs. (I was once being shown around an extremely secretive, elite Portuguese club when midway through my tour, my host suddenly asked, 'You're not a journalist, are you?', and went deathly pale when I answered, 'Yes.') Am I simply schizophrenic? I don't think so. Yet there is actually a golden thread running through it all: I like to empower people. I don't like sitting on knowledge and hoarding it for myself; I find that if I share what I learn, people often take me by surprise with their own very individual responses, and everybody has much more fun talking about the topic. It's almost like a club. So please do keep the letters and emails coming, and settle back, as I guide you through London Clubland today. At times, it can be a madhouse – but a thoroughly fascinating one.

London Clubland today: How we got here

Since I started publishing books on Clubland history, I've often found myself taken to one side by overseas visitors, who ask me to give something like 'a précis of the state of Clubland today'. This is not as easy as it sounds. As you will gather from this book, clubs are highly decentralised, idiosyncratic, eccentric organisations.

Moreover, clubs old and new tend to be a patchwork of many elements added over the years, so that one person's 'new' development is really some long-term adaptation, and another person's 'tradition' is really some recent affectation. To understand how London Clubland came into its present shape, it is necessary to understand something of its evolution.

This is particularly the case with the cultural divide between the 'old' and 'new' clubs. Members of long-standing establishments tend to be somewhat sniffy, or even dismissive, of any counterparts which are under a century old. (But then, members of most clubs tend to be dismissive about the majority of clubs to which they do not belong.) In reality, the dividing line can be vaguer. True, most (but not all) 'old' clubs are run as a not-for-profit business owned by their members, or else as a for-profit enterprise that keeps failing to turn a profit; and most (but not all) 'new' clubs are run by an external landlord as a for-profit business. But ownership alone does not define a club; and, indeed, until the early nineteenth century, *all* London clubs were run by external landlords as for-profit enterprises. Moreover, members are just as likely to be concerned with matters of taste, facilities, staff and their fellow membership, than the minutiae of governance. And the facilities can increasingly blur and overlap – recent years have seen the traditional clubs with floorspace to spare begin adding gyms, private hire rooms and co-working spaces, in a bid to compete with the newer clubs.

'New' clubs never stopped being set up. Even in the doldrum years of the 1960s and 1970s, when Victorian clubs were going bust by the dozen, chic new Mayfair establishments like Quent's and the Clermont Club were established, for the purpose of extracting as much money as possible from anyone who stepped over the thresholds.

But since the 1980s and 1990s, there has been a noticeable club 'boom' in the city, with dozens of new establishments being set up. On average, they have had a short lifespan; yet as the listing in Section 4 attests, this has not been any greater than the short lifespan of many 'traditional' clubs.

The seventeenth- and eighteenth-century origins of clubs were informal, verging on the scandalous: a room around the back of a 'legitimate' coffee house or hot-chocolate shop; in that room, fashionable (but illegal) gambling went on, with games often continuing for days at a time. Terming the back room a 'private members' club' raised all manner of jurisdiction headaches for the authorities, making it nigh impossible to raid. As these establishments grew ever more in vogue through the Georgian era, their aristocratic members became more demanding about entertainment and refreshment. With the professionalisation of club servants – originally the club steward, and then the chef – clubs

Introduction

began to rival restaurants for serving food and wine, often at more convenient serving times, and with more exotic menus.

The nineteenth century saw an explosion of clubs, from barely a dozen at the start of the century to around four hundred by its end. And it is during this era that London became the global capital of clubs, with more than any other city. Clubland became a recognisable, physical entity. The new clubs were increasingly middle class, and later lower middle class. Their premises became ever more elaborate, looking to outdo one another for opulence and splendour. A newfound Victorian focus on propriety made them more sober establishments than their Georgian predecessors (at least on the surface). A popular working-class spin-off – the working men's club – sprouted up, with thousands spreading around the country.

This rise and rise came to a messy end after the First World War. Clubland went into a long, steady decline for most of the twentieth century. The reasons for this were numerous. Many clubs stopped recruiting new members in large numbers, until they became a demographic time bomb, the bulk of their membership dying of old age within a decade. Food rationing during and after the Second World War seriously dented the clubs' ability to offer fine dining, and an expectation of serving up slop remained the norm for decades afterwards. Historic failures to invest in the maintenance of clubhouse buildings meant that clubs were presented with ruinous repair bills, catching up on a century or more of neglect. Serious governance flaws in clubs made them a tempting and vulnerable target to all manner of scammers, thieves and asset strippers. And many member-owned clubs folded through choice: as central London's land values soared, members often preferred to demutualise; or to put it another way, they dissolved their own clubs and flogged off the building for millions of pounds, retiring on their cut of the proceeds.

Clubland was in a depressing state by the post-war years, and it is this gloomy picture of decline that still comes to mind when people mention traditional London clubs – rather than the thrusting, dynamic, playful and experimental places they had been in the eighteenth and nineteenth centuries. The rejuvenation of Clubland over the last thirty or forty years is therefore to be welcomed – especially the role of the new clubs in triggering that.

Against that, not all new clubs are created equal. The caricature, of a gauche, tasteless, drugged-up, 'loadsamoney' culture aimed at fleecing *nouveau riche* oligarchs, has certainly had the ring of truth in some cases – although some of the more conspicuous examples of that have already folded. And some of the newer clubs can be delightfully unpretentious bohemian corners of London, dripping with as much character as their historic forebears.

London's clubs tend to be better organised than they used to be at recognising shared issues. Formal and informal communications networks between the managements of different clubs are extensive, and most club staff recognise that what may be a new problem for them has been tackled a hundred times over by their colleagues.

Some problems have been particularly new. The Covid-19 pandemic has cast a long shadow, particularly with the mandatory closure of all clubhouses for months of 2020 and 2021. Several clubs never reopened (including the Devonshire Club in Spitalfields, Fox Club in Mayfair, h-Club in Covent Garden and AllBright Fitzrovia), while a great many were saved by assorted government subsidies, from furlough pay for their staff, to participation in the 'Eat Out to Help Out' scheme (although the latter may, with hindsight, have further spread Covid).

The more long-term effects of the pandemic were subtler, and took a while to become noticeable. During the long lockdowns of 2020–1, many members continued to socialise remotely via Zoom, often arranging online literary talks or remote wine tastings. Online participation was not all sweetness and light. A certain impatience, bordering on intolerance, began to accompany many Zoom meetings. Previously, committee meetings had been held in person, and members tended to self-censor with great tact, not least because they all repaired to the bar or dining room after meetings – it would have been inconceivable to be rude in person. Online, people sometimes behaved differently. They would snap in the middle of Zoom meetings, having their say on long-festering grudges, and then disconnecting the call rather than facing

Introduction

the music. Anecdotally, these scenes were repeated across quite a few clubs – and once members returned to clubs in person, the ill temper often stayed. Consequently, while the members of clubs may not know it, the governance has in many cases become less kind, more aggressive, more suspicious, more opinionated and more stand-offish. This has been rarer in proprietary clubs, where the owner's iron fist in a velvet glove rules the day; but in a number of members' clubs, it has made matters increasingly unruly.

Feeding into this has been a newfound level of concern and polarisation around the 'culture war'. On the one hand, members and management keen to take steps towards greater diversity or modernisation of facilities have been denounced by traditionalists as 'woke'. On the other hand, members with scepticism about specific plans have been incensed to find themselves painted as bigots and reactionaries. While there have been times when such accusations have been fully justified, more often they have been down to needless vilification; the result has been a less patient, less forgiving atmosphere in the clubs. Most members just want peace and quiet. Simply 'agreeing to disagree' is no longer enough. Where clubs have their work cut out is in balancing an atmosphere which welcomes vigorous debate in a respectful way, with members and management still having a handle on what constitutes the 'red lines' for members of their own particular club, with its own unique culture.

Red lines have been particularly drawn on the topic of single-sex clubs, with the *Guardian*'s Amelia Gentleman having focused since 2015 on London's remaining men-only clubs. This came to a head with the leaking, in March 2024, of a Garrick Club membership list, and the *Guardian* serialising the names of prominent members in the arts, civil service and judiciary, where there was a suggestion of hypocrisy. Several individuals who were named promptly offered their resignations, and it was reported that the Club had urged members not to resign while the issue was being resolved. The resolution proved surprisingly swift: by April, the Garrick's Committee voted for women to be elected as members, in May this was endorsed by 59.98 per cent of members voting at a special general meeting, and the Club's first two women were elected as honorary members in July.

The newspaper furore over the Garrick prompted wider debates about the ongoing existence of single-sex clubs. Depending on one's view, it is argued either that restricting club membership to men limits significant career advantages to men; or that no work-related discussion whatsoever happens in clubs.

This is not a recent debate. Women have been a staple of Clubland since its foundation – London's oldest club, White's, was founded by husband-and-wife team Francesco and Elisabetta Bianco, while the first club with women members opened in 1770. There have been eighty-six women-only clubs in the city, peaking with several dozen in the Edwardian era, so that even though Clubland always had plenty of men-only clubs, Clubland as a whole was seldom a men-only space until the 1950s – and that was down to the financial collapse of the women's and mixed-sex clubs in the post-war years. Since then, clubs have frequently debated a range of related issues from admitting women, to the gender ratio of their members. Most of the historic gentlemen's clubs have become mixed sex, typically by the 1990s, with a dozen or so more traditional clubs resisting any change.

Where the 2024 Garrick controversy has longer-term implications for single-sex clubs is in the legal advice offered. This suggested that even when club rulebooks refer to a member as 'he', under English contract law this normally implies 'he or she', unless otherwise explicitly stated. Accordingly, gentlemen's clubs could end up breaching the Equality Act 2010 if they simply refuse to process applications from women candidates.

That said, the legal advice did *not* suggest that single-sex clubs were in themselves unlawful – that is clear from the Equality Act. The result, already quietly undertaken in some of the more aristocratic clubs, has been to pass an amendment to their own rules, explicitly stating that they are henceforth only open to men. Where things have become more ambiguous has been when the membership is so divided over the issue that this kind of clarifying motion on the status quo is not possible.

Introduction

Without enough support to either open up to women members, or to codify the Club as a men-only club, this 'no man's land' is fraught with uncertainty.

As long as there are single-sex clubs – and there are currently about a dozen men-only ones in London, and one women-only one – the issue is not likely to go away. What is likely to decide it is the culture of each club: some are still likely to make the change, with significant pressure from men who feel that reform is long overdue. Others are likely to resist any change whatsoever; and indeed currently attract members who joined because they wanted a single-sex environment. Each time a gentlemen's club opens up to women, there is a modest exodus of disgruntled members towards the remaining men-only clubs, further entrenching attitudes within them.

Yet while press coverage in the last year focused on women at the Garrick, most London clubs today have barely been affected by the issue. Most clubs are mixed sex; indeed, a majority today have always been so. More bread-and-butter issues have tended to be around the day-to-day running of the Club: whether the food is as good as it used to be, whether the members are as impressive as they used to be, and similar subjective judgements.

It is worth remembering that the early clubs were not founded in luxury. They were quite simple affairs, often just one room, and the remaining small dining clubs like the Beefsteak or Pratt's give a strong sense of their intimate atmosphere. Over time, some clubs – the ones that didn't go bankrupt – could build up substantial assets in terms of art, architecture, staffing, investments and intellectual property. The historic clubs we see today are the lucky 10 per cent that survived, and usually flourished. (The remaining 90 per cent went bust.) The result is that when we think of clubs today, we tend to think of luxury. Accordingly, new members can have very lofty expectations, not always matched by a preparedness to pay. And it is not simply students, the retired and the precariously employed who lobby for more affordable clubs and club meals. There are plenty of distressed aristocrats, too, much though they prefer to keep quiet about it.

These expectations also make things particularly difficult for the new clubs: they need to arrange for a clubhouse in one of the most expensive cities on earth, when a number of their older rivals bought a freehold at bargain-basement prices over a century ago, while they fork out for a ruinous lease; and they usually need to endeavour to outdo the traditional clubs, and can offer facilities including gyms, saunas, nightclubs. With all of these pressures, it is perhaps unsurprising that so many of them focus on 'new' money.

Why do people tolerate such spiralling costs? Snobbery only goes so far in explaining the appeal. And sometimes, members do not realise the true cost of the facilities they seek. There is certainly an enduring mystique among those outside the lofty portals of these establishments, if only to have a peek inside – a sentiment shared by many members who know their own club like the back of their hand, yet are curious about their peers. Moreover, at least some clubs must be doing something right to retain so many fee-paying members, year in, year out. It is because they speak to a very human need, for stimulation in congenial company, that the clubs are so enduring; and if many have come and gone, there is never a shortage of successors. Outsiders tend to characterise clubs by their physical trappings. But what most insiders tend to value about them is the human relationships forged within. I hope this book gives some insight into both.

SECTION 1

CLUB DIRECTORY

PART I

Historic Clubs

One of the striking features about clubs is how influential they have been on other social organisations – and how they have been influenced by others. Over the centuries, this has led to many groupings (like the Inns of Court for barristers, or the livery companies in the City of London) offering distinctly club-like facilities and hospitality; but for the purposes of brevity as much as anything else, those organisations are not included in this book. See 'Rules of Engagement' towards the end of the book for the method to my madness.

THE ARISTOCRATIC CLUBS

Boodle's – Brooks's – Buck's – Turf Club – White's

Just because they have membership lists suffused with aristocracy, this does not necessarily mean that they are the 'best' clubs. Some can be among the crustiest, stalest establishments. They can often underwhelm members of fellow London clubs used to more extensive premises, although they have not lost the power to impress visiting reciprocal members from overseas, who are excited at the thought of dining with a bona fide English earl.

Nevertheless, they are synonymous with quality. They have – on average – smaller memberships and greater accompanying intimacy, with

Club Directory: Historic Clubs

a much greater chance of having members' names remembered by the staff (and vice versa). They are the clubs which (along with the Cavalry and Guards and the Garrick) tend to have a tent at Ascot. They cultivate some of the very best wine lists in Clubland. The silverware tends to be of excellent quality, and reassuringly battered and dented with a patina that tells you it is centuries old. Hard to get into as either a member or a guest, but extremely convivial once you are there, they epitomise everything that is envied, lauded, resented and spoofed about London clubs.

The clubs in this category are also entirely men only – or 'gentlemen only', as more than one of them was keen to stress to me when I was preparing this book: Victorian notions of 'gentlemanliness' can mean a great deal to the members. A number of other men-only clubs with higher public profiles face significant pressure to open their doors to women – in the case of clubs like the East India, they have already had a majority of members repeatedly vote for integration, and it is surely only a matter of time. But the aristocratic establishments below are likely to be the last bastion of 'London gentlemen's clubs' (rather than private members' clubs).

Beefsteak Club – see THE DINING CLUBS

Boodle's
Address: 28 St James's Street, London, SW1A 1HJ.
Tel.: 020 7930 7166.
Founded: 1762.
Objects: Social.
Approx. no. of members: 1,400.
Sex: Gentlemen only.
Dress code: Suit and tie at all times for men, equivalent for women guests. The most formal of London clubs, with a dark suit required.
Type: Unincorporated association.
Reciprocal clubs: 26 clubs, across 11 countries.
Culture: Country pursuits, esp. hunting, shooting, fishing.
Architect: John Crunden, with alterations by John Buonarotti Papworth. (Long misattributed to the work of Robert Adam.)

Facilities: Entry hall, staircase, morning room (in three parts), coffee room (dining room), No. 27 dining room, billiard room, smoking terrace, 26 bedrooms.

What they want you to know: The London club of the country squirearchy; Ian Fleming's club, upon which he based Blade's club in the James Bond books.

What they probably don't want you to know: A member once shot himself in what is now the billiard room.

Short history: Founded by 25 members meeting in premises managed by Edward Boodle at 50 Pall Mall. Confusingly, the establishment began under the name Almack's, after its original proprietor William Almack, who also gave his name to the (entirely separate) nearby Salon on King Street. In time, service came to be so synonymous with Boodle's hospitality that the Club came to use his name. Boodle's settled in 1783 at its current mansion, best known for its iconic bow window. The house had originally been built in 1775 for the short-lived Savoir Vivre Club. Boodle's remained a proprietary club for over 130 years, but after the death of its last owner, the barrister and cricketer William Gayner, in 1892, the Club staged a management buyout by its members the following year. Always more of a club for landowners, Boodle's has long been light on politicians but heavy on aristocracy and squirearchy. Probably the best-preserved eighteenth-century clubhouse, with sympathetic restoration in recent decades. Its composition is largely unchanged; like Brooks's, a browse through the membership list today shows a significant number of descendants of members from earlier centuries.

Further reading:
Marcus Binney and David Mann (eds), *Boodle's: Celebrating 250 Years, 1762–2012* (Marlborough: Libanus Press, 2012).
Roger Fulford, *Boodle's, 1762–1962: A Short History* (London: Boodle's, 1962).
Stephen Hill, *Boodle's Apocrypha: A Story of Men and Their Club in London* (London: Duckworth, 2009).

Brooks's

Address: [Unnumbered; between 60 and 61] St James's Street, London, SW1A 1LN.
Tel.: 020 7493 4411.

Founded: 1764.
Objects: Social.
Approx. no. of members: 1,300.
Sex: Gentlemen only.
Dress code: Coat and tie at all times for gentlemen, equivalent formality for guest ladies.
Type: Unincorporated association.
Reciprocal clubs: 26 clubs, across 14 countries.
Culture: Whiggish; 'Establishment'.
Architect: Henry Holland, with Victorian alterations by John Macvicar Anderson, and further inter-war alterations by Sir Albert Richardson.
Facilities: Main hall and staircase, morning room, coffee room (dining room), Great Subscription Room, library, function rooms, 13 bedrooms.
Clubs within a club:

- The **Fox Club** has been a dining society since 1813, founded in memoriam to the celebrated Brooks's member Charles James Fox. Since the early twentieth century, it has been meeting at Brooks's. Membership is limited to 50, of whom all but 2 must be members of Brooks's.
- The **St James's Club**, a social club for diplomats which had a heavily aristocratic flavour and a strong gambling culture, was based on Piccadilly for over a century. Many (though not all) of its members joined Brooks's when that club folded in 1975. It no longer has an independent existence, but is fondly recalled by several members.
- The eighteenth-century **Society of Dilettanti** was hosted by the St James's Club, and in turn Brooks's. They brought with them a fine collection of paintings, including 23 members' portraits displayed in the library, and two large group portraits of the Society by Joshua Reynolds, now hanging in the Great Subscription Room. They continue as a dining society, but their members are not automatically elected to Brooks's. Walpole wrote of the Dilettanti, 'The nominal qualification for membership is having been in Italy, and the real one, being drunk.'

What they want you to know: One of the most cultured club memberships in London.
What they probably don't want you to know: They were the first major

London club to be prominently shown in a feature film location shoot, although Brooks's stopped short of allowing the crew in. The Club can be seen in *Sebastian* (1968), in which its exterior doubled as Dirk Bogarde's club, with Susannah York and him pacing out of the front doors.

Short history: Originally established on Pall Mall, and occupying Holland's mansion since 1778, the Club came into its own in the later years of its hero, Charles James Fox, when it came to be synonymous with the Whig cause. It remained a bastion of Whiggery until the early twentieth century. Whiggery – a creed that placed as much emphasis on aristocratic breeding and classical education as on political ideas such as civil and religious liberty – continues to be suffused through the building. At its peak influence in the 1830s and 1840s, most of the cabinet, and over half the Liberal/Reform/Whig MPs, were members – although this was subsequently dented by competition from the Reform Club. While the Club is in no way a political club any more, the Whig tradition has left its mark in the Club being one of the more literary clubs, with an exceptional library. The core of the building has been faithfully maintained, with the addition of an annexe on Park Place added in the 1850s (which hosts the coffee room on the ground floor, and the library on the first floor), and the Edwardian-era refacing of the building. More than perhaps any other London club today, family antecedents count for a great deal, with a quick browse of the present membership list showing numerous direct descendants of the Club's eighteenth- and nineteenth-century membership.

Further reading:
Henry S. Eeles and Earl Spencer, *Brooks's, 1764–1964* (London: Country Life, 1964).
Charles Sebag-Montefiore and J. Mordaunt Crook (eds), *Brooks's, 1764–2014: The Story of a Whig Club* (London: Paul Holberton, 2013).
Philip Ziegler and Desmond Seward (eds), *Brooks's: A Social History* (London: Constable, 1991).

Buck's

Address: 18 Clifford Street, Mayfair, London, W1S 3RF.
Tel.: 020 7734 2337.
Founded: 1919.
Objects: Reunion from the Great War (originally); social (today).
Approx. no. of members: 760.

Sex: Gentlemen only.
Dress code: Jacket and tie at all times for men, equivalent for women guests.
Type: Incorporated in 1996, as Buck's Club Ltd, a private company limited by guarantee, with the current members of the Club being the members of the company.
Reciprocal clubs: 23 clubs, across 8 countries.
Culture: Relaxed, unfussy.
Architect: Joseph Stallwood and Benjamin Timbrell.
Facilities: Hall and staircase, American Bar, gallery, dining room, library, function rooms, smoking terrace, 3 bedrooms.
What they want you to know: If you want the full Wodehousian Drones Club experience, this is the place to start. The cocktail 'Buck's Fizz' (champagne and orange juice – with a twist) originated here.
What they probably don't want you to know: Despite having formally structured themselves in recent years as a gentlemen's club, there is precedent for women members: both Margaret Thatcher and the late Queen Mother were members.
Short history: The Club started as a wartime reunion society founded by Captain Herbert Buckmaster, who loomed large for the first five decades, lodging in an upstairs bedroom of his club. Buck's rapidly gained a reputation in the 1920s as the *dernier cri* in style, with its American cocktail bar seeming unimaginably exotic in the post-war gloom. (Remember that Prohibition was in full swing in the USA at the same time, giving the Club even more of a *frisson*.) Buck's was badly damaged amidst wartime bombing in 1940, and the immediate post-war years saw decline, as with many other London clubs – where Buckmaster had been an innovative proprietor, showing great flair in the inter-war years, a number of bad practices set in during his later years. Members have long undertaken the practice of playing cricket in the bar – for which a wicket has been painted on the counter.
Further reading:
Henry Buckmaster, *Buck's Book: Ventures-Adventures and Misadventures* (London: Grayson & Grayson, 1933).

Cavalry and Guards Club – see THE MILITARY CLUBS

London Clubland

Pratt's – see THE DINING CLUBS

Travellers Club – see THE PALL MALL CLUBS

Turf Club

Address: 5 Carlton House Terrace, St James's, London, SW1Y 5AQ.
Tel.: 020 7930 8555.
Founded: 1861.
Objects: Horse racing, social, country pursuits.
Approx. no. of members: 1,300.
Sex: Gentlemen only (full membership), and associate ladies.
Dress code: Jacket and tie at all times for men, equivalent for women.
Type: Unincorporated association.
Reciprocal clubs: 11 clubs, across 9 countries.
Culture: Old-world, patrician, courteous, discreet.
Architect: John Nash, with alterations by Decimus Burton.
Facilities: Entry hall, bar, main staircase, morning room (in two parts), members' and ladies' dining rooms, ladies' sitting room, committee room, 11 bedrooms.
What they want you to know: That they are one of London's most intensely private clubs. They even took down their own website, after realising that none of their members used it, and did not want to draw outside attention.
What they probably don't want you to know: The seldom-explored rooftop view is spectacular, looking towards St James's Park and along the Mall, between Admiralty Arch and Buckingham Palace – but is something of a carefully guarded secret.
Short history: The Turf is possibly the most overlooked club of London. The members like it just that way. They are not literary men, like Brooks's, so almost uniquely for such a historic establishment, there are no history books published on the Turf. Instead, the Club, made up of racehorse enthusiasts and huntsmen, maintains a strong oral tradition. It began as the Arlington Club on Bennett Street off St James's Street, as a club dedicated to equestrianism and cards. Transferring to 47 Clarges Street in 1875, the Club spent 90 years developing a unique architectural style – Edwardian journalist Ralph Nevill thought the clubhouse had 'no particular interest from an

artistic point of view', but was 'comfortable in the extreme', marked by a fondness for candlelight over electrical light, and a fine collection of paintings of racehorses. When the Club moved to its present location in 1965, acquiring a late-Georgian Nash terrace overlooking the Mall, it brought all these items with it, and it remains hard to believe they were ever anywhere else. Sandwiched between the Royal Society and the Royal Academy of Engineering, and located on the street of London's most expensive home (the Hinduja brothers live a few doors along), the building has five storeys, and is larger than seems apparent, due to its capacious basement and the Mall being at a lower level around the back. Racing provides a broad stream of interest throughout the Club, and while not all members are devotees, a high number not only live and breathe horse racing, but own racehorses, too.

White's

Address: 37–38 St James's Street, London, SW1A 1JG.
Tel.: 020 7493 6671.
Founded: 1693 (as a coffee house); 1736 (as a club).
Objects: Social.
Approx. no. of members: 1,500.
Sex: Gentlemen only. No women guests permitted.
Dress code: Jacket and tie at all times for men.
Type: Unincorporated association.
Reciprocal clubs: Theoretically, none – White's does not enter into formal reciprocal agreements. But it does have an informal understanding with one overseas club.
Culture: Haughty, aloof, prosperous.
Architect: James Wyatt, with Victorian alterations by James Lockyer.
Facilities: Main hall, staircase, bar, coffee room (dining room), billiard room, morning room (for periodicals), card room, private dining room, roof deck.
What they want you to know: The oldest club in London.
What they probably don't want you to know: Nowhere near as aristocratic today as its reputation suggests. Yes, there are plenty of titled members, and those drawn from the gentry; but as the Club's own in-house historian Anthony Lejeune cattily observed thirty years ago, 'The

trouble really is not that stockbrokers have become members of White's but that members of White's have become stockbrokers.' Today's members are just as likely to have made a bundle at a merchant bank in the 1970s or 1980s, or an investment bank in the 1990s or 2000s, and be settling down to a comfortable retirement.

Short history: Beginning life as the gambling room around the back of White's hot-chocolate and coffee shop at 28 St James's Street (now the site of Boodle's), five years later White's moved to 69 St James's Street – the site now occupied by the Carlton Club. For many years it remained an informal club, until a 1733 fire burned down the building, and prompted its reconstruction and reconstitution as a club in 1736, without any chocolate shop. For nearly five decades, 'old club' and 'new club' existed side-by-side, until the last of the 'old club' died out in 1781, and White's became one solitary club. Initially non-political with a strong Whig element, it became heavily identified with the Tories during William Pitt the Younger's premiership, providing a strong counterpoint to the Whig domination of Brooks's across the road. Yet over time, aristocracy came to trump politics, and by the mid-nineteenth century around a third of the Club was drawn from the Whig families. Since the late nineteenth century, it has reverted to being culturally Tory, but non-partisan. It remained a proprietary club until 1891, when the members organised a buyout. The present building was heavily altered in 1811 (with further late-Victorian alterations), giving it its iconic bow window, at which Beau Brummell famously sat in the 1810s. The Club remains London's most resistant to women, with the opposite sex still barred from even entering as visitors – although exceptions are made for members of the royal family: the late Queen Elizabeth II visited in 1991 and 2016. For her Platinum Jubilee in 2022, the Club organised six jubilee dinners, at which members (for the only time in the Club's history) were allowed to bring their wives; and in more recent years, Catherine, Princess of Wales, has been seen lunching there.

Further reading:
Algernon Bourke, *The History of White's, with the Betting Book from 1743 to 1878 and a List of Members from 1736 to 1892*, 2 vols (London: privately published, 1892).
Percy Colson, *White's: 1693–1950* (London: Heinemann, 1951).
Anthony Lejeune, *White's: The First Three Hundred Years* (London: A. & C. Black, 1993).

Club Directory: Historic Clubs

THE PALL MALL CLUBS

The Athenæum – Oxford and Cambridge Club – Reform Club – Travellers Club

Redolent of the newly empowered, increasingly professional middle classes of the nineteenth century, these stand as temples to Clubland. Whereas the older aristocratic clubs had been small, intimate houses, the nineteenth-century clubs of Pall Mall were built as palaces to be noticed. They still stand aloof today; and even the defunct establishments like John Nash's palatial Roman-style United Service Club at 116 Pall Mall, and the brutalist 1960s concrete block of the Junior Carlton Club at 94 Pall Mall, have their former clubhouses standing conspicuously today.

Army and Navy Club – see THE MILITARY CLUBS

The Athenæum

Address: 107 Pall Mall, St James's, London, SW1Y 5ER.
Tel.: 020 7930 4843.
Founded: 1824.
Objects: Distinction in the arts, literature, science or engineering.
Approx. no. of members: 2,300.
Sex: Mixed sex.
Dress code: Jacket at all times for men, equivalent for women. Ties optional before 7 p.m.
Type: Unincorporated association.
Reciprocal clubs: 23 clubs, across 10 countries.
Culture: Academics, primarily, but also 'The Establishment', with a profusion of civil servants and experts.
Architect: Decimus Burton, with late Victorian alterations by Sir Lawrence Alma-Tadema and Sir Edward Poynter, and additional storey by Thomas Edward Collcutt.
Facilities: Morning room (main bar), coffee room (dining room), drawing room, smoking room, libraries (across several rooms – including the

three-storey members-only South Library), function rooms, archive room, 15 bedrooms, garden.

What they want you to know: 'The brainiest club in London' (*Baltimore Sun*).
What they probably don't want you to know: Named 'the club of last resort' by Ben Schott, owing to the traditionally frosty reception offered by some members, particularly towards those they don't deem to be their intellectual equals.

Short history: Founded from the outset to be Britain's premier club for the arts and sciences, it was the brainchild of John Wilson Croker. While the Club denies that it is some form of national honour society, election to membership has nonetheless long been seen in that vein, and the Club has served as a snapshot of Britain's evolving 'Establishment' over the last two centuries. The Athenæum was intended to have members from across the political divide, and still maintains a strong cross-party tradition. It is slightly baffling how the Club's long-established reputation for being packed with bishops came about – there are 108 Anglican bishops in England and Wales, so even if they all joined (and they certainly haven't), they would make up just 4 per cent of the membership. Nonetheless, this has contributed to a slightly crusty image, which the Club tries its best to defy with *bonhomie*. Built on part of the site of the old Carlton House, the neo-classical Grecian clubhouse proved highly influential on London clubhouses thereafter, as the first of its kind to be set around a large, central atrium. A statue of Athena stands over the front portico.

Further reading:
Frank Richard Cowell, *The Athenæum: Club and Social Life in London, 1824–1974* (London: Heinemann, 1975).
Felipe Fernández-Armesto (ed.), *Armchair Athenians: Essays from the Athenæum* (London: Athenæum, 2001).
Hugh Tait and Richard Walker, *The Athenæum Collection* (London: Athenæum, 2000).
Humphry Ward, *History of the Athenæum, 1824–1925* (London: Athenæum, 1926).
Francis G. Waugh, *The Athenæum and its Associations* (London: Athenæum, 1895).
Michael Wheeler, *The Athenæum: 'More Than Just Another London Club'* (New Haven: Yale University Press, 2020).

Oxford and Cambridge Club

Address: 71–77 Pall Mall, St James's, London, SW1Y 5HD.
Tel.: 020 7930 5151.

Club Directory: Historic Clubs

Founded: 1821 (United University Club); 1830 (Oxford and Cambridge Club); 1972 (merger into United Oxford and Cambridge Club, renamed in 2001 as Oxford and Cambridge Club).
Objects: Social; for alumni of the universities of Oxford and Cambridge.
Approx. no. of members: 4,500.
Sex: Mixed sex.
Dress code: Jacket and tie for men, and equivalent for women, at peak hours; some relaxation to 'smart-casual' on weekends before 6 p.m.
Type: Unincorporated association.
Reciprocal clubs: 155 clubs, across 38 countries.
Culture: Academic; members tend to be polarised between the sizeable number of recently graduated younger members and the large contingent of older alumni.
Architect: Robert Smirke.
Facilities: Front hall and staircase, morning room (bar), coffee room (dining room), Blomfield Room (brasserie), library (across three rooms), reading room (previously the smoking room), drawing room, squash courts and viewing gallery, billiard room, 4 function rooms, workspace, rooftop terrace, 42 bedrooms.
Clubs within a club:
- **United University Club** (1822–1971) merged into the Oxford and Cambridge Club, selling its Pall Mall East clubhouse just off Trafalgar Square, which is now the UK campus of Notre Dame University.
- **New University Club** (1864–1938) on St James's Street merged into the Oxford and Cambridge Club.

What they want you to know: The home of Oxbridge alumni in Pall Mall.
What they probably don't want you to know: For a brief period in 1970–1, the United University Club admitted graduates of universities other than Oxford and Cambridge. This practice was stopped upon the merger of 1971.
Short history: Part of the early wave of middle-class clubs around the professions in the 1810s and 1820s, the United University Club catered for graduates of England's two oldest universities, with a clubhouse at the north-eastern end of Pall Mall. A waiting list rapidly spiralled in size, and so the Oxford and Cambridge Club was set up nine years later to the

south-west end of Pall Mall, as a way of tackling the waiting list. With both clubs ailing by the late 1960s, a merger between the two resulted in the Oxford and Cambridge Club's building being retained. The Club's involvement with the universities (heads of colleges are routinely offered honorary membership) means that it has been subjected to more public scrutiny than most clubs – the 1990s battle over women's admission was particularly heated, with articles in the national press, and several protest resignations by Oxbridge academics. Matters have calmed since then, and serious redevelopment of the building has seen both the refurbishment of its bedrooms in the attic, and a flurry of sports facilities in the basement, from squash courts to a billiard room.

Further reading:
Francesca Herrick, *A Guide to the Art Collections of the Oxford and Cambridge Club* (London: Oxford and Cambridge Club, 2012).
John Thole, *The Oxford and Cambridge Clubs in London* (Henley-on-Thames: Alfred Waller/ United Oxford and Cambridge University Club, 1992).

Reform Club

Address: 104–105 Pall Mall, St James's, London, SW1Y 5EW.
Tel.: 020 7930 9374.
Founded: 1836.
Objects: Political reform; the principles of the 'Great Reform Act' of 1832.
Approx. no. of members: 2,850.
Sex: Mixed sex.
Dress code: Jacket at all times for men, equivalent for women. Ties encouraged for men, but not compulsory.
Type: Unincorporated association.
Reciprocal clubs: 82 clubs, across 25 countries.
Culture: A smorgasbord of left-leaning lawyers, academics, parliamentarians, economists, civil servants, authors, artists, adventurers, scientists, journalists and think tankers.
Architect: Charles Barry.
Facilities: Saloon, bar, coffee room (dining room), smoking room, library, card room, billiard room, business suite, function rooms, exhibition, 46 bedrooms, garden.

What they want you to know: Where Phileas Fogg is meant to have started and ended his journey in *Around the World in Eighty Days* (1872). Also one of the most filmed clubhouses in cinema, including several James Bond films.

What they probably don't want you to know: *Penthouse* magazine managed to book the Club for a nude photoshoot with a nineteen-year-old Paula Yates in 1978, sprawled all over the furniture, staircase and busts.

Short history: The Club was founded as a response to the conservative Carlton Club then based on Pall Mall; to provide a headquarters for the Whigs and Radicals (and later Liberals) who supported political reform, upholding the principles of the 1832 Reform Act. Originally conceived as an election headquarters that would fund campaigns, print election leaflets and recruit election candidates, its political role was reduced after further extensions of the franchise in the 1860s, 1880s and 1910s. The eclipse of the Liberal Party meant that, by the mid-twentieth century, it had ceased to be a political club (although it still has an active Political Committee – but along non-partisan lines), and it became synonymous with economists and technocrats. In more recent years, its status as 'a great theatre for politics' means that it continues to attract people interested in public policy, ranging from Blair-era New Labour politicians who wanted a traditional club with a more progressive ethos, to libertarian free-marketeers identified with the Institute of Economic Affairs. Possibly the best-maintained original Victorian clubhouse in London, it has undergone extensive restoration over the last two decades.

Further reading:
Russell Burlingham and Roger Billis (eds), *Reformed Characters: The Reform Club in History and Literature, an Anthology with Commentary* (London: Reform Club, 2005).
Louis Fagan, *The Reform Club: Its Founders and Architect* (London: Bernard Quaritch, 1887).
J. Mordaunt Crook, *The Reform Club* (London: Reform Club, 1973).
Michael Sharpe, *The Political Committee of the Reform Club* (London: Reform Club, 1996).
Peter Urbach, *The Reform Club: Some Twentieth Century Members – A Photographic Collection* (London: Reform Club, 1999).
—, *Reform! Reform! Reform! An Exhibition* (London: Reform Club, 2007).
George Woodbridge, *The Reform Club, 1836–1978: A History from the Club's Records* (New York: Clearwater, 1978).

Royal Automobile Club – see THE MASS-MEMBERSHIP CLUBS

Travellers Club

Address: 106 Pall Mall, St James's, London, SW1Y 5EP.
Tel.: 020 7930 8688.
Founded: 1819.
Objects: Travel; diplomacy; members need to have travelled somewhere at least 500 miles from London.
Approx. no. of members: 1,200.
Sex: Gentlemen only.
Dress code: Jacket and tie at all times for men, equivalent for women guests.
Type: Unincorporated association.
Reciprocal clubs: 152 clubs, across 41 countries.
Culture: Members tend to fall into two broad types: the diplomats, who are polite but circumspect; and the 'young fogeys', who are somewhat more gregarious.
Architect: Charles Barry.
Facilities: Bar, front hall, morning room (in two parts), smoking room, grand staircase, coffee room (dining room), library, 17 bedrooms, chapel, business room, Bramall Room (garden lobby), garden. (Open court at the centre is not usually accessible to members.)
What they want you to know: Traditionally the bastion of diplomats and spies, living the existence of an aristocratic townhouse in central London.
What they probably don't want you to know: The Club's historic links to the diplomatic service have been under strain in recent years, with the non-admission of women prompting opposition from some civil servants and diplomats, and an accompanying reduction in the proportion of members drawn from these walks of life.
Short history: The British foreign secretary, Viscount Castlereagh, played a pivotal role in the diplomatic efforts to remould Europe after Napoleon. He envisioned the Travellers Club as a place to meet diplomats from all over the continent – and further afield – who were engaged in global affairs. Charles Barry was engaged as architect, drawing his inspiration from Raphael's Palazzo Pandolfini in Florence, with a frieze above the library replicating the Bassae Frieze on the Temple of Apollo in the Peloponnese.

The clubhouse embodies a unique transition between the 'country house' style of eighteenth-century clubs and the grander mansions of nineteenth-century clubhouses. Barry himself later joined the Club. The Club has long been popular with British career diplomats as well as ambassadors to the UK resident in London, and has a well-earned reputation as home for numerous spies, too – for many years it was dubbed the 'Foreign Office works canteen'. Since the 1980s, this traditional diplomatic element has been balanced with a sizeable 'young fogey' contingent, who have moved the Club into a more politicised, small-c conservative direction.

Further reading:
Graham Binns, Hugh Massingberd and Sheila Markham, *A House of the First Class: The Travellers Club and its Members* (London: Travellers Club, 2003).
Almeric FitzRoy, *History of the Travellers Club* (London: George Allen & Unwin, 1927).
Franks Herrmann and Michael Allen (eds), *Travellers' Tales: By Members of the Travellers Club* (London: Castlereagh, 1999).
—, *More Tales from the Travellers: A Further Collection of Tales by Members of the Travellers Club, London* (London: Michel Tomkinson, 2005).
John Martin Robinson, *The Travellers Club: A Bicentennial History, 1819–2019* (Marlborough: Libanus Press/Travellers Club, 2018).
Julian Tunnicliffe (ed.), *Brave Lives: The Members and Staff of the Travellers Club Who Fell in the Great War* (Barnsley: Pen & Sword Military, 2016).

THE MILITARY CLUBS

Army and Navy Club – Cavalry and Guards Club – East India Club – Naval and Military Club – Oriental Club – Special Forces Club – Yeoman Warders Club

The military clubs are marked by the camaraderie of the armed forces, combined with the formality of military tradition. It was the military clubs in the nineteenth century which helped transform the rather louche, informal institutions of the early clubs into the stricter Victorian clubs. The emphasis today is on current and former serving officers – though most today have a majority of members who are civilians, the military members subsidised by discounted fees. Nevertheless, it is the military-themed membership, décor and events of these clubs which give them their distinctive identity.

Army and Navy Club, aka 'The Rag'

Address: 36–39 Pall Mall, St James's, London, SW1Y 5JN.
Tel.: 020 7930 9721.
Founded: 1837.
Objects: Army and navy officers.
Approx. no. of members: 4,500.
Sex: Mixed sex.
Dress code: Jacket at all times for men, equivalent for women. Ties encouraged for men, but not compulsory.
Type: Incorporated in 2013, as a private company limited by guarantee, as Army and Navy Club Ltd, with full members of the Club being members of the company.
Reciprocal clubs: 112 clubs, across 30 countries.
Culture: Authentic, military.
Architect: Sir Thomas Bennett.
Facilities: Bar, coffee room (dining room), smoking room, drawing room, library, Ribbon Bar and Terrace, business suite, gym, swimming pool, sauna, function rooms, 77 bedrooms, garage.
Clubs within a club:
- The **Portland Club** has been a long-standing club with its own independent existence since 1814. Based in a wing of the In and Out Club for 30 years from 1969, and then the Savile Club for 15 years, it has been based in the Army and Navy Club since 2014.
- The **Naval Club** – previously known as the RNVR Club for the Royal Naval Voluntary Reserve – closed in 2021, and its membership merged into the Army and Navy Club.

What they want you to know: The clubhouse has an enviable number of facilities, right down to the swimming pool.
What they probably don't want you to know: The little-loved 1960s clubhouse design has frequently been mooted for demolition and redevelopment by the members – including as recently as 2017.
Short history: Originally intended as an army club, the intervention of the Duke of Wellington resulted in it being launched as an army *and* navy club, with the two services on equal terms. At the time, the United Service

Club was London's leading military club, but only catered to senior officers (majors, commanders and above), and so the Army and Navy Club was intended to blend junior and senior officers. The Club's sobriquet, 'The Rag', comes from a nineteenth-century insult describing it as a 'Rag and famish affair', meaning a dingy gambling house – a description which the members accepted as a compliment. For over a century the Club was blessed with a grand neoclassical clubhouse built by George Tattersall in the 1840s, although there was widespread dissatisfaction at the poor use of space (which prioritised grand hallways and staircases over clubrooms); and years of neglect, bomb damage and internal politics all took their toll, resulting in a decision in the late 1950s to demolish the building. The current clubhouse, completed in 1963, has had its fair share of critics over its brutalist aesthetic; but from its garage to its swimming pool, it comes with a comprehensive array of facilities which few other central London clubs can match.

Further reading:
Anthony Keith Dixon, *The Army & Navy Club 1837–2008* (London: Army and Navy Club, 2009).
C. W. Firebrace, *The Army & Navy Club 1837–1933* (London: John Murray, 1934).

Cavalry and Guards Club

Address: 127 Piccadilly, Mayfair, London, W1J 7PX.
Tel.: 020 7499 1261.
Founded: 1810 (Guards Club); 1890 (Cavalry Club); 1976 (merged Cavalry and Guards Club).
Objects: British Army officers who have served in the Cavalry, Guards, Rifles or (historically) Royal Green Jackets regiments; or the Honourable Artillery Company.
Approx. no. of members: 3,000.
Sex: Mixed sex.
Dress code: Jacket and tie at all times for men, equivalent for women.
Type: Unincorporated association.
Reciprocal clubs: 54 clubs, across 20 countries.
Culture: Raucous, convivial, partygoing.
Architects: Charles Mewès and Arthur Joseph Davis.

Facilities: Main hall, staircase, bar, coffee room (dining room), drawing room, morning room, waiting room, conservatory, 7 function rooms, 38 bedrooms.

What they want you to know: The longest-standing of the historic clubs that used to line Piccadilly.

What they probably don't want you to know: The merger of the two clubs in the 1970s was somewhat traumatic and involved the sale of many Guards Club assets.

Short history: As its name suggests, the Club has its roots in two separate clubs, each themed around members of socially elite regiments of the British Army. The older of the two, the Guards Club, pre-dates Waterloo. After its first premises, on the corner of St James's Street, spontaneously collapsed, it relocated to Pall Mall for nine decades, before leading a slightly peripatetic existence around several Mayfair addresses. The Cavalry Club, by contrast, has always been based at this address. When both clubs came under the financial pressures of the 1970s, a merger resulted, with the Guards moving in with the Cavalry. Since then, a membership heavily skewed towards the social has resulted – but the presence of non-military members has not detracted from the ever-present military theme. The cavalry influence continues to be strong, with the Club organising an annual syndicate for a racehorse at Royal Ascot.

Further reading:
Val Horsler, *Cavalry & Guards: A London Home* (London: Third Millennium, 2009).

East India, Devonshire, Sports and Public Schools Club, aka East India Club

Address: 16 St James's Square, St James's, London, SW1Y 4LH.
Tel.: 020 7930 1000.
Founded: 1849.
Objects: Social, military, sports, public schools.
Approx. no. of members: 4,500.
Sex: Gentlemen only.
Dress code: Jacket and tie at all times for gentlemen, equivalent for lady guests.

Club Directory: Historic Clubs

Type: Incorporated, 1925, as the Sports Club Ltd (renamed in 1976 as the East India, Devonshire, Sports and Public Schools Club Ltd), a private company limited by shares, with the members as joint shareholders.
Reciprocal clubs: 114 clubs, across 29 countries.
Culture: Public school young fogey-ish, frivolous.
Architect: Charles Lee.
Facilities: Two bars (American Bar and Waterloo Room), dining room, drawing room, library, cigar sampling room, snooker room, function rooms, business centre, gym, 67 bedrooms.
Clubs within a club: As its full name suggests, the present-day club is a merger of four clubs. As well as the eponymous East India Club, whose clubhouse remains the base, it incorporates the following defunct clubs:
- **Sports Club** (1893–1938). A one-time neighbour on St James's Square, the amalgamation with the Sports Club and its members not only strengthened the EIC's tradition for sports teams, but an emphasis on sporting and gymnasium facilities followed.
- **Public Schools Club** (1919–72). The demise of this club provided the EIC with a large infusion of young men, courtesy of inheriting the 'J7' scheme (since replicated by the Oriental Club). Under this scheme, school leavers at Headmasters' Conference public schools can be elected for up to 7 years of membership for a bulk fee. Consequently, the Club has a much higher percentage of 18-to-25-year-old members than most other London clubs.
- **Devonshire Club** (1874–1976). It had originally been founded as a political club for Liberals, but after the Home Rule split of 1886 it became increasingly Liberal Unionist, and then Unionist (Conservative).
- Additionally, when the **Eccentric Club** (1890–1982) was wound up, many of its members migrated to the East India Club, but this was not a formal merger.

What they want you to know: That great rarity, a full-services, seven-days-a-week, traditional London club. And the EIC takes its traditions very seriously.
What they probably don't want you to know: The widely told tale about the Prince Regent being given the Waterloo despatch in the Waterloo Room at the front of the Club is somewhat embellished – as

is the claim on the plaque, 'The room has changed little from that day' in 1815. The whole building was demolished and replaced with a new building in 1866; while a contemporary floor plan confirms that the Waterloo despatch happened on that site, but on the ground floor, at the rear.

Short history: The East India United Service Club was founded in response to a memorandum from the Three Presidencies of British India, which complained that the East India Company did not have a loud enough voice in London. Taking over the clubhouse of the recently defunct Free Trade Club, and then acquiring the house next door, by the 1860s the site was comprehensively redeveloped into one of the larger clubhouses. The infusion of several merged clubs has added numerous aspects to the EIC's personality, most notably the old Public Schools Club, which means it has a younger-than-average membership. Wartime bomb damage led to renovated rooms being named in honour of the overseas troops billeted at the Club, particularly the Canadian Room.

Further reading:
Denys Forrest, *Foursome in St James's: The Story of the East India, Devonshire, Sports and Public Schools Club* (London: East India Club, 1982).
Charlie Jacoby, *The East India Club: A History* (London: East India Club, 2009).

Naval and Military Club, aka 'In and Out Club'

Address: 4 St James's Square, London, SW1Y 4JU.
Tel.: 020 7827 5757.
Founded: 1862.
Objects: Military officers (originally); social (contemporary).
Approx. no. of members: 3,150.
Sex: Mixed sex.
Dress code: Jacket and tie for men, equivalent for women in formal areas, smart-casual in informal areas.
Type: Incorporated in 1993, as In and Out Ltd, a private company limited by shares, with the current members of the Club being the shareholders.
Reciprocal clubs: 117 clubs, across 34 countries.

Club Directory: Historic Clubs

Culture: Officers' mess, combined with relaxed hospitality.
Architect: Edward Shepherd.
Facilities: Long Bar, Canning Room (bar), main hallway, grand staircase, coffee room (dining room), library, outdoor courtyard and smoking terrace, The Goat brasserie, gym, 4 treatment rooms, squash court, swimming pool, sauna, steam room, hairdresser, 4 function rooms, 53 bedrooms.
Clubs within a club: Over the years, the In and Out has absorbed a cornucopia of other clubs. This has included:

- **Junior Naval and Military Club**, which for many years occupied the building next door on Piccadilly, acting as a club for those on the In and Out's waiting list, operating in 1870–1939.
- **Ladies' Carlton Club**, a conservative political club for women, in 1910–58.
- **Royal Cruising Club**, a yacht club which still exists today, but had its own clubhouse in 1880–1959.
- **Goat Club**, for Royal Navy officers, in 1915–68. It is commemorated at the In and Out with The Goat, an informal brasserie off the inner hallway.
- **Junior Army and Navy Club**, another military club, in 1911–68. They chose to merge with the In and Out rather than their namesake, the Army and Navy.
- **Cowdray Club**, a club for nurses and professional women, in 1922–74.
- **United Service Club**, aka 'The Senior', a club for senior army and navy officers, in 1815–1977. Its former premises on the corner of Pall Mall and Waterloo Place are now the Institute of Directors.
- **Den Norske Klub**, for Norwegian expatriates, founded in 1887. They had their own clubhouse until 1997, and since 1999 have been hosted by the In and Out, continuing an independent existence within.
- **Canning Club**, originally founded as the **Argentine Club** in 1910, for South American expatriates, had its own clubhouse until 1970, when it merged into the In and Out. It is commemorated with the Canning Room bar.
- **New Cavendish Club**, originally the **Voluntary Aid Detachment Ladies' Club**, a club for female officers founded in 1920; it changed names after it became a mixed-sex club, continuing until 2014. Its former premises are now the Home Grown club (see p. 118).

What they want you to know: A full-services club with a homely atmosphere in the heart of St James's.

What they probably don't want you to know: The membership list has been on the brink of closing for some time, due to the Club being oversubscribed.

Short history: The 'In and Out', as it is still known, has had a picaresque existence. The Club had humble beginnings, being originally set up as an overflow for some of the oversubscribed armed services clubs of the day. Nonetheless, it has evolved a character of its own. The Club was closely identified with the palatial Cambridge House on Piccadilly, its former premises for over 130 years, marked with 'In' and 'Out' on its two driveways, giving the Club its sobriquet. It was plunged into crisis in the 1990s with the non-renewal of its lease; but thanks to some long-term planning and prudent investment, emerged from the chaos of 30 years ago to relative calm. A mortgage was taken out on a historic townhouse in St James's Square, once the London residence of Nancy Astor, with the handover ceremony of clubhouses involving a bagpipe-accompanied march of several hundred club members, fronted by bowler-hatted Guardsmen. While the new building had never been a club before, it proved well-suited to the conversion, as the square's only Georgian house with a surviving yard, with the outbuildings being converted to accommodation and sporting facilities. This is a club where its military roots give it a strong theme, but do not predominate. The eclectic mix of members is a balance between military and civilian.

Further reading:
Tim Newark, *The In & Out: A History of the Naval and Military Club* (London: Osprey Publishing, 2015).

Oriental Club

Address: Stratford House, 11 Stratford Place, London, W1C 1ES.
Tel.: 020 7629 5126.
Founded: 1824.
Objects: Military officers and East India Company civil servants (originally); social (contemporary).

Approx. no. of members: 3,000.
Sex: Mixed sex.
Dress code: Smart-casual in most of the Club. In the dining room and members' bar the dress code is 'Elegantly casual', with tailored jackets required for gentlemen.
Type: Incorporated in 2014, as Oriental Club (1824) Ltd, a private company limited by guarantee, with members of the Club being members of the company.
Reciprocal clubs: 68 clubs, across 22 countries.
Culture: Gregarious, sociable, adventurous.
Architect: Richard Edwin.
Facilities: 2 bars, dining room, drawing room, library, billiard room, 2 smoking rooms, private dining rooms, business room, courtyard terrace, 40 bedrooms.
Clubs within a club: The **Alfred Club**, a gambling club founded in 1808, merged into the Oriental in 1854, but is now fully absorbed.
What they want you to know: The Club marked its bicentenary year with a series of celebrations, and a renovation of its dining room by Russell Sage Studio.
What they probably don't want you to know: Some of the Club's paintings were 'adapted' to fit Stratford House, following the move from its former home in Hanover Square.
Short history: One of numerous clubs to have been founded or co-founded by the Duke of Wellington, the Oriental Club was established to cater to officers of one of the largest of British armed forces, who had hitherto been excluded from the existing clubs: the private army of the East India Company (EIC). However, the Club rapidly broadened its remit to soldiers and civil servants with Indian connections; so that by the time of the EIC's downscaling and eventual abolition, the Club was well-placed to survive. For many years, it was based on Hanover Square, but in 1960 it purchased the freehold of Stratford House, which had once served as the Stratford Club, a gambling establishment. Of all the London clubs, the Oriental adapted most effortlessly to the Covid-19 pandemic, launching Oriental Dine at Home, which arranged national home delivery of their famous

curries. The Club now recruits a sizeable intake of younger members with the 'OC7+' scheme, which gives public school leavers from a list of public schools with which it has a relationship (along with sons and daughters of current members) 13 years of membership for ages 18–31, for a lump sum (currently £850). The Club has a notable culinary heritage and, in the nineteenth century, its chef Richard Terry was the author of one of Britain's Indian cookery books, which continues to influence the menus of the Club today.

Further reading:
Hugh Riches, *History of the Oriental Club* (London: Oriental Club, 1998).

Royal Air Force Club – see THE MASS-MEMBERSHIP CLUBS

Special Forces Club, aka 'SF Club'

Address: 8 Herbert Crescent, Knightsbridge, London, SW1X 0EZ.
Tel.: 020 7589 9483.
Founded: 1945.
Objects: Membership is drawn primarily from the intelligence and security communities, military and civilian, and Special Forces, along with other organisations and individuals whose work reflects the ethos of the Club.
Approx. no. of members: 1,900.
Sex: Mixed sex.
Dress code: Smart-casual.
Type: Incorporated in 2009, as 8HC Ltd, a private company limited by guarantee, with members of the Club being members of the company.
Reciprocal clubs: None.
Culture: Improving.
Architect: John James Stevenson.
Facilities: Bar, dining room, library, bedrooms.
What they want you to know: Nothing. They tend to keep a very low profile: predictably, there is no plaque on the door, and the security may be the tightest of any London club. What goes on in the Club stays in the Club.
What they probably don't want you to know: A decade ago, membership requirements were reportedly relaxed to allow current and former police

officers who had worked on counter-terrorism programmes to join. The Club disputes this, arguing 'Membership was not relaxed, but broadened to reflect the ever increasing and international role of some specialist units in counter terrorism and international security.'

Short history: Established after the Second World War as a meeting place for those who had served in the Special Operations Executive (SOE) who had conducted behind-enemy-lines covert operations in occupied Europe throughout the war. The Club broadened its membership to members of the Special Forces and intelligence agencies. The Club remains remarkably low key, resembling a residential house. It proudly displays rows of photographs commemorating distinguished members along the staircase, with those who died on active service framed in black.

Further reading:
Sean Rayment, *Tales from the Special Forces Club* (London: Collins, 2013).

Union Jack Club – see THE MASS-MEMBERSHIP CLUBS

Victory Services Club – see THE MASS-MEMBERSHIP CLUBS

Yeoman Warders Club, aka the Tower of London Club, or 'The Keys'

Address: Tower Bridge Approach, Tower of London, London, E1W 1LE.
Tel.: None.
Founded: 1874.
Objects: Current Yeoman Warders of the Tower of London.
Approx. no. of members: 37.
Sex: Mixed sex.
Dress code: Jacket and tie at all times for men, equivalent for women; or military dress.
Type: Unincorporated association.
Reciprocal clubs: None.
Culture: Officers' mess.
Architect: Anthony Salvin.
Facilities: Bar.

What they want you to know: The only club inside the Tower of London, with membership restricted to the current 'Beefeaters'.

What they probably don't want you to know: It really is just a bar, modelled on an English pub.

Short history: For centuries, the Yeoman Warder 'Beefeaters', who live in the Tower of London with their families and guard it with their lives, have had an array of pubs and taverns. The last survivor of these is the Club, which became a private members' establishment in 1874. To qualify, Beefeaters must have at least 22 years' military service, retiring with at least the rank of warrant officer, and must also hold the Good Conduct and Long Service Medal. Taking up membership of the Club still involves a ritual with a large bowl of port, and a tankard each, swearing allegiance and pledging, 'May you never die a Yeoman Warder.' Drinks served include Beefeater gin, Beefeater bitter and Yeoman 1485 lager.

THE ARTISTIC AND CULTURAL CLUBS

Arts Club – Chelsea Arts Club – The Club for Acts and Actors – Garrick Club – London Sketch Club – The Magic Circle – Royal Kennel Club – Savage Club – Savile Club – University Women's Club

Arts Club

Address: 40 Dover Street, Mayfair, London, W1S 4NP.
Tel.: 020 7499 8581.
Founded: 1863.
Objects: Practising artists and patrons of the arts.
Approx. no. of members: 2,500.
Sex: Mixed sex.
Dress code: 'Elegant'.
Type: Proprietary; incorporated in 1896, as the Arts Club (London) Ltd, a private company limited by shares; principal shareholders since 2016 are

the Waney family, with Arjun Waney listed as the person with significant control.
Reciprocal clubs: 11 clubs, across 3 countries.
Culture: Mega-rich.
Architect: Unknown.
Facilities: Bar, 3 restaurants (including a ground-floor Brasserie, a first-floor members' lounge, 'Ofelia Members' Lounge', third-floor Japanese restaurant, 'Kyubi'), conservatory, function rooms, cigar lounge, nightclub, 8 bedrooms, garden.
What they want you to know: The last survivor of the historic clubs of Dover Street.
What they probably don't want you to know: Much of the Club's historic art collection was disposed of in the 2010s; though the Club points out that under the Waney family's ownership, significant contemporary acquisitions have been made.
Short history: For much of its history, the Arts Club was a somewhat raffish establishment, with numerous creative luminaries in the nineteenth century. After 30 years on Hanover Square, it settled on its current building in 1893. Until the early twenty-first century, the Club was dogged by financial difficulties, now resolved; changes of ownership since 2010 have brought about significant transformations; the Club is now trendier (with the addition of a nightclub), more affluent and better connected; but this came somewhat at the expense of its sleepy-but-unpretentious traditional ethos. The Club still holds quarterly art exhibitions, showcasing emerging and established artists alike. In 2020, a lucrative second branch of the Arts Club opened in Dubai in DIFC, the city's main financial centre, with the patronage of the Emirate's ruler, Sheikh Mohammed bin Rashid Al Maktoum.

Further reading:
Bernard Denvir, *A Most Agreeable Society: A Hundred and Twenty Five Years of the Arts Club* (London: Arts Club/Studio Editions, 1989).
G. A. F. Rogers, *The Arts Club and its Members* (London: Truslove and Hanson, 1920).

The Athenæum – see THE PALL MALL CLUBS

Chelsea Arts Club

Address: 143 Old Church Street, Chelsea, London, SW3 6EB.
Tel.: 020 7376 3311.
Founded: 1890.
Objects: Artists and the arts.
Approx. no. of members: 4,000.
Sex: Mixed sex.
Dress code: None.
Type: Unincorporated mutual.
Reciprocal clubs: Undisclosed.
Culture: Creative arts.
Architect: Robert Gunter; with alterations by Harrison Townsend and Gilbert Jenkins.
Facilities: Bar, dining room, billiard room, function room, garden, 12 bedrooms.
What they want you to know: There is a rolling programme of painting the clubhouse front with murals in drastically different styles.
What they probably don't want you to know: However attractive the wall murals that you see, you will never see them again once they move on to the next one.
Short history: Originally founded by James McNeill Whistler as a bohemian breakaway from the Arts Club in Mayfair, in 1902 the Club settled on its current building, the former Bolton Lodge, which retains the feel of a series of snug, convivial, interconnected cottages in which the members are brought close together. It still enjoys an informal, raucous spirit, and remains closely tied to the creative arts – a minimum of two-thirds of members elected each year are required to be practising artists, which not only makes 'social' membership sought-after, but gives the Club the feeling of a community of peers.
Further reading:
Tom Cross, *Artists and Bohemians: 100 Years with the Chelsea Arts Club* (London: Quiller, 1991).
Don Grant, *Private Parts: The Secret History of the Chelsea Arts Club* (London: Unicorn, 2019).

The Club for Acts and Actors

Address: 20 Bedford Street, Covent Garden, London, WC2E 9HP.
Tel.: 020 7836 3172.

Founded: 1897.
Objects: Current and retired actors.
Approx. no. of members: 1,200.
Sex: Mixed sex.
Dress code: Smart-casual.
Type: Unincorporated association.
Reciprocal clubs: None.
Culture: Informal, cultured.
Architect: William Howard.
Facilities: Jester Bar, hall, green room.
What they want you to know: One of the most relaxed clubs in London, for professional actors.
What they probably don't want you to know: There is more overlap with the Garrick Club membership than members might like to admit.
Short history: The Club had humble beginnings as the Concert Artistes' Association, which for its first five decades maintained a series of offices in the entertainment districts of London, from the Strand to Tottenham Court Road. It was during the years 1926–49 that it acquired more of the character of a club, as it shared its premises over Leicester Square Underground Station on Cranbourn Street, first with the Playgoers' Club and then with the Rehearsal Club, both of them for actors and actresses. A crisis in 1949, when their landlord forced them to vacate, was happily overcome as actor Jack Warner persuaded impresario J. Arthur Rank to loan the Club the money to buy the freehold on their present premises.

Further reading:
Larry Parker, *But – What Do You Do in the Winter? A History of the Concert Artistes' Association, 1897–1997* (London: Concert Artistes' Association, 1996).

Garrick Club

Address: 15 Garrick Street, Covent Garden, London, WC2E 9AY.
Tel.: 020 7379 6478.
Founded: 1831.
Objects: Theatre; 'the general patronage of the drama ... combining the use of a Club ... with the advantages of a Literary Society' (Geoffrey Wansell).
Approx. no. of members: 1,500.

Sex: Mixed sex.
Dress code: Jacket at all times for men, equivalent for women; men are asked to wear a necktie when dining in the coffee room.
Type: Unincorporated association.
Reciprocal clubs: 39 clubs, across 13 countries.
Culture: A mix of actors, writers, journalists, lawyers, doctors and other professions.
Architect: Frederick Marrable.
Facilities: Entry hall, grand staircase, cocktail bar, coffee room (dining room), morning room, reading room, library, card room, billiard room, function rooms, roof terrace, smoking balconies, 17 bedrooms.
What they want you to know: A London club closely concerned with the theatrical arts. It has an important theatrical library and the world's greatest collection of British theatrical portraits.
What they probably don't want you to know: The site of some of the most acrimonious scenes across Clubland in recent years, with recriminations and resignations over the non-admission (and then admission) of women.
Short history: Named in honour of eighteenth-century actor-manager David Garrick, who ran the Theatre Royal Drury Lane, the Garrick Club broke new ground. At a time when acting was still considered to be a somewhat disreputable profession, the Garrick was established so that actors and their patrons could engage on equal terms. Having outgrown their original clubhouse of the 1830s, the present building was completed in 1864, building on the pattern of the earlier Pall Mall clubs – but still located in the heart of London's Theatreland. The Club has a theatrical library of more than 10,000 books, together with archives, playbills and programmes. The walls are lined with over 400 oil paintings and several thousand sketches, a collection begun by actor Charles Mathews, and expanded upon by subsequent generations of members. It is the most substantial art collection of any London club. In 1956, the Club was the beneficiary of a quarter of the estate of *Winnie the Pooh* author A. A. Milne, and a 1990s copyright windfall from Disney, which holds

the film, TV and licensing rights following changes to US copyright law, which saw the Garrick receive a reported £40 million, making it 'one of the richest members' clubs in the world', in the words of Geoffrey Wansell. The Garrick Club is also well-known as a club for lawyers, not least because of the link between performances in the courtroom and on the stage – as Robert Low argues, 'some of our most distinguished lawyers over the past century and a half have been actors at heart'.

Further reading:
Geoffrey Ashton, *Pictures in the Garrick Club: A Catalogue of the Paintings, Drawings, Watercolours and Sculpture* (London: Garrick Club, 1997 [rev. 2002]).
R. H. Barham, *The Garrick Club: Notes of 135 of its Former Members* (London: Garrick Club, 1896).
John Baskett, *Brief Lives: Biographies of Sitters and Artists in the Garrick Club Collection* (London: Unicorn, 2005).
Guy Boas, *The Garrick Club, 1831–1964* (London: Garrick Club, 1948 [rev. 1964]).
Percy Fitzgerald, *The Garrick Club* (London: Elliot Stock, 1904).
Richard Hough, *The Ace of Clubs: A History of the Garrick* (London: Andre Deutsch, 1986).
Robert Low, *The Lawyers* (London: Garrick Club, 2011).
Desmond Shawe-Taylor, *Dramatic Art: Theatrical Paintings from the Garrick Club* (London: Dulwich Picture Gallery, 1997).
Geoffrey Wansell, *The Garrick: Story of a Club*, 2nd ed. (London: Garrick Club, 2013).

London Sketch Club

Address: 7 Dilke Street, Chelsea, London, SW3 4JE.
Tel.: 020 7352 8209.
Founded: 1898.
Objects: Sketch artists.
Approx. no. of members: 300.
Sex: Mixed sex.
Dress code: None.
Type: Unincorporated association.
Reciprocal clubs: None; although there are informal links to groups like the Savage Club.
Culture: Artistic.
Architect: Richard Phené Spiers.
Facilities: Main hallway and staircase, bar, studio.
Clubs within a club: Ironically, given it was founded as a spin-off from the **Langham Club**, the Langham long met as a society within the London Sketch Club, but now sketches independently.

What they want you to know: An authentic Victorian artists' club, occupying the garret of their clubhouse.

What they probably don't want you to know: Women were only admitted as recently as 2022.

Short history: The birth of the London Sketch Club lay in an improbable feud among London's Langham Sketch Club, between those artists who favoured the traditional cold buffet dinner, and those 'Young Turks' who argued for a more substantial hot meal after the group had its drawing sessions. From this esoteric feud, the rebels formed the London Sketch Club. Many of the early members were poster artists, and by the Edwardian era, two distinct LSC 'house styles' had emerged, one stressing stark lines, the other more ethereal in approach. For its first six decades, the Club had a slightly peripatetic existence, but since 1957 it has been ensconced in Chelsea, with a large, purpose-built Victorian artists' studio atop the building and the adjoining 'Sketcher's Arms' bar. The Club is lined with its members' historic artworks and organises seasonal exhibitions. Sketching is typically done twice weekly, while members' dinners are gala affairs with bohemian entertainments between courses, traditionally closing with the Club's dirge, 'Say, Watchman, What of the Night?', composed by Sir Arthur Sullivan.

Further reading:
Anthony Cohen, *The London Sketch Club, 1898–2023: A Visual Celebration* (London: London Sketch Club, 2024).
David Cuppleditch, *The London Sketch Club* (London: Dilke Press, 1978).

The Magic Circle

Address: 12 Stephenson Way, Euston, London, NW1 2HD.
Tel.: 020 7387 2222.
Founded: 1905.
Objects: Professional and amateur magicians.
Approx. no. of members: 1,700.
Sex: Mixed sex.
Dress code: None.
Type: Unincorporated Association (the Circle itself); but also incorporated

in 1987, as the Magic Circle Foundation Ltd, both as a registered charity and a private company limited by guarantee. The charity, which owns the freehold on the building, leases it to the unincorporated association on a long lease.

Reciprocal clubs: 1 club abroad; but it also affiliates with international magic societies operating across 50 countries.

Culture: Gregarious, cryptic – 'We're not a secret society, but we like to keep secrets.'

Architect: Jonathan Hampton.

Facilities: Lobby and staircase, bar, clubroom, museum, theatre, library, function room.

What they want you to know: The home of British magicians. The membership application process can be more onerous than for some Pall Mall establishments.

What they probably don't want you to know: A great deal. The nature of the magic trade depends upon secrecy, and the Club has some of the stiffest penalties (on pain of expulsion) around the revelation of trade secrets.

Short history: The Magic Circle, which traces its origins to assorted informal societies of magicians going back to 1791, founded a club in 1905. The Club presages well-known magic-themed clubs worldwide, like the Magic Castle in Los Angeles. For much of its history it had a peripatetic existence, meeting in theatres and taverns and inns. That changed when the current premises opened in 1998, in a purpose-built building. The charity looks to further the art of magic and organises public shows with the support of the Magic Circle in order to do so. The members of the Circle meet once weekly.

Further reading:
Michael Bailey, *The Magic Circle: Performing Magic Through the Ages* (Stroud: History Press, 2007).

Royal Kennel Club

Address: 10 Clarges Street, Mayfair, London, W1J 8AB.
Tel.: 020 7518 6874.
Founded: 1873.
Objects: The health, welfare and training of dogs.

Approx. no. of members: 1,200.
Sex: Mixed sex.
Dress code: Suit and tie at all times for men, equivalent for women.
Type: Incorporated in 2012, as The Kennel Club Ltd, a private company limited by guarantee, with members of the Club being members of the company; renamed in 2024 as The Royal Kennel Club Ltd. A separate Kennel Club Charitable Trust was set up in 1988.
Reciprocal clubs: 21 clubs, across 21 countries; all of them canine-themed.
Culture: Canine-friendly.
Architect: Unknown (original building); MCM Architecture (refurbishment).
Facilities: Bar, dining room, lounge, art gallery, library, conservatory, function rooms, 4 bedrooms.
What they want you to know: Since 1939, the Club has run the annual Crufts dog show.
What they probably don't want you to know: Following a costly IT programme, there were reports of extensive cutbacks in 2024, ranging from up to a fifth of staff being laid off, to terminating the Club's programme to help flat-faced dogs.
Short history: The Kennel Club was founded by Conservative MP and Irish landowner Sewallis Shirley, for the purpose of easing the organisation of dog shows and field trials. It was the first kennel club in any country. Moving between various premises in Victoria, Pall Mall, Piccadilly and Mayfair, it settled on Clarges Street in 1957. The club has since expanded across four sites: the headquarters in Mayfair, an administrative site in Aylesbury, and two country clubs at Stoneleigh Park in Warwickshire and on the Emblehope and Burngrange Estate in Northumberland. In 2012, the Club agreed to the sale of its previous clubhouse at 1–5 Clarges Street, using the proceeds to move to a new clubhouse a few doors away, which opened in 2016. In 2023, King Charles III granted the use of the 'Royal' prefix to mark the Club's 150th anniversary.

Savage Club

Address: 27 Great Queen Street, Covent Garden, London, WC2B 5BB.
Tel.: 07706 094 735.
Founded: 1857.

Club Directory: Historic Clubs

Objects: Art, drama, literature, music, science and law.
Approx. no. of members: 300.
Sex: Gentlemen only, though widows of members are allowed a form of associate membership, known as 'Rosemaries'.
Dress code: Jacket and tie at all times for men, equivalent for women.
Type: Unincorporated association.
Reciprocal clubs: 24 clubs, across 9 countries.
Culture: Bohemian, raucous.
Architect: Unknown.
Facilities: Club room, bar, library, meeting room with pantry and utility room, rehearsal space, co-working space, archive.
What they want you to know: The Club has a tradition of lively house dinners, chaired by a member, with a guest of honour, which involve a caricature-laden menu for each occasion, themed dishes and a singalong after the show.
What they probably don't want you to know: The Club downplays its historic links to the Masonic lodge, the Savage Lodge, No. 2190.
Short history: Author George Augustus Sala convened the first Savage Club meeting in 1857, with Richard Savage, a minor poet, being claimed as the source of inspiration for the name. The Club led an itinerant existence in its first three decades, convening in a succession of taverns and hotels, with the subscription 'just whatever the members choose to owe'. From 1889, however, the Savage began to be housed in a series of more substantial clubhouses and clubrooms within other clubs, though still wandering. Membership traditionally came in one of five categories: art, drama, music, literature and science, with a sixth category later added: law. The Club closed its previous premises at the end of 2021, and is about to open a major new clubhouse in Covent Garden.

Further reading:
Percy V. Bradshaw, *'Brother Savages and Guests': A History of the Savage Club, 1857–1957* (London: W. H. Allen, 1958).
Thomas Catling and Walter Jerrold, *A Savage Club Souvenir* (London: Savage Club, 1916).
Andrew Halliday (ed.), *The Savage Club Papers, First Series* (London: Tinsley Brothers, 1867).
—, *The Savage Club Papers for 1868* (London: Tinsley Brothers, 1868).
Mark Hambourg, *The Eighth Octave: Tones and Semi-Tones Concerning Piano-Playing, the Savage Club and Myself* (London: Williams & Norgate, 1951).

J. E. Muddock (ed.), *The Savage Club Papers* (London: Hutchinson, 1897).
Matthew Norgate and Alan Wykes, *Not So Savage* (London: Jupiter Books, 1976).
William Bernard Tegetmeier, *Reminiscences of the Savage Club* (London: Privately published, 1900).
John Wade, *Dining with Savages: A New Savage Miscellany* (Northam: Roundhouse, 2000).
Edwin A. Ward, *Recollections of a Savage, i.e. a Member of the Savage Club* (London: Frederick A. Stokes, 1923).
Aaron Watson and Mark Twain, *The Savage Club: A Medley of History, Anecdote and Reminiscence* (London: T. Fisher Unwin, 1907).
James Wilson, *Noble Savages: The Savage Club and the Great War, 1914–1918* (London: J. H. Productions, 2018).

Savile Club

Address: 69–71 Brook Street, Mayfair, London, W1K 4ER.

Tel.: 020 7629 5462.

Founded: 1868.

Objects: Literary, artistic and scientific.

Approx. no. of members: 950.

Sex: Gentlemen only.

Dress code: Jacket at all times for men, equivalent for women guests. Ties encouraged for men, but not compulsory.

Type: Incorporated in 1910, as Savile Club Ltd, as a private company limited by shares, with the Trustees of the Club being the shareholders on behalf of the members.

Reciprocal clubs: 69 clubs, across 23 countries.

Culture: Raffish, cultured, free thinking and free talking.

Architect: Thomas Cundy II (elevation of house at No. 69 *c.* 1850), unknown for Walter H. Burns (additional storey at No. 69 *c.* 1885), Trollope and Sons (No. 71, *c.* 1892–4), and Richard Bouwens van der Boijen and Jules Allard (interior decoration of No. 71).

Facilities: Entrance hall, main staircase, bar, salon (dining room), ballroom, ballroom lobby and staircase, morning room, drawing room, garden room and ante-room, library, snooker room/cards room, function rooms, 25 bedrooms, courtyard, terrace.

Clubs within a club: The **Flyfishers Club**, founded in 1884, is based on the second floor, with two rooms of its own, maintaining a voluminous library on the history and technique of fly fishing; with 600 members, it is a substantive club in its own right. The resurrected **Eccentric Club** also periodically meets at the Savile, though without a dedicated space of its own.

What they want you to know: One of the last of the traditional Mayfair clubs, possibly the closest to a Drones Club experience today, but more erudite.

What they probably don't want you to know: The *Evening Standard* once speculated upon the Club's library as a place of assignation.

Short history: The Club was originally styled 'the New Club' for its first two years at Spring Gardens off Trafalgar Square, until it changed its name on moving to premises on Savile Row. After a decade there, it spent over four decades in a former Rothschild mansion on Piccadilly overlooking Green Park, before acquiring the lease in 1927 of the Mayfair home of the daughter of Walter H. Burns and widow of Lewis, Viscount Harcourt, eccentrically put together from two adjoining houses. The result is an unconventional but ostentatious building, filled with hidden treasures. Long the home of the Clubland literati, it is also one of the more bohemian clubs, with a strong culture of indoor games. The size of around a thousand ensures the kind of club table where members know one another's names.

Further reading:
Anonymous [Sir Herbert Stephen], *The Savile Club, 1868–1923* (London: Savile Club, 1923).
Anonymous, *The Savile Club, 1868–1958* (London: Savile Club, 1957).
Garrett Anderson, *Hang Your Halo in the Hall: A History of the Savile Club* (London: Savile Club, 1993).
Monja Danischewsky, *The Savile Club, 1868–1968* (London: Savile Club, 1968).
Robert J. D. Harding, 'Founders of the Savile Club (*act.* 1868–1872)', *Oxford Dictionary of National Biography* (Oxford: Oxford University Press, 2024).
Patricia Reed, *A Brief History of No. 69 and 71 Brook Street, Mayfair* (London: Savile Club, 2009).
Sesquicentennial series:
Ken Allen and Robert J. D. Harding (eds), Michael Boulter and Neville Punchard, *The Savile Club Scientists* (London: Savile Club, 2019).
Michael Bloch, *Guide to the Savile Monument* (London, Savile Club, 2018).
Robert J. D. Harding (ed.), *Suggestions' Books: A Selection of Entries, 1869–1969* (London, Savile Club, 2018).
—, *The Savile Club 1914–1918 War Memorial* (London, Savile Club, 2018).
—, *A Sesquicentennial Miscellany* (London, Savile Club, 2019).
—, *The Savile Club 1939–1945 War Memorial* (London, Savile Club, 2023).

University Women's Club

Address: 2 Audley Square, Mayfair, London, W1K 1DB.
Tel.: 020 7499 2268.
Founded: 1886.
Objects: University graduates and professional women.
Approx. no. of members: 900.
Sex: Ladies only.
Dress code: Smart-casual.
Type: Unincorporated association.
Reciprocal clubs: 42 clubs, across 8 countries.
Culture: Thoughtful, professional, social.
Architect: Thomas Henry Wyatt.
Facilities: Entrance hall, main staircase, lobby and bar, dining room, drawing room, library, function rooms, garden, 21 bedrooms.
What they want you to know: The only remaining historic women's club in London.
What they probably don't want you to know: The Club recently faced local opposition to their application to change their licence from a Club Premises Certificate to a Full Premises Licence. (In the end, the licence was granted, subject to some restrictions.)
Short history: Rooted in the nineteenth-century movement for women's education, the University Club for Ladies – as it was originally called – was first convened by Gertrude Jackson, a graduate of Girton College, Cambridge. Her concern was that university-educated women were still significantly disadvantaged in the workplace if they were unable to access men-only clubs, and so the Club evolved. In 1921, it moved to its present building. Between the mid-Victorian era and the inter-war years, there were more than 80 women's clubs in London, mainly centred around Mayfair – the University Women's Club is the sole survivor of these historic clubs.

Further reading:
A. G. E. Carthew (ed.), *The University Women's Club: Extracts from Fifty Years of Minute Books, 1886–1936* (Eastbourne: Sumfield and Day, 1936, repr. 1985).
Evelyn Haselgrove, *University Women's Club: A History* (London: University Women's Club, 1994).

Club Directory: Historic Clubs

THE DINING CLUBS

Beefsteak Club – Pratt's

These occupy a unique corner of Clubland, not least because of their size: they are the smallest free-standing clubs in London, both in premises and in their number of members.

Beefsteak Club

Address: 9 Irving Street, Soho, London, WC2H 7AH.
Tel.: 020 7930 5722.
Founded: 1876.
Objects: Social: 'beef and liberty'.
Approx. no. of members: 500.
Sex: Gentlemen only.
Dress code: Jacket and tie at all times for men, equivalent for women.
Type: Unincorporated association. The Beef and Liberty Company Ltd, a dormant company limited by guarantee that was incorporated in 1999, acts as a trustee.
Reciprocal clubs: 8 clubs, across 5 countries.
Culture: Gregarious, inquisitive, literary.
Architect: Frank Verity (building); Roger Mears Architects (staircase).
Facilities: Dining room, grand staircase, one bedroom.
What they want you to know: That all the waiters are to be called 'Charles'.
What they probably don't want you to know: That the anonymous-looking entrance is sandwiched in between various chain Italian restaurants.
Short history: A throwback to an earlier age of dining clubs, the present-day Beefsteak Club was founded as a resurrection of a series of defunct beefsteak clubs which went back to the early eighteenth century, the last of which had closed its doors in 1867. Originally meeting for its first 20 years in a leased room of Folly's Theatre on King William IV Street, it had its current premises purpose-built in 1896, in what was then named Green Street (before it was renamed in honour of Henry Irving). Aside from the kitchen, the toilets, the office, a solitary bedroom and a very

small hallway, the Club consists of just one room on the first floor. The wood-panelled and silverware-lined clubroom is dominated by a long dining table, and exposed beams along the vaulted ceiling above, with the sole bay window overlooking Charing Cross Road and the Garrick Theatre opposite. Conversation turns more to the arts and current affairs than at Pratt's, where country pursuits tend to dominate. For over a century, the main clubroom was reached through a slightly scruffy winding staircase, shared with the offices occupying the rest of the building; but after a 2024 redesign, an old secondary kitchen staircase was converted into an extremely smart private staircase with a curved oak banister, lined with prints of past members.

Further reading:
John Martin Robinson, *History of the Beefsteak Club* (London: Beefsteak Club, 2024).

Pratt's

Address: 14 Park Place, St James's, London, SW1A 1LP.
Tel.: 020 7493 0397.
Founded: 1857.
Objects: Social.
Approx. no. of members: 800.
Sex: Mixed sex.
Dress code: Jacket and tie at all times for men, equivalent for women.
Type: Proprietary club; current proprietor is Bill Cavendish, Earl of Burlington.
Reciprocal clubs: None.
Culture: Aristocratic; 'One Nation' Tory.
Architect: Unknown; built by Robert, Joseph and John Rossington.
Facilities: Bar, dining room, private dining room, 2 bedrooms.
What they want you to know: That the steward and all the waiters are to be called 'George' or 'Georgina'.
What they probably don't want you to know: That they would struggle to accommodate more than 20 diners in a night.
Short history: Pratt's is unique among the historic London clubs, in that it remains a proprietary club; although the day-to-day management is

still overseen by an elected committee. Its roots go back 16 years prior to its official foundation, when in 1841 the 7th Duke of Beaufort began inviting his friends to the Park Place house of a local steward, William Steward Pratt, just off St James's Street. Pratt's hospitality in his basement kitchen proved so popular that this became a regular fixture, and by 1857 Pratt converted the hotel he operated above into a club. The Club remained in the Pratt family until 1908, changing hands several times in the early twentieth century, until its acquisition in 1926 by the 9th Duke of Devonshire, whose great-grandson still owns it today. Although Pratt's has a ground-floor lunch room and a first-floor private dining room for functions, it is to all intents and purposes focused on two small, interconnected rooms in the basement: the dining room, which is the heart of this supper club, and the ante-room, where members are called when their dinner is ready. The steward retains a flat at the top of the house. The décor is unfussy and unpretentious; rather than having any fine art on display it has more the appearance of a cosy countryside pub, with ephemera picked up over the years: tankards, plates, old prints, a taxidermised rhinoceros head, and a stuffed fish donated by Philip, Duke of Edinburgh. Pratt's recently surprised many, when, in 2023, this most conservative of establishments admitted women for the first time: it turned out to have come with not only the blessing of the proprietor Bill (Earl of) Burlington and the chairman Lord Soames, but was voted for unanimously by the committee.

THE 'EX-PAT' CLUBS

Caledonian Club – Ognisko Polskie

London has a long history of expatriate national groupings setting up their own clubs. Many, such as the American Club, French Club, German Athenæum, India Club, Irish Club, Royal Anglo-Belgian Club, Scandinavian Club and the West Indian Club, have become defunct. Others, such as the Canning Club (originally called the Argentine Club) and Den Norske Klub have merged into the Naval and Military Club. But there are two surviving 'national' clubs, from both within and without the United Kingdom.

Caledonian Club

Address: 9 Halkin Street, Belgravia, London, SW1X 7DR.
Tel.: 020 7235 5162.
Founded: 1891.
Objects: Social; Scots in London.
Approx. no. of members: 1,400.
Sex: Mixed sex.
Dress code: Jacket, collared shirt, smart trousers, dress or skirt required after 9.30 a.m. Ties optional, except at dinner in the dining room, where they are required.
Type: Incorporated in 1917, as the Caledonian Club Trust Ltd, now a private company limited by guarantee, with the members of the Club being the members of the company.
Reciprocal clubs: 72 clubs, across 25 countries.
Culture: Patriotically Scots, but low key.
Architect: Detmar Jellings Blow.
Facilities: Bar, smoking room, drawing room, dining room, library, snooker room, terrace, ballroom, function rooms, business centre, 39 bedrooms.
What they want you to know: The home-from-home for Scots in London, organising some of the best Burns Suppers in the capital.
What they probably don't want you to know: Aside from the tartan carpets, the Club is surprisingly English in its aesthetics.
Short history: Established for Scots living in London, the Club began as a proprietary club on Charles II Street, just off St James's Square, before a management buyout by the members near the end of the First World War turned it into a members-owned club. The Club was on St James's Square during the inter-war years, but suffered a direct hit in the Blitz, and after several years of lodging with its neighbours on the square moved to its present clubhouse in Belgravia in 1946. A large extension annexe, opened

in 2006, provides substantial events facilities including a ballroom with a sprung floor for ceilidhs and reeling.

Further reading:
Jan Coughtrie, *The Caledonian Club, Belgravia, London: A History of the Club and its Collection of Art and Artefacts* (London: The Caledonian Club, 2014).

Ognisko Polskie, aka 'The Polish Hearth'

Address: 55 Princes Gate, South Kensington, London, SW7 2PN.
Tel.: 020 7589 4670.
Founded: 1939 (informally); 1940 (officially inaugurated).
Objects: 'To encourage and promote within the United Kingdom wider knowledge of Poland and to promote the welfare of Poles residing in or visiting the United Kingdom … developing a closer relationship between British and Polish people … non-political.'
Approx. no. of members: Undisclosed.
Sex: Mixed sex.
Dress code: Smart-casual to formal, depending on the event.
Type: Incorporated in 1952, as Ognisko Polskie (Polish Hearth) Ltd, a private company limited by shares.
Reciprocal clubs: None.
Culture: Sociable; literary.
Architect: William Tasker and Charles James Freake.
Facilities: Bar and restaurant (open to public), ballroom, theatre, exhibition gallery, function rooms, terrace.
What they want you to know: They serve some of the best Eastern European cocktails in London, and many of their events are open to the public.
What they probably don't want you to know: Between the restaurant and bar being public, and most events being open to non-members, there are limited incentives to join.
Short history: Established by expatriate Polish officers and the British Council early in the Second World War, with the Duke of Kent helping them to secure premises, Ognisko Polskie rapidly became the focal point of Polish cultural and social life in the UK, with other Polish organisations

growing from its hub. Airmen serving in the RAF's Polish squadrons used Ognisko Polskie for some of their earliest social meetings and dances, and the Club took on a military flavour, especially with the arrival of General Władysław Anders. The Polish Free Theatre also had its home at Ognisko Polskie from 1942, and continues to this day. The Club has been based in South Kensington's 'Museumland' for most of its history, acquiring its present building from the University of London in 1978. The Club continues to serve as a major Polish cultural centre in London, but is Polish-British, with most events held in English. Since 2013, the ground-floor bar and restaurant have been leased to restauranteur Prince Jan Woroniecki, who operates the popular Ognisko establishment from there.

THE POLITICAL CLUBS

Carlton Club – House of Commons – House of Lords – National Liberal Club – Winchester House Club

Once upon a time, there used to be scores of political clubs in central London. Most were Conservative: the City Carlton, the Conservative, the Constitutional, the Junior Carlton, the Junior Conservative, the Junior Constitutional, the Ladies' Carlton. But there were also Liberal clubs like the Devonshire, and the City Liberal Club; and there was even once a National Labour Club on Westminster's Romney Street in the inter-war years. Many of the once-heavily political clubs, like Brooks's, the Reform and White's, have long since shed any formal affiliation. But going against the grain have been two party-affiliated survivors, one Conservative, the other Liberal.

However, Britain's club-like politics of the nineteenth century left a deep and lasting impression on its parliament, particularly after the Great Fire of 1834 almost entirely destroyed the old parliamentary estate. In the three decades before a new parliament was completed, many of the functions of government relocated to the clubs, while club architect Charles Barry was commissioned to create a new Houses of Parliament in the image of Clubland, complete with tearooms, smoking rooms and libraries. Indeed, Charles Dickens observed in 1864 that the new Houses of Parliament were 'the best club in London', and they remain so in many respects – including the wine lists (despite the best efforts of Robert Maxwell to asset strip the House of Commons wine cellars during his stint as chairman of the Commons' Refreshments Committee in the 1960s).* While parliamentarians can wander freely between them, each of the two Houses has its own distinctive culture and facilities.

Carlton Club

Address: 69 St James's Street, St James's, London, SW1A 1PJ.
Tel.: 020 7493 1164.
Founded: 1832.
Objects: Conservatism; support of the Conservative Party.
Approx. no. of members: 1,500.
Sex: Mixed sex.
Dress code: Jacket and tie at all times for men, equivalent for women.
Type: Incorporated in 1956, as Carlton Club Ltd, a private company limited by shares; with the Trustees of the Club ultimately being the persons with significant control, through the 99.97 per cent shareholding of Carlton Trustees (London) Ltd.
Reciprocal clubs: 134 clubs, across 36 countries.
Culture: Conservative activists, agents, candidates, councillors and MPs.
Architect: Thomas Hopper.
Facilities: Macmillan Bar, morning room, Thatcher Drawing Room, dining room (Wellington Room), four function rooms, smoking terrace, 24 bedrooms.
Clubs within a club: Such was the Carlton's lengthy waiting list in the nineteenth century that the **Junior Carlton Club** was set up in 1864, to

---

* Maxwell insisted upon selling at a fraction of their value thousands of bottles of the Houses of Parliament's finest nineteenth-century vintages, to an unidentified overseas buyer. The buyer was, of course, himself – something long suspected by his guests at Headington Hall, who noted for decades to come the excellent vintages he decanted from portcullis-crested bottles.

cater to three times as many members. When the Junior Carlton folded in 1977, it merged into the Carlton, bringing with it various paintings and artefacts, such as Benjamin Disraeli's table. The Junior Carlton had itself absorbed various clubs, including the staunchly Protestant **National Club** (which still meets as a dining society within the Carlton) and the apolitical **Thatched House Club**.

What they want you to know: The home of British conservatism.

What they probably don't want you to know: Government whip Chris Pincher's drunken groping spree here in 2022 brought down the government of Boris Johnson.

Short history: The Carlton, arguably the most significant political club in history, takes its name from the old royal palace, Carlton House, which had stood on the site of its first building. It has its roots in two groupings. The first was with the 'Charles Street Gang' – the St James's basement office of Tory election managers in the early 1830s was plagued by sympathetic noblemen wanting gossip and refreshment. The second was the effort to reorganise the broken Tory election machine after the Great Reform Act of 1832. Both elements were united when the Tories hit upon the idea of a club that combined a downstairs office to get on with the business of politics, with an upstairs salon to offer refreshment to politicking members. The Carlton hosted numerous political events over the years, most significantly the 1922 meeting which brought down the David Lloyd George coalition. For over a century, the Carlton occupied two clubhouses on Pall Mall, but this came to an end with the bombing of 1940, during the Blitz. Coincidentally, Arthur's, a Georgian gambling club, had just closed down, and so from 1943 the Carlton occupied the Arthur's building – initially temporarily and, since the 1960s, on a permanent basis. The Arthur's building, smaller than the previous Carlton clubhouse, has given the Club a more intimate feeling. Dating to the 1820s, the building is on the site occupied by White's in the early eighteenth century. The Club continues strictly to enforce its political creed – there is no such category as 'social membership', all members undertake to support the Conservative Party; and members who switch party affiliation are expected to resign, or they can (and will) be swiftly expelled – as politicians from Winston Churchill to Ann Widdecombe have found. In recent years, the library was replaced by a wine room.

Further reading:
Sir Charles Petrie and Alistair Cooke [Lord Lexden], *The Carlton Club, 1832–2007* (London: Carlton Club, 1955 [rev. 2007 and 2015]).
Barry Phelps, *Power and the Party: A History of the Carlton Club, 1832–1982* (London: Macmillan, 1983).

House of Commons

Address: Houses of Parliament, Parliament Square, London, SW1A 0AA.
Tel.: 020 7219 4272.
Founded: 1327 (as the House of Commons of England); 1800 (as the House of Commons of the United Kingdom); 1852 (as a club).
Objects: Representation of the British electorate.
Approx. no. of members: 650.
Sex: Mixed sex.
Dress code: In the chamber, jacket and tie at all times for men, equivalent for women. Smart-casual elsewhere.
Type: Legislature.
Reciprocal clubs: None.
Culture: Variable over the years, depending on elections. For much of the last decade, it was sleazy and boozy, with a high dose of sexual impropriety and recreational drugs. The incoming intake of earnest new MPs from 2024 has a more puritanical streak.
Architect: Charles Barry.
Facilities: Access to over a dozen bars across the parliamentary estate (including the Pugin Room and the riverside Strangers' Bar), Members' Dining Room, Members' Reading Room, Members' Smoking Room, Members' Tea-Room, Strangers' Dining Room, Churchill Room (restaurant), Terrace Dining Rooms, two permanent marquees (Terrace Pavilion and Thames Pavilion), House of Commons Library, assorted cafeterias and dining rooms across the parliamentary estate, committee rooms (often used as meeting rooms), riverside terrace (largest in London).
Clubs within a club: For over a century, the **Sports and Social Club** was a members-only pub directly under the central lobby, with membership

limited to current and former MPs and their staff; but after developing a reputation for drunken brawls, it was closed in 2017 and taken in-house by the parliamentary authorities as a regular bar. It has now been transferred to the House of Lords (see below) and renamed the Woolsack.

What they want you to know: The democratic part of 'the mother of Parliaments' (John Bright, 1865).

What they probably don't want you to know: They have tried very hard, for decades, to live down the club image ('Parliament cannot continue as a gentlemen's club', Gordon Brown, 2009), but items like the House of Commons snuff box continue to undermine this. Approached for comment for this book, the Commons' Press Office denied that it operates as a club: 'I'm not aware of any private members' club which welcomes over 1 million people as visitors each year. I would argue that you've also misrepresented our catering facilities – the majority of our venues are open to not just MPs but also their staff, the Peers and journalists who work here – and more importantly, the thousands of staff who keep Parliament running 24 hours a day.'

Short history: Parliament evolved from informal medieval beginnings, being summoned irregularly whenever the monarch needed money, 'An event rather than an institution' (Conrad Russell). The aftermath of the English Civil War saw the House of Commons' permanence guaranteed, with major extensions of the franchise in the nineteenth and twentieth centuries resulting in a less aristocratic and more representative intake. The result – after the rebuild from the 1840s to the 1860s, with its club facilities – has been the largest and most luxurious club in London, to which election can only be secured by standing for public office. Accommodation is not provided, but there is a very generous system of allowances and expenses to pay for travel and a second home. Nomination still requires a proposer and seconder, with ten supporting signatures (from within the prospective member's constituency).

Further reading:
Paul Flynn, *How to Be an MP: Learning the Commons Knowledge*, 2nd ed. (London: Biteback, 2012).
Clyve Jones (ed.), *A Short History of Parliament* (London: Boydell Press, 2012).
Various, *The History of Parliament: The House of Commons, 1386–1832*, 57 volumes (Various, 1964–2023).

Club Directory: Historic Clubs

House of Lords

Address: Houses of Parliament, Parliament Square, London, SW1A 0PW.
Tel.: 020 7219 3000.
Founded: Tenth century (as the Magnum Concilium or 'Great Council'); 1800 (as the House of Lords of the United Kingdom); 1847 (as a club).
Objects: Revision of legislation; secondary chamber.
Approx. no. of members: 850.
Sex: Mixed sex.
Dress code: In the chamber, jacket at all times for men and women, with men's ties welcome but not mandatory. Jacket and tie for men at all times in the Peers' Dining Room, Peers' Guest Room and the Barry Room. Smart-casual elsewhere.
Type: Legislature.
Reciprocal clubs: None.
Culture: A combination of pensioned-off party hacks, ageing experts whose knowledge may be decades out of date, and wealthy party donors, plus a smattering of bishops and hereditary peers (the latter proposed for abolition by the present government).
Architect: Charles Barry.
Facilities: Access to 30 bars across the parliamentary estate, Barry Room (members-only dining room), Peers' Dining Room, Peers' Guest Room, Peers' Tea-Room, House of Lords Library, assorted cafeterias and dining rooms across the parliamentary estate, function rooms (Attlee Room, Reid Room, Home Room, Cholmondeley Room), committee rooms (often used as meeting rooms), riverside terrace.
What they want you to know: The revising chamber of Parliament, with a wealth of expertise to hand.
What they probably don't want you to know: Peerages have been sold for centuries – initially by the Crown, and in the last two centuries by the political parties. This is therefore a club in which it is quite possible to buy one's way in.
Short history: For centuries, the House of Lords represented the feudal interests of the barons. The nineteenth-century construction of the present Houses of Parliament saw its reconstitution along consciously

'clubbable' lines, mirroring the rebuild of the House of Commons. Recent decades have seen major cultural changes: life peerages, introduced in 1958, have become the norm, and have seen a profusion of new peerage creations, while the 1999 abolition of the sitting rights of most hereditary peerages (barring a rump of 92, who have been allowed to sit until now) has resulted in a chamber that is less traditionally aristocratic, more plutocratic, and almost entirely based on the patronage of the political party leaders of the day. Accommodation is not provided, but peers can collect a tax-free daily attendance allowance of £342 per sitting day.

Further reading:
Clive Aslet and Derry Moore, *Inside the House of Lords* (London: HarperCollins, 1998).
Emma Crewe, *Lords of Parliament: Manners, Rituals and Politics* (Manchester: Manchester University Press, 2005).
John Wells, *The House of Lords* (London: Hodder & Stoughton, 1997).

National Liberal Club, aka 'NLC'

Address: 1 Whitehall Place, Whitehall, London, SW1A 2HE.
Tel.: 020 7930 9871.
Founded: 1882.
Objects: The promotion of an inexpensive and accessible home for Liberals.
Approx. no. of members: 2,500.
Sex: Mixed sex.
Dress code: Smart-casual. Jacket and tie for men are encouraged in the dining room, but not compulsory.
Type: Hybrid; unincorporated association, wholly owning through a nominated third party the 100 per cent shareholding in a private company limited by shares, National Liberal Club Ltd, incorporated in 1978.
Reciprocal clubs: 343 clubs, across 53 countries.
Culture: Earnest, multicultural liberals; mingled with apolitical freeloaders looking for a cheap club.
Architect: Alfred Waterhouse (building); Clyde Young and Bernard Engle (staircase).
Facilities: Bar, dining room, smoking room, terrace, workspace/lounge, 5 function rooms, snooker room.

Clubs within a club: The **Authors Club**, founded in 1891, has been based here since 2014, which has been something of a homecoming for them to Whitehall; they originally had a clubhouse of their own in one of the neighbouring converted flats up until 1966, and then spent a decade lodging with the NLC, before dalliances with the Lansdowne Club, Arts Club and Black's.

What they want you to know: A club that trades on its inclusivity, rather than exclusivity.

What they probably don't want you to know: One of the more contentious governance setups you will encounter in London Clubland, marred by long-running disputes in recent years.

Short history: Founded by rank-and-file Liberal Party activists during Gladstone's third government, the intention was to create a mass-membership club to help popularise liberal philosophy and politics among people who would not normally belong to a London club. For its first three decades, it occupied the largest London clubhouse ever built, with the largest membership of any London club (until superseded by the RAC). The collapse of the Liberal Party as a national political force from the 1910s, however, precipitated a long, slow decline in the Club across much of the twentieth century, much of it marked by cack-handed attempts to turn the Club into a more elite institution, modelled on the Pall Mall clubs. This culminated in a scandal in the 1970s, during which the Club was run by a confidence trickster who asset stripped the premises under the members' very noses. The Club arguably never fully recovered, selling off its building to a neighbouring hotel, and sub-letting a fifth of its old rooms back. A series of governance disputes rocked the Club in the early 2020s.

Further reading:
Anonymous, *The National Liberal Club* (London: National Liberal Club, 1933).
Coss Bilson (ed.), *The National Liberal Club, 1882–1982* (London: National Liberal Club, 1982).
Michael Meadowcroft, *A Guide to the Works of Art of the National Liberal Club, London, Second Edition* (London: National Liberal Club, 2011).
Robert Steven, *The National Liberal Club: Politics and Persons* (London: Robert Houghton, 1925).

Reform Club – see THE PALL MALL CLUBS

Winchester House Club

Address: 10 Lower Richmond Road, Putney, London, SW15 1JN.

Tel.: 07701 336 183.

Founded: 1892.

Objects: Conservative politics (originally); social (today).

Approx. no. of members: 1,000.

Sex: Mixed sex.

Dress code: Smart-casual.

Type: Incorporated, 1892, as Putney Constitutional Club Company Ltd (renamed in 1997 as Winchester House Club Ltd), a private company limited by guarantee, with the members of the Club being members of the company.

Reciprocal clubs: 122 clubs, across 27 countries.

Culture: Relaxed.

Architect: Unknown (seventeenth-century original building); Jacques Badouin (eighteenth-century extension).

Facilities: Bar, bistro, Whitehouse Room (snooker room), reading room, function room, garden.

What they want you to know: A premier riverside club; the Oxford vs Cambridge Boat Race is a particular annual highlight, with the Club's lawn overlooking the starting point.

What they probably don't want you to know: The Club's political roots have been quietly forgotten about.

Short history: The Winchester House Club is a survivor of a largely vanished breed of clubs. It was founded in 1892 as the Putney Constitutional Club, originally aligned with the Conservative and Unionist cause, one of many local political clubs up and down the country which supported election campaigns – an intermediate tier between the working men's clubs and the clubs of Pall Mall. They took as their home Winchester House, a seventeenth-century riverside lodge. Like many one-time political clubs, the politics was gradually dropped, making way for a purely social club, reflected in the name change.

Club Directory: Historic Clubs

THE CITY CLUBS

City of London Club – City University Club – Guildhall Club – Little Ship Club

The City of London – the capital's financial district – has its own unique customs dating back to the Middle Ages, and Clubland here is as much a product of 'City' culture as the norms of the West End.

City of London Club

Address: 19 Old Broad Street, City of London, London, EC2N 1DS.
Tel.: 020 7588 7991.
Founded: 1832.
Objects: Financial services.
Approx. no. of members: 1,800.
Sex: Mixed sex.
Dress code: Smart-casual in much of the Club; in the bar and dining room, jacket and tie for men, equivalent for women.
Type: Unincorporated association.
Reciprocal clubs: 42 clubs, across 14 countries.
Culture: City of London; luncheon club.
Architect: Philip Hardwick.
Facilities: Bar, coffee room (dining room), function rooms, 20 bedrooms.
What they want you to know: The oldest and largest club in the City.
What they probably don't want you to know: The bedrooms are also leased to non-members, on Booking.com.
Short history: A long-term staple of the City's lunching culture, the Club was founded in 1832 under the chairmanship of John Masterman MP, with its formidable clubhouse maintained and preserved. Small, but with all the essential facilities of a London club, it is one of the least changed clubs in the City: still buzzing at lunchtime, but quiet in the evenings.

Further reading:
J. Owen Unwin, *The City of London Club: Centenary Notes on its History and Traditions, 1832–1932* (London: City of London Club, 1932).

City University Club
Address: 42 Crutched Friars, City of London, London, EC3N 2AP.
Tel.: 020 7167 6682.
Founded: 1895.
Objects: University graduates working in the City of London.
Approx. no. of members: 500.
Sex: Mixed sex.
Dress code: Jacket and tie at all times for men, equivalent for women.
Type: Unincorporated association.
Reciprocal clubs: 602 clubs, across 59 countries.
Culture: Relaxed, businesslike.
Architect: Unknown (early seventeenth century).
Facilities: Bar, dining room, function rooms.
What they want you to know: The most extensive reciprocals list of any London club.
What they probably don't want you to know: They are sometimes mistaken for something to do with City University, which they pre-date by seven decades.
Short history: The City University Club was founded for graduates of Oxford and Cambridge universities working in the City of London – though being a university alumnus is no longer an entry requirement. For over a century, the Club was a fixture on Cornhill, by the Bank of England, as a luncheon club with the bar on one floor and the dining room on another, until its lease was terminated by the new landlord. In 2018, it moved in with the Lloyds Club at Crutched Friars, with which it merged.

Guildhall Club
Address: Guildhall, West Wing, Gresham Street, City of London, London, EC2V 7HH.
Tel.: 020 7332 1889.
Founded: 1899.
Objects: Refreshment for members of the Corporation of London.
Approx. no. of members: 125.

Sex: Mixed sex.
Dress code: Jacket and tie for men, equivalent for women.
Type: Unincorporated association.
Reciprocal clubs: None.
Culture: City of London; luncheon club.
Architect: Richard Gilbert Scott.
Facilities: Bar, dining room, 2 function rooms.
What they want you to know: The smallest club in the City.
What they probably don't want you to know: The prices are heavily subsidised by the 'City's Cash', the Corporation of London's endowment fund, which has brought adverse press attention over the years (although it does mean relieving the taxpayer of covering any subsidies).
Short history: Charles Dickens's dictum that the Houses of Parliament were 'the best club in London' still applies to this singular institution from the late Victorian era – a private members' club to which the only way of securing membership is by standing for election to public office. The members are the Aldermen and Court of Common Council of the Corporation of London, which runs the City. Established to provide refreshment for members of the Corporation, it is based in the 1970s brutalist West Wing of the Guildhall, overlooking the fifteenth-century core of the complex. Club life centres around the main dining room. Despite being built into the Guildhall, the Club maintains its own structures and elections.

Little Ship Club

Address: Bell Wharf Lane, Upper Thames Street, City of London, London, EC4R 3TB.
Tel.: 020 7236 7729.
Founded: 1926.
Objects: Social; yachting; training.
Approx. no. of members: 400.
Sex: Mixed sex.
Dress code: Smart-casual.
Type: Incorporated in 1930, as Little Ship Club (Members) Ltd, renamed in 2002 as Little Ship Club Ltd; now a private company limited by

guarantee, with guaranteeing members of the Club being members of the company.

Reciprocal clubs: 32 clubs, across 16 countries, all of them yacht clubs.

Culture: Informal.

Architect: Unknown; the building of the Club was at the behest of developers Eagle Star, and its main contractor, Kumagai Gumi. The fitting out of the Club was separately managed by members.

Facilities: Bar, dining room, lounge, chart room (for passage planning), function rooms, cabins (for overnight accommodation).

Clubs within a club: The **City Livery Club**, which has moved between different sites over the decades, was founded in 1914 for liverymen of the various Guilds of London. It first lodged with the Little Ship Club in 2010–20 and, after a three-year stint with the City University Club, moved back to the Little Ship Club in 2023.

What they want you to know: The only City club with premises on the river.

What they probably don't want you to know: The Club stands atop the site of Dick Whittington's Long House – the City's first public lavatory.

Short history: The Club's original purpose was to provide a winter meeting place for London's leisure sailors, including for a seasonal programme of lectures, although it now offers a programme all year round. It admitted women relatively early on – 1927, when it was only a year old – and has long been viewed as one of the more progressive and informal yacht clubs. It settled within Beaver Hall in the late 1920s, and regular weekly talks and the world's first properly organised training scheme were initiated; a long association with the Royal Navy began in the 1930s. It acquired its own premises in Bell Wharf Lane in 1962 from where it now provides a large programme of training, social events and on-the water activities around the year.

Further reading:
Rachel Hedley and Dick Negus, *Little Ship Club – The First 75 Years* (London: Little Ship Club, 2001).

Club Directory: Historic Clubs

THE MASS-MEMBERSHIP CLUBS

Civil Service Club – Farmers Club – Lansdowne Club – Royal Air Force Club – Royal Automobile Club – Royal Over-Seas League – Union Jack Club – Victory Services Club

These are the clubs that typically have 5,000 or more members. Mass-membership clubs have their own advantages and disadvantages. On the one hand, they can practise economies of scale, and offer facilities of which other clubs can only dream. On the other hand, critical mass can come at the expense of intimacy, and as a general rule of thumb, the larger the club, the less likely it is that most of the members will know most of the other members, and there can be more scope for rivalry and factionalism. It is more likely that a member's affiliation will be to some group within the club where they are a fixture – whether the golfing circle or the literary society – than for there to be a tangible, club-wide identity.

It should be conversely noted that not all clubs are smaller by choice – a number of the smaller clubs aspire to markedly larger memberships, and the healthy receipts they would no doubt bring, but have been singularly unsuccessful in recruiting and retaining enough like-minded individuals. Consequently, it should be admitted that large numbers of people wouldn't be joining these larger clubs if they weren't doing something right.

Civil Service Club

Address: 13–15 Great Scotland Yard, Whitehall, London, SW1A 2HJ.
Tel.: 020 7930 4881.
Founded: 1953.
Objects: To provide current and former civil servants with an affordable social facility.
Approx. no. of members: 14,000.
Sex: Mixed sex.
Dress code: None.
Type: Unincorporated association.
Reciprocal clubs: 2 clubs, across 2 countries.

Culture: Informal, approachable, with a vibrant wine circle; more of a canteen than a traditional club, but a very convivial one.

Architect: Richard Redding.

Facilities: Lobby, bar, function rooms, terrace, 26 bedrooms.

What they want you to know: The magnificent exterior is one of the most stately looking buildings in Whitehall.

What they probably don't want you to know: While the interior is comfortable enough, it looks like a 1980s conference centre.

Short history: The Civil Service and Foreign Service gave the future Queen Elizabeth II a generous wedding gift in 1947. Five years later, shortly after ascending to the throne, she reciprocated by offering up funds – collected from the surplus of her Wedding Fund – towards a club that would be at the disposal of the entire British civil service and diplomatic service. Although there had been various nineteenth-century attempts at clubs aimed at all or some civil servants, none had been particularly long lasting, but Queen Elizabeth's initiative enjoyed the support of the cabinet secretary, Sir Edward Bridges. A site was found in the heart of Whitehall, in a former 1880s fire station, and in 1953, the Club opened in time for its original patron's coronation. The Club exists today as a social hub for civil servants – unpretentious but convivial, and there are few better places to learn what is afoot in the halls of government.

Further reading:
Mark Quinlan, *A Brief History of the Civil Service Club, Great Scotland Yard, Whitehall* (London: Civil Service Club, 2020).
Norman Seymour, *The Story of 13–15 Great Scotland Yard, compiled for the Civil Service Club* (London: Civil Service Club, 1992).

Farmers Club

Address: 3 Whitehall Court, Whitehall, London, SW1A 2EL.

Tel.: 020 7930 3557.

Founded: 1842.

Objects: Farmers and farming.

Approx. no. of members: 5,000.

Sex: Mixed sex.

Dress code: Jacket and tie after 10 a.m. for men, equivalent for women. Smart-casual in the morning.
Type: Unincorporated association.
Reciprocal clubs: 13 clubs, across 5 countries.
Culture: Relaxed, subdued, squirearchical.
Architects: Thomas Archer and Arthur Green.
Facilities: Lobby, bar, restaurant, morning room, clubroom, function rooms, 50 bedrooms, terrace.
What they want you to know: The freshest food in Clubland – often sourced from their own members.
What they probably don't want you to know: The building is converted from a series of adjoining flats.
Short history: The Club had an erratic beginning, alternating between various hotels and taverns in its first few decades; but since 1904 it has been based in the Whitehall Court complex. It has always been a club for working farmers – offering discounts for those professionally engaged in agriculture – and members continue to be drawn from across the agricultural sector, and have long organised debates and seminars on the issues facing British farming. A vibrant under-30s section, created in 1964, ensures that it is one of the youngest feeling of the traditional London clubs. The Club also organises agricultural shows around the UK.

Further reading:
Charles Abel, *The Farmers Club, 1842–2017: A Brief History of a Fascinating Club* (London: Farmers Club, 2018).
Kevin Fitzgerald, *Ahead of Their Time: A Short History of the Farmers' Club, 1842–1967* (London: Heinemann, 1968).

Hurlingham Club – see THE SPORTS CLUBS

Lansdowne Club

Address: Lansdowne House, 9 Fitzmaurice Place, Mayfair, London, W1J 5JD.
Tel.: 020 7629 7200.
Founded: 1935.
Objects: Social; sporting.
Approx. no. of members: 7,500.

Sex: Mixed sex.

Dress code: Smart-casual in much of the clubhouse, shirt or polo with structured collar for men in lounges and bars. Jacket for men, equivalent for women, at all times in the dining room. Sportswear only in the sports facilities.

Type: Incorporated in 1961, as Fitzmaurice House Ltd, now a private company limited by guarantee, with the members of the Club as members of the company.

Reciprocal clubs: 250 clubs, across 40 countries.

Culture: Young, sporting, active social scene.

Architect: Robert Adam (original house); Charles Fox (modifications).

Facilities: Lobby, Round Room Bar, Adam Room (drawing room), courtyard brasserie, dining room, ballroom and long gallery, function rooms, gym, 3 squash courts, 25-yard swimming pool, aqua bar, fencing salle, exercise studio, steam room, 73 bedrooms.

What they want you to know: Some of the most formidable sporting facilities of any club in London, including a distinctive art deco swimming pool with curved edges.

What they probably don't want you to know: The Club owes its formation to a planning decision by Westminster council to improve access to nearby Berkeley Square, by bulldozing much of the building to create a new road. The remainder was given a new façade and opened as a club in 1935.

Short history: The building is converted from the surviving half of the Adam-designed London mansion of the Marquesses of Lansdowne, which famously hosted Benjamin Franklin for the 1782 signing of the treaty recognising American independence. The Club's first incarnation was as the short-lived Bruton Club, based in Bruton Mews around the back. The Bruton Club acquired Lansdowne House, oversaw its extensive redevelopment into a cutting-edge, largely art deco design, packed off some of the disassembled rooms to museums in New York and Philadelphia, and then merged into the newly formed club upon completion of the redevelopment in 1935. From the outset, it was a club with a strong sporting tradition, with film stars like James Mason being coached by the Club's fencing instructors.

Further reading:
Maria Perry, *The House in Berkeley Square: A History of the Lansdowne Club* (London: Lansdowne Club, 2003).

Club Directory: Historic Clubs

Marylebone Cricket Club – see THE SPORTS CLUBS

Roehampton Club – see THE SPORTS CLUBS

Royal Air Force Club, aka RAF Club
Address: 120 Piccadilly, Mayfair, London, W1J 7PY.
Tel.: 020 7399 1000.
Founded: 1918.
Objects: Royal Air Force officers.
Approx. no. of members: 25,000.
Sex: Mixed sex.
Dress code: Smart-casual on Fridays, weekends and before 6 p.m. on Mondays to Thursdays. After 6 p.m. on Mondays to Thursdays, jacket and tie for men, equivalent for women.
Type: Incorporated in 2004, as the Royal Air Force Club, a private company limited by guarantee, with the Trustees of the Club being trustees of the company; also registered in 2005 as a charity.
Reciprocal clubs: 54 clubs, across 19 countries.
Culture: A lively service club, where traditions and camaraderie reign.
Architect: Maurice Webb.
Facilities: Entrance hall, dining room, Cowdray Lounge, Running Horse bar, library, gym, business suite, function rooms, 110 bedrooms.
What they want you to know: The club hosts an exceptionally large collection of RAF-themed art, encompassing portraits of pilots and planes alike, as well as the badges of squadrons past and present, the latter lining the 'Badge Corridor'.
What they probably don't want you to know: Some of the more modern furniture can look a little at odds with the historic building.
Short history: Originally founded for the Royal Flying Corps, as it then was, the RAF acquired and redeveloped the Piccadilly clubhouse of the Lyceum Club, one of the more ambitious of London's ladies' club, opening on the site in 1922. Take-up among RAF officers was – and remains – high, thanks to low subscriptions for serving officers (well over half of whom are members) and fees equivalent to half a day's pay, based on their rank. Recent years have seen pressure on the building grow, so that it has

withdrawn from some reciprocal arrangements, specifically with other London clubs, to keep giving priority to its RAF-based membership.

Further reading:
Henry Probert and Michael Gilbert, *'128': The Story of the Royal Air Force Club* (London: Royal Air Force Club, 2004).

Royal Automobile Club, aka 'RAC'

Address: 89 Pall Mall, St James's, London, SW1Y 5HS.
Tel.: 020 7930 2345.
Founded: 1897.
Objects: Automobile enthusiasts.
Approx. no. of members: 17,000.
Sex: Mixed sex.
Dress code: Varies depending on the room and the time of day; but broadly speaking, in most of the clubhouse, men are required to wear a jacket and tie, and women the equivalent. There is less formality at weekends, with smart-casual permitted in some rooms.
Type: Incorporated in 1998, as the Royal Automobile Club Ltd, a private company limited by guarantee, with the full members of the Club being members of the company.
Reciprocal clubs: 80 clubs, across 27 countries.
Culture: Middle class, suburban.
Architects: Charles Mewès and Arthur Joseph Davis.
Facilities: Cocktail bar; the main clubroom; drawing room; three dining rooms (the Great Gallery – including the Minstrels' Gallery area – for formal dining, the art deco Brooklands Room for semi-formal dining, and the underground Long Bar for informal dining); the library heavily focused on automobile literature; Turkish baths; basement Italianate marble swimming pool with poolside café; 4 squash courts; gym; barber's shop; billiard room (with five snooker tables); business centre; gift shop; 108 bedrooms; 7 function rooms of varying sizes. Second clubhouse in the country at Epsom.
What they want you to know: 'It has better facilities [than other London clubs]. So I see no reason to join another club,' Andrew Neil. Without a doubt the most sumptuous facilities of any central London club; the swimming pool in particular is the envy of every other club – even the Lansdowne's

fine art deco pool – to say nothing of the second clubhouse in the country.

What they probably don't want you to know: The Club is so large that few people seem to know one another; so you or your host will be asked for your membership card at every transaction to prove that you are who you say you are.

Short history: Founded in the late-Victorian age, when motor sports were decidedly exotic; indeed, in its early years, the RAC played a crucial role in regulating and supporting motor racing – most famously, through international car rallies, such as at Monte Carlo. The Club originally had small beginnings, spending its first five years in a converted apartment in Whitehall Court, before being upgraded to the splendour of a Piccadilly mansion for over a decade. Finally, in 1913, the Club moved to its present home on Pall Mall: the largest clubhouse ever built in the UK – as the above summary makes clear, it offers an enviable array of facilities, though perhaps somewhat at the expense of the intimacy found in smaller clubs. In 1913, the Club was also bolstered by the acquisition of Woodcote Park, offering members a country club in Surrey, complete with an 18-hole golf course and gym. For many years, the Club also ran the nationwide breakdown service RAC as a wholly owned subsidiary. The 1997 sell-off of RAC breakdown services resulted in a £437 million bounty, which equated to a reported £34,000 dividend for each member of the Club. The RAC's membership today is less London-centric than many other nearby clubs, and both more suburban and more international. The Club retains to this day its long-standing tradition of displaying a prized motor car – often a vintage number – in the central lobby, on rotating exhibition.

Further reading:
Piers Brendon, *The Motoring Century: The Story of the Royal Automobile Club* (London: Bloomsbury, 1997).
Dudley Noble (ed.), *The Jubilee Book of the Royal Automobile Club, 1897–1947* (London: Royal Automobile Club, 1947).

Royal Over-Seas League, aka 'ROSL'

Address: 6 Park Place, St James's, London, SW1A 1LR.
Tel.: 020 7408 0214.
Founded: 1910.
Objects: Social.

Approx. no. of members: 8,000, mostly overseas.

Sex: Mixed sex.

Dress code: Smart-casual.

Type: Incorporated, 1922, as a Royal Charter company, as the Royal Over-Seas League.

Reciprocal clubs: 130 clubs, across 31 countries.

Culture: Internationalist.

Architect: James Gibbs (Rutland House).

Facilities: Entry hall, bar, 1910 Dining Room, function rooms, 2 lecture theatre, garden, 83 bedrooms.

What they want you to know: More than a club, an organisation with a mandate to promote international friendship.

What they probably don't want you to know: A second clubhouse in Edinburgh closed down in 2018, after 91 years in operation.

Short history: ROSL was originally founded as the Over-Seas Club by Sir John Evelyn Wrench, with the patronage of his employer Alfred Harmsworth (Lord Northcliffe). Wrench later founded the English-Speaking Union; and both projects were intended to bring the British Empire closer together, with Wrench advocating for the empire to move in the direction of democracy, self-determination and anti-racialism. With a view to furthering these aims, the Club was expanded into a League in 1918 (after a merger with the Patriotic League of Britons Over-Seas), securing a Royal Charter four years later – and settling on its current name. Straddling the divide between a pan-empire (and later pan-Commonwealth) membership organisation and traditional London club, ROSL has long had a particularly international membership, and maintains numerous overseas branches of members. The clubhouse is made up of three adjoining buildings knocked through into one: the eighteenth-century Rutland House, the nineteenth-century Vernon House (remodelled in the Edwardian era), and the inter-war Westminster Wing in art deco style. The older two buildings are some of the last survivors of the Victorian aristocratic mansions which used to overlook Green Park. The organisation has since its inception always had the monarch as patron, most recently King Charles III.

Further reading:
Adele Smith, *The Royal Over-Seas League: From Empire into Commonwealth, a History of the First 200 Years* (London: I. B. Tauris, 2010).

Union Jack Club

Address: 1 Sandell Street, Waterloo, London, SE1 8UJ.
Tel.: 020 7902 6000.
Founded: 1904.
Objects: Current officers and enlisted personnel in the armed forces, and veterans.
Approx. no. of members: 26,000.
Sex: Mixed sex.
Dress code: Casual.
Type: Incorporated in 1904, as the Union Jack Club, now a company limited by guarantee, with the members of the Club being members of the company (and with a wholly owned subsidiary, The Union Jack Club [Trading] Ltd); also registered in 1962 as a charity.
Reciprocal clubs: 9 clubs, across 6 countries.
Culture: Informal.
Architect: Fitzroy Robinson.
Facilities: Lobby, bars, restaurant, café, reading room, library, office hot-desk work, function rooms, 261 bedrooms.
What they want you to know: A club open to all ranks in the armed forces, and welcoming their families as well.
What they probably don't want you to know: The current building is a rather charmless 1970s tower block.
Short history: Founded at the instigation of Red Cross nurse Ethel McCaul, who noted that officers were well-catered for by clubs, but enlisted soldiers were not. The Club's palatial first clubhouse opened in 1907, enjoying patronage from the likes of Arthur Conan Doyle and King George V. Extensive bomb damage in the Second World War posed a series of long-term structural problems, leading to a wholesale redevelopment of the site with a purpose-built new building completed in 1975.
Further reading:
Major H. F. Trippel (ed.), *The Flag: The Book of the Union Jack Club* (London: Daily Mail, 1907).

Victory Services Club

Address: 63–79 Seymour Street, Tyburnia, London, W2 2HF.
Tel.: 020 7723 4474.

Founded: 1907.
Objects: Veterans and serving members of Commonwealth and NATO armed services.
Approx. no. of members: 60,000.
Sex: Mixed sex.
Dress code: None.
Type: Incorporated, 1952, as a registered charity, as the Victory (Services) Association.
Reciprocal clubs: 8 clubs, across 6 countries.
Culture: Informal.
Architect: Unknown.
Facilities: Lobby, lounge bar, coffee bar, The Grill restaurant, lecture theatre (Carisbrooke Hall), function rooms, 202 bedrooms.
What they want you to know: A club for all ranks, open to NATO and Commonwealth allies as well as British forces.
What they probably don't want you to know: By far the largest club membership in London, and therefore the club in which you are least likely to bump into a familiar face.
Short history: Founded the same year as the opening of the Union Jack Club, the Veterans' Club initially catered solely for retired servicemen, being renamed the Victory Services Club in 1936; and since the 1970s, it has been open to serving personnel as well. Based in Marble Arch since 1948, the estate has undergone extensive redevelopment in recent years, including provision of a lecture theatre.

THE SPORTS CLUBS

All England Lawn Tennis and Croquet Club –
Ham Polo Club – Hurlingham Club – Marylebone Cricket Club –
Queen's Club – Roehampton Club – Royal Ocean Racing Club –
Royal Thames Yacht Club

What follows is – necessarily – an incomplete list of sports clubs. Anything like an exhaustive directory of London's sports clubs would number in the hundreds, and take in a great many local golf courses, large and small. The clubs set out here all have a substantial social following by members and guests who are not necessarily aficionados of the sports hosted. Some host major international tournaments. These are also some of the most expensive clubs in London, with some of the longest waiting lists. None of them are based in the very centre – though they are outlying to differing degrees – allowing them sizeable grounds for their chosen sports.

All England Lawn Tennis and Croquet Club, aka 'All England Club'

Address: Church Road, Wimbledon, London, SW19 5AE.
Tel.: 020 8946 6131.
Founded: 1868.
Objects: Tennis and croquet.
Approx. no. of members: 375 (+ 125 associate and honorary members).
Sex: Mixed sex.
Dress code: Jacket and tie for men, equivalent for women.
Type: Unincorporated association.
Reciprocal clubs: None.
Culture: Summery, ebullient.
Architect: Charles Stanley Peach.
Facilities: Bars, 5 restaurants (The Wingfield, Centenary Brasserie, Centenary Seafood Bar, Café Pergola, Parkside Kitchen), 2 acrylic courts, 8 clay courts, 18 grass courts, 22 practice courts, 42 acres of grounds.
What they want you to know: The venue for the annual Wimbledon Championships tennis tournaments.
What they probably don't want you to know: Membership is near-impossible to secure, short of winning the Men's or Ladies' Singles Championship (and even then can be elusive), with a waiting list of over 1,000 at any one time.
Short history: One of the best-known sports clubs on Earth, the Club's grounds have hosted the annual Wimbledon Championships since 1877. Originally founded as the All-England Croquet Club, it changed its name once it began hosting tennis tournaments. The Club remains notoriously

elusive to join – even past tennis championship winners are not guaranteed election. Since 1920, the Club has operated a system of selling debentures for tickets, for five years at a time – only debenture holders can sell on their tickets.

Ham Polo Club

Address: Petersham Road, Richmond, Surrey, TW10 7AH.
Tel.: 020 8334 0000.
Founded: 1926.
Objects: Polo.
Approx. no. of members: 250 (+ 300 family memberships).
Sex: Mixed sex.
Dress code: Jacket and tie for men, equivalent for women.
Type: Incorporated in 2020, as Ham Polo Club Ltd, a private company limited by guarantee, with the members of the Club being members of the company.
Reciprocal clubs: Undisclosed.
Culture: The Club itself notes, 'The average annual income of members exceeds £100,000 p.a. ... [members include] company owners and directors, bankers, accountants, investors, publishers, advertisers, architects, importers, property developers, doctors, brokers, solicitors.'
Architect: Unknown
Facilities: Bar, restaurant, terrace, 23 acres of polo grounds.
What they want you to know: London's premier polo club (although still eclipsed by the Guards Polo Club outside London, in Windsor).
What they probably don't want you to know: Very much a seasonal club, with little going on in the winter months.
Short history: The Club began life as the Ham Common Polo Club, an informal seasonal gathering in the inter-war years. Revived in 1946, matches continued from the following year. The seventeenth-century stately home Ham House was built for the Duke of Lauderdale, and had latterly been the seat of the Earls of Dysart, but by the 1950s it had been turned over to the National Trust. In 1956, the orchard of Ham House was converted into the clubhouse and grounds, where the Club has been based ever since.

Hurlingham Club

Address: Ranelagh Gardens, Fulham, London, SW6 3PR.
Tel.: 020 7610 7400.
Founded: 1869.
Objects: Sports.
Approx. no. of members: 13,000.
Sex: Mixed sex.
Dress code: 'A clean and tidy manner when at the Club', including sportswear for much of the grounds, and 'smart' attire for the restaurant and carvery.
Type: Unincorporated association.
Reciprocal clubs: 40 clubs, across 19 countries.
Culture: Affluent, ostentatious.
Architect: George Byfield and John Ellis; Sir Edwin Lutyens (alterations).
Facilities: Bars, restaurant, carvery, quadrangle, conservatory, Palm Court, theatre, function rooms, fitness centre, gym, racquet centre, tennis pavilion, 22 all-weather tennis courts, 20 grass courts, cricket pitch, 9-hole golf course, indoor and outdoor swimming pools, 10 croquet lawns, 2 bowls greens, lake, 42 acres of grounds and gardens.
What they want you to know: The closest thing London has to an American-style 'country club', with a multiplicity of sports offered across its grounds.
What they probably don't want you to know: Several acres of the Club's grounds were compulsorily purchased by the local council in 1948, to build the neighbouring five-storey Sulivan Court housing estate and Hurlingham Park, on the Club's former polo grounds.
Short history: The Club was a pioneer of numerous sports from the outset, including polo, publishing its rules in 1873. The 1908 Olympics, hosted by London, had their polo tournament played at the Hurlingham. Always a sought-after club with a long waiting list, many people have been refused membership over the years: it is the only club to have ever blackballed Winston Churchill (in 1905 – although he was elected an honorary life member 15 years later). Today, the waiting list stands at some 30 years, with existing members' immediate families given priority, and the list

was closed to new applications some years ago. A 2013 offer from (later sanctioned) Russian oligarch Roman Abramovich to buy the Club for £1 billion was laughed off.

Further reading:
Taprell Dorling, *The Hurlingham Club, 1869–1953* (London: Hurlingham Club, 1953).
Nigel Miskin, *Pigeons, Polo, and Other Pastimes: A History of the Hurlingham Club* (London: Hurlingham Club, 2000).

Little Ship Club – see THE CITY CLUBS

Marylebone Cricket Club

Address: Lord's Cricket Ground, St John's Wood Road, St John's Wood, London, NW8 8QN.
Tel.: 020 7616 8500.
Founded: 1787.
Objects: Cricket.
Approx. no. of members: 23,000 (including 5,000 associate members).
Sex: Mixed sex.
Dress code: Jacket and tie at most times for men, equivalent for women.
Type: Incorporated, 2013, as a Royal Charter company, as the Marylebone Cricket Club.
Reciprocal clubs: 14 clubs, across 7 countries.
Culture: Sedate, boozy, eccentric.
Architect: Frank Verity (Verity Stand); Sir Herbert Baker (Grace Gates); Nicholas Grimshaw (Grand Stand); Sir Michael Hopkins (Mound Stand); Wilkinson Eyre (Compton and Edrich Stands); Populous (Warner Stand).
Facilities: Bars, dining rooms, function rooms, grounds of the Lord's Pavilion, 17 acres of grounds.
What they want you to know: The spiritual home of English cricket, renowned around the world, with a 29-year waiting list for membership.
What they probably don't want you to know: Tempers were so flared during an Ashes Test match in 2023 that an altercation in the Long Room resulted in one member being expelled and two others being suspended.
Short history: The MCC was conceived as a club from the beginning, its members meeting in the Star and Garter pub on Pall Mall that hosted many

other informal clubs of the eighteenth century. Its first dedicated premises were on Dorset Fields (now Dorset Square), and within a year of creation it issued a set of the Laws of Cricket – which continue to be copyright of the Club. In 1810, the Club moved to the St John's Wood district, settling four years later on its current site at Lord's, where it has been based for over two centuries. For decades, it campaigned for a Royal Charter in recognition of its unique role in cricket, which it was finally granted in 2013.

Further reading:
Patrick Eager, *Marylebone Cricket Club: 33 Years and 50 Tests Through the Lens of Patrick Eager* (London: MCC, 2005).
Henry Perkins, *The Centenary of the Marylebone Cricket Club: A Short Summary of the History of the Club* (London: G. H. Whittmann, 1887).
William H. Slatter, *Recollections of Lord's and the Marylebone Cricket Club* (Ewell: J. W. Mackenzie, 1914).

Queen's Club

Address: Palliser Road, West Kensington, London, W14 9EQ.

Tel.: 020 7386 3400.

Founded: 1886.

Objects: Tennis and rackets.

Approx. no. of members: 4,000.

Sex: Mixed sex.

Dress code: Smart-casual in most of the Club; in the President's Room, jacket and tie preferred for men, equivalent for women.

Type: Incorporated in 1886, as The Queen's Club Ltd, a private company limited by shares. One special non-voting share may only ever be held on behalf of the All-England Lawn Tennis and Croquet Club.

Reciprocal clubs: 90 clubs, across 28 countries, through affiliation with the Centenary Tennis Clubs network.

Culture: 'Sloane Ranger'.

Architect: William Marshall.

Facilities: Members' bar, Grille (restaurant), real tennis museum, function rooms, 12 grass lawn tennis courts, 6 shale courts, 6 plexi courts, 4 artificial grass courts, 10 indoor tennis courts, 2 real tennis courts, 2 racket courts, 3 squash courts, gym, treatment rooms, sauna, steam rooms, 'Junior Club' (for ages 6–16), 40 acres of grounds.

What they want you to know: London's premier tennis club outside of Wimbledon – and arguably its best-equipped.

What they probably don't want you to know: It is more sports club than social club.

Short history: In the summer of 1886, the demolition of the 32-year-old Prince's Club (to make way for what is now much of Chelsea) yielded interest in a successor club. The Prince's had been Britain's first multi-purpose sports club, and the new Queen's Club was only the second. Like the Hurlingham Club, it was a venue for the 1908 London Olympics, specifically the racquet and tennis events. From 1953 to 2007, it was a proprietary club owned by the Lawn Tennis Association; but after a management buyout, it has since reverted to being owned by its members. Applications for full membership have been suspended since 2019, due to the existing size of the waiting list.

Further reading:
Roy McKelvie, *The Queen's Club Story, 1886–1986* (London: Stanley Paul, 1986).

Roehampton Club

Address: Roehampton Lane, Roehampton, London, SW15 5LR.
Tel.: 020 8480 4200.
Founded: 1901.
Objects: Sports.
Approx. no. of members: 5,000.
Sex: Mixed sex.
Dress code: Smart-casual.
Type: Incorporated in 1929, as Roehampton Club Ltd, a private company limited by shares; in which all the shares are held by Roehampton Club Members Ltd, formed in 1989 as a private company limited by shares in which all members of the Club are shareholders.
Reciprocal clubs: 94 clubs across 29 countries; principally (though not exclusively) through affiliation to the Centenary Tennis Clubs network.
Culture: Sporting.
Architect: Scott Brownrigg and Turner.
Facilities: Bar, restaurant, bridge room, function rooms, indoor swimming pool, outdoor swimming pool, 28 tennis courts, 2 padel tennis courts,

6 squash courts, 4 croquet lawns, 18-hole golf course, gym, fitness studio, 100 acres of grounds.

What they want you to know: The most extensive grounds of any London sports club.

What they probably don't want you to know: The 1960s brutalist clubhouse is an acquired taste.

Short history: Set up by army officers as a polo club, when the Hurlingham Club and its main rival the Ranelagh Club were both thought civilian-heavy. It rapidly expanded into a multi-sports club also open to civilians, with croquet and golf being particularly popular in the early years. The original one-storey wooden clubhouse was deemed unfit for purpose by the 1960s, and replaced by the current structure in 1969, with additional facilities like the indoor swimming pool in the 1980s. In recent years, it has been a premier club in tennis, squash, padel tennis and pickleball, with Grand Slam champions as members.

Further reading:
Elizabeth Hennessy, *A History of the Roehampton Club, 1901 to 2001* (London: Roehampton Club, 2001).

Royal Ocean Racing Club

Address: 20 St James's Place, St James's, London, SW1A 1NN.
Tel.: 020 7493 2248.
Founded: 1925.
Objects: Yachting.
Approx. no. of members: 4,000.
Sex: Mixed sex.
Dress code: None; but dress tends to be smart-casual or crew uniform.
Type: Incorporated in 2006, as Royal Ocean Racing Club Ltd, a private company limited by guarantee, with the members of the Club as the members of the company.
Reciprocal clubs: The Club does not have formal reciprocal arrangements, but welcomes members of bona fide yacht clubs worldwide, subject to a letter of introduction.
Culture: Prosperous, sporting.
Architect: John Rossington.

Facilities: Bar, dining room, function rooms, 16 bedrooms.

What they want you to know: The place to go, if you want to see someone about a boat.

What they probably don't want you to know: The clubhouse is easily overlooked, down the end of a cul-de-sac by the Stafford Hotel.

Short history: Originally founded as the Ocean Racing Club, it received its royal patronage (and name change) six years later. A new clubhouse on Pall Mall was destroyed in the Blitz, with the Club being based at its present building on St James's Place since 1941. The Club plays a major role in organising some of the main yacht races held in the UK, such as the Fastnet Race, Admiral's Cup and the Commodore's Cup. A second clubhouse is maintained at Cowes, with yachting facilities.

Further reading:
Ian Dear, *The Royal Ocean Racing Club: The First 75 Years* (London: Adlard Coles Nautical, 2000).

Royal Thames Yacht Club

Address: 60 Knightsbridge, Knightsbridge, London, SW1X 7LF.

Tel.: 020 7235 2121.

Founded: 1775.

Objects: Yachting.

Approx. no. of members: 1,800.

Sex: Mixed sex.

Dress code: Smart-casual during weekday daytimes. After 7 p.m. on the Quarterdeck, Cumberland Bar and Coffee Room, a jacket and tie for men, and equivalent for women, are required.

Type: Incorporated in 2003, as Royal Thames Yacht Club Ltd, a private company limited by guarantee, with the members of the Club being members of the company.

Reciprocal clubs: 95 clubs, across 30 countries.

Culture: Affluent.

Architect: Guy Morgan.

Facilities: Cumberland Bar, Coffee Room (dining room), Britannia Bar and Deck, Britannia Bistro, library, function rooms, 33 bedrooms ('Cabins').

What they want you to know: Britain's pioneering yachting establishment – 'the senior yacht club in the country'.

What they probably don't want you to know: They only admitted women as full members in 2014.

Short history: The Club's early beginnings were as an informal association, called the Cumberland Fleet, meeting in coffee houses. In 1823, it was renamed the Thames Yacht Club, continuing to lease rooms in coffee houses. In 1857, the Club acquired its first dedicated clubhouse, and remained in the Mayfair area until 1923, when it moved to its present location in Knightsbridge. A major redevelopment followed in 1961–3, with the present building being constructed, occupying the lower floors of a nine-storey office block.

Further reading:
A. R. Ward, *The Chronicles of the Royal Thames Yacht Club* (Oxford: John Wiley, 1999).

PART II
Modern Clubs

W hile there is an obvious cultural divide between 'old' and 'new' clubs, there is no widespread agreement on the distinction. The long-standing definition (adopted here) has been that anything since the Second World War is a 'modern' club, but some of these venerable establishments are nearly eighty years old. In practice, most 'new' clubs have cropped up since the 'club boom' which followed the Groucho Club in 1985; and indeed, the vast majority have launched in the last decade.

Club Directory: Modern Clubs

A more obvious dividing line is that almost every single one of the modern institutions is a proprietary club, run by a private landlord. 'Something is afoot in clubland,' observes Ben Schott, 'the absurd proliferation of enterprises that walk like clubs and talk like clubs but are not clubs at all. Such sleight of brand covers everything from the sublime 5 Hertford Street (ruled by the velvet fist of Robin Birley) to the ridiculous Soho House (which boasts a global waiting list of 98,000).' Schott points to '*genuine* clubs' as being owned and run by their members, whereas 'ersatz establishments . . . are for-profit businesses operated for the benefit of their owners. Perhaps pseudo-club members don't realise they're paying for someone else's mortgage, perhaps they don't care."

However, the division is a little blurrier than Schott argues. This is partly due to London's oldest clubs of the eighteenth century all having started out as proprietary clubs, run for profit (before the members staged management buyouts, decades later). It is also worth noting that the 'old' clubs do not necessarily have permanence of tenure, either, with numerous recent closures of traditional clubs, too.

And some of the founders of the newer proprietary clubs have shown great taste. The late Andrew Edmunds founded the Academy Club above his Hogarthian print shop and restaurant in 1985, partly in response to the vanishing of 'old Soho'. He observed, 'We've kept our décor close to how we found it for two reasons: idleness and economy. It's so shabby now that high fashion wants to use it for photo shoots: we've gone full circle. I'm happy to say there is an extraordinary age range here, a new generation who find us romantic, and old farts like me who simply come here because the meals are sensibly priced. A good top and tail.'†

What unites these 'modern' clubs is a greater degree of informality – something that was found in London's oldest clubs in their early days, before Victorian priggishness set in. Some are noble endeavours to support a creative and cultured community of like-minded individuals. A few are shameless attempts to fleece the super-rich for cash, preying on their sense

---

* Ben Schott, 'Where are all the proper members' clubs?', *Spectator*, 16 December 2023.
† Tom Bolger, 'The last bastion', *Port*, 9 November 2022.

of boredom, with a gaggle of sex workers soliciting for clients. The new clubs embrace the full range of establishments, from the earnest and the bohemian, to the tasteless and the gauche. Where Schott has a point is in the eagerness to trot out the tired phrase, 'the best-kept secret in London', to describe so many of them.

THE SOHO DRINKING CLUBS

Academy Club – BBC Club – Gerry's – New Evaristo Club – Phoenix Arts Club

These are creative, bohemian clubs that are in many ways the spiritual successor to the original Georgian clubs; and no shortage of spirits have been known to be consumed. A strong literary and creative element prevails, but they are less smart and fussy than some of the more recent modern clubs. Long gone is the most famous Soho haunt of all, the old Colony Room Club (although a reconstruction has made a comeback since 2023, but as a pop-up).

Academy Club
Address: 46 Lexington Street, Soho, London, W1F 0LP.
Tel.: 020 7437 5708.
Founded: 1985.
Objects: Literary; journalistic.
Approx. no. of members: Undisclosed.
Sex: Mixed sex.
Dress code: None.
Type: Proprietary; owned by the late Andrew Edmunds's neighbouring restaurant.
Reciprocal clubs: None.
Culture: Erudite, literary.
Architect: Unknown.
Facilities: Dining room, one function room.

What they want you to know: The Club takes a 'zero-tolerance' approach to bores.

What they probably don't want you to know: The facilities are rather modest, though that is part of the charm.

Short history: Homely and shambolic, the Academy is a delightful throwback to the supper clubs of the eighteenth century. Centred around just one upstairs room above the late Andrew Edmunds's eponymous Soho restaurant and Hogarthian print shop, a stone's throw from Carnaby Street, the Academy was the brainchild of the late Auberon Waugh, and retains a strong journalistic element. One of the rules is 'No poets'. The wine list is particularly treasured.

BBC Club

Address: London Broadcasting House, Portland Place, Marylebone, London, W1A 1AA.

Tel.: 020 7765 3620.

Founded: 1924.

Objects: Current and former employees of the BBC and its production partners.

Approx. no. of members: 3,000.

Sex: Mixed sex.

Dress code: None.

Type: Incorporated in 2010, as BBC Club Sports and Leisure Ltd, a private company limited by guarantee, with the members of the Club being members of the company.

Reciprocal clubs: None.

Culture: Creative.

Architect: HOK, MacCormac Jamieson Prichard and Sheppard Robson.

Facilities: Bar, media café, gym.

What they want you to know: The BBC's own in-house club.

What they probably don't want you to know: Nowhere near as exciting as its louche historic reputation; today, members tend to talk shop.

Short history: With the BBC having begun radio broadcasting in 1922, it was as early as 1924 that its staff launched their own club. For many years it was a notoriously boozy media hangout. (Terrance Dicks, longtime

Doctor Who scriptwriter, blamed the show's production difficulties in the late 1960s on its producers almost permanently hanging out in the BBC Club, several sheets to the wind.) These days, the Club has a more sedate cafeteria feel to it. For many years based in the old television centre in Wood Lane, and transferred to an outbuilding near New Broadcasting House, the closure of Woburn House in 2024 has meant it has reopened inside the main BBC studio building. While technically in Marylebone, it is very much spiritually one of the Soho clubs – with considerable overlap in membership. Additionally, members have access to two further facilities attached to TV studios, the BBC Club Elstree just north-west of London, and the BBC Club North in Salford.

Gerry's

Address: 52 Dean Street, Soho, London, W1D 5BJ.
Tel.: 020 7437 4160.
Founded: 1955.
Objects: Social.
Approx. no. of members: Undisclosed.
Sex: Mixed sex.
Dress code: None.
Type: Proprietary; incorporated in 1972 as Gerry's Club Ltd, a private company limited by shares; the person with significant control is Elliott Rogers.
Reciprocal clubs: None.
Culture: Boozy, discreet, respectful, artistic.
Architect: Benjamin Simpson.
Facilities: Bar.
What they want you to know: One of the last bastions of 'old Soho'.
What they probably don't want you to know: Sometimes mistaken for the (completely unrelated) Gerry's off-licence around the corner.
Short history: A venerable watering hole synonymous with actors and journalists, the Club was known by the seventies for its out-of-hours drinking, unpretentious, welcoming atmosphere in which members and guests freely mingled in the one small room, and the occasional raid. It is more genteel

today, but still has a raffish air. A small band crammed into a corner plays live jazz on most nights.

New Evaristo Club, aka 'Trisha's', aka 'The Hideout'
Address: 57 Greek Street, Soho, London, W1D 3DX.
Tel.: 020 7437 9536.
Founded: 1948.
Objects: Social.
Approx. no. of members: Under 500.
Sex: Mixed sex.
Dress code: None.
Type: Proprietary; owner is Trisha Bergonzi.
Reciprocal clubs: None.
Culture: Raucous, honest, unpretentious.
Architect: Unknown.
Facilities: Bar, smokers' yard.
What they want you to know: Many clubs use the label, 'the best-kept secret in London', but this is probably the most deserving recipient.
What they probably don't want you to know: Westminster City Council nearly closed the Club in 2023, citing a string of alleged licensing breaches; the Club received a reprieve after a series of improvements were recognised.
Short history: Universally known today as Trisha's, after Trisha Bergonzi, the Club's proprietor since 1988, although she has stepped back from day-to-day management since 2023. The Club itself began life 40 years before she acquired it, as a basement drinking den reached through the stairwell of an unassuming residential building. It retains the authentic atmosphere of 'Old Soho', with its unpretentious plastic tablecloths, pictures of Italian popes and gangsters on the walls, and simple décor. A solitary sub-basement open-air smokers' yard in a light-well is the only space other than the main bar room, and the clientele is a convivial mix of regular drinkers propping up the bar and the occasional media figure. Fridays and Saturdays are predictably heaving; but it remains a very quiet space the rest of the week. Subscriptions

recently skyrocketed 400 per cent – from the previous £5 a year, to the current £20 a year.

Phoenix Arts Club, aka the Phoenix Artist Club

Address: 1 Phoenix Street, Covent Garden, London, WC2H 8BU.
Tel.: 020 7836 1077.
Founded: 1988.
Objects: Social.
Approx. no. of members: Undisclosed.
Sex: Mixed sex.
Dress code: None.
Type: Proprietary; incorporated in 1988 as Brent Contracts Ltd, changed name in 2006 to The Phoenix Artist Club Ltd, a private company limited by shares, with the current persons with significant control being Colin Savage and Ken Wright.
Reciprocal clubs: None.
Culture: Camp, theatrical, gregarious.
Architect: Bertie Crewe, Sir Giles Gilbert Scott and Cecil Massey.
Facilities: Bar; private theatre with cabaret-style restaurant seating.
What they want you to know: Famous for its nightly cabaret show.
What they probably don't want you to know: A surprisingly large number of the venue's casual patrons wander in by accident.
Short history: Located beneath the West End's Phoenix Theatre, the small side entrance marked by a red awning reading 'Phoenix Artist Club' (which remains its legal name), the Club was founded by entrepreneur John Mahoney. True to the literary roots of the area, most of the second-hand booksellers on Charing Cross Road have long enjoyed complimentary membership. After the death in 2011 of its previous proprietor, Soho character Maurice Huggett, regulars Colin Savage and Ken Wright were pleasantly stunned to find they had inherited ownership of the Club. Today it organises 600 events a year, as well as offering members scope for daytime working.

Club Directory: Modern Clubs

THE MARK BIRLEY CLUBS

Annabel's – Bath and Racquets Club – George – Harry's Bar – Mark's Club – Walbrook Club

Whereas the future King Charles III had his 1981 'stag night' at the more traditional White's, Princess Diana had her 'hen night' at Annabel's. The juxtaposition highlighted the difference between 'old' and 'new' Clubland. Entrepreneur Mark Birley was at the forefront of the 'new' clubs of the late twentieth and early twenty-first century, either launching or designing half a dozen clubs, each of them quite distinct, with a widely acknowledged attention to detail. Mark Birley's later years were dominated by ill health, during which his children stepped in with the day-to-day running of his clubs. A feud between father and son resulted in Mark Birley disinheriting Robin Birley; and in 2007, shortly before his death, he sold to Richard Caring the Birley Group, being five of the clubs which he operated. In the ensuing two decades, the five clubs have had varying degrees of renovation and makeover. The sixth club designed by Mark Birley, the Walbrook Club, was undertaken as a private commission for the Palumbo family, where it remains today.

The Birley Group, running all but the Walbrook, was shown a draft of the below entries, and offered the following comment: 'There is quite a lot of incorrect information regarding our Clubs'; but they did not respond to repeated further requests for elaboration or correction.

Annabel's

Address: 46 Berkeley Square, Mayfair, London, W1J 5AT.
Tel.: 020 3915 4046.
Founded: 1963.
Objects: Social; international.
Approx. no. of members: 8,000.
Sex: Mixed sex.
Dress code: Smart-casual; men are asked to wear a jacket after 6 p.m.
Type: Proprietary; part of the Birley Group, owned by Richard Caring.

Reciprocal clubs: Other clubs within the Birley Group.
Culture: Relaxed, louche, affluent, cosmopolitan.
Architect: Henry Flitcroft.
Facilities: 6 bars, 4 restaurants, cigar terrace, cigar shop, garden courtyard, wine shop, function rooms.
What they want you to know: The move next door has made Annabel's bigger than ever, with it being possible to lose yourself 24/7 in the world of the Club.
What they probably don't want you to know: These days, it is more a celebrity hangout frequented by Instagram influencers and reality TV stars, than the aristocratic nightclub of Mark Birley's day.
Short history: The first of Birley's clubs, it was situated for over half a century in the cavernous basement of the old Clermont Club on Berkeley Square. Birley declared at the opening in 1963, 'It must smell of exclusivity and sex', and its combination of secluded, candlelit corner passages and membership drawn from Birley's extensive contacts book made it a chic destination for decades to come; famously, it was the only nightclub in which Queen Elizabeth II ever set foot. A change of landlord for the old premises in 2018 prompted a move, two doors away, occupying a vast house, complete with a yard reclaimed as a restaurant beneath a barrel-vaulted glass roof.

Bath and Racquets Club
Address: 49 Brook's Mews, Mayfair, London, W1K 4EB.
Tel.: 020 7499 9044.
Founded: 1989.
Objects: Racquet and health club.
Approx. no. of members: 300.
Sex: Gentlemen only.
Dress code: White sportswear.
Type: Proprietary; Birley Group, owned by Richard Caring.
Reciprocal clubs: Other clubs within the Birley Group.
Culture: Preppy, gossipy, masculine. Members mostly work in nearby Mayfair hedge funds.
Architect: David Champion and Anthony Collett.

Facilities: Lounge and bar, changing rooms, squash courts, gym, barber, steam room.

What they want you to know: One of London's most expensive clubs.

What they probably don't want you to know: During a 1990s dispute between publisher Condé Nast and Harrods proprietor Mohamed Al-Fayed over a *Vanity Fair* exposé of Fayed, their representatives met in the Club's steam room to ensure they were not being bugged.

Short history: Modelled on the men's athletic clubs found in the big North American cities, specifically the vast Racquet and Tennis Club on New York's Park Avenue. This is – by choice – one of the smallest club memberships in London, as well as the most expensive. Built into the basement of an office building, it combines a full gym and squash courts with a bar that is the Club's social centre.

George

Address: 88–89 Mount Street, Mayfair, London, W1K 2SU.
Tel.: 020 7491 4433.
Founded: 2001.
Objects: Social; Mediterranean food.
Approx. no. of members: Undisclosed.
Sex: Mixed sex.
Dress code: Smart-casual. Jackets are encouraged when dining.
Type: Proprietary; Birley Group, owned by Richard Caring.
Reciprocal clubs: Harry's Bar and Mark's Club, within the Birley Group.
Culture: International, opulent.
Architect: Unknown.
Facilities: Bar, restaurant, outdoor heated terrace (the largest in Mayfair), function rooms, basement 'nighterie' (nightclub), basement private bar.

What they want you to know: The most dog-friendly club in London, with a dog menu, specially designed dog seating, and a committee that oversees the welfare of canine guests.

What they probably don't want you to know: It's a very chic restaurant; but it is essentially just a restaurant.

Short history: Envisioned by Mark Birley as a more generically Mediterranean dining experience than Harry's Bar, it was the last of the Mayfair clubs he founded. David Hockney was commissioned to provide much of the artwork which lines the main restaurant. Birley aimed it towards young urban professionals – yuppies – in their 30s, as a place they might like to take a date. The Club remains avowedly dog-friendly, with a dog menu and dog artwork throughout, including two bronze German shepherd statues by the main entrance. The Club temporarily closed after the Covid-19 pandemic, but reopened in 2023 after a major renovation.

Harry's Bar

Address: 26 South Audley Street, Mayfair, London, W1K 2PD.
Tel.: 020 7408 0844.
Founded: 1979.
Objects: Social; Italian cuisine.
Approx. no. of members: Undisclosed.
Sex: Mixed sex.
Dress code: Jackets for men, the equivalent for women.
Type: Proprietary; Birley Group, owned by Richard Caring.
Reciprocal clubs: George and Mark's Club, within the Birley Group.
Culture: Discreet.
Architect: Albert J. Bolton.
Facilities: Bar, restaurant, function rooms.
What they want you to know: Some of the most authentic Italian cuisine in town, with particularly fresh ingredients.
What they probably don't want you to know: It is essentially just a restaurant.
Short history: A lifelong Italophile, Mark Birley created Harry's Bar as a private club aimed at serving contemporary Italian food to a more female clientele, in an environment inspired by the famous Venice restaurant of that name. Birley's silent partner in the enterprise was James Sherwood, CEO of Orient-Express Hotels, who originally owned 49 per cent to Birley's 51 per cent. After a lengthy dispute between Birley and Sherwood over the direction of the Club, Birley bought out Sherwood's stake in 2006, a year prior to his

death. With Richard Caring's franchising of the Birley clubs after Mark Birley's death, spinoff Harry's Bar restaurants that are open to the public have cropped up in the last decade in Marylebone and Cannon Street.

Mark's Club

Address: 46 Charles Street, Mayfair, London, W1J 5EJ.
Tel.: 020 7499 2936.
Founded: 1973.
Objects: Social.
Approx. no. of members: 1,500.
Sex: Mixed sex.
Dress code: Jackets for men at all times, the equivalent for women.
Type: Proprietary; Birley Group, owned by Richard Caring.
Reciprocal clubs: George and Harry's Bar, within the Birley Group.
Culture: Eclectic, aristocratic, international.
Architect: John Phillips and George Shakespear.
Facilities: Front lobby, 'green room' dining room and dining terrace, bar, lounge, smoking terrace, two function rooms.
What they want you to know: A decade ago, they took the 'nuclear option' to slim down their members' list from 2,500 to 1,500, expelling the entire membership and inviting them to reapply.
What they probably don't want you to know: Recent plans for a much-anticipated relocation to a bigger clubhouse on nearby Berkeley Square were quietly dropped.
Short history: Buoyed by the success of Annabel's in its first decade, Mark Birley sought to start a more traditional gentlemen's club nearby. Since 1950, Polish entrepreneur Siegi Sessler had run 46 Charles Street as a chic, celebrity-laden Mayfair restaurant called Siegi's Club; but after Sessler's early death in 1969, the premises came up for sale, and Birley bought them for his new, low-key club. The aim was to convey a traditional, Edwardian-era establishment replete with prints and caricatures on the walls, from the likes of Max Beerbohm, H. M. Bateman and George du Maurier. Subsequent redecorations have given it a more contemporary feel.

Walbrook Club

Address: 37A Walbrook, City of London, London, EC4N 8BS.
Tel.: 020 7623 6100.
Founded: 2000.
Objects: Social.
Approx. no. of members: 400.
Sex: Mixed sex.
Dress code: Smart-casual; men are encouraged to wear jackets and ties, but it is not compulsory.
Type: Proprietary; owners are the Palumbo family.
Reciprocal clubs: 47 clubs, across 20 countries.
Culture: City workers, particularly busy around lunchtime.
Architect: Rudolph Palumbo.
Facilities: Bar, dining room, function rooms, terrace.
What they want you to know: The City of London's only family-run private members' club.
What they probably don't want you to know: Mark Birley, already ailing by the time he worked on the Club, had no involvement beyond the initial design.
Short history: The singular neo-Georgian house by St Stephen's Walbrook church, near Bank, was built in the early 1950s by Rudolph Palumbo to house the offices of the family's property firm. In the late 1990s, his son Peter, Lord Palumbo, set about converting the building into a club, and hired Mark Birley to design it – though not to run it. It has been a family affair for the Palumbos, with one of Lord Palumbo's sons, Philip, running the Club since 2018. The result is an elegant, idiosyncratic Georgian-style clubhouse that is extremely small; but the narrow dimensions of the rooms only encourage sociability in this corner of the City.

Club Directory: Modern Clubs

THE ROBIN BIRLEY CLUBS

5 Hertford Street – Oswald's

Robin Birley used to manage a string of his father's clubs in the 1990s and 2000s, but after the sale of the Birley empire, he began planning a club of his own, launched in 2012. The runaway success of that first club, 5 Hertford Street, led to a further Mayfair spin-off club in 2018, Oswald's, and a New York spin-off club, Maxime's, launched in 2025.

5 Hertford Street

Address: 2–5 Hertford Street, Mayfair, London, W1J 7RB.
Tel.: 020 4513 1555.
Founded: 2012.
Objects: Social.
Approx. no. of members: Undisclosed.
Sex: Mixed sex.
Dress code: Jackets are required for men at all times, the equivalent for women.
Type: Proprietary; owned by Robin Birley. Incorporated in 2009 as a private company limited by shares, now as 5 Hertford Street Ltd (originally Birley Club Ltd), with Birley as the person with significant control. The company is part of a wider network of companies, including 5 Hertford Street (Trading) Ltd, 10 Pembridge Crescent Ltd, Bar at 5 Hertford Street Ltd, Late Night Dining at 5 Hertford Street Ltd, Birley Pastry Holdings Ltd, Private Dining at 5 Hertford Street Ltd, Restaurant at 5 Hertford Street Ltd, 5 Hertford Street Nominees Ltd, Retail at 5 Hertford Street Ltd, Santa Maria (London) Ltd, Sicasa Ltd, and Upper Floors at 5 Hertford Street Ltd.
Reciprocal clubs: Members also have use of Oswald's.
Culture: Posh, louche, right wing.
Architect: Unknown (architect); Rifat Ozbek (designer).
Facilities: 3 bars, 2 restaurants, function rooms, cinema, cigar shop, nightclub (Loulou's).
What they want you to know: The trendiest of London's modern clubs; much emulated, with its trademark floral-pattern wallpaper.

What they probably don't want you to know: More political than they might like to be, owing to its popularity and identification with a series of Brexiteers, including Nigel Farage, Arron Banks, Boris Johnson and Liz Truss.

Short history: After several years of development – and an aborted attempt to go by the name 'Birley's' – 5 Hertford Street launched in 2012. A staple of gossip magazines, owing to its reputation as a celebrity hangout, within five years the Club was full and operating a waiting list. The in-house nightclub, Loulou's (named after Birley's aunt, the fashion designer Loulou de la Falaise), gives the Club a strong party vibe, with plenty of singing and dancing.

Oswald's

Address: 25 Albemarle Street, Mayfair, London, W1S 4HU.
Tel.: 020 3794 6320.
Founded: 2018.
Objects: Social; oenophiles.
Approx. no. of members: 2,000.
Sex: Mixed sex.
Dress code: Smart-casual.
Type: Proprietary; incorporated in 2017 as Winter Restaurants Ltd, a private company limited by shares, with Robin Birley as the person with significant control. The company is part of a wider network of companies, including Winter Restaurants Holdings Ltd and Winter Restaurants Nominees Ltd; see the above listing for 5 Hertford Street for some of the other companies in Birley's empire.
Reciprocal clubs: None.
Culture: Aristocratic, oenophile.
Architect: Unknown (architect); Tom Bell and Bruce Cavell (designers).
Facilities: Bar, restaurant (La Loma), function rooms, wine cellars.
What they want you to know: One of London's best wine lists – and at surprisingly inexpensive prices for Mayfair.
What they probably don't want you to know: Many members have simply joined as a way of getting into 5 Hertford Street.
Short history: A spin-off club from 5 Hertford Street, this club was launched in a converted hair salon. The ground floor takes as its inspiration the Hall of

Mirrors at Versailles, while the main Mediterranean-themed restaurant is on the first floor. Members can store up to a dozen of their own bottles on-site, enjoying free corkage. The *Mail on Sunday*'s diary editor, Charlotte Griffiths, observed that Birley set up Oswald's specifically to attract an aristocratic crowd: 'He figured that the way to do it was to make the wine there very, very good, but at very reasonable prices. He clearly understands that real toffs like a drink or two – but have less ready money than the Euro[sceptic] crowd. And from what I can see, it's worked,' noting that Prince Andrew's daughters, Beatrice and Eugenie, 'introduced more senior Royals to Oswald's'. To cap it all, 5 Hertford Street now has a waiting list, and the only route to membership involves first taking out a membership of Oswald's.

THE SOHO HOUSE EMPIRE

40 Greek Street – 76 Dean Street – 180 House – Electric House – High Road House – Little House, Balham – Little House, Mayfair – Ned's Club – Shoreditch House – Soho Mews House – White City House

When people speak of 'modern clubs', it is often Soho House that comes to mind. Or rather, *a* Soho House, since the chain now numbers forty-three branches and counting worldwide, with plans to expand to some eighty clubs. The group started in 1995 with just one club in Soho – then already a fashionable area for the media and creative industries, but also more down-at-heel than it is now. The year 2003 saw the opening of the first Soho House abroad, in New York; and by the end of the decade, the Club began expanding into a full-blown global chain of clubs, with members able to buy either a membership of just one house, or the whole chain of houses. Membership numbers for individual houses are undisclosed. Over a quarter of a million members are now found across the whole network worldwide (185,000 for the Houses, and a further 70,000 enjoying access through groups such as Soho Friends, Soho Works and Soho

Home+) – which averages at between 4,400 and 6,000 members per Soho House. Current clubhouses in the business empire include Amsterdam, Austin, Bangkok, Barcelona, Berlin, Brighton, Canouan, Chicago, Copenhagen, Hong Kong, Istanbul, Los Angeles, Malibu, Mexico City, Miami, Mumbai, Mykonos, Nashville, Paris, Portland, Rome, São Paulo, Stockholm, Tel Aviv and Toronto, with plans to open in Glasgow and Manchester in 2025. And London alone has eleven Soho House ventures. Additionally, Soho House owns Soho Works, a series of co-working spaces across the capital.

A major shift came in 2021, when Soho House went from being a private company to being floated on the stock exchange for the first time. Today, the Soho House Group is a complicated web of companies, including Soho House UK Ltd (the original company, incorporated in 1993 as Soho House), Soho House Ltd, Soho House CWH Ltd, Soho House (Management Services) Ltd, Soho House Properties Ltd, Soho House Toronto Ltd, Soho Works Ltd, Ned-Soho House LLP, the holding company SHG Acquisition (UK) Ltd, the Delaware-based parent company Soho House & Co Inc, and the charity The Soho House Foundation registered in 2022. Among Soho House & Co Inc's Class A shares (common stock, non-voting), the major shareholders at the time of writing are Goldman Sachs & Co LLC (29 per cent), founder Nick Jones (19 per cent), and hedge funds Lansdowne Partners (UK) LLP, Scoggin Management LP and Pelham Capital Ltd (between 3 and 5 per cent each). Among the Class B shares (voting), the majority shareholder is The Yucaipa Cos LLC (the investment firm of US billionaire Ron Burkle, who serves as Soho House's executive chairman); and other major Class B shareholders include the restaurateur Richard Caring who also owns the Birley Group of clubs (29 per cent), Burkle in a personal capacity (7 per cent) and Jones (6 per cent). At one stage, Caring owned 80 per cent of Soho House's shares, after a 2008 deal, but his stake has been much smaller since the 2021 flotation. It took twenty-eight years for the company to turn a profit, and then only in the final quarter of 2022. At the time of writing, it has yet to report a profit for an entire financial year. As of December 2024, Burkle has given his support to a $1.75 billion bid for the Soho House Group, by an as-yet-unnamed buyer. If successful, it would see Soho House return to private ownership.

In 2024, Soho House became locked in a dispute with New York-based short-sellers GlassHouse, who produced a report suggesting that Soho House had become overstretched, was unprofitable and was heavily indebted. This was strenuously contested by Soho House, which argued that the report, 'contains factual inaccuracies, analytical errors and false and misleading statements, all designed to adversely impact the company's stock price for the benefit of the short-seller', and indeed the report dented Soho House's share price, though it then went on to recover. Soho House responded to a suggestion of overcrowding by closing new applications for several of its London, New York and Los Angeles clubhouses.

40 Greek Street

Address: 40 Greek Street, Soho, London, W1D 4EB.
Tel.: 020 7734 5188.
Founded: 1995.
Objects: Media; creative arts.
Approx. no. of members: Undisclosed.
Sex: Mixed sex.
Dress code: Smart-casual.
Type: Proprietary; Soho House Group.
Reciprocal clubs: Rest of the Soho House chain.
Culture: Media trendies, flanked by hedge funders and investment bankers. Seems perennially busy.
Architect: Unknown (original); SODA (Studio of Design & Architecture) Studio (conversion); Soho House Design (interior design).
Facilities: Circle Bar, Morning Room, Red and Blue Drawing Rooms, function rooms, courtyard (with bar), rooftop terrace.
What they want you to know: The original club of what has grown into a $300-million-a-year empire.
What they probably don't want you to know: Has often been satirised by comedians, who have lampooned some of the members as coked-up parvenus.
Short history: The original Soho House. At the time, the group's founder

Nick Jones was operating the Café Boheme on Old Compton Street, when he was offered the lease on the rooms above it, approached from a Greek Street side entrance. Tapping into the creative theme of the café's regular clientele, Jones modelled the ramshackle three houses knocked together into a space that epitomised 'Britpop' and the 'Cool Britannia' of the 1990s. By the late 2000s, new houses were opened – initially in London and New York – while this original clubhouse was extensively renovated in 2016–18, bolstered by the Soho House Group's acquisition of Kettner's restaurant around the back, with the upstairs rooms of Kettner's added to the members' complex. A large collection of works by modern British artists is embedded throughout the building.

Further reading:
Anonymous, *Eat, Drink, Nap: Bringing the House Home* (London: Preface Publishing, 2014).
Anonymous, *Morning, Noon, Night: A Way of Living* (London: Preface Publishing, 2016).

76 Dean Street

Address: 76 Dean Street, Soho, London, W1D 3SQ.
Tel.: 020 3006 0076.
Founded: 2009.
Objects: Media; creative arts.
Approx. no. of members: Undisclosed.
Sex: Mixed sex.
Dress code: Smart-casual.
Type: Proprietary; Soho House Group.
Reciprocal clubs: Rest of the Soho House chain.
Culture: Much the same as 40 Greek Street.
Architect: Thomas Richmond (original); SODA (Studio of Design & Architecture) Studio (conversion); Soho House Design (interior design).
Facilities: Library bar, restaurant and separate dining room, drawing room, function rooms, 43-seat screening room, rooftop bar and terrace.
What they want you to know: Prince Harry and Meghan Markle reportedly went on their first date here.
What they probably don't want you to know: The building was badly damaged in a devastating 2009 fire.
Short history: With ever-present pressure on the nearby 40 Greek Street for membership, this Soho House opened 20 years after the original. Unusually

for the modern Soho House chain, the clubhouse retains a number of original eighteenth-century features, such as naval murals by John Devoto and much period décor including fireplaces and chandeliers, giving it the feel of a blend between an 'old' and 'new' club. During the 2016–18 refurbishment of the original Soho House, its members were decanted into 76 Dean Street.

180 House
Address: 180 Strand, Embankment, London, WC2R 1EA.
Tel.: 020 3985 0000.
Founded: 2020.
Objects: Media; creative arts.
Approx. no. of members: Undisclosed.
Sex: Mixed sex.
Dress code: Smart-casual.
Type: Proprietary; Soho House Group.
Reciprocal clubs: Rest of the Soho House chain.
Culture: Similar to other Soho Houses, though also popular with academics at the nearby London School of Economics and King's College London.
Architect: Sir Frederick Gibberd.
Facilities: Bar, restaurant, 12 function rooms including a dining room, sitting room and kitchen, with rooftop terrace and swimming pool.
What they want you to know: 5,000 square feet of clubhouse, with riverside views.
What they probably don't want you to know: Much of the building is given over to other businesses, with the Club only occupying the top two floors (of nine).
Short history: Converted from a large 1970s brutalist office block, located on the bend of the River Thames, with views stretching from Tower Bridge to Big Ben. The launch of 180 House on the Strand, originally slated for the spring of 2020, was impacted by the 2020–1 global Covid-19 pandemic; but after intermittent lockdowns, the Club opened permanently in 2022.

Electric House
Address: 191 Portobello Road, Notting Hill, London, W11 2ED.
Tel.: 020 7908 9696.

Founded: 2001.
Objects: Media; creative arts.
Approx. no. of members: Undisclosed.
Sex: Mixed sex.
Dress code: Smart-casual.
Type: Proprietary; Soho House Group.
Reciprocal clubs: Rest of the Soho House chain.
Culture: Indeed, very cultured, with an emphasis on the performing arts.
Architect: Gerald Seymour Valentin.
Facilities: Library bar, The Snug lounging space, Electric Diner (also open to the public), function rooms, roof garden, 98-seater Electric Cinema (also open to the public).
What they want you to know: London's only club to also run a premier independent cinema.
What they probably don't want you to know: The most interesting features are already open to the public.
Short history: Adjoining the historic Electric Cinema built in 1910, Electric House was the Soho House empire's second London clubhouse, and its first venture into Notting Hill. Much of the clubhouse takes a cinema theme.

High Road House
Address: 162–170 Chiswick High Road, Chiswick, London, W4 1PR.
Tel.: 020 8742 1717.
Founded: 2006.
Objects: Media; creative arts.
Approx. no. of members: Undisclosed.
Sex: Mixed sex.
Dress code: Smart-casual.
Type: Proprietary; Soho House Group.
Reciprocal clubs: Rest of the Soho House chain.
Culture: Café culture chic.
Architect: Gebler Tooth.
Facilities: Bar, brasserie, function rooms, basement nightclub, shop, 14 bedrooms.

What they want you to know: Suburban west London's premier club.
What they probably don't want you to know: Sometimes confused for a high-street chain, the brasserie is open to the public.
Short history: The first of London's Soho Houses to be founded outside the city centre, High Road House was decorated in an art deco/mid-twentieth-century style.

Little House, Balham
Address: 15–19 Bedford Hill, Balham, London, SW12 9DS.
Tel.: 020 3728 0002.
Founded: 2022.
Objects: Creative; Balham community.
Approx. no. of members: Undisclosed.
Sex: Mixed sex.
Dress code: Smart-casual.
Type: Proprietary; Soho House Group.
Reciprocal clubs: Rest of the Soho House chain.
Culture: Cosmopolitan, diverse.
Architect: Unknown.
Facilities: Bar with lounge, Cecconi's restaurant, mezzanine snug, function rooms.
What they want you to know: Balham's first ever club.
What they probably don't want you to know: Like High Road House, the restaurant (a branch of the Cecconi's chain) is open to the public.
Short history: Inspired by the large number of existing Soho House members living in London, and modelled on its namesake in Mayfair (below). The ceiling murals by Miranda Forrester focus on Black and LGBTQ+ history, and are part of a focus on local Balham artists, embedded into retro 1940s décor.

Little House, Mayfair
Address: 2 Queen Street, Mayfair, London, W1J 5PA.
Tel.: 020 7961 1200.
Founded: 2014.

Objects: Media; hedge funds.
Approx. no. of members: Undisclosed.
Sex: Mixed sex.
Dress code: Smart-casual.
Type: Proprietary; Soho House Group.
Reciprocal clubs: Rest of the Soho House chain.
Culture: Affluent.
Architect: Unknown.
Facilities: Salon bar, restaurant, drawing room, 4 apartments.
What they want you to know: Soho House's first Mayfair clubhouse.
What they probably don't want you to know: The smallest of the Soho Houses.
Short history: A compact clubhouse near Shepherd Market. Much of the building is given over to the 4 apartments, one taking up each floor. The communal areas for members are on the ground floor.

Ned's Club
Address: 27 Poultry, City of London, London, EC2R 8AJ.
Tel.: 020 7437 9585.
Founded: 2017.
Objects: Dining club.
Approx. no. of members: 2,500.
Sex: Mixed sex.
Dress code: Smart-casual.
Type: Proprietary; incorporated in 2012 as Ned-Soho House LLP, a limited liability partnership.
Reciprocal clubs: 2 clubs, across 2 countries. Access to Soho House clubs, depending on membership type.
Culture: Affluent, contemporary, trendy.
Architect: Sir Edwin Lutyens.
Facilities: Rooftop restaurant, bar and terrace with swimming pool, gym, spa, cocktail bar, basement bar in bank vault, 250 hotel bedrooms, function rooms.
What they want you to know: The best rooftop swimming pool in the City of London.

What they probably don't want you to know: So extensive is the ground-floor maze of bars and restaurants, and the facilities of the hotel, that the public are spoiled for choice without needing to be paying members.

Short history: Set up as a Soho House business venture which would combine a hotel and independent restaurants, the Ned was launched by the redevelopment of the old Midland Bank headquarters in the City of London. It was named after its architect Edwin Lutyens, known to his friends as 'Ned'. Seven restaurants and three bars are open to the public across the ground floor, with the rest of the six storeys of the building being given over to the hotel and Ned's Club. The Ned has since expanded to set up new branches in New York (called NoMad, on Broadway) and Doha (in the old Ministry of the Interior building). The involvement of Soho House provides both club management expertise and limited reciprocation with its clubhouses worldwide.

Shoreditch House

Address: 1 Ebor Street, Shoreditch, London, E1 6AW.
Tel.: 020 7739 5040.
Founded: 2007.
Objects: Creative; media.
Approx. no. of members: Undisclosed.
Sex: Mixed sex.
Dress code: Smart-casual.
Type: Proprietary; Soho House Group.
Reciprocal clubs: Rest of the Soho House chain.
Culture: More hipster than the rest of London's Soho Houses, as befits Shoreditch.
Architect: Hal Williams (original building); Stephen Archer (conversion).
Facilities: Bar, 3 restaurants (House for British food, Pen Yen for Japanese cuisine, and Maya for Mexican dishes), function rooms, gym, rooftop pool, Cowshed spa, screening room, 2 function rooms, 26 bedrooms.
What they want you to know: Noted for its rooftop swimming pool with views of London.
What they probably don't want you to know: The Cowshed spa is open to the public.

Short history: Located on the fifth and sixth floors of Shoreditch's Tea Building, a historic local landmark, once operated by Lipton, which was opened in the 1930s.

Soho Mews House

Address: 8 Lancashire Court, Mayfair, London, W1S 1EY.
Tel.: 020 3989 3222.
Founded: 2024.
Objects: Media and televisual arts.
Approx. no. of members: Undisclosed.
Sex: Mixed sex.
Dress code: Smart-casual.
Type: Proprietary; Soho House Group.
Reciprocal clubs: Rest of the Soho House chain.
Culture: Trendy, creative.
Architect: Unknown.
Facilities: Bar, ground-floor lounge, first-floor dining room, second-floor event space, outdoor terrace, 3 bedrooms.
What they want you to know: Soho House's latest London venture, opened in September 2024, with a 'no laptops' policy to differentiate it from the others.
What they probably don't want you to know: 'The new [Soho House] club is purely for old members who want a bit of quiet these days. The days of Britpop debauchery are well and truly over.' (*Popbitch*)
Short history: Early in 2024, Soho House acquired the space of a former 1930s-style restaurant in Mayfair, opposite Handel Hendrix House – the museum dedicated to both George Frideric Handel and Jimi Hendrix – and opened it later that year as its latest club.

White City House

Address: 2 Television Centre, 101 Wood Lane, White City, London, W12 7FR.
Tel.: 020 7870 0000.
Founded: 2018.

Objects: Media and televisual arts.
Approx. no. of members: Undisclosed.
Sex: Mixed sex.
Dress code: Smart-casual.
Type: Proprietary; Soho House Group.
Reciprocal clubs: Rest of the Soho House chain.
Culture: Trendy, creative.
Architect: Graham Dawbarn.
Facilities: Bar, 3 restaurants (Studio Kitchen for light meals, Pen Yen for Japanese food, House for British cuisine), function rooms, rooftop swimming pool, gym, 45 bedrooms.
What they want you to know: Unique views over a landmark courtyard.
What they probably don't want you to know: Parts of the building show its age.
Short history: Television Centre was the BBC's distinctive, iconic home from 1960, and the world's first purpose-built television studio. Its eventual closure in 2013 led to its conversion into a multi-purpose complex, including offices, apartments, cafés, bars and studios (some of which are still hired by the BBC). White City House is located in one wing of the Helios Building, aimed at creatives working in the surrounding area.

THE HOME HOUSE CHAIN

Home House – Home Grown

Soho House's stablemate as one of the trendy clubs of the 'Britpop' era was Home House in Marylebone, launched in 1998. Such was the Club's success that a nearby further spin-off club, Home Grown, followed in 2019. Ownership is an international affair: the holding company for Berkeley Adam Ltd, House Collections Ltd, lists its persons with significant control as Salah Eddin Osseiran of Lebanon, Saleh Mohammed Al Hajaj of Saudi Arabia, and Bengt Algot Dahl of Sweden.

Home House

Address: 19–21 Portman Square, Marylebone, London, W1H 6LW.
Tel.: 020 7670 2000.
Founded: 1998.
Objects: Social.
Approx. no. of members: 5,000.
Sex: Mixed sex.
Dress code: Smart-casual.
Type: Proprietary; incorporated in 1995 as Berkeley Adam Ltd.
Reciprocal clubs: 16 clubs, across 8 countries (shared with Home Grown).
Culture: 'Civilised hedonism', according to its managing director.
Architect: James Wyatt and Robert Adam.
Facilities: Bison Bar, main brasserie restaurant, House 21 restaurant, 4 drawing rooms, grand staircase, function rooms, 23 bedrooms, garden.
What they want you to know: Perennially fashionable.
What they probably don't want you to know: Bedrooms can be booked via Booking.com.
Short history: Built in the eighteenth century as the London residence of the Countess of Home, the building had a colourful history as a private address and literary salon, as well as the home of the Courtauld Institute of Art, although it lay abandoned for much of the 1990s prior to its refurbishment. The Club combines contemporary design with preserved architectural features, and has long been synonymous with louche parties, making the various entrances a favourite for gossip columnists.

Home Grown

Address: 44 Great Cumberland Place, Marylebone, London, W1H 7BS.
Tel.: 020 3928 8000.
Founded: 2019.
Objects: 'High-growth entrepreneurs, investors and world class business leaders.' Entrepreneurs and investors in growing businesses.
Approx. no. of members: 1,200.
Sex: Mixed sex.

Club Directory: Modern Clubs

Dress code: Smart-casual.
Type: Proprietary; incorporated, as Berkeley Adam Ltd.
Reciprocal clubs: 16 clubs, across 8 countries (shared with Home House).
Culture: Entrepreneurial.
Architect: Unknown (original); Russell Sage Studio (redevelopment).
Facilities: Bar, restaurant, 7 function rooms, 35 bedrooms.
What they want you to know: A spin-off of the highly successful Home House, with joint membership of both clubs an option.
What they probably don't want you to know: The contrast between Georgian architecture and modern artworks can be an acquired taste.
Short history: Prompted by the number of members and applicants wanting to use Home House for business, this was spun off as a business-oriented club. The six-storey premises were for many years the clubhouse of the Voluntary Aid Detachment Ladies' Club, which became the New Cavendish Club on becoming mixed sex in the 1970s, but which closed in 2014. Five years later, Home House opened this business club on the site.

THE CASINO CLUBS

Les Ambassadeurs – Aspinall's

Gambling used to be synonymous with the earliest clubs of the eighteenth century – gambling was both highly fashionable and illegal at the time, giving the earliest clubs a frisson. Since the nineteenth century, gambling culture in clubs has been complicated. On the one hand, successive waves of legalisation and liberalisation in the 1860s, 1960s and 2000s have theoretically made it easier to gamble, and a series of 'tribute' clubs have paid homage to the early Georgian clubs. On the other hand, the world of gambling clubs has long straddled a wide arc from the chic to the shady – and everything in between. Periodic raids of supposedly reputable clubs were a hallmark of Victorian and inter-war Britain. At one stage, the 1960s saw a new profusion of fashionable gambling clubs, from Quent's to the revived Crockford's. But these suffered heavily from a Metropolitan Police crackdown on irregularities in the late 1970s and early 1980s, and saw the most profitable casinos of all, run by Playboy Enterprises, closed down. The modern-day casino clubs are rather tamer affairs, combining a restaurant with gaming tables. The fees, however, are astronomical compared to the £1,000–£2,000 charged by most of the non-sporting London clubs; premium membership of Les Ambassadeurs comes in at £25,000 a year, not including any sums spent in the casino, putting it out of the means of most members of Clubland. The aftermath of the Covid-19 pandemic was particularly challenging for London's casino clubs, with the Ritz Club closing in 2020 (initially temporarily, and then permanently) and Crockford's closing in 2023. Les Ambassadeurs and Aspinall's are therefore the two survivors of what was once a much larger *demi-monde*.

Les Ambassadeurs

Address: 5 Hamilton Place, Mayfair, London, W1J 7ED.
Tel.: 020 7495 5555.
Founded: 1941.
Objects: Gambling.
Approx. no. of members: Undisclosed.
Sex: Mixed sex.
Dress code: Smart-casual.
Type: Proprietary; incorporated in 1992, as Les Ambassadeurs Club Ltd, a private company limited by shares, with the person of significant control being Hong Kong-based Chinese businessman Paul Suen Cho Hung.
Reciprocal clubs: None, but has a series of arrangements with five-star Mayfair hotels.
Culture: International, discreet.
Architect: Thomas Leverton, with late-Victorian alterations by William Rogers.
Facilities: Bar, restaurant, library (drawing room), gaming rooms, smoking garden.
What they want you to know: James Bond's club.
What they probably don't want you to know: The representation of Les Ambassadeurs seen in *Dr No* (1962) was a studio set in Pinewood.

Short history: 'Bond, James Bond.' The endurance of this Blitz-era club owes much to its connection with the James Bond franchise; while the literary Bond was associated with the fictitious Blades club (modelled on Ian Fleming's own club, Boodle's), the first Bond film introduces the character with his soon-to-be trademark introduction at Les Ambassadeurs, engaged in a game of chemin de fer. This reflected the popularity of the Club in the early 1960s, having outgrown its original wartime premises on Hanover Square, and moved to Hamilton Place in 1950, where it has remained ever since. Gaming today tends to focus on baccarat, blackjack, poker and roulette.

Aspinall's

Address: 27–28 Curzon Street, Mayfair, London, W1J 7TJ.
Tel.: 020 7499 4599.
Founded: 1992.
Objects: Gambling.
Approx. no. of members: Undisclosed.
Sex: Mixed sex.
Dress code: Smart-casual.
Type: Proprietary; incorporated in 1990, as Aspinall's Club Ltd, a private company limited by shares, whose person of significant control is Crown UK Investments Ltd, a subsidiary of Australian gambling consortium Crown Resorts, which is in turn owned by US-based alternative investment fund Blackstone.
Reciprocal clubs: None.
Culture: International, traditional.
Architect: Unknown.
Facilities: Bar, restaurant, gaming rooms, garden terrace.
What they want you to know: The bust by the entrance of Lord Lucan (who famously disappeared in 1974 after the murder of his family's nanny) was inserted at the insistence of John Aspinall, a close friend and patron of Lucan's.
What they probably don't want you to know: Under its previous management, the Club faced legal difficulties; a change in ownership came about after a scandal engulfed Crown Resorts over money laundering and other

irregularities, with its billionaire CEO at the time admitting before an Australian parliamentary inquiry that he had been involved in 'shameful' and 'disgraceful' conduct. None of the Australian proceedings around Crown Resorts involved Aspinall's; but they did lead to the buyout of the firm, and its new management under new ownership.

Short history: Aspinall's, or Crown London Aspinall's to give its full name, provides a link to the 1960s resurgence of London casino clubs. The millionaire entrepreneur John Aspinall had operated the Clermont Club in Berkeley Square for a decade from 1962 (with Annabel's run separately in the basement), emphasising a blend of British aristocracy and Arab money, before selling the Clermont to Playboy Enterprises. Missing the proprietorship of a gambling establishment by the late 1970s, he opened a new club, Aspinall's, in 1978, with branches in Knightsbridge's Hans Place and Mayfair's Curzon Street, selling the business in 1983. The present club, also called Aspinall's, was launched in 1992, after Aspinall needed to raise further capital, and was successfully run by him before being sold to Crown Resorts. Gaming today focuses on baccarat, blackjack, poker and roulette. At the time of going to press, Crown Resorts was in the process of selling Aspinall's to Las Vegas-based hotel and casino consortium Wynn Resorts, subject to regulatory approval.

THE MASLOW'S CLUBS

1 Warwick – Mortimer House

The Maslow's Group derive their name from the psychologist Abraham Maslow's proposed 'hierarchy of needs', setting out how human behaviour prioritised some needs above others. A relatively recent entry to Clubland, they followed the 2017 opening of Mortimer House in Fitzrovia with a new club, 1 Warwick, in Soho. Maslow's Group LLP was founded by Guy Ivesha and lists its persons with significant control as New York-based Todd Boehly and (via a holding company, Holne Investments) Jonathan and Sharon Goldstein. Boehly also owns women's club AllBright in Mayfair. Boehly also owned women's club AllBright prior to it going into administration in 2025.

1 Warwick

Address: 1 Warwick Street, Soho, London, SW1W 0QH.
Tel.: 020 7337 7400.
Founded: 2023.
Objects: Social.
Approx. no. of members: Undisclosed.
Sex: Mixed sex.
Dress code: Smart-casual.
Type: Proprietary; incorporated as part of Maslow's Group LLP, a limited liability partnership.
Reciprocal clubs: None.
Culture: Trendy, media, creative.
Architect: Unknown (original building); Fettle Studio with Denton Corker Marshall (interior design).
Facilities: Bar, Living Room and Den, Nessa bistro, Pied-à-Terre workspace, members' lounges, 9 function rooms, gym. Also hosts Yasmin, a members' rooftop restaurant, bar and terrace.
What they want you to know: Six floors with every facility modern club members would need.
What they probably don't want you to know: The ground-floor restaurant and bar are open to the public.
Short history: The sister club of Mortimer House in Fitzrovia, Maslow's say their aim is 'creating premium multi-faceted hospitality solutions'. The menu draws inspiration from Istanbul.

Mortimer House

Address: 37–41 Mortimer Street, Fitzrovia, London, W1T 3JH.
Tel.: 020 7139 4400.
Founded: 2017.
Objects: Social.
Approx. no. of members: Undisclosed.

Sex: Mixed sex.
Dress code: Smart-casual.
Type: Proprietary; incorporated in 2016 as Maslow's Group LLP, a limited liability partnership.
Reciprocal clubs: None.
Culture: Commercial.
Architect: Unknown (original); MATA Architects (conversion).
Facilities: Bar, restaurants, members' lounges, co-working spaces, function rooms, gym.
What they want you to know: The premium £5,600-a-year subscription grants you your own private office space in the heart of Fitzrovia.
What they probably don't want you to know: It is as much of a co-working space as a club.
Short history: The first of the Maslow's clubs, set across seven floors, with the emphasis on co-working spaces, this converted 1930s office block emphasises art deco design elements.

THE CREATIVE CLUBS

Academicians' Room – BAFTA – Brydges Place Club – Century – The Conduit – The Dally – Frontline Club – Groucho Club – Shoreditch Arts Club – Union Club – Upstairs at the Department Store – Vout-O-Reenee's

A number of the recent clubs have been aimed at those in the creative industries, particularly around Soho and Shoreditch. Each has stretched the boundaries of Clubland in terms of what clubs do, but has also resisted the temptation to become a franchise. Most are the product of the renewed 'boom' in modern-day London Clubland since the mid-1980s; indeed, one of these clubs, the Groucho, can lay claim more than any other to being responsible for generating interest in 'clubbism', among a new generation.

Club Directory: Modern Clubs

Academicians' Room

Address: The Keeper's House, Burlington House, Piccadilly, Mayfair, London, W1J 0BD.
Tel.: 020 7300 8090.
Founded: 2015.
Objects: Practitioners in the visual, fine, applied and performing arts, or creative industries.
Approx. no. of members: 1,000.
Sex: Mixed sex.
Dress code: None.
Type: Incorporated in 2007, as the Royal Academy of Arts, a private company limited by guarantee, with the elected Royal Academicians being members of the company; and also as a charity, registered in 2008.
Reciprocal clubs: None.
Culture: Art aficionados.
Architect: Sydney Smirke (original space); major 2013 redevelopment by David Chipperfield Architects, with later additions by Martin Brudnizki.
Facilities: Clubroom, cocktail bar, reading room, all-day café.
What they want you to know: The inside track on the Royal Academy's exhibitions and events.
What they probably don't want you to know: The Royal Academy concedes, 'Don't expect five-star luxury', though adds, 'the Keeper's House has a Bohemian charm of its own'.
Short history: The Royal Academy of Arts was established in 1768, and has occupied purpose-built premises in Burlington House since 1868. At its heart is the Keeper's House, originally a residence for the keeper of the Royal Academy Schools. A redecoration in 1883 saw the creation of the Academicians' Room, providing common-room facilities for the 80 Royal Academicians (RAs) who form the Academy's governing body. A 2015 revamp saw the Academicians' Room renovated and relaunched as a private members' club, with members sharing the facilities with Academicians, and having full run of the Keeper's House.

BAFTA, aka British Academy of Film and Television Arts
Address: 195 Piccadilly, St James's, London, W1J 9LN.
Tel.: 020 7734 0022.
Founded: 2022.
Objects: Film, television and screen arts.
Approx. no. of members: 6,500.
Sex: Mixed sex.
Dress code: None.
Type: Incorporated in 1958 as the British Academy of Film and Television Arts, a company limited by guarantee, with the members of the Academy being members of the company; also a registered charity since 1963.
Reciprocal clubs: None.
Culture: Media, the creative arts.
Architect: Edward Robert Robson (original building); Renato Benedetti and Carla Sorrentino (conversion of clubhouse area).
Facilities: Richard Attenborough Rooms: café-bar area, 2 screening rooms, roof terrace, function rooms.
What they want you to know: The place to meet the movers and shakers in the creative arts.
What they probably don't want you to know: The members' area is really just one big room.
Short history: BAFTA has been operating since 1947 – originally as the British Film Academy, founded by the country's leading directors, with David Lean as the first chairman. A separate Guild of Television Producers and Directors was formed in 1954, and the two organisations merged four years later. BAFTA continues as the UK's main trade association for those working in the film industry. A major 2022 renovation of its Piccadilly headquarters saw it launch a private members' club on the top floor.

Brydges Place Club
Address: 2 Brydges Place, Covent Garden, London, WC2N 4HP.
Tel.: 020 7240 7659.
Founded: 1982.
Objects: Social; arts; media.

Approx. no. of members: 1,300.
Sex: Mixed sex.
Dress code: None.
Type: Proprietary; incorporated in 2019 as Honeydon Ltd, a private company limited by shares, with the persons with significant control as Nicholas Turner and John Steans.
Reciprocal clubs: None.
Culture: Louche, relaxed.
Architect: Unknown.
Facilities: Bar, dining room, Chandos Lounge, function rooms.
What they want you to know: As close to the bohemian atmosphere of the old Colony Room as you will find in London today.
What they probably don't want you to know: Accessed down a urine-strewn alley only 15 inches wide at its narrowest point, it is easy to miss.
Short history: The premises first opened as a club in 1951, as the Festival Club, ostensibly named after that year's Festival of Britain, occupying the rabbit's warren of rooms set across five floors. Originally a discreet gay club, that incarnation of the Club folded in the late 1970s; but it was revived on the same premises by former employee Rod Lane, who bought the building and opened it as Two Brydges in 1982, running it for the next 30 years. In recent years, the Club has become rather chic as a broader arts club, with plenty of writers, journalists, actors and actresses, not to mention opera singers from the Coliseum next door. Financial troubles briefly hit, with the Club closing in 2018, but reopening in 2019 under its present name.

Century

Address: 61–63 Shaftesbury Avenue, Soho, London, W1D 6LQ.
Tel.: 020 7534 3080.
Founded: 2001.
Objects: Arts and culture.
Approx. no. of members: 2,500.
Sex: Mixed sex.
Dress code: Smart-casual.
Type: Proprietary; incorporated as two private companies limited by

shares; firstly, Century Club Ltd in 2012; and secondly, CCL Shaftesbury Holdings (London) Ltd in 2021; both have Stephen D'Alton as the person with significant control.
Reciprocal clubs: 35 clubs, across 19 countries.
Culture: Media, the creative arts.
Architect: Unknown.
Facilities: 4 bars including a cocktail lounge, 3 restaurants, 3 roof terraces (main terrace, outer terrace, top terrace), Green Room (theatre/cinema), Club Room and Tap Room galleries, function rooms.
What they want you to know: Blessed with one of the best roof terraces in Soho, particularly in demand during Pride.
What they probably don't want you to know: Inside it's very, very dark.
Short history: A TARDIS-like building across five floors, in a building that once housed General Motors, this trendy club on the outskirts of Soho remains extremely popular with creatives. The Club hosts an exceptionally large number of musical and theatrical performances, highbrow and lowbrow.

The Conduit

Address: 6 Langley Street, Covent Garden, London, WC2H 9JA.
Tel.: 020 3912 8400.
Founded: 2018.
Objects: Changemakers.
Approx. no. of members: 2,500.
Sex: Mixed sex.
Dress code: Smart-casual.
Type: Proprietary; incorporated in 2020 as Conduit Club Ltd, a private company limited by shares; the person with significant control was formerly American investor Rowan Finnegan, via The Conduit Holdco Ltd registered in 2017, but there is currently no registrable PSC.
Reciprocal clubs: None, but a sister club has launched in Oslo.
Culture: Entrepreneurial.
Architect: Unknown (original); Feix&Merlin Architects (conversion).
Facilities: Bar, Rucola rooftop restaurant, function rooms.

What they want you to know: A meeting point for changemakers.
What they probably don't want you to know: Rishi Sunak was a member, during the Club's first incarnation.
Short history: The Conduit has had a short but colourful existence. It first launched in 2018, in Mayfair's Conduit Street, aimed at entrepreneurs with a social conscience. It was one of numerous clubs to be victims of the Covid-19 pandemic in 2020; but it relaunched two years later, in a converted nineteenth-century Covent Garden warehouse that had originally been part of a brewery complex. The Club offers its members an academy with online skills courses.

The Dally

Address: 181 Upper Street, Islington, London, N1 1RQ.
Tel.: 020 4553 5367.
Founded: 2024.
Objects: A home away from home for the Islington neighbourhood.
Approx. no. of members: Undisclosed.
Sex: Mixed sex.
Dress code: None.
Type: Proprietary; incorporated as The Dally Club Ltd in 2022; the person with significant control is ultimately (via The Bee Club Ltd) Caroline Baldwin.
Reciprocal clubs: 18 clubs, across 11 countries.
Culture: Community-led.
Architect: Unknown (building); BusbyWebb (interior design).
Facilities: Cocktail bar, Margo's (restaurant), living room, loft event space.
What they want you to know: 'Your stylish best friend's house ... without having to do the dishes.'
What they probably don't want you to know: Members have a smaller guest allowance than at some other clubs, being limited to three.
Short history: The Club's two globe-trotting founders met in 2016, after both had recently returned to the UK – Caroline Baldwin from Ghana and Claire Ilardi-Crow from New York and Sydney. Musing ensued about how people managed to meet new friends without a shared space

or activity, and Ilardi-Crow was already a veteran of working in members' clubs. After the Covid-19 pandemic, they noticed changes in commuting patterns, with Londoners spending less time in the city centre, while local neighbourhoods were coming into their own; and they were convinced there was an appetite for community-based social clubs. The first branch of the Dally opened in 2024, converted from a period Victorian pub building in Islington. However, at the time of going to press, the Club abruptly closed down after some nine months in operation, reopening as a pub.

Frontline Club

Address: 13 Norfolk Place, Tyburnia, London, W2 1QJ.
Tel.: 020 7046 7050.
Founded: 2003.
Objects: Independent journalism.
Approx. no. of members: 1,500.
Sex: Mixed sex.
Dress code: None.
Type: Proprietary; incorporated in 2002 as Barbridge Flyover Company Ltd, a private company limited by shares; persons with significant control are Vaughan Smith and his ex-wife Pranvera Smith.
Reciprocal clubs: 8 media partners, across 8 countries.
Culture: Journalistic, connected, informal.
Architect: Skene Catling de la Peña.
Facilities: Bar, restaurant (open to public), function rooms, 12 bedrooms.
What they want you to know: 'Small, funky, very focused but rather cool' (Peter York).
What they probably don't want you to know: Julian Assange stayed at the Club for several months, and then lived with its proprietor in Norfolk for nearly a year, while Assange was tagged.
Short history: Founded by former Guards officer and veteran war correspondent Vaughan Smith, the Frontline Club celebrates and supports independent journalism worldwide, particularly in nations and regions where press freedom is under assault. Smith named it after Frontline television news agency, for whom several of his colleagues were killed in

war zones. The Club combines something of the feel of early, informal clubs – the private area above the public restaurant – with a contemporary atmosphere, blending a modern restaurant, and exposed brickwork in the members' areas above. Some of the produce grown on Smith's own Norfolk rural estate supplies the restaurant.

Groucho Club

Address: 45 Dean Street, Soho, London, W1D 4QB.
Tel.: 020 7439 4685.
Founded: 1985.
Objects: An 'anti-club' for creatives.
Approx. no. of members: 5,000.
Sex: Mixed sex.
Dress code: Smart-casual. 'The wearing of string vests is fully unacceptable and wholly proscribed by the Club Rules.'
Type: Proprietary; incorporated, 2015, as the Groucho Club Ltd, a private company limited by shares, with its persons with significant control (via holding companies Oval (2287) Ltd and Artfarm Group Ltd) ultimately being Swiss couple Iwan Wirth and Manuela Wirth-Hauser.
Reciprocal clubs: 14 clubs, across 9 countries.
Culture: Media, arts, banking.
Architect: Unknown (original); Tchaik Chassay and Melissa North (original interior design); Michaelis Boyd (2015 refurbishment).
Facilities: Soho Bar, dining room, 8 function rooms, snooker room, 22 bedrooms.
What they want you to know: Stephen Fry wrote the original rulebook.
What they probably don't want you to know: Columnist Toby Young, already notorious among the membership for being spotted leaving an amorous meeting with a Princess Diana lookalike in a Groucho Club toilet cubicle, was expelled in 2001 after writing an article in *Vanity Fair* in which he described taking drugs with other members in the Club.
Short history: Conceived by Carmen Callil, Liz Calder, Michael Sissons and Ed Victor as an antidote to stuffy, traditional clubs, just as Clubland was at its most stale in the 1980s, the Groucho has become a Clubland

institution, and helped revitalise interest in clubs more generally. It remains as much a literary salon. It takes its name from the well-known Groucho Marx quip about not wanting to belong to a club that would have him as a member. The Club's ownership has changed hands four times in the 40 years since its foundation, with past proprietors including Rupert Murdoch's then son-in-law Matthew Freud, and private equity group Graphite Capital, with the most recent change of ownership in 2022.

Further reading:
Alice Patten, *The Groucho Club – 30th Anniversary* (London: Preface Publishing, 2015).

Shoreditch Arts Club

Address: 6 Redchurch Street, Shoreditch, London, E2 7DD.
Tel.: 020 3376 0383.
Founded: 2023.
Objects: Artistic.
Approx. no. of members: Undisclosed.
Sex: Mixed sex.
Dress code: None.
Type: Proprietary; incorporated in 2020 as The Shoreditch Arts Club Ltd; persons with significant control are ultimately the members of Buckley Gray Yeoman Employee Trustee Ltd.
Reciprocal clubs: None.
Culture: Creative, artistic.
Architect: Unknown (original building); Buckley Gray Yeoman (design of conversion into a club).
Facilities: Kitchen, bar, café, screening lounge, 24-seat cinema, gallery, 2 function rooms.
What they want you to know: An authentically trendy club capturing the Shoreditch zeitgeist.
What they probably don't want you to know: There is no sit-down restaurant for a full meal; the kitchen serves snacks and small plates.
Short history: Converted from a 5,000-foot former loading bay in the centre of Shoreditch, the Club takes its inspiration from the homes of art collectors and the history of the East End, with a seasonal gallery programme.

Union Club

Address: 50 Greek Street, Soho, London, W1D 4EQ.
Tel.: 020 7437 4002.
Founded: 1993.
Objects: Social; arts.
Approx. no. of members: Under 1,000.
Sex: Mixed sex.
Dress code: Smart-casual.
Type: Proprietary; owners are Pete Cross and Carolyn Dawson, who founded the Club.
Reciprocal clubs: 15 clubs, across 5 countries.
Culture: Literary, journalistic, media.
Architect: Unknown.
Facilities: Bar, dining room, function rooms.
What they want you to know: An authentic, family-run club which remains a powerhouse for creatives.
What they probably don't want you to know: The recent annexe can feel more like a co-working space.
Short history: The Club was set up in 1993 by former North Sea oil rigger Pete Cross and chef Carolyn Dawson, who converted a derelict building. The décor varies from the modern to the eclectic, with a strong emphasis on creative industries among the members. The Club significantly expanded in 2015, acquiring the warehouse premises next door, opening a workspace area for members. It remains popular with writers and creatives, with well-attended lunches as well as low-key events like backgammon.

Upstairs at the Department Store

Address: 10 Stockwell Avenue, Brixton, London, SW9 8BQ.
Tel.: 020 3598 6970.
Founded: 2018.
Objects: Social.
Approx. no. of members: 3,000.
Sex: Mixed sex.

Dress code: Smart-casual.

Type: Proprietary; incorporated in 2017 as Squire and Partners Architects, a private company limited by shares; changed name in 2018 to The Department Store Ltd; the person with significant control is Henry Squire.

Reciprocal clubs: None.

Culture: Relaxed ('no laptop' policy).

Architect: James Smith (original building); Squire and Partners (conversion).

Facilities: Bar, restaurant, rooftop terrace, 3 function rooms.

What they want you to know: An organically grown members' club, which began as an entertaining space, and which proved such a hit that it was spun off after a year into a membership club.

What they probably don't want you to know: Much of the building is given over to, and shared with, a variety of other businesses.

Short history: The building was constructed in 1876 as the Bon Marché department store. Over the years, parts of the complex have been used as offices, a horse-and-cart fire station, a wartime bomb shelter, and the headquarters of the British Refugee Council. With the building abandoned and occupied by squatters in the early 2010s, its 2015 acquisition by architects Squire and Partners saw a major renovation and reopening of the complex in 2017, with the Club sitting atop the building.

Vout-O-Reenee's

Address: The Crypt, 30 Prescot Street, Whitechapel, London, E1 8BB.

Tel.: 020 3598 6970.

Founded: 2014.

Objects: Artistic, jazz and visual arts.

Approx. no. of members: 200.

Sex: Mixed sex.

Dress code: Smart-casual.

Type: Proprietary; incorporated in 2013 as Vout-O-Reenee's Ltd, a private company limited by shares; the person with significant control was originally Sophie Parkin; since 2021, it has been her ex-husband, Jan Vink.

Reciprocal clubs: 1 club.

Culture: Creative, eccentric, informal.

Architect: Edward Welby Pugin.
Facilities: Bar, Stash art gallery, function rooms.
What they want you to know: 'A private members' club for the surrealistically distinguished.'
What they probably don't want you to know: It can be hard to find, amidst a tangle of narrow streets in the direction of Whitechapel.
Short history: The brainchild of Sophie Parkin, the renaissance woman and writer-novelist-artist-poet who wrote a history of Soho's vanished Colony Club and yearned for a similar artistic atmosphere, the Club is named after the jazz slang of Slim Gaillard. It is the archetypal bohemian poet's club, in the crypt beneath a Catholic church near the Tower of London, just a stone's throw from the boundary of the City. The Stash Gallery hosts a rotating programme of exhibitions.

THE GASTRONOMIC CLUBS

67 Pall Mall – Le Beaujolais Club – Ivy Club – Mosimann's – Quo Vadis – Snail Club – UnHerd Club

Going back to the roots of Clubland is the idea of a private upstairs room, atop public premises for refreshment. This has had a new lease of life in the twenty-first century, and these clubs are either known for their gastronomic experience – as with Mosimann's – or else are spun off from (and based atop) a well-known public restaurant – as with the Ivy Club, Quo Vadis, the Snail Club and the UnHerd Club.

67 Pall Mall
Address: 67 Pall Mall, St James's, London, SW1Y 5ES.
Tel.: 020 3000 6767.
Founded: 2015.
Objects: Social; oenophilia.
Approx. no. of members: 4,000.
Sex: Mixed sex.

Dress code: Smart-casual.

Type: Proprietary; incorporated in 2010 as PMWineBar Ltd (subsequently renamed 67 Pall Mall Ltd in 2013), a private company limited by shares; the person with significant control is Singapore-based Grant Ashton. Connected companies, also controlled by Ashton, include 67 Pall Mall Media Ltd in 2020, and 67 Pall Mall London Ltd in 2023.

Reciprocal clubs: 12 clubs, across 8 countries.

Culture: Cosmopolitan.

Architect: Sir Edwin Lutyens.

Facilities: Wine-bar clubroom, dining room, 2 function rooms.

What they want you to know: The club of choice for oenophiles, boasting 5,000 wines from 42 countries, with 1,000 available by the glass.

What they probably don't want you to know: The site may be cursed, having previously hosted at least three defunct clubs in the nineteenth and twentieth centuries.

Short history: Converted from the old Hambros Bank building, 67 Pall Mall was founded in 2015 as London's first club dedicated wholly to wine. Since 2022, the Club has spun off into an international franchise, the 67 Pall Mall Group, which operates clubhouses in Switzerland's Verbier region as well as Singapore, and plans to open branches in Beaune, Bordeaux and Melbourne.

Academy Club – see THE SOHO DRINKING CLUBS

Le Beaujolais Club

Address: 25 Litchfield Street, Covent Garden, London, WC2H 9NJ.

Tel.: 020 7240 3776.

Founded: 1972.

Objects: French cuisine.

Approx. no. of members: 1,500.

Sex: Mixed sex.

Dress code: None.

Type: Proprietary; incorporated in 1970, as Le Beaujolais Ltd, a private company limited by shares; persons with significant control are father-and-son Jean-Yves and Terence Darcel.

Reciprocal clubs: None.
Culture: Chic and quirky.
Architect: Unknown.
Facilities: Bar, restaurant.
What they want you to know: Outstanding, hearty French cuisine, paired with optimal wines.
What they probably don't want you to know: The members' area is just one room in the basement.
Short history: The Club has its origins in the Free French Officers' Club founded in 1940, which met on these premises throughout the Second World War, in the heart of London's Theatreland and around the corner from the Ivy. The building, an unassuming terraced house, dates to 1685. After the Second World War, it morphed into a succession of French restaurants. In 1970, Le Beaujolais was incorporated, with the members' club opening in the basement below in 1972. Then in 1976, Lou Hart, who operated the Bunjies Coffee House and Folk Cellar at No. 25 next door, converted the ground-floor restaurant into Winkle's Wine Bar, specialising in French wines sourced by the Club below. That bar in turn became Le Beaujolais – a public-facing, street-level wine bar, decorated with rustic charm, and strewn with bric-a-brac including tankards, pans and ties hanging from the ceiling. The wine bar offers much of the menu from downstairs; while the members-only basement dining room offers an authentic French dining experience.

Ivy Club

Address: 1–5 West Street, Covent Garden, London, WC2H 9NE.
Tel.: 020 7557 6095.
Founded: 2008.
Objects: Dining club.
Approx. no. of members: Undisclosed.
Sex: Mixed sex.
Dress code: Smart-casual.
Type: Proprietary; acquired by and operated through Caprice Holdings Ltd, a private company limited by shares since 1982, whose accounts state that Richard Caring is the ultimate controlling party.

Reciprocal clubs: 10 clubs, across 10 countries.
Culture: Thespy and theatrical, with journalists.
Architect: Unknown (original building); Martin Brudnizki (designer).
Facilities: Piano bar, Drawing Room (dining room), The Loft (screening room), cigar terrace, plus 1 private room.
What they want you to know: Membership is 'as hard to get as a table at The Ivy itself.' (A. A. Gill).
What they probably don't want you to know: The secret entrance, which is through a lift next door to the Ivy.
Short history: The Ivy has prospered as a staple restaurant of London's Theatreland since 1917, situated opposite the Ambassadors Theatre, and the St Martin's Theatre (which has been continuously staging Agatha Christie's *The Mousetrap* since 1974). In 2005, the Ivy's holding company, Caprice Holdings, was taken over by Richard Caring – the same hospitality impresario who would go on to buy the Mark Birley clubs, and remains a major shareholder in Soho House. Three years later, an expansion of the restaurant followed, with the opening of 'The Club at the Ivy', since renamed the Ivy Club. Located across three floors above and next door to the restaurant, the Club replicates the décor of the restaurant's stained glass as a motif throughout, with art deco interiors. Artwork emphasises modern British artists, including Maggi Hambling, Tracey Emin and Damien Hirst. Since the Club opened, the Ivy brand has undergone extensive expansion as a franchise with dozens of brasseries – the first branches opened in Covent Garden in 2014 and Chelsea in 2015, and since 2018 these have extended to Asia; but the Club is run by Caprice Holdings, which manages the restaurant itself – the spin-off restaurants are part of the Ivy Collection.

Further reading:
Fernando Peire and Gary Lee, *The Ivy Now* (London: Quadrille, 2020).

Mosimann's

Address: 11B West Halkin Street, Belgravia, London, SW1X 8JL.
Tel.: 020 7235 9625.
Founded: 1988.
Objects: Fine dining.

Approx. no. of members: Undisclosed.
Sex: Mixed sex.
Dress code: Jacket required for men at all times, with tie preferred, equivalent for women.
Type: Proprietary; incorporated in 1987 as Mosimann's Ltd, a private company limited by shares, with the person with significant control being Anton Mosimann.
Reciprocal clubs: Yes, but undisclosed.
Culture: Business.
Architect: Seth Smith.
Facilities: Balcony bar, restaurant, 7 private dining rooms.
What they want you to know: Still some of the finest cuisine in London today, and fully deserving of its reputation as one of the great restaurants of the world (with prices to match).
What they probably don't want you to know: The restaurant is the Club; there is much less 'club life' than found at other establishments covered in this guide.
Short history: Set up by Swiss restaurateur Anton Mosimann in a converted church in the heart of Belgravia, Mosimann's runs a restaurant along the lines of a private members' club. The building had been constructed as an Episcopal church in 1830, but spent most of its lifespan as the Belgrave Presbyterian Church, and was deconsecrated as early as 1924, when it was converted into a private residence, the Belfry. In 1935, the Belfry became a restaurant, changing owners several times over the ensuing half-century, until Mosimann acquired it in 1988. Set around a multi-levelled, galleried dining room, with a balcony bar overlooking the diners and private areas around the back, the Club is popular for its discretion. The Club remains a family business, run by Anton with his sons, Philipp and Mark Mosimann.
Further reading:
Anton Mosimann, *25 Years of Mosimann's* (London: Elliot & Thompson, 2013).

Quo Vadis
Address: 26–29 Dean Street, Soho, London, W1D 3LL.
Founded: 2012.
Objects: Dining club.

Approx. no. of members: Undisclosed.
Sex: Mixed sex.
Dress code: Casual.
Type: Proprietary; incorporated in 2008 as Quo Vadis Collections Ltd, renamed in 2018 as Harts Group Ltd, a private company limited by shares; the person with significant control is winegrower Rollo Gabb.
Reciprocal clubs: None.
Culture: Relaxed, media-friendly.
Architect: Unknown (original buildings); Andy Martin (conversion to a club).
Facilities: Two bars, private restaurant (over the ground-floor brasseries open to the public), snooker room, three private dining rooms.
What they want you to know: Karl Marx once lived at this address.
What they probably don't want you to know: Closer to a subscription restaurant along the lines of Mosimann's.
Short history: The long-established Soho restaurant was launched in 1926 by Peppino Leoni, an Italian former head waiter at the Savoy, in a house with a louche historic reputation, easily spotted by its trademark neon sign on Dean Street. Leoni continued to run the restaurant for over 30 years (with an interval during the war, when he was interned by the British government as a fascist sympathiser), since when it has continued through a string of owners. Much of the building is early Georgian in origin, though with No. 29 being a survivor of the Stuart era. The restaurant was purchased in 2008 by a company, now the Harts Group, which also operates restaurants in King's Cross, Borough and Soho, and which was run by the Hart brothers. Four years later, Quo Vadis saw a major relaunch, and the upper rooms were opened as the Club, with a main dining room across the first floor, and smaller function rooms on the floors above.
Further reading:
P. G. Leoni, *Recipes of Specialities from Leoni's Quo Vadis Restaurant* (London: Quo Vadis, 1937).

Snail Club
Address: 48 Greek Street, Soho, London, W1D 4EF.
Tel.: 020 7439 7474.
Founded: 2024.

Objects: 'All walks of life ... for individuals seeking comfort, space, art, and fine dining ... Bores will not be entertained.'
Approx. no. of members: 200.
Sex: Mixed sex.
Dress code: Relaxed, 'Soho' smart-casual.
Type: Proprietary; incorporated in 2023 as The Snail Restaurant Ltd, a private company limited by shares, ultimately controlled (via The Snail Restaurant Holding Ltd) by the Munich-based firm Left Peg Holding GmbH.
Reciprocal clubs: 24 clubs, across 8 countries.
Culture: Artistic.
Architect: William Halfpenny.
Facilities: 6 upstairs rooms, centred around the Salon Grande Siècle.
What they want you to know: The restaurant below was the first in London to serve snails, keeping a snail farm in the basement for snails bred in and imported from Burgundy.
What they probably don't want you to know: The restaurant briefly closed in 2023, before a restructuring led to a reopening three months later.
Short history: L'Escargot was founded as a restaurant in 1927 by Georges Gaudin. Since 1896, he had been operating Bienvenue, a French restaurant at the foot of Greek Street; it was so well-known for its signature dish of snails that, upon moving premises three decades later, Gaudin called the new restaurant L'Escargot Bienvenue. It continued to be a family-run restaurant, owned by Gaudin's son Alex until 1962, since when it has changed hands numerous times. After the present management took over in 2014, a club opened on the top floor, 'The Upstairs Club at L'Escargot', but folded in 2016. In 2024, the Snail Club opened on these upper floors, led by restauranteur Brian Clivaz, former footballer Thomas Hitzlsperger and Eccentric Club secretary Ima von Wenden.

UnHerd Club
Address: 2 Old Queen Street, Westminster, London, SW1H 9HP.
Tel.: 020 3005 2320.
Founded: 2022.

Objects: Free speech; non-mainstream, controversial opinions.
Approx. no. of members: 500.
Sex: Mixed sex.
Dress code: None.
Type: Proprietary; incorporated in 2019 as UnHerd Ventures Ltd, a private company limited by shares, with hedge-fund billionaire Sir Paul Marshall as person with significant control.
Reciprocal clubs: None.
Culture: Heterodox, Eurosceptic.
Architect: Unknown.
Facilities: Restaurant (open to the public as the Old Queen Street Cafe), clubroom, plus one private room.
What they want you to know: Avowedly anti-'woke' and anti-'political correctness'.
What they probably don't want you to know: While cheaper than many other clubs, the Club premises are essentially just one room.
Short history: The brainchild of investor Paul Marshall, who has helped bankroll a range of political initiatives from the Vote Leave campaign for Brexit to the GB News channel, UnHerd launched as a website in 2017, aimed at giving a platform to non-mainstream voices. In 2022, UnHerd bought the building for a headquarters in the heart of Westminster, just a stone's throw from HM Treasury and Parliament. The building is split into three areas: a café that is open to the public, selling traditional British fare; an editorial office for UnHerd's website; and a clubroom, which is mainly used to host talks. They object to being viewed as conservatives, preferring to eschew labels, and point to a range of influences ranging from Karl Marx to Roger Scruton – both of whose pictures are found on their staircase. The Club was already particularly popular with the staff of the *Spectator* (whose offices are only a few doors away), and which was also purchased by Paul Marshall in 2024, for a reported £100 million.

Club Directory: Modern Clubs

THE HOTEL CLUBS

Admiralty Arch Club – Cambridge House – Dartmouth House – The Other House – St James's Hotel and Club – Sloane Club – Ten Trinity Square – The Twenty Two

Often dismissed as a new-fangled gimmick, the hotel–club combination was actually a well-trodden path in the nineteenth century. Many of the facilities in a club are already provided in a hotel, so it is little surprise that some hotels open a club within.

Admiralty Arch Club

Address: The Mall, St James's, London, SW1A 2WH.
Tel.: TBC.
Founded: 2026 (forthcoming).
Objects: Social.
Approx. no. of members: TBC.
Sex: Mixed sex.
Dress code: Smart-casual.
Type: Proprietary; incorporated in 2022 as Admiralty Arch Holdings Ltd, a private company limited by shares, whose person with significant control is property developer Simon Reuben.
Reciprocal clubs: None.
Culture: New money – lots of it.
Architect: Aston Webb.
Facilities: TBC.
What they want you to know: One of London's most sought-after views, with Buckingham Palace on one side, and Trafalgar Square on the other.
What they probably don't want you to know: The launch date, originally slated for 2022, keeps being pushed back.
Short history: A new club, due to open in 2026. The iconic building over the Mall, originally an Edwardian annexe of the Admiralty, was sold off by the British government on a 125-year-lease in 2012, and is now being converted by the Reuben brothers, Simon and David, into a luxury hotel,

the Admiralty Arch Waldorf Astoria, with a club within. Hotel concierges are already touting membership across London.

Cambridge House

Address: 94 Piccadilly, Mayfair, London, W1J 7BP.
Tel.: TBC.
Founded: 2025.
Objects: Social.
Approx. no. of members: TBC.
Sex: Mixed sex.
Dress code: None.
Type: Proprietary; ultimate beneficial owners are Simon and David Reuben; day-to-day operations are run by Auberge Resorts, the California- and Maryland-headquartered hospitality group.
Reciprocal clubs: None.
Culture: International.
Architect: Matthew Brettingham.
Facilities: Bar, restaurant, lounge, courtyard, 102 bedrooms in adjoining hotel.
What they want you to know: London's newest club, in a renovated nineteenth-century clubhouse.
What they probably don't want you to know: For much of the last quarter-century, this architectural gem has lain abandoned, languishing and rotting, with extensive damage to the old American Club during that time.
Short history: Cambridge House began its life as Egremont House, constructed in 1756 as the Palladian London mansion of the Earls of Egremont. It was renamed Cambridge House after serving as the home of the Duke of Cambridge, George III's youngest son, in 1829–50. After his death, it served as the 3rd Viscount Palmerston's residence during the last 15 years of his life, including during his stints as home secretary, foreign secretary and prime minister. From 1865 to 1999 it took its most famous guise, housing the Naval and Military (In and Out) Club. Their then-landlord refused to renew their lease in 1999, but successive plans for a luxury hotel, luxury flats, mansion and casino all came to nothing, as

the building passed through the hands of several developers. Eventually, current freehold owners Simon and David Reuben developed the latest plan for the five-star Cambridge House Hotel and Residences, embedding a club. This includes redevelopment of adjoining buildings at 90–93 and 95 Piccadilly, with the latter once having housed the American Club. There is also a substantial new residential building at the back; but the Club is centred around the clubrooms of the old Cambridge House, which has been restored, following the original floorplan. In 2025, the Reubens announced that one of the rear buildings would be developed as a separate business club called The Carrington, as a collaboration with Robin Birley.

Dartmouth House

Address: 37–38 Charles Street, Mayfair, London, W1J 5ED.
Tel.: 020 7529 1554.
Founded: 2023.
Objects: Social.
Approx. no. of members: Undisclosed.
Sex: Mixed sex.
Dress code: None.
Type: Incorporated in 1977, originally as ESU Dartmouth House Club Ltd, and now as ESU Trading Ltd, a private company limited by guarantee; ultimate beneficial owner is the English Speaking Union of the Commonwealth, a registered charity with a Royal Charter dating to 1957.
Reciprocal clubs: None.
Culture: A combination of hotel guests with earnest student debaters.
Architect: William Allwright; with alterations by Clough Williams-Ellis.
Facilities: Bar, restaurant, lounge, courtyard, 38 hotel bedrooms.
What they want you to know: The spiritual home of free speech.
What they probably don't want you to know: The Club, the hotel and the Union are essentially separate enterprises sharing the same building.
Short history: Since 1926, Dartmouth House has been occupied by the English-Speaking Union, which had been founded eight years earlier by Sir Evelyn Wrench to promote debating and public speaking across the

Anglosphere. The organisation has long had a club-like element. A 2020s redevelopment converted much of the building into a hotel, with a category of membership of the building, while the ESU continues to be headquartered there.

The Other House

Address: 15–17 Harrington Gardens, South Kensington, London, SW7 4JJ (South Kensington branch); 25 Wellington Street, Covent Garden, London, WC2E 7PX (Covent Garden branch).
Tel.: 020 3846 6000.
Founded: 2022.
Objects: Medium-term residential club.
Approx. no. of members: Undisclosed.
Sex: Mixed sex.
Dress code: None.
Type: Proprietary; incorporated in 2019 as The Portfolio Club Opco Holdings (subsequently renamed in 2022 as The Other House Opco Holdings Ltd), a private company limited by shares, with subsidiaries including The Other House Opco 1 Ltd, The Other House Opco 2 Ltd, The Other House Ipco Ltd; and the Jersey-based affiliates The Other House Propco 1 Ltd and The Other House Propco 2 Ltd. The person with significant control is ultimately (via LCP Hospitality Holdings Ltd and LCP Corp Ltd) Naomi Heaton.
Reciprocal clubs: None.
Culture: High-end tourism.
Architect: Unknown.
Facilities: 4 bars (Owl and Monkey, Hogsmire, The Keeping Room and The Den), The Other Kitchen (café), House Blend (restaurant), gym, steam room, sauna, vitality pool, wellbeing studio, function rooms, over 200 Club Flats in the adjoining hotel.
What they want you to know: The ladies' lavatories have strokable armadillo wallpaper.
What they probably don't want you to know: Hotel guests have full access to the Club as well as the members.

Short history: The Club opened in 2022 when a complex of 11 South Kensington townhouses was converted into a long-stay hotel, with Club Flats of up to five bedrooms, suitable for occupation for weeks or months at a time. A second clubhouse, with 146 flats, is due to open in Covent Garden in 2025.

St James's Hotel and Club

Address: 7–8 Park Place, St James's, London, SW1A 1LS.
Tel.: 020 7316 1608.
Founded: 1980.
Objects: Social.
Approx. no. of members: Undisclosed.
Sex: Mixed sex.
Dress code: None.
Type: Proprietary; owners are husband-and-wife German hoteliers Thomas H. Althoff and Elke Diefenbach-Althoff, via Althoff Hotels.
Reciprocal clubs: 616 clubs, across 54 countries.
Culture: International travellers; visiting reciprocal members.
Architect: Hyman Henry and Marcus Evelyn Collins.
Facilities: Bar, restaurant, 60 hotel bedrooms.
What they want you to know: The most extensive reciprocals list of any London club.
What they probably don't want you to know: Despite claiming a lineage with the old St James's Club on Piccadilly (many of whose members joined Brooks's after their club's closure in 1978), the old club of that name had no connection whatsoever to this one; and so their claim to be 'est. 1857', and to have 'changed our home and our décor several times since then' may be taken with a pinch of salt; at best regarded as an homage.
Short history: In the late 1970s, the entrepreneur Peter de Savary began opening a mini-chain of St James's Clubs in Antigua, London, Los Angeles and Paris. The London branch was opened in 1980 as the St James's Hotel, embedding a club within it, in a converted late-Victorian block of flats on the same street as Pratt's and the Royal Over-Seas League. De Savary sold

the clubs in the late 1980s to fund his acquisition of Skibo Castle, which he turned into the members-only Carnegie Club. The St James's Hotel and Club were sold on in 2010 to Pakistan-based Mian Mohammad Mansha, via the Nishat Group; and in 2024, he sold it on to the present owners. The hotel is currently rated as five stars.

Sloane Club

Address: 52 Lower Sloane Street, Chelsea, London, SW1W 8BP.
Tel.: 020 7730 9131.
Founded: 1976.
Objects: Social.
Approx. no. of members: 4,000.
Sex: Mixed sex.
Dress code: None in most of the Club; at lunch and dinner in the restaurant, jacket and tie for men, and the equivalent for women.
Type: Proprietary; incorporated in 1991, as Sloane Club Management Limited; a private company limited by shares; whose ultimate beneficial owner is Clearbell Capital LLP, a real estate and fund management advisory, which lists directors, but does not disclose any registrable persons with significant control.
Reciprocal clubs: 100 clubs, across 20 countries.
Culture: Transient, with much traffic with the hotel.
Architect: William Willet.
Facilities: Bar, restaurant, co-working space (Chelsea Room), function rooms, 138 hotel bedrooms.
What they want you to know: 'The Sloane Club empowers all of you, in spaces you can be your whole self.'
What they probably don't want you to know: Much of the building is now given over to the (club-owned) hotel next door, with hotel guests given the free run of the place.
Short history: Once upon a time, London had a multitude of ladies' residential clubs, such as the Beechwood Club, the Columbia Club, the Connaught House Club, the Minerva Club, the Twentieth Century Club and the Ladies' Town and Country Club. These catered to young, educated,

professional women working in the capital, who needed a safe and reliable home, emulating the gentlemen's clubs of the day, but with a core community of permanent residents. It was in this spirit that, in 1922, the building opened as the Service Women's Club. Yet after half a century, the Club met with the same fate as the other Victorian- and Edwardian-era ladies' residential clubs – an attempted 1972 rebrand, as the Helena Club, named after its former patron, did little to reverse its fortunes, and the Club folded three years later. In its place, the building reopened under new management as the Sloane Club, now open to men as well as women, with the former Club chambers now being a hotel with serviced apartments; but the ground floor still operates a suite of clubrooms open to members and hotel guests alike.

Ten Trinity Square

Address: 10 Trinity Square, City of London, London, EC3N 4AJ.
Tel.: 020 3297 9330.
Founded: 2017.
Objects: Social.
Approx. no. of members: Undisclosed.
Sex: Mixed sex.
Dress code: Smart-casual.
Type: Proprietary; part of the Canada-headquartered Four Seasons Hotels and Resorts, with US-based Bill Gates and Saudi-based Prince Al-Waleed bin Talal being the majority shareholders.
Reciprocal clubs: 5 clubs, across 3 countries.
Culture: Opulent, expensive.
Architect: Edwin Cooper.
Facilities: Bar, restaurant, dining room, lounge, function rooms, cigar shop, 100 hotel bedrooms, 41 hotel apartments, hotel spa.
What they want you to know: 'The pinnacle of luxury.'
What they probably don't want you to know: It feels more a luxury hotel than a club.
Short history: In 2017, the Four Seasons hotel chain opened their Tower Hill branch in the old Port of London Authority's Beaux Arts building, which had opened in 1922. After extensive wartime bomb damage, it spent

most of the ensuing decades hosting a series of offices, until the recent renovation, where the Club is within the hotel.

The Twenty Two

Address: 22 Grosvenor Square, Mayfair, London, W1K 6LF.
Tel.: 020 3988 5022.
Founded: 2022.
Objects: Social.
Approx. no. of members: Undisclosed.
Sex: Mixed sex.
Dress code: None.
Type: Proprietary; incorporated in 2018 as 22 Hotel Management Ltd, a private company limited by shares. There is no current registerable person with significant control, although it was previously investor Jamie Reuben.
Reciprocal clubs: None.
Culture: International.
Architect: Unknown (original); ReardonSmith Architects (conversion); Natalia Miyar (design).
Facilities: 4 bars, basement clubrooms, main restaurant, evening dining room, 2 terraces, 31 bedrooms and suites in the adjoining hotel.
What they want you to know: 'A hotel and cultural space dedicated to the art of lingering.'
What they probably don't want you to know: It is primarily a hotel.
Short history: Founded by hotelier and restauranteur Navid Mirtorabi and property tycoon Jamie Reuben, the Twenty Two redeveloped an Edwardian residence on Grosvenor Square into a luxury hotel with a club attached to it. A second branch opened in New York in 2024.

Club Directory: Modern Clubs

THE BUSINESS NETWORKING CLUBS

12 Hay Hill – Albert's – Arboretum – CEO Club London – The Clubhouse – Eight – The Ministry – Pasley Tyler – Pavilion Club

The 2010s and 2020s have seen a boom in business-oriented clubs, many of them combining the characteristics of a co-working space. While many have closed down in recent years, in line with difficulties across the co-working sector since the Covid-19 pandemic, a number continue to this day. Several of them emphasise mixing business with pleasure.

12 Hay Hill

Address: 12 Hay Hill, Mayfair, London, W1J 8NR.
Tel.: 020 7952 6000.
Founded: 2014.
Objects: Business.
Approx. no. of members: Undisclosed.
Sex: Mixed sex.
Dress code: None.
Type: Proprietary; incorporated in 2014 as Cabinet Lounge UK Ltd, a private company limited by shares, renamed in 2015 as 12 Hay Hill Ltd; the person with significant control is ultimately the Greek entrepreneur Stephanos Issaias, via holding company Club Working Ltd.
Reciprocal clubs: None.
Culture: Professional, managerial.
Architect: Sidell Architects (original building); Architects of Innovation (renovation).
Facilities: Bar, restaurant, co-working spaces, quiet zone, business lounges, 9 function rooms, serviced offices.
What they want you to know: 'Pioneering the concept of clubworking.'
What they probably don't want you to know: Less of a club, and more of an office.

Short history: Launched in 2014, this experimental club combines a full suite of office facilities with paid membership.

Albert's, aka Albert's at Beaufort House

Address: Beaufort House, 354 King's Road, Chelsea, London, SW3 5UZ.
Tel.: 020 7352 2828.
Founded: 2016.
Objects: Social.
Approx. no. of members: Undisclosed.
Sex: Mixed sex.
Dress code: Smart-casual.
Type: Proprietary; incorporated in 2009 as Beaufort House Chelsea Ltd, a private company limited by shares; persons with significant control are Simon Oldham and Louis Hysa.
Reciprocal clubs: None.
Culture: 'Sloane Ranger'.
Architect: Unknown.
Facilities: Cocktail bar, attic champagne bar, brasserie, clubroom, function room, private dining room.
What they want you to know: 'The King's Road premier brasserie, cocktail bar and private members' club.'
What they probably don't want you to know: The first incarnation of Albert's club floundered.
Short history: Albert's originally launched in South Kensington, in 2016; but the Club's life was short, folding in 2018. A year later, it reopened, having relocated to the upstairs rooms of Beaufort House in Chelsea.

Arboretum

Address: Cavell House, 2A Charing Cross Road, Covent Garden, London, WC2H 2HF.
Tel.: 020 3876 2317.
Founded: 2019.
Objects: Co-working, for people who care about the planet.
Approx. no. of members: Undisclosed.

Sex: Mixed sex.
Dress code: Smart-casual.
Type: Proprietary; incorporated in 2019 as Penway Holdings Ltd, a private company limited by shares; the person with significant control is Derek Neerkin, managing director of serviced office provider Pennine Way.
Reciprocal clubs: Yes, but undisclosed.
Culture: Trendy, casual.
Architect: John Walker (original Victorian building); A. W. Murray (Edwardian enlargement).
Facilities: Main lounge, The Hub on the Square, meeting room, gym.
What they want you to know: 'We are taking the "private" out of membership and accept all applications.'
What they probably don't want you to know: Just as its short-lived sister club, Library, was a library-themed club without a library, Arboretum is an arboretum-themed club with relatively few plants – a 'living green wall' is its main contribution.
Short history: The Club opened as a spin-off of the nearby Library club on St Martin's Lane, which had opened five years earlier but did not survive the pandemic. Membership can be annual, seasonal, or even on day passes.

CEO Club London

Address: 120 Pall Mall, St James's, London, SW1Y 5EA.
Tel.: TBC.
Founded: 2025.
Objects: Business; candidates are expected to be successful senior executives of high-turnover companies.
Approx. no. of members: 50 (United Kingdom); 250 (Ukraine).
Sex: Mixed sex.
Dress code: Smart-casual.
Type: Proprietary; incorporated in 2023 as CEO Club London Ltd, a private company limited by shares; Serhiy Haydaychuk is the person with significant control.
Reciprocal clubs: None, but affiliated to the CEO Club in Kyiv.

Culture: Discreet, informed, with an emphasis on high-level briefings.
Architect: Sir Edwin Lutyens (original building); MCM Architecture (refurbishment).
Facilities: Bar, restaurant, function rooms.
What they want you to know: Building bridges between the UK and Ukraine, and developing ties between the progressive business communities of both countries.
What they probably don't want you to know: Until they acquired their own clubhouse in 2024, meetings were held in other London clubs.
Short history: CEO Club was set up in Ukraine in 2011, initially as an informal networking association for connecting business leaders and experts. Six years later, it opened a physical clubhouse in an 1896 building in central Kyiv. In November 2022, CEO Club London was established as a bridgehead for the Ukrainian business and diplomatic community in London with their British counterparts, fully backed by the Ukrainian Embassy. In 2024 it acquired the lease on 120 Pall Mall, next to the Institute of Directors, making it the latest club on the thoroughfare.

The Clubhouse

Address: 8 St James's Square, Mayfair, London, SW1Y 4JU (St James's branch); 20 St Andrew Street, City of London, London, EC4A 3AG (Holborn Circus branch).
Tel.: 0800 756 2911.
Founded: 2011 (original Mayfair branch); 2018 (Holborn Circus and St James's branches).
Objects: Business.
Approx. no. of members: 1,000.
Sex: Mixed sex.
Dress code: None.
Type: Proprietary; incorporated in 2016 as Express 042 Ltd, a private company limited by shares, renamed in 2019 as The New Clubhouse London Ltd; persons with significant control are ultimately French lender Lance Mysyrowicz (via Boost&Co Limited) and Monaco-based Mark Dixon (via

IWG Clubhouse Partner Limited, a subsidiary of Swiss co-working giant IWC plc).

Reciprocal clubs: None.

Culture: Work-oriented.

Architect: Eric Parry Architects (St James's branch); DLA Design (Holborn Circus branch).

Facilities: Deli, flexible meeting areas, hot desks, private offices.

What they want you to know: 'Created by business leaders for business leaders.'

What they probably don't want you to know: Two previous branches, in Mayfair and Bank, have closed down.

Short history: Part of the 2010s boom in co-working spaces that also doubled as private members' clubs, The Clubhouse originally opened in Mayfair in 2011, with a further three branches opening in 2017. Cash-flow difficulties, however, forced the original company into administration in 2019 amidst a reported £74 million in debt, and half of the four branches liquidated, while the remaining two passed into new ownership.

Eight

Address: 1 Change Alley, City of London, London, EC3V 3ND (Bank branch); 1 Dysart Street, City of London, London, EC2A 2BX (Moorgate branch); 49 Clifton Street, City of London, London, EC2A 4EX (gym).

Tel.: 020 7621 0808 (Bank branch); 020 7392 9410 (Moorgate branch).

Founded: 2006 (Moorgate branch); 2009 (Bank branch).

Objects: City workers.

Approx. no. of members: Undisclosed.

Sex: Mixed sex.

Dress code: Smart-casual.

Type: Proprietary; incorporated in 2005 as Five Eights Account Ltd, a private company limited by shares; renamed in 2012 as Eight Members Club Ltd; no registrable person with significant control.

Reciprocal clubs: Yes, but undisclosed.

Culture: Cosmopolitan, international.

Architect: Unknown.

Facilities: Rooftop lounge, bar, restaurant, private dining room, terrace, function rooms (Moorgate branch); basement lounge, bar, conference room, cinema/theatre, 7 function rooms (Bank branch).

What they want you to know: The perfect place to do business in the City.

What they probably don't want you to know: Less suited for those who wish to get away from the office.

Short history: Eight was the brainchild of its founder and CEO Brandon Kinsman, who envisioned an informal office-lounge setup where workers would stick around for entertaining in the evenings. The two branches are deliberately quite different in ambience, so as to complement one another.

Home Grown – see THE HOME HOUSE CHAIN

The Ministry

Address: 79–81 Borough Road, Bermondsey, London, SE1 1DN.

Tel.: 020 7740 8611.

Founded: 2018.

Objects: Social; creative.

Approx. no. of members: Undisclosed.

Sex: Mixed sex.

Dress code: None, though they reserve the right to refuse admission if 'inappropriate'.

Type: Proprietary; Jersey-based Submin Holdings Ltd, incorporated in 2016, runs the Club (as well as the nearby nightclub); no registrable person with significant control.

Reciprocal clubs: None.

Culture: Trendy, creative.

Architect: Unknown (original building); Squire and Partners (conversion).

Facilities: Bar, restaurant, gym, cinema, sound studio, terrace, function rooms, offices, co-working spaces.

What they want you to know: 'The first social workspace and private members club for creative industries.'

What they probably don't want you to know: Most of the building is given

over to co-working space, with members largely limited to the ground floor.
Short history: The family of Jamie Palumbo, Lord Palumbo of Southwark, had already dabbled in club management – his property developer father Lord Palumbo launched the Walbrook Club in 2000, which is now operated by his half-brother. Since 1991, Jamie has operated the Ministry of Sound nightclub; 27 years later he launched this nearby private members' club, in a converted former Victorian printworks.

Pasley Tyler

Address: 42 Berkeley Square, Mayfair, London, W1J 5AW.
Tel.: 020 7318 0800.
Founded: 2019.
Objects: Global senior executives.
Approx. no. of members: Undisclosed.
Sex: Mixed sex.
Dress code: Smart-casual.
Type: Proprietary; incorporated in 1997 as Pasley Tyler & Company Ltd, a private company limited by shares; no registrable persons with significant control.
Reciprocal clubs: None.
Culture: Secretive, formal.
Architect: Edward Cock and Francis Hillyard.
Facilities: Dining room, private studies, offices, function rooms.
What they want you to know: 'A homely, secure, safe space within which to conduct matters, both personal and professional . . . Our ethos – provide members with what they want, when they want it.'
What they probably don't want you to know: A great deal. Much emphasis is placed on discretion, with the highly secretive Club operating 'mediation and safe house policies' which allow for the filtering of guests and visitors out of sight from one another.
Short history: Pasley Tyler opened in 1997, created by several former Kleinwort Benson bankers as a suite of offices tailored to the needs of sensitive businesses. In 2019, Pasley Tyler rolled out club membership.

Pavilion Club

Address: 64 Knightsbridge, London, SW1X 7JF (Knightsbridge branch); Cannon Green, 27 Bush Lane, London, EC4R 0AA (City branch); 96 Kensington High Street, London, W8 4SG (Kensington branch); 69–79 Fulham High Street, London, SW6 3JW (Fulham branch).

Tel.: 020 7484 5755.

Founded: 2012 (Kensington); 2017 (City); 2022 (Knightsbridge); 2024 (Fulham).

Objects: Co-working.

Approx. no. of members: Undisclosed.

Sex: Mixed sex.

Dress code: None.

Type: Proprietary; incorporated in 2007 as Heven Ltd, a private company limited by shares; the person with significant control is Jon Hunt.

Reciprocal clubs: None.

Culture: Ostentatious.

Architect: Russell Sage Studio (Knightsbridge branch); Nissen Richards Studio (Kensington branch).

Facilities: Bars, lounges, dining rooms, terraces, serviced offices, function rooms.

What they want you to know: 'An eclectic blend of luxury workspace and exquisite private members' facilities.'

What they probably don't want you to know: There can be something of a culture clash between the 'office' parts and 'club' parts of the buildings.

Short history: Foxton's property billionaire Jon Hunt described moving into the co-working business as 'a total accident'; but after operating a Battersea office building, he developed the concept of a combined co-working space and club. The first branch, in Kensington, originally opened as Dryland, before changing its name to Pavilion in 2014. Three further branches have followed.

Club Directory: Modern Clubs

THE NIGHTCLUB CLUBS

The House of KOKO – Maison Estelle – The Roof Gardens – Tramp

The link between nightclubs and the establishments covered in this book is not as random as it may seem – in the early-to-mid-twentieth century, a number of nightclubs structured themselves as private members' clubs as a licensing convenience. These days, this is no longer necessary, but there are still numerous members' clubs that operate in conjunction with a nightclub, typically in the basement.

5 Hertford Street (Loulou's) – see THE ROBIN BIRLEY CLUBS

Annabel's – see THE MARK BIRLEY CLUBS

Arts Club – see THE ARTISTIC CLUBS

George – see THE MARK BIRLEY CLUBS

Gerry's – see THE SOHO DRINKING CLUBS

High Road House – see THE SOHO HOUSE EMPIRE

The House of KOKO
Address: 74 Crowndale Road, Mornington Crescent, London, NW1 1TP.
Tel.: 020 7388 3222.
Founded: 2022.
Objects: Music, arts and theatre.
Approx. no. of members: 1,500.
Sex: Mixed sex.
Dress code: Smart-casual.
Type: Proprietary; incorporated in 2021 as the Koko Foundation, a private company limited by guarantee; no current registrable person with significant control.
Reciprocal clubs: None.

Culture: Musical, artistic.
Architect: William G. R. Sprague (original building); Archer Humphryes Architects (conversion).
Facilities: Dome Cocktail Bar, Battens Bar, Stage Kitchen (restaurant), penthouse lounge, roof terrace, Vinyl Rooms, theatre.
What they want you to know: 'Sixteen beautiful spaces . . . steeped in over 122 years of history.'
What they probably don't want you to know: You can still visit the music venue downstairs without being a member of the Club.
Short history: KOKO is a music venue and nightclub in a 1900-built theatre which has gone by many names over the years, including the Camden Hippodrome Theatre and the Camden Palace. *The Goon Show* was recorded here in the 1950s, when the BBC occupied the building. Since 2004, entrepreneur Olly Bengough has operated the premises as KOKO. A massive fire in 2020 saw major refurbishment, including the rear areas of the theatre opened as an arts-themed private members' club run by Bengough. The space combines parts of a piano factory from the 1800s, a pub from the 1860s and the late-Victorian theatre. Members have a 24-hour advance booking window on the music venue below.

Maison Estelle

Address: 6 Grafton Street, Mayfair, London, W1S 4EQ.
Tel.: 020 7623 6100.
Founded: 2021.
Objects: Social.
Approx. no. of members: Undisclosed.
Sex: Mixed sex.
Dress code: None; indeed, they say there are 'No rules', although this is not entirely the case (see the photography rule below).
Type: Proprietary; incorporated in 2017 as Maison Estelle Ltd, a private company limited by guarantee; it is a subsidiary of GH Holdings 2 Ltd, and ultimately GH Holdings 1 Ltd, neither of which have any registrable persons with significant control.
Reciprocal clubs: One; its sister country club, Estelle Manor.

Culture: Affluent.
Architect: Sir Robert Taylor (original building); C2J Architects (conversion).
Facilities: 11 bars, 4 restaurants, study, lounges, event spaces, nightclub.
What they want you to know: 'A place of celebration and sanctuary, of fine dining and daily discourse.'
What they probably don't want you to know: What the Club looks like inside; there is a strict 'no photography' policy, with the posting of any images to social media being particularly *verboten*. All mobile phones have their cameras stickered on arrival.
Short history: Maison Estelle is the brainchild of Sharan Pasricha, founder of the Ennismore group which runs Scotland's Gleneagles hotel and the Hoxton Hotels chain. Conversion of the historic building into a club posed some challenges, due to the River Tyburn flowing directly beneath it. The Club places a big premium on secrecy. They have since branched out into a rural spin-off, Estelle Manor, a country hotel and club in Oxfordshire.

New Evaristo Club – see THE SOHO DRINKING CLUBS

The Roof Gardens
Address: 99 Kensington High Street, Kensington, London, W8 5SA.
Tel.: 020 3837 5727.
Founded: 2024.
Objects: Social.
Approx. no. of members: 3,000.
Sex: Mixed sex.
Dress code: None.
Type: Proprietary; incorporated in 2020 as Kensington RG Ltd, a private company limited by shares. The person with significant control is ultimately (via Imagination Industries Ltd, and its holding company Imagination Industries Holdings Ltd) Stephen Fitzpatrick.
Reciprocal clubs: None.
Culture: 'Sloane Ranger'.
Architect: Ralph Hancock.

Facilities: Three rooftop gardens (Woodland Garden, Spanish Garden and Tudor Garden, with a Tudor Walk linking the latter two), four restaurants (sixth-floor clubroom restaurant, seventh-floor Asian-inspired dining room, rooftop North African- and southern European-inspired grill in the Spanish Garden, and al fresco Italian restaurant in the Tudor Garden), dance floor, 'meandering stream', 6,000 square metres of space.

What they want you to know: The Club's unofficial motto is 'head in the clouds, feet on the dance floor' (Sue Walter, chief executive).

What they probably don't want you to know: Gone are the four resident flamingos from its days as a public restaurant.

Short history: The Derry & Tom's department store was constructed on Kensington High Street in 1933, and five years later the Kensington Roof Gardens opened atop it. Initially conceived of as a pleasure garden with paid admission, the gardens changed hands several times in the decades following Derry & Tom's 1973 closure, including stints as a nightclub and a restaurant, latterly operated by Richard Branson's Virgin Group, until they closed in 2018. In 2021, it was acquired by Stephen Fitzpatrick, founder of OVO Energy, who converted it into a private members' club, which opened three years later.

Tramp

Address: 40 Jermyn Street, St James's, London, SW1Y 6DN.
Tel.: 020 7734 0565.
Founded: 1969.
Objects: Social; nightclub.
Approx. no. of members: About to start anew; only the handful of still-living founding members, still paying £10.50 a year in perpetuity, will be retained. Everyone else will have to reapply.
Sex: Mixed sex.
Dress code: None.
Type: Proprietary; the Club closed some time ago, but reopened late in 2024 under Italian entrepreneur Luca Maggiore.
Reciprocal clubs: None.
Culture: Adrenalin-fuelled, debauched.
Architect: Stephen Egan.

Club Directory: Modern Clubs

Facilities: Bar, dance floor, dining room, function rooms.
What they want you to know: Where celebrities from Jack Nicholson to Princess Margaret have been seen partying.
What they probably don't want you to know: Long-time regular Prince Andrew definitely did not sweat here.
Short history: Some might query whether Tramp even belongs in this listing, since it's primarily a nightclub. But then, exactly the same thing could have been said about Annabel's for its first half-century. Tramp was opened by Johnny Gold, Bill Ofner and Oscar Lerman in 1969, as an aristocrat-friendly nightclub run as a private members' club, complete with surprisingly traditional, wood-panelled décor for a disco, complete with chandeliers. It rapidly became a chic haunt for Hollywood celebrities in London: in the opening year, the Beatles, Roman Polanski and Peter Sellers all visited, the latter holding his third wedding there in 1970. Joan Collins, a long-standing member whose sister was married to one of the co-founders, booked it as the filming location for her trashy 1978 flick *The Stud*. Porn baron Paul Raymond, a nightly fixture in the 1980s, gave it a sleazy veneer for many years, but it has never entirely lost its reputation as somewhere the rich and famous let their hair down, helped by decades of paparazzi snaps of guests entering and leaving. A strict ban on photography inside the Club remains enforced, and is a key component of its reputation for discretion, along with its unpretentious house burgers. Gold's sale of his stake in the business in 1998 has seen it change ownership several times since.

Further reading:
Johnny Gold, *Tramp's Gold* (London: Robson Books, 2001).

THE FAMILY CLUBS

Cloud Twelve – Little Houses – NEXUS Club – Purple Dragon

The concept of the family club, welcoming people of all ages, is rooted in the gymkhana clubs of Asia, where young children are welcome from an early age to be part of the club experience. In Britain, the Maggie and

Rose chain of four clubs (2007–24) introduced the notion of a private members' club focused around childcare, with the members' children being given nursery facilities. Since then, some other clubs have striven to be exceptionally child-friendly.

Cloud Twelve

Address: 2–5 Colville Mews, Notting Hill, London, W11 2DA.
Tel.: 020 3301 1012.
Founded: 2018.
Objects: 'Wellness, Spa and Kids' Club.'
Approx. no. of members: Kids' Club membership is capped at *c.* 200, while the Spa and Wellness Clinic do not have a membership limit.
Sex: Mixed sex.
Dress code: Smart-casual.
Type: Proprietary; incorporated in 2015 as Cloud Twelve Club Ltd, a private company limited by shares; with Russian-British Jenya Di Pierro, née Evgenia Emets, listed as the person with significant control.
Reciprocal clubs: None.
Culture: A focus on family well-being.
Architect: Melt Architecture and Construction.
Facilities: Brasserie, spa, wellness clinic, botanical pharmacy and kids' club.
What they want you to know: The only place in London to offer revolutionary Head Spa Treatments.
What they probably don't want you to know: Easily missed in a residential mews reached via a low-hanging alley off a residential street.
Short history: Founded by former fund manager and qualified herbalist Jenya Di Pierro, Cloud Twelve is a wellness and lifestyle club in Notting Hill, extending over three floors with an interactive play and learning zone for families with children, including a spa, luxury salon, nutritionally focused brasserie and holistic wellness clinic.

Little Houses

Address: 557 Harrow Road, Kensal Green, London, W10 4RH (Jaego's House); 8–10 Heathman's Road, Parsons Green, London, SW6 4TJ (Jesse's House).

Tel.: 020 3910 8816.
Founded: 2022 (Jaego's House); 2024 (Jesse's House).
Objects: Whole-family social clubs, for parents or guardians of children aged up to 9.
Approx. no. of members: Undisclosed.
Sex: Mixed sex.
Dress code: None.
Type: Proprietary; incorporated in 2020 as The Little Houses Group Ltd, a private company limited by shares; persons with significant control are hospitality impresario Charlie Gardiner and investment firm Imbiba Growth 2 LP.
Reciprocal clubs: None.
Culture: Familial.
Architect: ZAP Architecture (Jaego's House); Myrtha Pools and Barr + Wray (aquatic areas of Jesse's House).
Facilities: Restaurant, gym, spin and fitness studio, nursery, crèche, jungle gym for children (both houses); waterside café, co-working space, study, cinema (Jaego's House only); living room, courtyard café, terrace, outdoor playground, indoor and outdoor swimming pools, kids' club, the den and games room, kids' studio, kids' cinema (Jesse's House only).
What they want you to know: 'Where children can play and adults can work, workout and unwind.'
What they probably don't want you to know: Perhaps not the club of choice for people averse to boisterous young children.
Short history: The Little Houses Group offers a full suite of club facilities aimed at parents and their children, seven days a week. A third club, Orly's House in East Sheen, is shortly due to open.

NEXUS Club
Address: 38–42 Harrington Road, South Kensington, London, SW7 3ND.
Tel.: 020 3005 5555.
Founded: 2025.
Objects: Whole-family social club.
Approx. no. of members: Undisclosed.

Sex: Mixed sex.

Dress code: None.

Type: Proprietary; incorporated in 2023 as The Nexus Club London Ltd, a private company limited by shares; persons with significant control are ultimately (via Nexus Luxury Collection UK Holdings Ltd) Isle of Man-based Anthony Markham and Bahamas-based Joseph Lewis.

Reciprocal clubs: None.

Culture: Familial.

Architect: Unknown.

Facilities: Ronnie's Bar, restaurant, gym, private dining room, children's den, games room for teens.

What they want you to know: NEXUS has a 'collection of luxury assets, experiences and services in New York, the Bahamas, Florida and beyond'.

What they probably don't want you to know: Perhaps more of a concierge service than a club.

Short history: In 2010, The Albany opened as a luxury Bahamas resort. A decade later, they branched out into opening a family-oriented clubhouse in New York City, the NEXUS Club. In 2023, London's South Kensington Club closed down, and the building was acquired and converted into a London branch of the NEXUS Club.

Purple Dragon

Address: Bramagh House, 30 Gatliff Road, Chelsea, London, SW1W 8DP.

Tel.: 020 3906 8601.

Founded: 2008 (original branch); 2011 (Chelsea branch).

Objects: Social, childcare.

Approx. no. of members: Undisclosed.

Sex: Mixed sex.

Dress code: None.

Type: Proprietary; incorporated in 2007 as Purple Dragon Play Ltd, a private company limited by shares; persons with significant control are ultimately (via Purple Dragon (Holdings) Ltd) Sharai Meyers and investment firm Imbiba Growth 1 LP.

Reciprocal clubs: None.

Culture: Family-oriented.
Architects: EPOC/Keen and Able.
Facilities: Lounge, restaurant, crèche, art studio, cooking lab, music lab, sports area, indoor swimming pool, function rooms.
What they want you to know: 'The place for children that loves adults.'
What they probably don't want you to know: Previous branches in Battersea and Putney have closed down.
Short history: Launched by entrepreneur Sharai Meyers in Battersea in 2008, Purple Dragon set up a further two branches, later consolidating around the flagship branch in Chelsea. Meyers notes the emphasis is on including the whole family: 'I found that there were great places for children that were pretty awful for adults and great places for adults that really didn't like having children in them.'

Queen's Club – see THE SPORTS CLUBS

THE CLUB BARS

Apollo's Muse – Keystone Crescent – Nikita

Some establishments combine the closeness of a single main lounge supplied by a bar, with the model of private members' club. This can make for great intimacy, with members and guests being within close earshot of one another.

Apollo's Muse
Address: 1–3 Mount Street, Mayfair, London, W1K 3NB.
Tel.: 020 3161 9720.
Founded: 2022.
Objects: Social.
Approx. no. of members: 500.
Sex: Mixed sex.
Dress code: Smart-casual.

Type: Proprietary; and operated through Richard Caring's Caprice Holdings Ltd, a private company limited by shares since 1982, the same firm which owns the Ivy Club.

Reciprocal clubs: None.

Culture: Opulent, super-rich, with cash to flash.

Architect: Frederick Thomas Pilkington (original Victorian building); Richard Caring (interior design).

Facilities: Bar and lounge.

What they want you to know: 'The world's most private of private members' clubs.'

What they probably don't want you to know: At one stage, it was called Apollo's Mews.

Short history: Richard Caring, who has operated the Birley Group of clubs since 2007, remains a major shareholder in Soho House and also owns the Ivy Club, converted a hidden room of his Bacchanalia restaurant into the Apollo's Muse club, with marble-and-gold-adorned décor designed to emulate classical Greek and Roman motifs, embedding original antique artefacts.

Gerry's – see THE SOHO DRINKING CLUBS

Keystone Crescent

Address: Grey Door, 28 Caledonian Road, King's Cross, London, N1 9DT.

Tel.: 07496 642 391.

Founded: 2015.

Objects: Social; cocktail bar.

Approx. no. of members: Undisclosed.

Sex: Mixed sex.

Dress code: 'Casual elegant'.

Type: Proprietary; incorporated in 2013 as Base Club Ltd, a private company limited by shares; the person with significant control is Diwayta Gilzene.

Reciprocal clubs: None.

Culture: Hipster, relaxed.

Architect: Robert James Stuckey.
Facilities: Basement cocktail bar.
What they want you to know: 'As we don't pay for PR, our community has been built from our friends and friends of friends.'
What they probably don't want you to know: The keycode on the front door – it changes every month.
Short history: Founded by Kristie Bishop and Coralie Sleap, this speakeasy-style basement club positively relishes its anonymity on a residential street off the Caledonian Road, reached through an unmarked and unnumbered grey side door. The décor evokes the 1950s and 1960s. Members must display their gold keyring at the bar to place orders.

New Evaristo Club – see THE SOHO DRINKING CLUBS

Nikita
Address: 22 Davies Street, Mayfair, London, W1K 3DT.
Tel.: 020 3839 0000.
Founded: 2021.
Objects: Social; cocktail bar.
Approx. no. of members: Undisclosed.
Sex: Mixed sex.
Dress code: Smart-casual.
Type: Proprietary; incorporated in 2021 as two companies, Nikita Lease Ltd and its subsidiary, Nikita Ops Ltd; the person with significant control (via two holding companies, Goodkat Ltd and Bad Dog Ltd) is ultimately the French entrepreneur and restauranteur Jean Philippe Kley.
Reciprocal clubs: None.
Culture: Popular with hedge funds.
Architect: Unknown (original building); Victoria Vogel (interior designer).
Facilities: Basement wine, champagne and cocktail bar, lounge.
What they want you to know: 'Unashamedly high-end' (*Evening Standard*).
What they probably don't want you to know: It serves as a private hire venue for much of the daytime.

Short history: Having opened in December 2021, Nikita is a small basement bar open in the evenings and into the small hours from Wednesdays to Saturdays, a few doors away from the proprietor's Mr Nice restaurant.

COUNTRY CLUBHOUSES OF LONDON CLUBS

Babington House – Bretton Hall – Emblehope and Burngrange Estate – Estelle Manor – Soho Farmhouse – Stoneleigh Park – Woodcote Park

Central London clubs existing in tandem with an outlying country club is not a new phenomenon. The earliest example was the Orleans Club in the 1870s – this combined a London clubhouse with a Twickenham-based country club on the grounds of Orleans House, home of the exiled French royal family, which gave the Club its name. Although the Twickenham country club proved short-lived, not surviving the decade, the London clubhouse continued until the mid-twentieth century.

The country club in England combines several influences: the evolution of golf clubs in nineteenth-century Scotland; the mid-nineteenth-century gymkhana clubs found across the British Empire; the late-nineteenth-century North American country clubs; and the country-house culture that flourished among the ruling class between the mid-eighteenth and early twentieth centuries. Britain's first standalone country club opened in 1908: Stoke Park, in Buckinghamshire (although that is now due to reopen as a golfing hotel).

Since then, London clubs have occasionally sought to establish country-club branches, most notably the RAC, though in recent years, the practice has proved popular among several proprietorial clubs. Because of the economics needed to maintain usage, a number of these clubs (indicated below) are open for bookings by the public, unlike their London clubhouses. The below list does not include seasonal pitches around events, or 'pop-ups' like the 2021 Soho House pop-up on the grounds of Oakley Court.

Club Directory: Modern Clubs

Babington House
Affiliated London club: Soho House chain.
Address: Charity Lane, Frome, Somerset, BA11 3RW.
Tel.: 01373 812 266.
Founded: 1999.
Sex: Mixed sex.
Dress code: Smart-casual.
Open to the public: Yes.
Architect: John Pinch the Elder.
Facilities: Bar, restaurant, function rooms, gym, spa, 33 bedrooms, indoor and outdoor swimming pools, tennis courts, croquet lawn, walled garden, 18 acres of grounds.
What they want you to know: The Georgian house is filled with period features, including an original ice house on the grounds.
What they probably don't want you to know: It is possibly better known as a celebrity wedding venue than as a hotel or club. As with many celebrity weddings, a number of them have ended in divorce.
Short history: As Soho House's first venture beyond London, which sparked the renewed twenty-first-century interest in London clubs opening up country clubs, Babington House was something of a trendsetter. A late eighteenth-century Somerset manor house, built on the site of an older house, the Grade II*-listed property has been sympathetically modernised.

Bretton Hall
Affiliated London club: Groucho Club.
Address: West Bretton, Wakefield, West Yorkshire, WF4 4LG.
Tel.: TBC.
Founded: 2026 (forthcoming).
Sex: Mixed sex.
Dress code: Smart-casual.
Open to the public: Yes.
Architect: William Wentworth and James Moyser (original building); John Carr (late eighteenth-century alterations).

Facilities: Bar, restaurant, function rooms, 40 bedrooms, 500 acres of grounds.
What they want you to know: The Groucho Club's first venture beyond its Dean Street townhouse.
What they probably don't want you to know: The nearest village, West Bretton, has no pub or shops, and has a population under 500.
Short history: Announced by the new owners of the Groucho Club in early 2024, as forthcoming in late 2026, it will involve the conversion of the Grade II*-listed Bretton Hall near Wakefield, dating to the early eighteenth century, on the site of an older manor house. For several generations, it was the seat of the Allendale barons, until it was sold to the local council in 1947. The building was used as a teacher training college in 1949–2001, and as a campus of the University of Leeds in 2001–7.

Emblehope and Burngrange Estate
Affiliated London club: Royal Kennel Club.
Address: Tarset, Hexham, Northumberland, NE48 1RX.
Tel.: 01296 318540, ext. 1290.
Founded: 2017.
Sex: Mixed sex.
Dress code: None.
Open to the public: No.
Architect: Unknown.
Facilities: Alan Rountree Lodge, Emblehope Farm, 7,750 acres of grounds.
What they want you to know: 'Absolutely ideal for walked up trialling and training for Retrievers, Spaniels and hunt, point, retrieve breeds (HPRs)', while the shooting estate offers both pheasant and partridge, and 'It is also a gundog training estate and has woodland cover which provides excellent hunting for Spaniels, while the stretching moorland is ideal for challenging retrieves and for the pointing breeds to show off their hunting abilities to the full.'
What they probably don't want you to know: While eminently practical, some of the facilities are more functional than luxurious: Alan Rountree Lodge lists its amenities as 'large sitting area, toilets, kitchen'.

Short history: The Kennel Club acquired the estate in 2016, opening the following year as a centre of excellence for working dogs, with Alan Rountree Lodge opening in 2018.

Estelle Manor
Affiliated London club: Maison Estelle.
Address: North Leigh, Eynsham Park, Oxfordshire, OX29 6PN.
Tel.: 01993 685 800.
Founded: 2023.
Sex: Mixed sex.
Dress code: Smart-casual.
Open to the public: Yes.
Architect: Ernest George.
Facilities: Bar, Brasserie (modern English restaurant), Billiards Room (traditional Chinese restaurant), Glasshouse (serving produce from the walled garden), living room, events spaces, gym, padel courts, 3,000 m² spa Eynsham Baths, 108 bedrooms, archery range, axe-throwing range, rifle-shooting range, 85 acres of grounds.
What they want you to know: With the London club remaining highly secretive, the country club and hotel is the closest many will get to a glimpse of Maison Estelle.
What they probably don't want you to know: The 'library' just has a smattering of books for show, and its walls are mainly taken up with an offering of tequila shots.
Short history: A year after the opening of their London club, Maison Estelle opened this country clubhouse and hotel in the Cotswolds, located in the early-twentieth-century Grade II-listed mansion, Eynsham Hall. The building had passed through various owners and been used as a wartime maternity ward, US Army Air Force recreation centre and police training college, before being converted to a hotel.

Soho Farmhouse
Affiliated London club: Soho House chain.
Address: Great Tew, Chipping Norton, Oxfordshire, OX7 4JS.

Tel.: 01608 691 000.
Founded: 2015.
Sex: Mixed sex.
Dress code: Smart-casual.
Open to the public: Yes.
Architect: Alex Michaelis.
Facilities: Bar, Mill Room (restaurant), hay barn, main barn, 10 function rooms, gym, studio, spa, 114 bedrooms (including a 7-bedroom farmhouse, a 4-bedroom cottage, 40 cabins and 20 farm huts), cinema, tennis courts, five-a-side football pitch, clay pigeon shooting range, Teeny Barn with camp, 100 acres of grounds.
What they want you to know: It is a working farm, complete with 40 piglets.
What they probably don't want you to know: Most of the accommodation isn't within the main house, but on cabins and huts on the grounds.
Short history: Soho House's second venture into rural properties, opened 16 years after Babington House. The clubhouse was based in a derelict Grade II-listed former farm, which was rebuilt around the style of 'upstate New York cabin culture'.

Stoneleigh Park

Affiliated London club: Royal Kennel Club.
Address: The Kennel Club Building, Stoneleigh Park, Stoneleigh, Kenilworth, Warwickshire, CV8 2LZ.
Tel.: 01296 318540.
Founded: 2009.
Sex: Mixed sex.
Dress code: None.
Open to the public: Yes.
Architect: Unknown.
Facilities: Restaurant, 2 meeting rooms, 2 halls, educational centre, showground facilities, 800 acres of grounds.
What they want you to know: 'The UK's only purpose-built, completely dog-friendly venue, suitable for a wide range of canine activities.'

What they probably don't want you to know: Seems to work as more of a conference centre than a club.

Short history: The grounds were once part of the Stoneleigh Abbey estate, and were opened in 1963 as the National Agricultural Centre. It has since been converted to a business park, with the Kennel Club opening their facility on the site in 2009.

Woodcote Park
Affiliated London club: Royal Automobile Club.
Address: Epsom, KT18 7EH.
Tel.: 01372 276 311.
Founded: 1913.
Sex: Mixed sex.
Dress code: Smart-casual.
Open to the public: Yes.
Architect: Charles Mewès and Arthur Joseph Davis.
Facilities: Bars, three restaurants, function rooms, gym, spa, squash courts, tennis courts, indoor swimming pool, 22 bedrooms, two 18-hole golf courses, motor house (housing the RAC heritage fleet), walled garden area for children (including children's pool and play areas), 350 acres of grounds.
What they want you to know: The oldest surviving country club tied to a London club.
What they probably don't want you to know: The house was burned down in 1934, with the current façade being a reconstruction of the original.
Short history: In 1913, the Royal Automobile Club purchased the seventeenth-century Woodcote Park for use as a golf course, although the First World War intervened, during which the building was seized for use as the training ground of the Universities and Public Schools Brigade. In the inter-war years, post-fire reconstruction of the building was undertaken by Mewès and Davis, whom two decades earlier had built the RAC's Pall Mall clubhouse. The current house is Grade II*-listed. During the Second World War, the clubhouse was again requisitioned

as a training camp, with 110 acres given over to food production. This meant the loss of the 'New' golf course, although the 'Old' golf course remains, and since 1953, a 'Coronation' golf course has been on the site of the 'New' course.

SECTION 2

CLUB CULTURE

JOINING A CLUB: A STEP-BY-STEP GUIDE

So you want to join a club? Depending on the club, this might vary from a hurriedly-filling-out-a-form-in-five-minutes affair, to a decade-long campaign of cultivation. But joining any London club can have the following stages:

─────────────── Proposers ───────────────

All clubs will require you to have an existing member act as a proposer (and the vast majority will insist on a seconder as well). It is a licensing requirement. The only way to get around this stipulation is to set up a club of your own, becoming a 'founder member' of a newly formed club.

Your choice of proposer is incredibly important, for they are the person who will vouch for you with other members. In an ideal world, they will combine being well-known in the Club with being well-known to you personally. But if you have to choose between the two, it is far preferable to have a relatively unknown armchair member of the Club who shall willingly sing your praises, than to have a prominent member who has only the vaguest acquaintance with you, and so will barely lift a finger to help.

It is often believed that a member who proposes an unsuccessful candidate will have to resign their own membership, on a point of honour. This is not true. What *is* true is that it reflects badly on a member to propose one or more candidates who don't complete the process. So do not waste a potential proposer's time: if you are only mildly considering

Joining a Club: A Step-by-Step Guide

the possibility of membership, make it abundantly clear that this is just a speculative query. If you are serious about it, then say so. Never say you want to join and then back out halfway through, whether for cost reasons or because you have decided to join another club. Your proposer, who is doing you a substantial favour, is going to put their time and credibility on the line. Please respect that.

If you do not believe you know any members, the Club may or may not be willing to help. The more inclusive clubs are often happy to take membership queries via the office, and to arrange an introduction to a member, typically in the form of a tour with a member of the committee, who may get to know you. Other clubs, however, shun such practices, and insist that only applicants who have been personally known to a member for many years should be proposed. Generally speaking, the larger the club, the more inclusive, though size is not the only factor at play.

The form

This varies considerably from club to club, but all clubs are required by law to have a written application process, and a 'cooling-off' period. Even if God were to turn up seeking membership, and were to be fast-tracked, they would still have to wait at least several days before their form was processed.

Some clubs only seek a half-page form to be presented with the bare essentials, others ask for considerable credentials to be provided, including a CV, character references, publications, honours and decorations, accompanied by mini-essays on topics such as what you could offer the Club. Your proposer and seconder will typically also be asked to provide references (unseen by you), testifying as to your general 'clubbability', or sociability.

What is written on the form matters, not least as anything remotely misleading could result in your instant expulsion years down the line; any inaccuracies could constitute a straightforward breach of the terms and conditions of membership, if it later transpires that the Club elected you under false pretences. So your application should be impressive, but *on no account whatsoever should it be embellished.*

Many clubs have adapted to the twenty-first century in welcoming a measure of online applications. The more traditional clubs, however, still insist on an entirely paper-based system. When dealing with paper applications, the process can be very slow, with hard copies being posted from applicant to proposer, to seconder, to club office, to club committee.

Gaining support

Just because you have a proposer and a seconder, it does not follow that you will proceed straight to election. What happens next is that your name will be circulated to all the members, inviting comments, concerns or expressions of support. Your name might go up on a noticeboard alongside other new candidates; or it might be entered into a candidates' book, which is available for inspection by members in a secure part of the Club; or it might be emailed out to the entire membership, or posted to a secure area of the Club's website.

Many clubs have a minimum threshold of support needed before an applicant can come up for election. This threshold is typically around ten or twelve members, although anything from six to fifty would not be unheard of. Support is shown by other members signing the applicant's entry in the candidates' book. There is nothing to stop additional members from continuing to sign the book long after the threshold has been reached: it is a way of denoting the popularity of an applicant, and that they should be brought up for a ballot as soon as possible. But even in meeting the minimum threshold, it can take time for support to build – typically a few months. (Joke entries in the candidates' book are not unheard of. In the 1980s, the Great Train Robber Ronnie Biggs, then living as a fugitive in Rio de Janeiro, was placed in the White's candidate book, and had attracted twenty signatures before his name was torn out.)

Building support is an exacting process. It is very much the responsibility of the proposer and the seconder to approach fellow members about soliciting support. *Under no circumstances should the applicant seek to lobby members directly* – in many clubs, that is grounds for instant dismissal of the application.

If the applicant knows other members of the Club, then they can ask their proposer or seconder to approach the members on their behalf; but in a catch-22 scenario, the applicant is not usually allowed to see a membership list, so they cannot know how many of their friends and acquaintances are already members. (Some clubs have been known to relax this stipulation, allowing the candidate to come in and view the list while supervised in a secure room, ensuring that they do not take any notes or copy the list.)

There are also opportunities for candidates to get to know members – many clubs will organise a dinner, or a drinks reception, so that applicants have a chance to meet more members. And existing members, in turn, can keep an eye on these events to be sure the quality of candidates is maintained, not least in case of any 'warning signs', such as a candidate who turns up drunk and incapable, or turns out to be excessively dull or unbearably pretentious in conversation.

The waiting list

Waiting lists are funny things. No club has ever set down a rule that there shall be a waiting list. Instead, waiting lists can crop up as a symptom of something else entirely: a cap on the number of members. When a club places a membership cap, whether it is of five hundred members or five thousand members, it deems itself to be 'full'. At that point, there are only two main ways that vacancies will come up: either through members resigning (typically because they have fallen behind with their subscriptions) or through members dying of old age. And that is where the waiting list comes in; when people speak of clubs with thirty-year waiting lists, they are describing the actuarial projected lifespan of the existing members; how soon they are expected to snuff it from old age, and a surfeit of port.

'Real' waiting lists are rare – these are where a new application is paused for years on end while the backlog of older applications is slowly cleared, as places only very slowly come up. What is sometimes mischaracterised as a waiting list – clubs waiting several months to process a form or put it to a committee – is merely the leisurely bureaucracy of an organisation heavily dependent on volunteers. Waiting lists are rare in London today because the underlying assumptions behind them are questionable. The nineteenth and twentieth centuries were filled with social clubs claiming that they were absolutely at full capacity, and could not possibly countenance any more members than the five hundred or seven hundred they contained. If those clubs are still in business, then they typically have memberships three or four times that size today. Membership caps are a choice, not a necessity (a club that is at full capacity during peak hours in the run-up to Christmas may still stand virtually empty 95 per cent of the time); and waiting lists are often thought desirable because of their connotation of having 'snob value'. Yet waiting lists often get in the way of injections of new blood – something that's almost impossible if the newest member has been on the waiting list for fifteen years. Furthermore, waiting lists are not exclusive, as is often thought, but simply obstructive. A genuinely exclusive – or exclusionary – course would be for a club to instantly say 'No' to most applicants, rather than waiting several decades to reach a decision.

It is also worth conceding that waiting lists can vary significantly among the clubs that have them. I know of one London club which currently has a three-year waiting list, another of between six and seven years, another of fifteen years, and several of thirty years. These are waits of very different magnitude, so that applying to some can be a highly speculative venture. Aside from a handful that insist on having a joining fee or application fee up-front, many have applicants who do not know what their financial circumstances will be when they finally come up for election, so that when they are elected, they can no longer afford the joining fee and subscription in one go. Some clubs are patient in allowing applicants to defer taking up their place, or to pay their subscription in instalments. Others rather brutally require an applicant to get to the back of the queue and start the whole process again.

Where waiting lists are prevalent now is in the sports clubs, from the Marylebone Cricket Club to the Hurlingham – here, as well as the Club having a social function, the concept of being 'full' has a quantifiable meaning, with tennis courts being solidly booked. In those instances, you may find yourself monitoring the obituaries columns for some time to come.

Usually, there is little you can do about the waiting list. Yet this is where the 'gaining support' stage counts for so much. If a club has a seven-year waiting list, and the threshold for applications is the support of twelve members, then the candidate whose application is signed by eighty-five members may well find themselves being rushed forward for a vote after only a year or two, leap-frogging ahead of dozens or even hundreds of candidates who command twelve to twenty supporters each.

Vetting

Before a candidate comes up for election, most clubs do some type of vetting, typically undertaken by members elected for that purpose. It may take the form of a simple Google search ('What is the public domain information on this candidate, which any reasonable person would expect us to have considered at the time of election?'), or even something more advanced, like a DBS (Disclosure and Barring Service) check for unspent criminal convictions. The vast majority of candidates yield no concerns whatsoever, but in a small minority of cases, the concerns raised can be very serious indeed. These may range from clear-cut instances of unspent criminal convictions to more borderline, can't-quite-put-my-finger-on-it factors.

Because of their immense prestige and wealth, clubs can attract all manner of chancers, charlatans, grifters, asset strippers and con artists, and so committee members are often on the lookout for anything that may seem amiss. You might be surprised by how many of these 'characters' apply to join certain clubs – and, indeed, how many of them get in.

Vetting enquiries are invariably conducted in great secrecy, with the findings only shared with committee members. In some clubs, the documents are shared in numbered paper copies only, which have to be handed back at the end of the meeting, and all copies destroyed thereafter. The Club is not seeking to publish its findings, nor to make any public representations on applicants. But it will often seek to use public-domain sources to determine whether anything about the candidate might embarrass the Club or makes them unsuitable for membership.

――――――― Interview ―――――――

Some clubs refuse point-blank to do any interviews, ever, placing their trust in the vetting process, and on an assumption that they are more likely to refuse ten reasonable members than to risk admitting one objectionable member. At the other end of the spectrum, some clubs insist that *all* applicants up for ballot should be interviewed, so as to place candidates on an equal footing. In between the two extremes are the clubs that only ask for an interview in specific cases, whether to clear up some minor ambiguity on the form ('It says here that you have two addresses, including one in town; but you're applying for the country membership discount?'), or when there is a more specific concern that has come up in vetting, and it is felt appropriate to give the candidate the right of reply. ('The name "John Smith" is fairly common; can we just check that you're not the same "John Smith" living in Paddington who is a convicted axe-murderer?')

The advantage to the Club of an interview is that it can pick up on 'intangibles'; the very eminent-sounding applicant who filled out the form beautifully may turn out to be mad as a March hare, something only apparent when they turn up for a chat. So bear in mind that if you are asked to an interview, you are likely to be assessed, first and foremost, for your suitability, i.e. 'Is this the kind of person we'd like to

Joining a Club: A Step-by-Step Guide

have hanging around the place? Are they convivial and engaging?' But moreover, your interviewers will be vigilant for any 'alarm bells' around your mannerisms. And while clubs need to be keenly aware that on no account can they engage in unlawful discrimination, *there is nothing to stop them from engaging in lawful discrimination* – indeed, the whole notion of a club is founded on that principle. Applicants can – and do – get rejected for simply being boring. (Not that a great many excessively boring individuals haven't sailed through the application process – *c'est la vie*.)

You should be prepared to respond to some basic questions. Be yourself – if you can only get into a club by putting on airs and graces, then it's not going to be much fun for anyone. (This may sound obvious, but you would be surprised at how many people put on the most elaborate charades for an interview, from putting on a preposterous Noël Coward accent that keeps slipping mid-sentence, to renting a Bentley for the day to be seen driving up to the Club in one.) And if you can't give a strong answer to, 'Why do you want to join?', then you may run into some trouble.

The ballot

The great day comes, and you are due for election. Any waiting list has sailed by, and it is surely all just down to counting the votes? Wrong.

This is where blackballing plays its part. The practice of literally electing each member by casting white balls for 'yes', and black balls for 'no', has ceased in all but the most traditional clubs. Nevertheless, the principle of blackballing remains. Contrary to popular belief, it has not been the practice in most clubs that a solitary rank-and-file member was single-handedly able to veto a new applicant.

However, it is certainly the case that a proportion of the committee members voting can veto an applicant. That proportion varies from club to club – the smaller the proportion for wielding a veto the more difficult it is to get elected. Most clubs today have a *one-in-three proportion* needed to veto an applicant – so a third of voting members opposed to an applicant would be enough to scupper their chances, even if a majority of members voted for them. But some clubs have as small a proportion as *one-in-ten*, which means that an applicant has to be a popular consensus choice. (Some clubs also give a veto to the club chairman.) Consequently, most clubs with a reputation to maintain tend to be risk-averse, avoiding applicants who seem overly controversial or disagreeable. Clubs that need the money will take anyone – but walk a perilous path as, once elected, 'rogue' members can be hard to get rid of.

If you are unsuccessful at the ballot, there is no right of appeal. Theoretically, there is nothing to stop you from immediately reapplying, if needs be ad infinitum; but Einstein's dictum is relevant here, that the definition of insanity is doing the same thing over and over again and expecting different results. Your two realistic courses of action are to give up entirely; or to make discreet enquiries as to the reason, and to see if you can wage a subtle campaign to assuage any misapprehensions, trying again in a year or two. Clubs are not required to give a reason for declining an application, and they almost never do. Applicants have occasionally tried to litigate their way into a club after having been blackballed. It never ends well.

Joining a Club: A Step-by-Step Guide

Election

Once you have been elected, there are a few formalities. You need to pay your first year's subscription, which is usually a pro rata reduction of the annual subscription until the end of the calendar year (so a candidate elected in late June should only pay for six months in their first year). You also need to pay a joining fee, which can vary wildly between clubs, from the nominal to the hefty. You should then be sent a welcoming pack, which typically includes your membership card and publications such as the members' list, members' handbook, rulebook and a list of reciprocal clubs. Of these, the most important is the rulebook: upon joining, you implicitly agree to abide by the rules; but a club cannot enforce its rules if it has not shared those rules with the members. You might also have some sort of welcome arranged for your first visit to the Club; for instance, a tour of the building, and maybe the presentation of a copy of the history of the Club.

The first visit(s)

On your first visit to your new club, you will probably be asked to sign the book for new members. It is good form to introduce yourself to each member of staff that you meet, and to make an effort to remember all of their names. Some of these people may be looking after you for years – or decades – to come; the least you can do is to pay them the courtesy of being polite. Always remember how they wish to be addressed (some insist on 'Mr' or 'Miss', others prefer Christian names); and remember to pay something into the annual staff fund at Christmas, even if you can only afford a nominal contribution. (Clubs typically post on a noticeboard a list of the members who have contributed so far, so that it becomes very obvious which names are absent. The list can remain on the noticeboard for many months afterwards.)

Most new members squander an excellent opportunity on their first visit: they understandably poke around nervously, naturally unsure of where to go, and in bluffing their way around a daunting and unfamiliar building, they pass up a unique chance to ask for a guided tour. Such an opportunity will never present itself again so well as when you can say, 'I am a new member, and this is my first visit.' You should therefore ask to be shown around. It is also helpful to be accompanied by a member or a staffer on your first visit, so that you can be warned of any unwritten rules – whether a room is traditionally silent, or a chair reserved for a long-standing member, etc. These gaffes can be easily avoided, if you take a few precautions.

Most clubs will periodically throw some sort of dinner for welcoming new members – these are spaced out across the year, so that if you cannot make the first one, then you can attend another, several months down the line. As a point of etiquette, invite your proposer and seconder to the dinner, and make sure to pay for their tickets – while it would be deeply improper to ever pay them while they are steering your application through, offering them a 'thank-you' dinner is only fair after they have put their reputations on the line for you.

Finally, as your friends gradually find out about your election to this club, you can expect to be inundated with sometimes-quite-pushy suggestions of, 'You can take me to lunch/dinner there.' Yes, by all means do so. However, in your first few months of membership, you will want to space out the visits of your guests. When you are still in the early stages of getting to know a club as a new member, the last thing you want to do is to gain a reputation as someone known by sight who only brings their own guests, and sits in a corner with their own company, never mixing with the other members. Far better form to mingle with new members on your own visits, making a beeline for the club table, where you can introduce yourself, and slowly start to build up acquaintances. That in turn will make for a much more convivial experience for your guests – as when they do eventually visit, their host will clearly be more deeply embedded in the Club.

VISITING THE CLUB

Getting there

People often imagine that visiting a club involves a procession of Rolls-Royces parking outside, or at the very least a gathering of taxis. Given the gridlock of London's traffic, nothing could be further from the truth. Most club members either visit on foot, working (or even living) locally; or else they use the London Underground.

For the largest concentration of clubs around Pall Mall, St James's Street and southern Mayfair, the holy trinity of the tube stations Green Park (Jubilee, Piccadilly and Victoria Lines), Piccadilly Circus (Bakerloo and Piccadilly Lines) and the labyrinthian Charing Cross (Bakerloo and Northern Lines, plus overground trains) serve the heart of Clubland. Further north in Mayfair, clubs like Buck's and the Savile are fed by Oxford Circus (Bakerloo, Central and Victoria Lines; the Golden Law of the Tube being, 'Everybody changes at Oxford Circus'); the station also supports, along with Tottenham Court Road (Central and Northern Lines), the more creative and bohemian clubs of Soho – although the Oriental Club, further west, is best reached via Bond Street (Central and Jubilee Lines). The west of Piccadilly, with clubs like the Cavalry and Guards and the RAF, is supported by Hyde Park Corner (Piccadilly Line). Further to the west, Knightsbridge (Piccadilly Line) caters to the likes of the Special Forces Club and the Royal Thames Yacht Club. As you might infer, the Piccadilly Line is the optimal line to live on for members/visitors of multiple clubs. The Whitehall clubs like the Farmers and the National Liberal are best reached from Embankment (Bakerloo, Circle, District and Northern Lines).

All of these stations are relatively close to one another, so that most central London clubs can be reached by foot within half an hour or less from any of the above stations. Further afield are the clubs of the City of London, reached via Mansion House or Cannon Street (both Circle and District Lines), or Bank/Monument (Central, Circle, District and Northern Lines), this latter one a Brobdingnagian behemoth of a super-station which is to be avoided on all accounts, owing to the ten-minute walking time routinely needed to navigate through it. The modern clubs of Shoreditch are best reached via Shoreditch High Street (London Overground and East London Line). Other outliers include the Frontline Club near Paddington (Bakerloo, Circle, District, and Hammersmith and City Lines). The sports clubs tend to be quite widely scattered, with the likes of the Hurlingham Club, Queen's Club and Roehampton Club being more likely to be visited by car.

Opening hours

While each club's opening hours vary, most are open on Mondays to Fridays, from breakfast time until late.

Closing times may be a moveable feast. There will be an 'official' closing time, around 11 p.m. or midnight, in line with most licensed drinking establishments. But the licensing arrangements of clubs allow them to maintain far longer opening hours, and many either serve alcohol into the small hours or, at the very least, allow members to stay on the premises, nursing the drinks already bought before the bar had shut; or else allowing a limited range of drinks to be purchased out-of-hours from the night porter.

Weekend opening is rare. The historical roots of this are long – and date back to the convention of gentlemen not being seen in town at the weekends, but traditionally retiring to their country estates. The more practical modern reason is that many clubs have tried weekend openings, with many an earnest member insisting that others would flock to use the place at the weekend – only to find that they do not. A small handful of traditional clubs run a truly seven-day-a-week operation. The rest either close at weekends or run a scaled-down operation, typically involving overnight guests still staying in the club, and one room offering a reduced weekend drinks service and bar snacks.

Guests

It is one thing to go to a club as a member, but infinitely more daunting to visit as a guest. Club staff – particularly porters – can be quick to decide whether they like the look and sound of an outsider and want to engage in some repartee with them, or whether they frostily regard them as an interloper, to whom they will reveal as little information as possible. This is true whether they be a reciprocal club member or a member's guest. And manifold are the tales of old, with guests left flummoxed and snubbed by cool passive-aggressive queries dispensed by sarcastic hall porters. Today, club staff (who increasingly have backgrounds in hospitality) tend to be infinitely more welcoming; though the members encountered can be a mixed bag.

The first thing for a guest is to make it absolutely clear on the front desk why you are there and who you are there to see. Try wandering in off your own back – even if you have every right to access the Club as a reciprocal member – and you will be swiftly pigeonholed as someone to watch for signs of absconding with the silverware.

The 'private' in private members' club is important. Members tend to value peace, quiet and discretion. It's one thing to be the life and soul of the party at the club table; but members infinitely prefer guests who do not draw attention, and do not make a fuss. Every member who knows your host (and plenty who don't even know your host's name, but are just on nodding terms with them) will be fascinated by you. They will probe you. They want to know if you are some secret business partner on a shady venture; or some hidden lover hinting at a hitherto-unsuspected sexual predilection of your host. They will eavesdrop your conversation, and study your body language from the next table. It is for this reason that club members think twice about bringing friends and partners into the club: the members may not be the most welcoming bunch, and one new guest may be gossiped about for weeks afterwards. Remember, the club is there for the convenience of its members, but seldom the members' guests. This in itself might be a factor cited as your host leans over after dinner and asks whether you've ever considered joining.

THE GOOD, THE BAD AND THE UGLY

"What's the point of private members' clubs?" recently asked the *Financial Times*.[*] There are many possible answers; but their appeal can be divided up between the good, the bad and the ugly. No one joins a club for all of these reasons, but many do so for several of them.

──────── The good ────────

Companionship: Humans are inherently social creatures, seeking one another out for company; and that is at the root of clubs. This is why club members who have emigrated very often set up clubs of their own. A sumptuous facility belonging to one person may be very exclusive – in the sense of excluding other people – but it is not a club.

Shared interests or values: This is at the root of all successful clubs; even if there is no formal theme, there should be a common bond to give the membership some cohesion. Without this, you simply have a marriage of convenience, with the members momentarily bartering around value for money. With this, you have a unique culture, which the members find is worth digging deep to preserve.

Intellectual stimulation: A club is a very dull place indeed if all the members share precisely the same outlook. Shared values are desirable; but so is

---

[*] Joy Lo Dico, 'What's the point of private members' clubs?', *Financial Times*, 30 March 2024.

each member bringing to the table something to stretch the horizons of their fellow members, beyond their comfort zone. This could be through one-off talks or events, or simply through interesting conversation at the bar or club table. The opposite of this is the Club Bore, regaling everyone in sight with the same anecdotes.

Convenience: There is no shame in a club fitting into a regular routine, whether daily or weekly. If it already provides companionship, shared values and intellectual stimulation, then making it a convenient place to drop into is a boon.

Conviviality: An underpinning of clubs is a welcoming, accepting disposition. This means that when there are differences of opinion – and wherever there are multiple people, there will be many – they can be openly discussed on the friendliest of terms. Agreeing to disagree is a step towards this; but actively welcoming differing perspectives is even better. If the members agree that they share fundamental values, then differences of opinion should be amicably and respectfully tackled. This has not always been the case, however.

Discretion: Secrets in Clubland are often vilified; but less recognised is the value of clubs being a space able to mediate sensitive conversations. Two people who may not usually want to be publicly seen together in the outside world may well be willing to bury the hatchet over a relaxed club lunch, to amiably thrash out their differences. Most clubs are *not* sitting on top of some great big hidden scandal waiting to blow the whole institution apart (whatever the more swivel-eyed malcontent getting up to offer 'Less of a question, and more of a comment ...' at the AGM may say). But clubs do respect the privacy of their members and staff, allowing people to be themselves, in a supportive environment.

Keeping subcultures alive: A corollary of allowing people to be themselves is that clubs act as a vital ecosystem, which keeps alive all manner of eccentricity, culture and subculture, much of it unique. This may be around some literary theme, or some otherwise-vanished culture that the Club helps sustain.

The bad

It's always been there: The complacency of being part of an institution because it is a family tradition, rather than any active engagement with the Club's overall aims or purpose, is never a very compelling reason to join. This makes for members who are both bored and boring.

Keeping up with the Joneses: This is a reasoning most common in sporting clubs, and is based on latent insecurity, wanting to show off to neighbours/co-workers/rivals that you have access to facilities at least as opulent as theirs, if not infinitely more extravagant and hard-to-access. Sporting facilities offer the most scope for showing off.

Conspicuous consumption: Another manifestation of latent insecurity, this is found among individuals with a hollow sense of inner self, who believe that the Club will afford them the scope to show off to their fellow members and guests. Since the whole point of a club is a shared experience, enhanced by the contributions of other members, showing off is not in the spirit of clubbing. That said, club committees and proprietors can be keen to pander to this because of the large sales and mark-ups involved in selling more expensive wines, cigars, etc.

Networking: Most clubs agree that they are very much against networking on their premises; yet paradoxically, most of their members network, whether formally or informally, and this has been a staple of club activity for centuries. What riles club members is not networking per se, but being flagrant about it: handing out business cards, covering communal tables with business papers, or working from a static laptop perched in a prominent spot of the smoking room from 9 a.m. to 5 p.m. on Mondays to Fridays. In reality, a great many conversations at club bars and dining tables have some work-related aspect to them; they may be a business lunch to firm up some forthcoming transaction. But above all, they are to be done discreetly.

Facilities: Yes, Section 1 of this book details a great many impressive facilities across a multitude of clubs, and it's jolly nice to have access to them. Yet simply sybaritically devouring the offerings of dining rooms and gyms and bars is not in itself clubbable behaviour, and you may not be invited back if you only sit in a corner with your host/guest. What makes a club is the conviviality of shared experiences with other members, some similar, some very different, but all sharing common interests or values. The facilities are just a shared way of expressing that, and some of the most agreeable times are to be spent in the most sparsely furnished clubs, where the human spirit is strong. Beware the member who 'only joined for the squash court'.

The ugly

Outsourcing your private life: This is quite sad, really, but increasingly common: the phenomenon of the idle super-wealthy looking to outsource their private lives, in search of *some* kind of excitement or stimulation, when they are jaded by already being able to buy their way into most things, and are seeking momentarily to alleviate their boredom with a fresh challenge. It is not a new phenomenon; indeed, Clubland's early beginnings are rooted in it. Today, the mystique of private members' clubs has an added lustre for the super-rich and super-bored – everything from the much-vaunted 'exclusivity' of these places, to the sense of acceptance that comes from gaining election to a secretive club. Needless to say, billionaire oligarchs who are used to always getting everything they want, without compromise, do not necessarily make the most convivial club members. And a whole ecosystem has been created to support this, including any number of hotel concierges and specialist concierge firms that have cropped up to cater to this lucrative market, on an unprecedented scale. A number of the newer clubs are consciously predicated on targeting High Net Worth Individuals, often at the expense of shared values or conviviality. Paradoxically, it is the unattainable nature of the older clubs that makes them particularly desirable among some HNWIs, and more difficult for conciergeries to engineer elections – they typically have to give a disclaimer to their clients that they can merely advise on applications, and do not guarantee elections. Older clubs tend to take a dim view of 'coached' applications facilitated by a concierge in this way; but will also weigh that against the desirability of having at least a smattering of super-rich members on the rolls, as a contingency against the periodic cash-flow crises found across Clubland.

Snobbery: Snobbery exists in most clubs. It takes many forms: social snobbery, financial snobbery, intellectual snobbery. But it is most evident in a vocal enthusiasm for 'keeping out the riff-raff', and rapidly latching on to minutiae of dress and custom to assert supposed superiority. Naturally, the loudest snobs in clubs are not usually bona fide aristocrats or people found in *Who's Who*. They are more typically rather mediocre, middle-aged, middle-ranking businessmen, often in corporate finance, who view their club as an opportunity to move in more exalted circles, and are aggressively proprietorial about its minutiae. Some clubs are absolutely steeped in snobbery; but the vast majority simply have a fringe veneer of it, with the handful of unpleasant and unclubbable snobs being shunned and disapproved of by most of their peers, who rue ever having elected them in the first place.

Lifestyle, and 'Elevating your experience': Anything involving 'lifestyle' is to be regarded with suspicion. (The late John Fortune insisted, 'But I don't have a lifestyle; I just sit in the pub all day.') The most entertaining club members are those who lead busy, active and varied lives in the wider world, and so bring insights from the outside world to their club visits. Be wary of the member looking fundamentally to change their whole lifestyle to revolve around their club: at best, it points to a hollowness of self or a mildly obsessive tendency and, at worst, the visits to the Club become an exercise in role play and cosplay. You want members who are comfortable just being themselves, warts and all, not those who are playing dress-up with affected mannerisms, trying to live a different lifestyle through the Club. Regard with extreme suspicion any establishment that promises to 'elevate your existence', or that claims to be 'curated' – it is likely to cater precisely to this kind of hollow, affected bore. It is the opposite of being a member of a club that has its own wider collective identity and culture.

CLUB PERSONALITY TYPES: THE MEMBERS*

The consummate clubman

What every club member, male or female, wants to be: ever-present, dependable, a patient listener, with an inexhaustible supply of amusing anecdotes that are seldom repeated.

The 'good thing' backwoodsman

Probably the most common type of member. This individual takes great pride in their club membership, but only visits the Club maybe once a year (if that). They nonetheless believe the Club is a 'good thing', and selflessly go on paying their subscription, even though they rarely use it. Visits are a special occasion, to be cherished.

The pedant

Tells the same four or five anecdotes about the Club, over and over again, pedantically taking great pains to point out where other people usually have the details wrong. Usually gets the details wrong.

---

* Each of these is a composite, combining and exaggerating characteristics and trends among a great many people, rather than based on any one individual. Long-term habitués of many clubs will recognise these traits across Clubland.

Club Personality Types: The Members

The partygoer

A nice-but-dim chinless wonder, whose keenest concern is the price of champagne and using the Club to keep themselves in cut-price bubbly at events. They have been known to repeatedly harass the committee on this topic, in the strongest possible terms. Typically inherited their club membership. Attends between four and seven parties a week, more than half of them in the Club, posting highlights on Instagram.

The spouse-seeker

Male or female (they come in both forms), the spouse-seeker is a twenty-something or thirty-something variant on the partygoer, but with little loyalty to any particular establishment: they will instead rotate from club to club, leaving each after a couple of years over some ticketing dispute, before settling on one of the larger, more facilities-laden clubs with the most obnoxiously rich members to clumsily attempt to seduce. They are looking to settle down to a life of idle ease with someone who is the heir to one-half of Clackmannanshire; but by their late thirties, they will eventually settle down in Fulham with someone equally pleasant-but-dull, who works in audit accountancy and thinks that Jordan Peterson is quite profound.

The hearty fellow

The ruddy-faced, 'hail fellow well-met' stout yeoman permanently propping up the Club bar, immediately identifiable by a bulbous, pock-marked nose streaked with throbbing purple veins, and a readiness to dispense quips and pleasantries at all hours. Was probably last sober sometime around 1979.

The eccentric

Highly amiable, this great British institution has an amusing series of largely harmless quirks. They may hum quietly to themselves, or remove sugar lumps from their sugar pot and place them in a line. The world outside is not as forgiving of their eccentricities as their club.

The frustrated retiree

Once at the top of their profession, as a chief executive, ambassador, professor or similar, they are now retired. They miss wielding power and influence. They cannot understand why the Club has not already made them its chairman, and they regularly circulate epic memoranda to their colleagues, spelling out in excessive detail everything that everyone else is doing wrong.

The bored middle-manager

Similar to the frustrated retiree, only instead of being motivated by a sense of declining importance, they are driven by a deep sense of personal inadequacy that they never quite 'made it' in their day job; and so they hope to seek high office in the Club to compensate for this. They spend a lot of time thinking about having their portrait commissioned, to hang up alongside the Club's most famous members.

The fantasist

A surprisingly common Clubland figure, who escapes from the tedium of their day job by coming into the Club to fantasise about being a James Bond figure, rubbing shoulders with spies, diplomats and statesmen. Very poor at small talk, and extremely awkward. Often fabricates highly elaborate tales about what they do outside the Club.

The alcoholic

A sad figure, alternately gregarious and lonely, whose alcohol dependence is turned a blind eye by the Club, which profits so well from feeding their addiction. Often works the committees in clubs, and uses that authority to organise 'lock-ins'. Tends to forget whatever they drunkenly declared the night before; and so does not fully comprehend why they are held in low esteem by their peers.

The status-seeking social climber

Sees club membership as a vital stepping stone on their way up to greater social prestige; will often spend years cultivating membership of a club, and once they are in, the very first thing they will do is home in on an even more prestigious club to try to move on to, trading in their existing club memberships along the way. Has little interest in any of the three ingredients of a club: members, staff or building.

The con artist

A more highly functioning version of the above; except that instead of seeking status, they seek money. Typically a smooth-tongued property developer or a management consultant, and often highly successful at charming their way up a club's hierarchy, their greatest goal is to asset strip the Club to enrich themselves. They are charismatic, deeply dishonest, highly litigious and extremely dangerous. Clubs are driven to ruin by these individuals.

The not-so-closet fascist

They see the Club as a place to 'banter', which they understand to mean freedom from any consequences, as they air a series of extreme right-wing views which they know could land them in jail in the wider world, but enjoy the freedom of the Club to goad others into a sort of contest as to who can say the most outrageously racist, sexist, homophobic or just generally disagreeable abuse. If questioned, they will claim that they are a 'traditional Tory', ignoring that traditional Tories would have no truck with this sort of nonsense. A bedside photograph of Augusto Pinochet is not unknown.

The left-wing contrarian

One of life's natural contrarians, they enjoy the frisson of being the most Bolshevik person in the room, despite not actually being that left wing, and having rather unremarkable, middle-of-the-road, moderate views. They have therefore contrived to join the most reactionary club they could find, for the stimulation of being in a state of near-constant argument with all the other members.

The consultant

Has a highly impressive curriculum vitae on paper, which conceals the fact that the reason why they are a daily fixture in the Club in the daytime is that they do not actually have a job, but instead attempt to practise some ill-defined 'consultancy' role from a writing table in the Club, wining and dining prospective clients over long, boozy lunches, all the while denying to the Club management that they are carrying out business on the premises. It is not unknown for the Club to be contacted for details of their whereabouts by HMRC, to whom they may owe substantial sums.

Club Personality Types: The Members

The obsessive anorak

These are found in every club that has a theme. The obsessive anorak is inordinately attached to that theme, and they can bore for England on the topic. Highly knowledgeable, with flashes of real insight – but not always terribly easy to talk to, due to their ongoing obsessions. The author of this book is several of the club personality types listed here, but most obviously an obsessive anorak.

The squeezed upper-middle

A broader variant on the partygoer; the squeezed upper-middle is addicted to the tropes of an upper-middle-class life which they can barely afford, though they are determined to do whatever it takes – however boring or morally questionable – to supply it. Their club membership primarily exists to offer them subsidies on aspects of their lifestyle: cheaper dining and alcohol, gym facilities, etc. The squeezed upper-middle flits from one club to another, shopping around for the cheapest subscription, and the largest spread of reciprocal clubs.

The uniform cosplayer

The uniform cosplayer is a young man who mainly joined a club so he could dress up. They most likely volunteer for the Territorial Army, the Naval Reserve or similar, so that they can don a snazzy uniform while denigrating the dress of everyone else in sight, deriding them as peasants. They will have a nervous breakdown by thirty, at which time they will discover sex for the first time and promptly resign from the Club.

The traveller

A frequent international globe-trotter, the traveller lives entirely out of clubs (whether their own ones spread across the globe, or a reciprocal club in each city). On arriving at a new destination, they immediately make a beeline for the bar, trading red-hot gossip from their last destination. More common in the press clubs of the world (the traveller is often a foreign correspondent), they will often stop off in London.

The duke

The duke – who may not literally be one of the UK's twenty-two remaining dukes – is a bona fide aristocrat. This gives them enormous leeway for anything they do to be dismissed as 'eccentric'; although being suffused with *noblesse oblige*, they will generally avoid pressing the point. Indeed, they're more often than not quite shy, modest, quiet, and shabbily dressed in their father's stylish but ill-fitting fifty-year-old tailored suit with moth-holes in it.

The more-money-than-sense

A trustafarian born to outrageous wealth, the more-money-than-sense is unaccustomed to anybody saying 'No' to them. They will belch loudly in the dining room, urinate in plain view in the garden and swear like a sailor, but nobody will dare say anything, because they own a substantial chunk of Lancashire, have a crumbling Irish castle, live in a Northamptonshire stately home, with a pied-à-terre in Chelsea, and keep a (relatively modest) yacht on the Riviera. Eventually, there is one incident too many, and words are had, resulting in their never being heard from again.

Club Personality Types: The Members

The freeloader

They joined the Club for free food and wine. They will be a regular fixture at dinners and drinks dos, forever having 'forgotten their wallet', and asking a passing acquaintance to stand them dinner or a drink. Nobody will have ever got a drink out of them. When they eventually expire, aged ninety-five, there will be general incredulity at the revelation in their obituary that they were a multi-millionaire all along.

The association freeloader

An offshoot of the above, the association freeloader isn't actually a member of the Club. Nevertheless, they are very adept at turning up to the Club more frequently than most of its own members, courtesy of having carefully studied the calendars of when various associations and societies are holding their own private events in the building – preferably free ones. You will usually see them elbowing their way into the bar straight after the event, scooping up any nibbles in sight, sometimes being swept into a conveniently extracted carrier bag.

The son of an oligarch

His much-referred-to father is never seen in the Club, as he is currently under sanctions from most European countries. But the son of the oligarch can be found frequenting the Club on most days, drinking alone in a corner, looking maudlin and usually conspicuously overdressed for any occasion – he'll turn up to an informal gathering in black tie, or to a black tie event in white tie and tails, invariably souped up with excessive quantities of jewellery-studded bling. His social skills leave something to be desired, and he sees no problem with offering paid introductions to the Club. He attempts to resolve most problems by slapping a wad of

£50 notes down on the table. His election to the Club was engineered by an external concierge for a hefty fee.

The permanent resident

Permanently lives in a cramped attic room of the Club. This makes no financial sense, as they pay a small fortune for the privilege; but they get a real buzz from effectively having the clubhouse as their living room. After their death at a venerable old age, the Club will probably erect a small bust or shrine to them.

The perennial bachelor

They never grew up. Growing old disgracefully, and clubs are the perfect place to do it.

The convenor

The backbone of club life, the convenor is a retired person who uses the convening power of the club as a social organisation, to throw themselves into arranging a never-ending range of talks, visits, concerts, theatricals, charity benefits and other cultural events. Genuinely selfless, they are the backbone of club life. Note also that the con artist often masquerades as a convenor, but is a very different beast.

The luncher

Born into money, generously divorced from more money, and remarried into even more money, they have never worked. Nor would they ever dream of working. Instead, they occupy themselves by organising a daily series of long lunches, opining strongly on what everyone else is doing wrong. Very much a champagne socialist (or rather, a Bollinger Bolshevik).

The declinist

One of the older members, they will spend every visit continuously insisting that 'Things aren't as good as they used to be', even when the food, wine and décor all show a marked improvement. They like to reminisce extensively, often somewhat embellishing their anecdotes on each fresh retelling.

The antiquarian

The antiquarian is motivated by many things: a love of knowledge, wisdom, reason and compassion. But mainly by a passion for fondling and caressing old books. They are one of the few members of the Club to use its library, diligently doing so on most weekdays, fuelled by regular cups of tea between serious bouts of scholarly study.

The opinionated malcontent

They are very, very angry. About everything. And they suspect some deep-rooted conspiracy lies at the heart of the Club, seeing themselves as a latter-day Woodward and Bernstein who is going to uncover it. They will pigeonhole passers-by the bar, launching into a monologue and asking them what they make of some lurid rumour they have semi-invented. Any denial of the rumour will only further convince them that they are close to uncovering the truth. They will usually get up to ask a hostile question at the AGM, and they often stand for committee. Staff regard them with distaste for their habit of telling everyone else how they should be doing their jobs.

The club bore

If you spend any time in a club, you will not need the club bore to be described to you. You do not need to wait long to find them; they will find you.

The dirty old man

Marked by a deep-throated cackle and an excessively natty series of pocket squares, the dirty old man will often dine in the Club with a succession of young men and/or women he is trying to seduce, in a bid to impress them. His lust will not be limited to his own guests, and he often casts lecherous glances at those around him, which can be a highly uncomfortable experience. The dirty old man's day job is nebulous, but extremely well-remunerated, and the Club has never dared to expel him. The club secretary has had words with him about his habit of leaving used condoms in the Club bedrooms.

The reciprocal fiddler

This individual has worked out that by joining a club halfway across the country (or planet), they can obtain full reciprocal rights with scores of London clubs, at a fraction of the cost of joining just one. They frequent lots of clubs, but are at home in none, effectively treating them as hotels. They will have their favourites, and you will often see them camped out as an almost-daily fixture, so that you are surprised to learn after a while that they are not a member at all. They will usually come unstuck, with a complaint back to their club resulting in their being stripped of all reciprocal privileges, and their swiftly resigning – only to start the process again with another far-flung reciprocal club.

Club Personality Types: The Members

──── The member who reads this book ────

This person is absolutely outraged that the book you are holding is *not* the following: a love letter to their own club, explaining to one and all why they have made the best decision in the world in joining their club, why it is simply 'the best' club in the whole world, and why all the other clubs must be markedly inferior to theirs.

They cannot believe that the book's references to their own club are not more fulsome, or that the references to other clubs are not more scathing.

CLUB PERSONALITY TYPES: THE STAFF*

The grizzled veteran

Experienced and professional, the grizzled veteran has worked in clubs (or the same club) for decades; possibly their whole adult life. They are affable to all, but give very little away. They know their patch, they know their members and they know their guests. Nothing surprises them, good or bad – they've seen it all.

The global professional

Part of the new breed of high-flying CEOs who have gradually supplemented and supplanted the traditional club secretary, the global professional's career sees them take distinct steps, maybe five years at a time, at major clubs in different countries, before moving on to the next appointment.

The omniscient

The omniscient is a highly observant staffer whose position, physical and managerial, allows them to know where every member in the

---

* As with the members' character types, each of these is a composite of wider trends, rather than based on any one individual.

Club Personality Types: The Staff

clubhouse can be found. Perhaps their desk gives them a view of the main hall where everyone enters and leaves. Perhaps they memorise the seating plans at club events. Perhaps they have sight of the CCTV system, which the Club denies having installed. Whatever the reason, the omniscient staff member is well-equipped to rival the best hotel concierge, remembering each member, their movements and their foibles. To the members, they seem a minor deity.

The self-assured

This staff member is permanently unflappable – and working in a club can involve a great deal of being flapped. They are stoically calm with immovable deadpan, whether dealing with irate diners or nosy journalists.

The charlatan

The charlatan has bitten off more than they can chew. They cannot do their job, and live in permanent dread of being found out. They typically seek refuge by bluffing it out in a dialect that no one else in the Club can understand. It is no use speaking in the language of the army, or the hospitality trade – both backgrounds that are common for those working in clubs. Instead, they choose something more niche, like the language of management consultancy, hoping to come across as impenetrably brilliant. They are easy to see through.

The bully

The bully has a similar deep-rooted insecurity to the charlatan over their inability to do the job. But in their case, it expresses itself through bullying and intimidating their juniors. They often mask this by deploying a superficial charm with members, which immediately drops when dealing with subordinate staff.

The toady

The toady has decided that the best way to navigate the choppy waters of committee politics, with frequent rows, rebellions, and committees being elected and unseated, is to deploy an obsequious silver tongue at all times. Consequently, no one trusts them. These are dictators in the making.

The temperamental professional

Something of a tortured genius, the temperamental professional is one of the Club's more creative staff members, typically as a chef or bar staff. Their skill is highly prized, but they can be prone to erratic fits and unreliability.

The overpromoted

The 'Peter Principle' can be well-established in Clubland: 'He's been a fine waiter here for twenty-eight years, he'll make an excellent dining-room manager.' And so the fallacy produces people promoted until the point where they cease to perform well.

The plodder

Clubs are very stable employers, priding themselves on large numbers of long-term staff who have worked there for years, or even decades. While this can provide stability and continuity for highly valued, high-skilled staff who know the members, it can also reward plodders. The plodder goes in every day, going through the motions doing the same thing, having grown jaded of it, their enthusiasm having fizzled out after their first decade of employment. Above all, the plodder hates a fuss and likes a quiet life. Questions are likely to be met with a shrug of indifference.

The seen-and-not-heard

'Children should be seen and not heard,' the Victorians maintained. The same might be said of many of the staff in a traditional club. This is not necessarily a bad thing. While members can bond with the porters, and the waiting and bar staff they meet, there is an army of chefs, accounts staff, maintenance staff and cleaners whom they almost never meet, who quietly go on efficiently keeping the plates spinning. These professionals are often the backbone of a well-run club.

The alarmed temp

They have been thrown in at the deep end. A much-valued member of long-term staff has either left or called in sick, and a temp agency has been rung up and asked to provide someone for this key role. Invariably inadequately briefed, the alarmed temp has a minefield to navigate, in the tastes and expectations of members. The longer they spend in the Club, the more they regard it as a madhouse. They may even walk out on the first day.

The asset stripper

They have realised they are on to a good thing. Typically someone recruited from a non-club background, it is not lost on the con artist that the Club is swimming in valuable assets, many of them poorly secured and ripe for the plucking. What they are doing may well be entirely legal. They may simply be flogging off bits of the Club to maintain the Club's own ruinously expensive and loss-making habits for a while longer. Or they may be working their way into a position where they might benefit from an equity release by the Club. Or they may be an out-and-out crook, conning their way into a position of trust and then pocketing the proceeds for their own gain. Clubs should be vigilant: left unchecked, the asset stripper will bring down a club.

The chairman's bit-on-the-side

Clubs are often one big, happy family, it is often observed. And so it has not been unknown for chairmen to install their lover – or lovers – as staff in key posts. After all, it is argued, they already know a number of the members, and have some idea of the expectations involved in the place. Irrespective of their merits or shortcomings in the role, tongues will be wagging for the rest of their time in post, about the suitability of their appointment – especially after the chairman has long since retired.

The mightily entertained

This individual knows that the Club is a madhouse, but they are strangely addicted to this ringside seat on all manner of human entertainment. For this reason, they usually become valued members of staff, remembering all the members' names and foibles – but never entirely losing their sense of the absurd.

The club-before-self

Clubs do not generally pay their staff as generously as commercial rivals, such as grand hotels. But a well-run club can deliver enormous job satisfaction. The club-before-self is the employee who could have easily left years ago and gone on to become one of the world's great practitioners in their field – as a chef, librarian, concierge, etc. – but who has remained at the Club for decades, because of the loving care for their members, which is sharply reciprocated. Clubs are lucky to have them.

SUBSCRIPTIONS EXPLAINED

There is a common misconception that subscriptions are raised to keep people out of clubs. In fact, their purpose is – or is supposed to be – to cover a club's overheads. In theory, this allows the Club to continue to exist, so that even if there were no trading business through the bar or dining room, the premises would still be maintained and the administrative office still open. However, whether this is true can vary considerably from club to club, depending on the scale and complexity of a club's premises and its business model. Some older clubs own their freehold outright, and many venerable institutions are on peppercorn rents with long leases (typically with the Crown Estate, or the Duke of Westminster's Grosvenor Estate), while a number of modern clubs can pay eye-watering commercial-rate fees for premium sites – and so the sums spent on rent or ground rent can vary wildly.

In practice, the removal of so many overheads should allow a club's food and beverage operations to charge significantly less than a West End restaurant would, as the non-club competitors' prices have to factor in these overheads. This also gives members a financial incentive to use their club. The member's outlay of several thousand pounds in subscription fees for the year is never going to be entirely made up, unless that member is dining every other night; but membership is a whole lot more cost-effective if the member pops in a couple of times a month, rather than a couple of times a year.

That said, not all clubs choose to reward their members with low food and drink prices. This is particularly true of the newer clubs, where the overheads are likely to be greater, and so the break-even point requires a greater contribution from each member, with larger mark-ups on every

Subscriptions Explained

transaction. There are also traditional clubs that choose to benchmark their prices against commercial restaurants, investing the profits back into the Club – which can make them financially sound, but not particularly affordable.

Subscriptions vary considerably across London clubs, and clubs in trouble often hike up their prices significantly in a short space of time (which can prompt mass resignations, and a net loss of revenue, compared to if the subscriptions had either been frozen, or gradually increased over the years); while complacency can set in among even the most well-run clubs. As of 2024, the major clubs of Pall Mall and St James's charge around £2,000 for a year's full membership, though many have very considerable discounts for country members, overseas members, and (usually on a phased basis) both the younger and older members, so that the average subscription per member may be closer to £1,000–£1,500; and such are the demographics that it is often the case that a majority of members are paying a reduced subscription of some form. A number of clubs – typically those not offering the full suite of club services like overnight accommodation, or those with restricted opening hours – charge several hundred pounds a year, or just over £1,000. Some of the cheaper mass-membership clubs come in at under £100 a year, as they are able to exercise economies of scale, although that comes at the expense of amenities offered by more expensive clubs, like fine dining. At the other end of the spectrum, the sporting clubs can charge significantly more than the St James's clubs – a range of £3,000 to £7,000 for sporting clubs is more typical if a club has tennis courts, squash courts, swimming pool(s) and sports grounds. Yet higher fees do not necessarily equate to more prestige, or more facilities, or greater longevity: the highest subscription for any London club so far (barring the gambling clubs) was the £7,900 annual fee charged by the short-lived Chief on Bedford Square, the London branch of a US chain of clubs for female CEOs, which closed early in 2024, after one year in business. The highest fees of all have been at gambling clubs, charging around £25,000 a year.

The one-off joining fees – otherwise known as entry fees – are a different matter altogether. For one thing, historically, when they have been high, they have been used actively to keep out new applicants, as a way of raising cash without inconveniencing a club's existing members. However, most prudent clubs have not treated that sum as regular income, but as a windfall, typically being ring-fenced and invested in a long-term refurbishment reserve for the building or for art collections. The problem with treating joining-fee income as 'regular' income is that it builds up a dependency on maintaining high levels of recruitment at all times, whereas in reality a club will wax or wane its admission numbers over the years as it goes in and out of fashion, or as the supply of places becomes available.

Joining fees are not static. Whereas subscriptions tend to have a certain continuity from one year to the next, typically rising either in line with inflation or slightly above inflation, joining fees are a device directly linked to whether a club feels it is 'full'. Consequently, a club that is actively recruiting new members usually has a low joining fee (or a number of exemptions, or even no fee at all), while a club that is not seeking new members often chooses to ratchet up the joining fee, occasionally to outrageously high levels. This may well be a temporary phase, however, dictated by the principles of supply and demand.

CLUBLAND FOUNDERS

Most of the notable club founders of the seventeenth, eighteenth and nineteenth centuries were not aristocrats, but enterprising, wheeler-dealer servants with widespread contacts in catering and hospitality, who had a firm, instinctive grasp of the wants and needs of their members, and, above all, of what made for style and good taste. Over time, however, as club types diversified, a wide variety of people went on to found clubs. Some of the more notable ones are below.

William Almack (1741–81)

A Yorkshireman from Thirsk, William Almack had been valet to the 5th Duke of Hamilton before branching out into business as a vintner, becoming landlord of the Thatched House Tavern on St James's Street where a number of informal clubs and societies met in the back room. In 1754, he opened a fashionable Mayfair coffee house on Curzon Street, and upon its closure in 1759, he opened a tavern at 49 Pall Mall. The next few years would see him launch three significant new establishments – all confusingly known as Almack's. Firstly, in 1762, he opened a clubhouse at 50 Pall Mall, next door to his pub. This was, 'a large new house ... for the sole use of the Society'. In time, this was to become known as Boodle's club. Secondly, in 1763, he opened on King Street a new establishment, Almack's Assembly Rooms – not a club, but a salon (although confusingly, several much later clubs would be named after it), which proved immensely fashionable. Thirdly, bolstered by the success of his first club and his salon, in 1764, Almack opened another club in rooms above the tavern at 49 Pall Mall. This came to be known as Brooks's. Almack also hosted other clubs, like the Female Coterie – otherwise known as Ladies' Boodle's – although they only leased part of his Pall Mall premises in 1769–71, before seeking a clubhouse of their own in Albemarle Street. Almack retired to Hounslow in some prosperity, bequeathing his salon and clubs to his niece.

John Arthur (d. 1736)

John Arthur was a waiter at the original White's, residing next door from 1701. He was the right-hand man to both Francesco Bianco and then Elisabetta Bianco, in the informal 'old club' behind the chocolate shop. After Elisabetta's death in 1729, Arthur took over the running of White's, only for it to be hit by a fire in 1733. It was Arthur who oversaw a temporary move to Gaunt's coffee house, further up St James's Street, for the three years while new premises were built; but he did not live to see them become a club.

Robert Arthur (d. 1761)

Robert Arthur was the man who turned White's coffee house into a club. He was the son of John Arthur (above), succeeding his father to open the 'new' White's club in 1736 – now wholly turned over to the Club, without any chocolate shop or coffee house. For some forty-five years that followed, the new club was confusingly known as Arthur's, while hosting the old society, still known as White's, until the two merged in 1781 under the name of White's. Arthur's daughter Mary was married to Robert Mackreth, who succeeded Arthur as the proprietor of Arthur's/White's. Half a century after Arthur's death, the site once occupied by White's during his management was redeveloped and opened as Arthur's club in 1811 – a gambling club named after him.

Clubland Founders

John Aspinall (1926–2000)

Born into a military family in British India, Aspinall was an inveterate gambler, who spent much of his youth as a bookmaker organising chic, illicit, high-stakes card games in temporarily rented premises that drew an upper-class clientele. With the Betting and Gaming Act 1960 having criminalised Aspinall's earlier practices, he switched to running casinos, opening the Clermont Club as a private members' club on Berkeley Square in 1962, with a membership focused on wealthy Arabs, plus a smattering of British aristocrats like Lord Lucan, to whom Aspinall paid a retainer. Aspinall ran the establishment for a decade, with his management marked by endemic cheating, fixing the tables and swindling his members out of millions. He sold the business to Playboy Enterprises in 1972; but due to a lavish personal lifestyle and the ruinous expense of maintaining his private zoos, he periodically required fresh influxes of cash, and so opened, operated and then sold successive casinos branded 'Aspinall's' from the 1970s to 1990s.

Elisabetta Bianco (d. 1729)

The wife of Francesco Bianco (below), Elisabetta would go on to single-handedly run the coffee house with its informal club for as long as her late husband had: eighteen years, from his death in 1711, until her own passing in 1729. 'The widow White', as she was known, would go on to remarry by 1724, Major Skene of Chelsea. During her tenure the private subscription gambling rooms above the chocolate shop became the place to obtain tickets to the fashionable salons of the day.

Francesco Bianco (d. 1711)

Much is still unknown about the founder of what would become London's first club, an Italian who anglicised his name as Francis White.

In his own lifetime, his establishment was not yet a club: it remained a coffee house specialising in hot chocolate, with a gambling room around the back, as the enterprising Bianco joined the coffee boom of the late seventeenth century, opening his shop in 1693. He managed the premises for eighteen years, with his 1711 will noting he was, 'weake and infirm in body, but in sound disposing mind and memory'. By the time Bianco died, he had built the fashionable shop into a profitable business. His will suggested his family hailed from Genoa.

Marcus Oswald Hornby Lecky 'Mark' Birley (1930–2007)

Born to two society artists, Old Etonian and Oxford dropout Birley worked for advertising agency J. Walter Thompson in the 1950s, where 'he honed his skill in convincing customers that spending large sums on trifles showed discernment' (Richard Davenport-Hines). He launched Annabel's in 1963 as an upmarket nightclub run as a private members' club, in the basement underneath the Clermont Club, leased from his friend John Aspinall. So successful was Annabel's that Birley launched a succession of clubs in the ensuing years – Mark's in 1973, in the style of a traditional gentlemen's club; Harry's Bar in 1979, inspired by the Venice brasserie; the Bath and Racquets Club in 1989, as an American-style athletics club; and George in 2000, as a members' restaurant in the style of Mosimann's. He also agreed to undertake design work in 2000 for the Walbrook Club. Noted for his taste, Birley ran his clubs as an empire, selling them to restauranteur Richard Caring for £90 million just months before his death.

Robin Marcus Birley (b. 1958)

The son of Mark Birley (above), Old Etonian Robin Birley was badly mauled as a teenager by a tiger in the private zoo of family friend John Aspinall (above). He began his working life developing a chain of sandwich shops in the 1980s. By the 1990s, he and his sister India Jane began assisting with the day-to-day running of their father's clubs. A family rift resulted in their being disinherited of the clubs, which were sold to Richard Caring shortly before Mark Birley's death; but in 2012, Robin Birley launched a club of his own. Initially announced as being called 'Birley's', litigation from Caring resulted in it using another name, and it launched as 5 Hertford Street. The success of 5 Hertford Street has led to Robin Birley opening a further London club for oenophiles, Oswald's, and a New York spin-off club, Maxime's.

Edward Boodle (1722–72)

Born in Oswestry, the son of the landlord of the Three Tuns pub, Boodle was the head waiter who managed the Club founded at 50 Pall Mall by William Almack (above) in 1762. An expert in procuring wine who sublet part of the premises, living on-site, he became so synonymous with the management of the Club that it came to be named after him, as Boodle's. He died still working at the Club, after it had been in business for a decade.

William Brooks (d. 1782)

In 1764, Brooks was installed by William Almack (above) as the manager of his new club at 49 Pall Mall, with Almack distracted by the running of his neighbouring club as 50 Pall Mall (later known as Boodle's), and nearby salon on King Street. Brooks came to be synonymous with the Club, so that before long, members were referring to it as Brooks's. He oversaw the design and construction of the present clubhouse in St James's Street, to which members moved in 1778. At this point, he also became the proprietor of the relocated club. However, the combination of the building's expense and personally underwriting the excessively expensive gambling in the Club meant that Brooks died in poverty, ruined by his venture.

Robert Stewart, Viscount Castlereagh, later 2nd Marquess of Londonderry (1769–1822)

A British statesman whose decade as foreign secretary and key role at the Congress of Vienna of 1814–15 made him a central figure in the moulding of post-Napoleonic Europe, Castlereagh also founded the Travellers Club. With the disruption of the Napoleonic Wars, Castlereagh envisioned a club for those who travelled widely, resuming the 'Grand Tours' of Italy and Greece from the previous century, with the Club being bolstered by diplomats and representatives of foreign governments residing in London. He inherited the title of 2nd Marquess of Londonderry in the final year of his life. He would not live to see the completed Travellers Club building; and suffering from stress and depression, he committed suicide, cutting his throat.

William Crockford (1776–1844)

Crockford began life in the family trade as a fishmonger in Temple, before branching out into a lucrative sideline providing food and drink for the clubs and salons of St James's. A skilled card player, Crockford used his winnings to launch a highly fashionable gambling club – widely known as Crockford's – on St James's Street in 1823. He continued to gamble, with considerable success, profiting greatly from his members before his retirement in 1840. His club would only outlive him by two years, although a succession of unrelated gambling clubs would later assume its name.

John Wilson Croker (1780–1857)

Born the son of an Irish civil servant and elected to parliament as a Tory in 1807, Croker gained a reputation for argumentativeness. A keen antiquarian, he bemoaned the aristocratic nature of London's leading clubs, and sought to convene one centred around the arts, sciences and culture, which inspired him to establish the Athenæum in 1824. Despite his strong political convictions, he was adamant that a majority of the committee should be drawn from the Whigs, to ensure balance.

John George Lambton, 1st Earl of Durham (1792–1840)

'Radical Jack' was the *true* founder of the Reform Club in 1836 – for decades, the Club was incorrectly reported as having been the brainchild of the Whig whip and MP Edward Ellice, the result of a face-saving compromise. In fact, Ellice had been strongly *opposed* to the Reform's creation, regarding it as a dangerously factional development in Whig politics, but strong lobbying from the 1st Earl of Durham saw Ellice relent. Having inherited the vast Lambton Castle estate, and being elected an MP in 1811, Lambton became chairman of the New Zealand Company, which attempted comprehensive colonisation in the 1820s, before serving as Lord Privy Seal in Earl Grey's reforming government, for which he was awarded his earldom in 1833. His foundation of the Reform Club was sandwiched between two assignments abroad, as British ambassador to Russia, and a stint in North America which culminated in his briefly serving as governor-general of British North America, as Canada and Bermuda were known. He died at the age of forty-eight.

Emily Langton Massingberd (1847–97)

Born the heiress of a substantial Lincolnshire estate, Massingberd was widowed by the age of thirty-four, and increasingly dedicated her time to temperance reform and the cause of women's suffrage. In 1892, as an outlet for her work, she set up the Pioneer Club in Mayfair, dedicated to the advancement of women in both education and suffrage. It remained one of the more socially well-connected women's clubs, though with a strong emphasis on a cross-class membership, and it outlived its founder by over four decades – she died aged forty-nine, from complications of an operation. Massingberd herself remained the proprietor and president of the Pioneer Club until her death, with her will providing for the Club's maintenance.

William Nathaniel Pratt (d. 1857)

A former croupier at Crockford's, William Pratt moved to a small house at 14 Park Place in 1841, letting out rooms within. Later that year, he began entertaining the 7th Duke of Beaufort's friends in his basement kitchen on a regular basis. Pratt professionalised the operation of his boarding house into a hotel, but as the informal basement club flourished, Pratt converted the house into a club in 1857, retaining a flat on the premises as the proprietor. After Pratt's death, the Club remained in the family until 1908, first run by his widow Sophie, then by his son Edwin. His club, uniquely among London's older clubs, remains a proprietary club to this day, having been acquired by the family of the Dukes of Devonshire in the 1950s.

Anne Constance Smedley (1876–1941)

Born in the West Midlands, Constance Smedley was a prolific playwright and author, achieving a measure of fame in her twenties. Convinced that clubs held the key to providing women with a place to socialise, in 1903 she founded the Lyceum Club, opening a clubhouse on Piccadilly two years later. Smedley made the London clubhouse the core of her network of International Lyceum Clubs for Women Artists and Writers, which spread worldwide. Although the London club closed in 1936, the global network of Lyceum Clubs flourished, and still exists to this day. Smedley travelled extensively worldwide, often encouraging the foundation of new branches. A devout Christian Scientist from the late 1900s, she declined medical treatment for her final illness.

The Revd Henry Solly (1813–1903)

A Unitarian minister, he came to see that the greatest vehicle for working-class self-improvement was the creation of working men's clubs, modelled on the Pall Mall clubs. Solly founded the Working Men's Club and Institute Union in 1858 to realise this ambition with thousands of clubs across Britain. However, his vision of abstemious, alcohol-free clubs, where the members would attend self-improving lectures in the evenings, was not universally popular; and within a decade, Solly was sacked from the running of his own union of clubs. He nonetheless lived to see their exponential growth in every part of the UK, strongly disapproving of their inclination towards cheap beer.

Arthur Wellesley, 1st Duke of Wellington (1769–1852)

With a reputation as Britain's most accomplished general in the Napoleonic Wars, Wellington was the toast of London society, belonging to no fewer than a dozen clubs; and when numerous clubs were launched, it was often considered the ultimate seal of approval to secure Wellington's participation, whether as a paying member or as an honorary member. He wrote to the proposed new United Service Club from the continent, accepting membership just five days before the Battle of Waterloo. He was a founder-member of two clubs that launched in 1824, the Oriental Club organised by his protégés in the East India Company, and the Athenæum, which sought to combine distinguished members in different disciplines. The new Army and Navy Club in 1837 was going to be an army club until Wellington opined that naval officers should be members as well. As the recently defeated Tory prime minister in 1830, Wellington was instrumental in the reorganisation of the Tory Party's St James's office around the 'Charles Street Gang', combining the group's official duties with a social club, which created the Carlton Club in 1832 – although he later came to regret the innovation. His deathbed advice was, 'Never write a letter to your mistress, and never join the Carlton Club.'

CLUBHOUSE TYPES: A BLUFFER'S GUIDE

The specially designed Georgian townhouse

The earliest clubhouses were really just large townhouses in London's St James's district. Splendidly well-proportioned, yes, but they were modelled for providing well-travelled aristocrats with comfortable, warm rooms offering geometrical simplicity and classical shapes, with plenty of wall space on which to display artwork acquired on Grand Tours of Italy and Greece – although the artwork itself is often a late addition. Notably, for much of their early existence, clubs such as Brooks's and the Travellers were positively denuded of artworks, with it being argued that the architecture should do the talking. White's also preceded this trend, though its move to new premises in 1778 offered more leeway. With the Victorian taste for clutter and ephemera, however, these clubs have steadily built up art matching the tastes of their members. Boodle's and the Turf focus more on hunting and horse racing in their choice of art, matching the squirearchical bent of their memberships. Charles Barry's Travellers Club occupies a particularly important phase in this design, embodying the transition between the Georgian townhouse and later palatial Victorian clubhouse.

The adapted Georgian townhouse

Quite simply a tall, narrow, well-designed late-Georgian residential house adapted from domestic use to serving as a club. Accordingly, domesticity and comfort are very high priorities. This type of clubhouse is under threat. It was once the mainstay of much of Clubland – particularly 'Ladies' Clubland', with the profusion of ladies-only and mixed-sex clubs north of Piccadilly – but relatively few instances have survived. The University Women's Club (heavily modified in the late Victorian period) and Buck's are probably the most prominent examples. The main advantage of this kind of building is a sort of forced intimacy, requiring members to be close to one another at all times, making for a much more sociable environment than many of the more palatial buildings. The Naval and Military ('In and Out') Club technically occupies one of these, but it is such a large residence, with a complex of outhouses around the rear yard, that it comes closer to the courtyard-based clubs of southern Spain. To this day, many modern clubs in Mayfair will acquire an old Georgian townhouse in this style and convert it to modern taste.

The neo-classical clubhouse

The trend towards grandiose neo-classicism came heavily to dominate nineteenth-century Clubland worldwide. Its influential early examples were several purpose-built clubhouses intended to create the impression of solidity and 'Establishment'. These pioneers included the dual building for the Union Club and the Royal College of Physicians completed in 1827 and designed by British Museum architect Sir Robert Smirke, which is now the Canadian High Commission in Trafalgar Square; the nearby United Service Club on the eastern end of Pall Mall completed in 1828 by John Nash (with later additional refacing and redecoration by Decimus Burton), which is now the Institute of Directors; and the Athenæum opposite, completed in 1830 to designs by Decimus Burton. These buildings went much further than the restrained neo-classicism of Boodle's and Brooks's, to make the Club a temple to its given purpose, dominated by major classical elements such as porticos. This school of architecture across Pall Mall was heavily influenced by Nash (and his pupils) in his pomp, part of the grand masterplan influenced by the Prince Regent, and the architecture of Carlton House which had previously stood on the site. Giant order columns dominate; but variation was created though the column capitals: the Union Club's columns were Ionic, the United Service Club's were Corinthian, and the Athenæum's were Doric. Later examples included the Oxford and Cambridge Club completed in 1838 by Sir Robert Smirke, and Charles Lee's East India Club completed in 1866, with its Roman-influenced friezes. (Passers-by may notice that the much earlier Brooks's clubhouse also has noticeable neo-classical touches like giant order pilasters, friezes and cornice – but most of these details date to a later Edwardian refacing of the building.)

The Italianate revival clubhouse

Charles Barry's Reform Club, completed in 1841, marked a departure from his Travellers Club next door, and indeed from anything else. Its ornate interiors are barely hinted at by the stately but subdued exterior, said to have been influenced by Michelangelo's Palazzo Farnese in Rome, a building closely studied by Barry. Other clubhouses influenced by the *palazzo* style, inside and out, included Pall Mall's (now-demolished) Army and Navy Club completed by Charles Octavius Parnell and Alfred Smith in 1851, and Frederick Marrable's Garrick Club completed in Covent Garden in 1864.

'Municipal bank' architecture

This is a peculiarly British style of architecture, blending elements of the Georgian and the Italianate revival, which proved tremendously popular in the second half of the nineteenth century, and reflecting the growth of both national and provincial wealth. It is not an acknowledged architectural term, but relates to the curious parallels between the architecture of municipal banks of the period up and down the country, and the clubhouses built at the same time, complete with an elevated ground floor with large windows offering a view down into the main street outside, without letting passers-by easily peer in. Examples include the (now-demolished) second Pall Mall clubhouse of the Carlton Club completed in 1856 by Sydney Smirke (younger brother of Sir Robert).

The small cottage

This style suits the more informal, bohemian clubs, such as the former Bolton Lodge occupied by the Chelsea Arts Club, and the Victorian artist's studio of the London Sketch Club. Like the adapted Georgian townhouse, the forced intimacy of such small premises makes these clubs extremely sociable.

Victorian pottery

A late-Victorian love of ceramics and potteries in the Midlands and the north of England, along with a deeply practical need for buildings housing a lot of smokers to have wipe-clean surfaces, combined to create an extensive use of decorative faience ceramics in the late nineteenth century. Some of the most notable examples, like Robert William Edis's Constitutional Club completed in 1887, are long gone. However, of the survivors, Alfred Waterhouse's National Liberal Club on Whitehall Place, which was also completed in 1887, and parts of Charles Mewès and Arthur Joseph Davis's Royal Automobile Club on Pall Mall (particularly around the swimming pool and Turkish baths) completed in 1913, offer particularly ostentatious examples.

The art deco

The futuristic inter-war style, with its clean, crisp lines and geometrical shapes, left its mark in Clubland. It can most clearly be seen in the

Lansdowne Club, on which Charles Fox put a new façade to Lansdowne House, and redecorated much of the interior in this way in 1935. Other inter-war art deco renovations include the Brooklands restaurant of the Royal Automobile Club, while Reginald Blomfield in 1924 and 1938 reworked the exterior of the old United University Club on Pall Mall (which is now the London campus of the University of Notre Dame).

The tavern

A throwback to the very earliest, informal clubs, which met in the 'snug' or back room of a pub or tavern; a number of clubs still embrace this style in whole or in part to maximise informality. Pratt's does this most authentically, still meeting in the old basement kitchen area of the seventeenth-century house that once belonged to William Pratt. The Beefsteak Club also emulates this, with a first-floor room in a four-storey building designed to suggest a wooden-beamed attic. Club bars lacking in natural sunlight can also sometimes be made over in this style – for instance, the American Bar in the East India Club, and the RAF Club's Running Horse tavern in the basement.

Gothic revival

Relatively rare among surviving clubhouses in London, although it used to predominate among many provincial clubs, like the Manchester Reform Club, and the Leeds and County Liberal Club. The prime London example, Alfred Waterhouse's New University Club completed in St James's Street in 1868, which was meant to evoke both Oxbridge colleges and redbrick universities, has long since been demolished.

Since its inception in 1919, Buck's has been in the same Georgian townhouse.

The former clubhouse of the United Service Club, now the Institute of Directors.

Clubhouse Types: A Bluffer's Guide

The former clubhouse of the Carlton Club on Pall Mall, as it appeared from its rebuild in 1856 until it was refaced in 1923. It was later bombed in 1940.

Boodle's, one of the most intact Adam-style mansions in London, originally built for the short-lived Savoir Vivre Club.

London Clubland

Bolton Lodge serves as the clubhouse of the Chelsea Arts Club.

The terracotta clubhouse of the former Constitutional Club on Northumberland Avenue.

Clubhouse Types: A Bluffer's Guide

The Lansdowne Club has a 1930s facade with art deco and neo-classical influences, over the surviving part of a Georgian mansion.

The Reform Club's Italianate revival clubhouse was highly influential on 19th-century club architecture.

LISTED CLUBHOUSES

Clubs having their buildings listed can be a double-edged sword. On the one hand, there is the immense prestige of a listing, and the certainty provided for posterity, that any alterations will be done sympathetically, in a like-for-like manner. On the other hand, many clubs have come to rue the ruinous expense of maintaining a listed building. A non-listed club can happily bumble along for decades making a loss, growing ever shabbier, and no one will care. A listed club will have a statutory duty to maintain their clubhouse, and will accordingly have to budget for significantly greater expenditure.

Below are details of when different clubhouses were listed, and whether they are Grade I, Grade II* or Grade II.

(Buildings marked *N* were not yet in use as clubhouses at the time of the listing.)

4 January 1950: City University Club *N* (II*).
24 October 1951: Savage Club *N* (II*).
6 May 1954: Hurlingham Club (II*).
9 September 1954: Home House *N* (I).
14 July 1955: Winchester House Club (II).
24 February 1958: Annabel's *N* (I); Brooks's (I); Cambridge House (I);* Maison Estelle *N* (I); Mosimann's *N* (II); Pasley Tyler *N* (II); Royal Over-Seas League (I); Soho House – 76 Dean Street *N* (II*); Union Club *N* (II); Snail Club *N* (II); White's (I).
14 April 1969: Chelsea Arts Club (II).
1 July 1969: RAF Club (II).

---

* At the time, Cambridge House was already a club, but as the home of the Naval and Military Club on Piccadilly, a site since vacated in 1999.

Listed Clubhouses

2 July 1969: Cavalry and Guards Club (II*).*
14 January 1970: Garrick Club (II*); Lansdowne Club (II*); Quo Vadis *N* (I).
5 February 1970: 67 Pall Mall *N* (II); Academicians' Room *N* (II*); Admiralty Arch *N* (I); Athenæum (I); Boodle's (I); Carlton Club (II*); East India Club (II); Farmers Club (II*);† National Liberal Club (II*); Oxford and Cambridge Club (II*); Pratt's (II); Reform Club (I); Royal Automobile Club (II*); Travellers Club (I).
3 March 1972: Ten Trinity Square *N* (II*).
15 January 1973: Le Beaujolais Club (II); Conduit Club *N* (II).
8 February 1974: Soho House – Electric House *N* (II*).
17 September 1975: Soho House – 40 Greek Street *N* (II).
17 December 1975: 5 Hertford Street *N* (II).
28 June 1976: Gerry's (II).
23 November 1978: Academy Club *N* (II).
8 June 1982: Arboretum *N* (II).
2 September 1982: Marylebone Cricket Club, Lord's Pavilion (II*).
1 December 1987: Dartmouth House *N* (II*); The Twenty Two *N* (II).
1 January 1988: Yeoman Warders Club (I).
6 October 1998: The Roof Gardens (II*).
8 July 2009: White City House *N* (II).‡

---

* Clubhouse of the Cavalry Club at the time of the listing. The merger with the Guards Club happened seven years later.
† The Farmers Club was included as part of the wider listing of the surrounding Whitehall Court building.
‡ As part of the wider listing for the old BBC Television Centre building.

FREEHOLDS

London clubs are often thought of as being permanent institutions, but relatively few of them own their own freehold outright. Some enjoy long leases of 100 or 150 years from favourable landlords such as the Crown Estate or the Grosvenor Estate; while others live a far more hand-to-mouth existence on a range of shorter leases, rentals and licences.

With London property prices booming, it is growing ever rarer for new clubs to own their freeholds. Indeed, it is no coincidence that seven of the twenty-six clubs below bought their freeholds within an eight-year span in 1919–27, when Britain was in the throes of a deep recession, and just before a surge in Mayfair and St James's property values in the 1930s. Indeed, with the capital's land prices continuing to grow stratospherically, only one London club has bought its freehold since 1999 – and that was because the Royal Kennel Club was able to make a profit on the 2012 sale of the freehold of their previous property.

The following clubs, however, are known to have owned their freeholds since the following dates:

- All England Lawn Tennis and Croquet Club (1868).
- Army and Navy Club (1851).
- Beefsteak (1927).
- Brooks's (1778).
- Cavalry and Guards Club (1987).
- City of London Club (1832).
- The Club for Acts and Actors (1950).
- East India Club (1849).
- Garrick Club (1864).
- Hurlingham Club (1869).
- Lansdowne Club (1935).
- London Sketch Club (1957).
- Magic Circle (1998).

Freeholds

- Marylebone Cricket Club (1814).
- Naval and Military ('In and Out') Club (1999).
- Ognisko Polskie (1978).
- Oriental Club (1962).
- Pratt's (1857).
- Roehampton Club (1927).
- Royal Air Force Club (1922).
- Royal Kennel Club (2012).
- Royal Ocean Racing Club (1942).
- Royal Over-Seas League (1921).
- Royal Thames Yacht Club (1923).
- University Women's Club (1921).
- White's (1778).

CLUB MOTTOS

Most London clubs do not have a motto, but some exceptions follow:

Army and Navy Club: Unitate Fortior. ('Strength in unity.')

Authors Club: Cedit Ensis Calamo. ('The pen is mightier than the sword.')

Beefsteak Club: Beef and Liberty; *motto was previously* Esto Perpetua ad Libitum. ('Be perpetual at will.')

Brydges Place Club: Main tien le droit. ('Hold on right.')

Caledonian Club: Floreat Caledonia. ('Let Scotland flourish.')

Cavalry and Guards Club: Tria Juncta in Uno. ('Three joined into one.' *Historic motto of the old Guards Club, prior to the merger; previously the motto of the Order of the Bath.*)

City Livery Club: Uniting the Livery, Promoting Fellowship.

City of London Club: Domine Dirige Nos. ('Lord, guide us.' *City of London Corporation motto.*)

East India Club: Concordia Crescimus. ('We grow in harmony.')

Eccentric Club: Nil Nisi Bonum. ('Nothing but good.')

Flyfishers' Club: Piscator Non Solum Piscatur. ('It is not all of flying to fish.')

Garrick Club: All the World's a Stage.

Magic Circle: Indocilis Privata Loqui. ('Keep mum.')

Naval and Military Club: Nunquam Dimoveas. ('Never move away.')

New Evaristo Club: Italia.

Royal Air Force Club: Per Ardua ad Astra. ('Through adversity to the stars.' *RAF motto.*)

Royal Kennel Club: Making a difference for dogs.

Royal Over-Seas League: Ubique Navigavimus. ('Travelling everywhere.')

Club Mottos

Savage Club: The pursuit of happiness.
Savile Club: Sodalitas Convivium. ('Conviviality and belonging.')
Snail Club: Slow but sure.
Special Forces Club: Spirit of Resistance.
White's: Cogit amor nummi. ('The love of money compels him.')
Winchester House Club: Think and Tank.

The White's motto was originally coined as a joke by Horace Walpole, Richard Edgecumbe, George Selwyn and George J. Williams in 1756, as part of a prank coat of arms that they created; but the object now hangs in the front hall of White's. The shield deliberately has a gap separating the word 'cogit' into two, as 'cog it' – a pun on the practice of sneakily cogging the dice. It can be described as being:

> On a green field (in allusion to the baize on a card table), three cards (aces); between a chevron sable (for a hazard table), two rouleaus of guineas in saltier, and a pair of dice; on a canton, sable, a white election-ball. The crest is an arm issuing from an earl's coronet, and shaking a dice-box. The arms are surrounded by a claret-bottle ticket and its chain; the supporters are an old and a young Knave of Clubs; and the motto, 'Cogit amor nummi'.*

---

* With thanks to Michael Hillman for his reading of this example of burlesque heraldry.

CLUBS WITH SOBRIQUETS FOR THEIR MEMBERS

Most London clubs simply refer to their members as 'Members'. Yet the following clubs have specific sobriquets that can be used when referring to them:

Academicians' Room: Academicians.
Athenæum: Athenians.
Boodle's: Noodles. *(Unofficial; archaic; derogatory.)*
Eccentric Club: Eccentrics.
Magic Circle: Magicians.
Reform Club: Reformers.
Savage Club: Brother Savages.
Savile Club: Savilians.
Travellers Club: Travellers.

CLUB SONGS

Edward Boodle's favourite Irish toping song

A drinking song from the early years of Boodle's club.

'There's the Day!'

(Innkeeper)
'A fitful sleep was mine last night,
Mid din and chat not of my choosing,
My daughter 'till the morning light
Upbraiding those who sat there boozing.'

(Chorus: Daughter and topers)
'There's the day!' 'It's not the day!'
'It is the day, the night is over!'
'It's not the day, whate'er you say,
But the moonbeams bright to light the rover!'

(Toper)
'Come, landlord, join us in the snug,
All drowsy thoughts of slumber scorning;
There's not a drop in jar or jug
That we won't drain before the morning!'

(Innkeeper)
'I'll stop in bed,' the landlord said,
'Though if I don't you'll go out quicker!
There's not a drop in jar or jug
That we won't drain before the morning!'

(Toper)
'The shebeen has my socks and shoes,
The tavern has my coat and breeches;
By daybreak I'll have nought to lose –
And then I'll snooze among my ditches!'

(Another toper)
'I still can lend to treat a friend,
And here's my guinea on the table;
So tilt the barrel on the end,
And let's be drinking while we're able!'

DONAL O'SULLIVAN

Reform Club song

Pre-dating the Club, and written in 1832 as 'Verses Celebrating the Triumph of the Reform Bill', the song was adopted by the Reform Club shortly after its foundation. Many of the politicians named in the song, including Earl Grey, Lord Brougham, Lord John Russell and Francis Burdett, were the Whig architects of the 1832 Reform Act, who went on to be founder members of the Club.

(Tune: 'Auld Lang Syne')

We, sons of proud Britannia! meet
On this auspicious day,

Club Songs

Our height of rapture to proclaim –
Our triumph to display.
We 'sound our trumpets, beat our drums',
And lift our voices high;
For we are crown'd, are crown'd, are crown'd,
With heav'n-born Liberty!
There was a time when Tyranny
Held its tremendous sway –
When we were banish'd from the blaze
Of Freedom's golden day;
But that, dark time has disappear'd,
And ne'er again shall be;
For we, &c.

Grey, Brougham, Russell and Burdett,
With their triumphant host,
Have, our once-formidable foe,
Into oblivion tost;
And there the vanquish'd tyrant shall,
In endless ruin lie,
For we, &c.

Our Nation shall no longer lie,
The dupe of haughty men –
Her late enlighten'd glorious eyes,
Shall ne'er be dimmed again.
But white-rob'd Truth and Justice shall,
Her sole instructers be;
For we, &c.

While millions of our countrymen,
Their victory display,
And tell that they are re-illum'd,
By Freedom's golden day;

We, with them, join to roll the note,
O'er hill and dale, and sea;
For we, &c.

(With thanks to Dr Peter Clark and Dr Peter Urbach for sharing this discovery.)

National Liberal Club song

The origins of 'The Land' were as a Georgist song first published in a Chicago journal in 1887. With the influence of Georgism on British Liberal ideas of taxation (focusing on the potential value of land, and taxing accordingly), and Henry George having been made a temporary member of the National Liberal Club when visiting London in 1888–9, the song was to become commonplace among British Liberals by the early 1890s, and is often sung in the NLC after banquets.

(Tune: 'Marching Through Georgia')

Sound a blast for Freedom, boys, and send it far and wide!
March along to victory, for God is on our side!
While the voice of Nature thunders o'er the rising tide –
'God made the Land for the People!'

(Chorus)
The Land! the Land!
'twas God who gave the Land!
The Land! the Land!
the ground on which we stand!
Why should we be beggars,
with the ballot in our hand?
'God gave the Land to the People!'

Club Songs

Hark! the shout is swelling from the East and from the West:
Why should we beg work and let the Landlords take the best?
Make them pay their taxes for the Land – we'll risk the rest;
The Land was meant for the People!

(Repeat chorus)

The banner has been raised on high to face the battle din:
The Army now is marching on the struggle to begin.
We'll never cease our efforts till the victory we win,
And the Land is free for the People!

(Repeat chorus)

Clear the way for liberty! the land must all be free!
True men will not falter in the fight, though stern it be,
Till the flag we love so well shall wave from sea to sea,
O'er land that's free for the People.

(Repeat chorus)

(With thanks to the *Liberator* Collective.)

ASSOCIATIONS OF ASSOCIATIONS

Clubs began life as unincorporated associations; but they can themselves form associations *of* the associations. This can be for various reasons:

Professional networks:

- The **Association of London Clubs** acts as a forum for shared interests among the management of most – though not all – of the historic London clubs. It has existed since 1942, though fell into abeyance by 1961. As they note, in 1966, 'one Club Secretary called a meeting to suggest the Secretaries of London Clubs formed an Association. There were around 20 Secretaries in attendance who listened patiently as the Secretary shared his thoughts. He was allowed to finish his rousing address before the Secretaries kindly informed him that there was already an Association in being with funds in the bank.' The ALC was promptly revived, and has remained active ever since. It currently has forty-eight participating clubs.
- The **Distinguished Clubs** emanated from the Distinguished Clubs of America nominated by *Boardroom* magazine since 1997, and run in partnership with *Forbes* travel guide, which regularly provides assessments of clubs worldwide. It bestows platinum status – the international club equivalent of a five-star rating. Nominated clubs must be at least seventy-five years old.
- The above is not to be confused with the (unrelated) **Distinguished Clubs of the World**, which is an elite group of no more than

twenty-five managers of leading clubs worldwide, of whom around five are drawn from London at any given time. Nominated clubs of this grouping must be member owned and at least 100 years old. Election of a club manager to this latter organisation is very much like election to a club; strictly by internal nomination and election, and subject to a joining fee and subscription. Participating London clubs have included the Athenæum, Boodle's, Brooks's, Caledonian, Carlton, Cavalry and Guards, Garrick, Oriental, Travellers and Whites.

- The **Club Managers Association of Europe** – provides training, coaching, mentoring and development for club management staff, with its own dedicated chapter in London.
- The **League of Club Chefs** began as an informal network of five club chefs in 1988 and was more formally established two years later. It combines the chefs of fourteen historic London clubs, with those of half a dozen other institutions ranging from livery companies, through an inn of court, to the House of Lords.
- **Le Réunion des Gastronomes**, set up in 1899, exists to promote excellence in hospitality and catering. It is drawn equally from restaurants, hotels and private members' clubs.

Shared younger members' groups:

- The **Inter-Club Younger Members' Group**, widely known as Inter-Club, was founded in 2005 and is the network for the younger members of some twenty leading London clubs. Organising a social calendar of events at one another's clubs all year round – and therefore acting as a convenient introduction for members of one participating club to visit the premises of others – Inter-Club often sells out its tickets within seconds. How clubs define 'Younger' can vary considerably, depending on a club's own demographics (from under twenty-five to under fifty), but Inter-Club generally recognises thirty-five as the demarcation point.
- **Gold Alliance**, founded in 2017, is the European-wide network for younger members of some sixty historic clubs across the continent.

It organises roughly annual events, typically combining several host clubs in the same European city, with events across a weekend. Membership goes up to the age of forty-five.

Reciprocation:

- **International Associate Clubs** is a global network founded in 1983, currently listing some 176 clubs both old and new. It offers participating clubs the opportunity of an instant reciprocals network upon joining the network; although it comes at a trade-off with clubs surrendering some of their autonomy in maintaining their own reciprocals lists. It also provides many of the forms of hospitality more normally associated with luxury hotels, including concierge service, corporate partnerships and arranging stays at some 2,500 villas worldwide.
- **ONDA** is a global network for modern clubs, founded by Luca del Bono, previously the co-founder of international concierge firm Quintessentially. ONDA says it offers, 'Worldwide access', to a 'unique community that calls hundreds of exclusive places home', listing seventy-two participating clubs, hotels and communal workspaces, including much of the Soho House chain.

COMPLAINTS

'It's not like it used to be . . .' If club members enjoy doing one thing, it's complaining. There is nothing quite like paying several hundred – or several thousand – pounds a year in subscription fees to give a member a sense of entitlement to speak freely. And speak *exceptionally* freely, they will. A glance through a club's 'Suggestion Book' will often reveal that it serves more as a 'grumble book', less given over to constructive suggestions, and more a forum for pointed critiques: tepid coffee, faded décor, lack of weekend opening, are all preferred grounds for a good gripe. Most of these are simple 'management' issues, either remedied through managerial action, or else mitigated with a conciliatory or apologetic approach to the member.

Most feared of all are complaints about individuals – for therein lies considerable risk of animosity, offence, escalation and even litigation. These are rightly regarded by clubs with dread. They can usually be subdivided into two broad categories: complaints against members and complaints against staff.

―――――― Complaints against members ――――――

There are any number of reasons why a member might be the subject of a complaint. They might have been snoring into their soup, in a manner which disturbed their fellow diners. Or they might have said or done something very serious indeed, in full view of witnesses in the clubhouse. Or there might be a general feeling that their prominent involvement in a front-page sex/drugs/financial scandal in all the tabloids reflects poorly on the Club's reputation, with their resignation being called for.

As noted, members can feel very entitled once they have paid a subscription. They feel that it buys them some rights, and even some social standing. Accordingly, when a member is the subject of a complaint, whether it is justified or not, the most common response is to go absolutely ballistic.

Once upon a time, the more honourable members might meekly raise their hands in the air, conceding, 'It's a fair cop,' and quietly offer up their resignation with no further fuss. And still, a few will do the honourable thing. But not most members. Today, they will more typically offer up a stout denial, a barrage of retaliatory abuse and counter-accusations against the complainant, and they will quite possibly even lawyer up. The more prestigious the club, the higher the stakes, because the member knows that if they give any ground, they may never walk through the Club's doors again.

Matters typically then go to the Club's complaints procedure. This may have been deftly redrafted by leading silks in the last few years; or it may have lain unchanged since 1843. The wiser clubs will often resort to some form of mediation, whether formal or informal, to see if things can be diffused before the complaint runs its course. If that cannot be done, then in the event of the Club deciding in favour of one member or the other, the most common outcome is for the dissatisfied member to quit the Club in protest. Given the explosive dynamic at play, it is understandable that clubs often prefer to defuse tension through mediation. Yet given the Club's need to protect its reputation, it is also essential to have in reserve the powers for a swift suspension and expulsion, including due process and an appeals process, for those handful of cases which merit it.

Clubs are often accused of being unduly cautious when it comes to electing new members. Yet the complaints procedure demonstrates why. If the members are to suffer some catastrophic falling out, then in a highly charged, litigious environment, the costs to a club can be ruinous. This is why many clubs prefer to play it safe and *not* elect controversial candidates. The alternative may be the doomsday scenario of spending a six- or seven-figure sum on legal bills relating to complaints about a hot-headed member of whom it's widely thought, 'We did have some warning signs when he applied ...'

Complaints against staff

Complaints against staff are a nightmare for clubs. They have been present for as long as clubs have existed. But the long-established habit of some members, blowing off steam 'because the staff don't understand the Club's traditions', sits uneasily with the modern niceties of HR.

Traditionally, the club servant has been voiceless, and in decades gone by could be expected to endure all manner of character assassination from the members, with their only viable options being to suffer in silence or to resign. In 1827, the secretary of the Junior United Service Club complained of:

> circumstances that would have destroyed almost any other man and which would have destroyed me had I not been supported by the consciousness of my own integrity and innocence while labouring under the foulest and most interested calumnies and slanders hurled against me in the dark by anonymous accusers.*

Today, of course, staff have the same employment rights enshrined in law as anyone else – something that committees often realise, but members might not. This means that careful, professional management and record keeping are essential; and only a healthy spirit of mutual respect can avert an intolerable situation.

Some complaints are implicit: over the quality of food, for instance – an especially common topic of gripes. This suggests that the kitchen is

---

* Quoted in Tom Girtin, *The Abominable Clubman* (London: Hutchinson, 1964), p. 59.

not doing its job properly (which may or may not be fully justified). Yet it can be hard to satisfactorily resolve for all parties.

Even trickier are the direct complaints about members of staff, especially if something cannot be proved. 'They were very rude to me, but there were no witnesses', is a typical complaint of this sort. If it comes down to one person's word against another, whether a member or staff, then it may be impossible to resolve, only incurring further ill feeling.

Feuds

Most feuds in clubs do not escalate to a formal complaint. They may be resolved amicably. Or they may simmer, for years (or decades) on end. The relationships from sharing a clubhouse can be much like the relationship between flat-sharers and housemates – only more long term. You eat and drink together under the same roof, unable to avoid one another; and as the decades go by, you might even see a succession of work colleagues and significant others wander through the door as guests. After a certain number of years, you can know your fellow members' tastes almost as well as their own spouse does (and you might even see them for more hours of the day than their spouse does), quite regardless of whether or not you cordially despise them.

Some clubs seem particularly well-attuned to disputes. Many clubs have either a membership focused on one age bracket, or a membership roughly evenly spread out across different age brackets. But I can think of one club with hefty subscription discounts for the very young and very old, which consequently has few middle-aged members in between. The result is two tribes that cannot abide each other and routinely question one another's very right to be in the same building. If you stand at the bar, you will often find the two groups sitting in diagonally opposite corners of the room, glowering at one another.

None of this is new. Clubs have long housed simmering feuds, and once tempers cool they can become subjects of lore. One of the most well-known tales – though often mangled in the retelling – was the dispute between Charles Dickens and William Makepeace Thackeray, which started at the Garrick in 1858, and ended at the Athenæum in 1863 (although Anthony Lejeune embellished it into an estrangement lasting '15 years').

Edmund Yates, scribbler of the 'Lounger at the Clubs' gossip column, wrote a less-than-flattering portrait of Thackeray, drawing heavily on his observations of the novelist in the Garrick Club, where they were both members. Thackeray wrote to Yates in disgust, alleging misuse of his private conversations in a private club, and complaining to the Garrick's General Committee – which promptly expelled Yates in a special meeting. But Yates had a doughty defender in Charles Dickens, who spoke in his support, and resigned from the Garrick on Yates's expulsion. Thackeray and Dickens did not speak for five years – until a chance encounter in the hall of the Athenæum, when according to one account, they shook hands and Thackeray added, 'I'm glad I have done this.'*

---

* For various versions with different perspectives, see Peter Ackroyd, *Dickens* (London: Sinclair-Stevenson, 1990), pp. 923–4; Anthony Lejeune, *The Gentlemen's Clubs of London* (London: MacDonald & Jane's, 1979), p. 127; Geoffrey Wansell, *The Garrick: Story of a Club*, 2nd ed. (London: Garrick Club, 2013), pp. 51–8; Michael Wheeler, *The Athenæum: More Than Just Another Club* (New Haven: Yale University Press, 2020), pp. 133–4.

GLOSSARY OF CLUBLAND SLANG

Account ... a means for clubs to remain largely cashless – 'Charge it to my account.' Members are typically billed monthly for all drinks, meals, etc. that have been charged to their account.

At home ... a sort of open evening for guests to sample a club, traditional in some theatrical clubs.

Backwoodsman ... a club member who only visits once or twice a year.

Ball ... a *real* ball – none of this 'a dinner followed dancing, and taxis at 1 a.m.' nonsense. A ball will typically last no fewer than twelve hours, kicking off with pre-dinner drinks at 6 p.m., and although it *will* involve a dinner and dancing, it will also take in multiple shifting entertainments across a club and its grounds throughout the night, from ceilidhs to stage plays, with unlimited food and drink provided. 'Chickening out' before dawn is frowned upon, as is napping. Gorged members and their guests are often near comatose by the time they are served a hearty breakfast at 7 a.m. the next day, at the close of proceedings.

Billiard room ... a place where cue sports are played with billiard balls on a baize-covered table. Paradoxically, billiards is almost never played in the billiard rooms of London clubs any more; most are equipped with a snooker table or pool table.

Blackball ... the practice of vetoing an application for membership, by deploying enough votes against a candidate, historically by using black balls to vote 'No'.

Boiled change ... a now largely retired practice of spare change being boiled to ensure cleanliness.

Glossary of Clubland Slang

Chambers ... bedrooms.

Club ... literally to 'club together' to defray the cost; splitting the bill. The word comes from the mid-seventeenth-century word 'unclubbable', to describe someone who could not be relied upon to pay their fair share of the bill in a pub, tavern or inn; and from that comes the reverse idea of being 'clubbable', with all the virtues of being reliable, good company.

Club bore ... a member best avoided; typically given to delivering opinionated monologues and/or anecdotes, over and over again. Often notorious within the Club. As the saying goes, 'If you can't name the Club bore, you must be the Club bore yourself.'

Club secretary ... chief executive. They have better things to do than to read your email complaining about the fish.

Club table ... a long, central table, where you will be seated next to other members, regardless of whether or not you already know them. The idea is to encourage members to dine together, and to meet one another. Different clubs have different conventions – some very much welcome guests, others insist that the club table remains members only.

Clubland ... originally, this referred to a strict geographical area of London in a grid, containing most of the main clubs: a square formed by Pall Mall in the south, St James's Street in the west, Piccadilly in the north, and Trafalgar Square in the east. As clubs grew more numerous worldwide, the word 'Clubland' came to refer to more of an abstract idea, of clubs wherever they may be found.

Clubman ... a man who belongs to multiple clubs, and who regularly attends them.

Coffee room ... the dining room. Coffee is not served here; you have to retire elsewhere for it.

Conversazione ... a learned discussion around the arts and/or sciences; typically a lecture or talk followed by questions and then dinner.

Exclusive ... the most overused – and meaningless – word in Clubland. Few establishments that describe themselves as 'exclusive' are actually defined by excluding people. Generally used as a synonym for 'snob value'.

Papers ... the periodicals and

newspapers subscribed to by a club, typically focused on the theme of the Club. Traditionally ironed, to ensure crispness, this practice has fallen into disuse.

Petticoat Alley ... the area around Dover Street, spilling over into nearby Grafton Street and Albemarle Street, well-known for its concentration of ladies-only clubs and mixed-sex clubs from the mid-nineteenth to the mid-twentieth centuries.

Pilled ... to be blackballed.

Plodge ... an Oxbridge term, also applied to Clubland; abbreviation of 'porter's lodge'.

Reciprocal clubs ... two or more clubs, typically in different countries or cities, which have signed a contract to let one another's members use each club as if it were their own, for a limited number of days a year.

Smoker ... now largely discontinued since the 2007 smoking ban, the smoker was a traditional supper where members smoked during dinner. Only now legally feasible in clubs with large outdoor seating areas, or else a specially designated cigar-tasting room (which is exempted under the 2007 legislation, subject to conditions).

Smoking room ... the drawing room, which has been strictly 'no smoking' since 2007.

Snifter ... a cocktail.

Steward ... a senior club servant; the modern equivalent would be the house manager, a sort of chief operating officer, reporting directly to the secretary.

Suburb ... something most club members will pretend to be completely unfamiliar with, despite three-quarters of them living in one.

Tourist ... a reciprocal member.

Trencherman ... glutton.

There are also words that are taboo. On no account is the language of the hospitality industry to be used, and so referring to table places at dinner as 'covers' is likely to attract opprobrium.

ETYMOLOGICAL ROOTS

The place names of Clubland contain numerous words with very specific linguistic roots.

- **Club:** originally 'unclubbable' in its seventeenth-century form, denoting someone who ducks their round in the pub; evolved to 'clubbable', to describe the attributes of an ideal convivial companion, and from this, 'club'.
- **Mayfair:** named after the annual May Fair of the seventeenth and eighteenth centuries, in the area which is now Shepherd Market.
- **Pall Mall:** named after pell-mell, a seventeenth-century ball game adapted from the Italian game pallamaglio.
- **Piccadilly:** originally rendered as 'Piggadillo', in the seventeenth century the street bordered open fields where pigs were kept.
- **St James's:** the district is named after St James's Palace, which in turn was named after it was constructed in the sixteenth century on the site of a leper hospital named for St James the Less.

SOMETHING FOR THE WEEKEND

Traditional London clubs are a weekday affair. The historical reasons for this were social – gentlemen were thought of as retiring to the country at weekends, owning or staying in rural estates. Although this practice was never as widespread as popularly perceived, the prevailing wisdom continued for clubs.

The modern reason for London clubs closing at weekends is rather more practical: weekend closure is considered to be an easy economy, cutting staffing and operating costs for two days of the week. Assorted weekend 'trial openings', occasionally carried out, do seem to have borne out the suspicion that weekend business is unprofitable – unless a club is willing significantly to raise its subscriptions to subsidise the activity. This is not something many members have responded to with favour.

The result is that very few historic clubs are fully open at weekends: namely, the East India Club, the Lansdowne Club, the Oxford and Cambridge Club, the RAF Club, the Union Jack Club and the Victory Services Club, each of which have larger memberships, a large number of bedrooms, and maintain a full internal hotel operation seven days a week. Weekend visitation rights to these clubs are popular with other historic London clubs, and it is not uncommon to wander through them at weekends and encounter far more reciprocal members than members.

A handful of other historic clubs maintain some reduced service at weekends, whether it is breakfast only, or access (and sometimes minor meals) for overnight guests only. For weekend service, members are far better catered for in the modern clubs, found in Part II of Section 1 of this book.

EVENTS OF 'THE SEASON'

'The Season', whereby rural-based aristocrats would relocate to London over the spring and summer for several sporting and social occasions, has had varying definitions. Traditionally, it coincided with the parliamentary session, which ran from February to August, ending in time for the 'Glorious Twelfth' of August, when the shooting season would begin. Today, events of 'the Season' span the whole year, with the principal dates set out below. Most London clubs will celebrate some or most 'Season' events, whether in organising outings or in holding tie-in events of their own. As can be seen, many are nineteenth-century festivals whose creation was synonymous with the growth of clubs.

Clubs do not, by and large, celebrate religious festivals such as Christmas and Easter in and of themselves – members return to their families for those. However, a great many Christmas dinners are given in the run-up to the event, before the traditional Christmas closure, which usually lasts around a fortnight until the beginning of January.

Event	Inaugurated	Location
Lord Mayor's New Year's Parade.	1987.	City of London.
Burns Night.	1801.	Universal.
St David's Day.	12th century.	Universal.
Oxford and Cambridge Varsity Rugby Match.	1872.	StoneX Stadium, Hendon (since 2024); Twickenham (historically, 1921–2023).
St Patrick's Day.	1631.	Universal.
Oxford and Cambridge Boat Race.	1827.	Championship Thames route: Putney to Mortlake.
Crufts dog show.	1891.	National Exhibition Centre, Solihull, West Midlands.
Cheltenham Festival.	1860.	Cheltenham Racecourse, Gloucestershire.
Grand National.	1839.	Aintree Racecourse, Merseyside.
St George's Day.	5th century.	Universal.
Royal Caledonian Ball.	1849.	Grosvenor House Hotel, Park Lane.
Royal Windsor Horse Show.	1943.	Home Park, Windsor.
Glyndebourne Festival.	1934.	Glyndebourne, West Sussex.
Badminton Horse Trials.	1949.	Badminton House, Gloucestershire.
Chelsea Flower Show.	1912.	Royal Hospital Chelsea.
Epsom Derby.	1780.	Epsom Downs Racecourse, Surrey.
Chestertons Polo in the Park.	2009.	Hurlingham Club.
Royal Academy Summer Exhibition.	1769.	Burlington House, Piccadilly.
Trooping the Colour.	1748.	Horseguards Parade, St James's Park.
Garsington Opera.	1989.	Garsington Manor, Oxfordshire.
Royal Ascot.	1768.	Ascot Racecourse, Berkshire.
Cartier Queen's Cup – International Polo.	1960.	Guards Polo Club, Berkshire.
Wimbledon Championships.	1877.	All England Lawn Tennis and Croquet Club, Wimbledon.
Garter Service of the Order of the Garter.	1348.	Windsor Castle.
Pride in London.	1972.	Hyde Park Corner to Trafalgar Square.

Events of 'the Season'

Date
1 January.
25 January.
1 March.
A Saturday in March.
17 March.
The Saturday between Good Friday and Easter Sunday.
Four days encompassing the second weekend in March, from the preceding Thursday to the Sunday.
Four days from Tuesday to Friday, typically in the second full week of March.
A Saturday in the first half of April.
23 April, unless it clashes with the Octave of Easter, in which case it is the first Monday afterwards.
A Friday in mid-May.
Four or five days in mid-May, running until the Sunday.
May to August.
Five days in May, including one weekend.
Five or six days in late May, running up to the Saturday.
First Saturday in June.
Three days in early June, from Friday to Sunday.
Mid-June to late August.
King's Official Birthday (third Saturday in June for Charles III).
Late May to late July.
Five days in June, running from Tuesday to Saturday.
Three weeks in May and June.
Two weeks in late June and early July.
Garter Day, a Monday in June.
A Saturday in late June.

Event	Inaugurated	Location
British Grand Prix.	1926.	Silverstone Circuit, Northamptonshire.
Henley Royal Regatta.	1839.	Henley-on-Thames, Buckinghamshire and Berkshire.
Hampton Court Garden Festival.	1990.	Hampton Court Palace.
The Game Fair.	1958.	Variable.
Glorious Goodwood.	1802.	Goodwood Racecourse, West Sussex.
London Athletics Meet.	1953.	Variable.
Lord's Test Matches.	1892.	Marylebone Cricket Club, Lord's Cricket Ground, St John's Wood.
The Proms.	1895.	Royal Albert Hall, South Kensington.
Cowes Week.	1826.	Cowes, Isle of Wight.
Edinburgh Festival.	1947.	Edinburgh.
Royal Edinburgh Military Tattoo.	1949.	Edinburgh Castle.
Notting Hill Carnival.	1966.	Notting Hill.
Braemar Highland Gathering – The Games.	1832.	Braemar, Aberdeenshire.
Goodwood Revival.	1998.	Goodwood Circuit, West Sussex.
LAPADA Art and Antiques Fair.	2009.	Berkeley Square.
London Open House Festival.	1992.	London-wide.
Royal Ballet and Opera – Covent Garden season.	1734.	Royal Opera House, Covent Garden.
Horse of the Year Show.	1949.	National Exhibition Centre, Birmingham.
BFI London Film Festival.	1957.	Screens across central London; hosted by the British Film Institute.
Trafalgar Day.	1896.	Universal.
Royal Shakespeare Company Stratford season.	1827.	Royal Shakespeare Theatre and Swan Theatre, Stratford-upon-Avon, Warwickshire.
Lord Mayor's Show.	13th century.	City of London, from Guildhall to the Royal Courts of Justice.
St Andrew's Day.	11th century.	Universal.

Events of 'the Season'

Date
A Sunday in early July.
Six days on the first weekend in July, running from Tuesday to Sunday.
Six days in early July, running from Tuesday to Sunday.
Three days in late July, from Friday to Sunday.
Five days in late July and/or early August, running from Tuesday to Saturday.
July to August.
July to September.
Mid-July to early September.
First week in August, from Saturday to Friday.
Final three weeks in August.
August, during the Edinburgh Festival.
August Bank Holiday weekend.
First Saturday in September.
Three days in early September, from Friday to Sunday.
Six days in September or October, from Tuesday to Sunday.
Two consecutive weekends, in mid-to-late September.
September to July.
Five days in early October, from Wednesday to Sunday.
Eleven days in mid-October.
21 October.
October to May.
Second Saturday in November.
30 November.

SELECTED BETTING BOOK ENTRIES

Common topics of early bets included the chances of whether they or their mutual acquaintances would outlive one another, the odds of wives having babies, the chances of mutual acquaintances marrying, the political fortunes of governments, and the outcomes of by-elections.

'Octr. ye 5, 1743. Ld. Lincoln bets Ld. Winchilsea One hundred Guineas to fifty guineas, that the Dutchess Dowager of Marlborough does not survive the Dutchess Dowager of Cleveland.' – White's.

This was typical of many early bets that compared the likely lifespans of mutual acquaintances.

'April ye 17, 1744. Lord Coke betts Sr. Henry Liddell Five Guineas, that there is an engagement between ten ships, French and English before this day two months. [Added later:] Expired and paid.' – White's.

Many early bets focused on wars and battles. This trend would only continue up to and including the Napoleonic Wars.

'Feb. 10th, 1749. Mr. Fanshawe betts Sr. W. Stanhope twenty guineas, that there was not a play acted at Covent Garden Play house twenty years ago.' – White's.

Although the Theatre Royal, Covent Garden was not constructed until 1732, it was inspired by the premiere of The Beggar's Opera *in Lincoln's Inn Fields, 1728, so there had been plays performed near Covent Garden over twenty years earlier, but not on the site of the theatre.*

Selected Betting Book Entries

'March ye 31st, 1753. Mr. Fanshawe wagers Mr. O'Brien Ten guineas to one guinea, that the French Ambassador's Lady at Constantinople has not paid a visit to any of the Grand Vizier's Ladys.' – White's.

Diplomatic gossip was also a popular topic for bets.

'Octr. 15th, 1751. Mr. O'Brien betts Mr. Reynolds ten guineas, that Ld. Downe beats Ld. Northumberland in the raffle for the Dresden China.' – White's.

There was often gambling about gambling.

'29th June 1777. Mr. Boothby bets Mr. Townshend 50 Guineas that the American war is over before Christmas 1779, without America's being independent of the Crown of Britain.' – Brooks's.

'[No date – *c.* 1780s.] Lord Cholmondeley bets Mr St John five guineas that a ball fired out of a cannon horizontally does not rise before it falls. To be decided by a demonstration.' – Brooks's.

'[No date, but variously estimated as 1785 or May 1794.] Lord Cholmondeley has given two guineas to Lord Derby to receive 500 guineas whenever his Lordship fuck[s] a woman in a balloon one thousand yards from the earth. [Added later:] Off by consent.' – Brooks's.

Probably one of the best-known – and most notorious – bets in club history. The bet was later called off, by mutual agreement.

'June 1792. Colonel Fitzpatrick bets Colonel Tarleton that the slave trade is abolished before Episocopacy.' – Brooks's.

Political issues were a popular topic of bets.

'[No date, but *c.* 1790s.] Mr. W. Hanger bets Mr. Fox 50 guineas that the latter has the gout before the first.' – Brooks's.

'[No date, but *c.* 27 April 1807] Col. J. Osborn bets Sir J. Copley ten guineas to one, that he is returned for the County of Bedford in the

Parliament on the present Election, and ten guineas even that if another candidate joins him, they both come in.' – White's.

Not paid, as the Tory Sir John Osborn was unseated by two Whig candidates for this two-member constituency. From the 1800s onwards, bets on the outcome of elections became much more popular for the remainder of the nineteenth century, especially when at least one of the candidates was a club member.

'Jany. 21st, 1810. Mr. W[illiam]. Howard bets Mr. [Charles] Bouverie 5gs. that he is not elected a member of Watier's Club the first time he is balloted for. [Added later:] Paid.' – White's.

Betting on the chances of people navigating a waiting list to become a member of another club – or of being blackballed – was another popular topic for wagers.

'16th Novr. [1810]. Sweepstakes for the vacant office of Lord Chamberlain. 5gs. each.

Ld. Grimston	names	Lord Pembroke	pd.
Mr. Stanhope	"	Lord Salisbury	paid.
Mr. Brodrick	"	Lord Chesterfield	pd.
Sir J. Copley	"	Lord Aylesford	pd.
Mr. Chas. Jenkinson	"	Lord Hertford	
Col. Osborn	"	Duke of Montrose	pd.
Mr. Berkeley Paget	"	Lord Chatham	pd.
Lord H. Moore	"	Lord Winchilsea	pd.
N. B. This sweepstakes is closed.			
Nobody		Lord Limerick.' – White's.	

Guessing on prospective officeholders of government posts grew in popularity in the nineteenth century. In this instance, the office of Lord Chamberlain remained vacant for two years, until the appointment of the 2nd Marquess of Hertford in 1812, indicating Charles Jenkinson eventually won the sweepstake.

Selected Betting Book Entries

'January 1811. Mr. Howarth to give 50 Guineas to Sir John Copley whenever the King is sufficiently recovered to set aside the Regent.' – Brooks's.

King George III never recovered.

'May 4th, 1813. Lord de Clifford bets Sir G. Talbot five guineas, that there are not fifty new members elected at White's, between this day and the eleventh of July, 1813.

        G. Talbot.
        De Clifford. paid.

[Added later:] Lost July 6.' – White's.

'22nd March 1815. Colonel Ponsonby has given Mr. Howarth Ten Guineas to receive 100 Guineas should Louis XVIII or any Bourbon be reinstated on the Throne of France in the course of 12 months. (He being at this period dethroned.)' – Brooks's.

Louis XVIII was reinstated four months later, in the aftermath of Waterloo.

'March 1815. Mr. Brummell bets Mr. Raikes one hundred guineas to fifty guineas, that the Bourbons are on the throne of France on the 1st of May next. [Added later:] not paid 20th Jan. 1816.' – White's.

This was the final reference to Beau Brummell in the White's betting book, prior to his fleeing the country over accumulated debts. Brummell was due to pay up on this bet, as 1 May 1815 fell in the middle of the exile of Louis XVIII during the Hundred Days; and while he would be restored to the throne as Brummell predicted, it would not happen until 8 July 1815.

'[Not dated, early 1818.] Sir Joseph Copley bets Mr. Horace Seymour ten guineas, that six members of White's club die between the 9th Feby. 1818, and 9th Feby, 1819.

[Added later:] Name, Name, Name! Horace Seymour.
             Jos. Copley.' – White's.

A curiously undiplomatic bet.

'18th March 1825. Lord Sefton bets Lord Kensington 100 Guineas that he does not ride a horse now in his possession from London to Oxford between Sunrise and Sunset on the first day of June next.' – Brooks's.

'[Not dated, but 1827.] Mr. Raikes wagers Sir Joseph Sebright that in pronouncing the French word oeufs, the plural for eggs, the F is sounded. Five sovereigns. [Added later:] Mr. Raikes wagers the same with Lord Clonmell.' – White's.

'2nd Aug. 1833. Lord Ailsa bets Sir Robert Wilson ten sovereigns that Don Miguel is not on the throne of Portugal this day four months. [Added later:] Ailsa off.' – White's.

Although Portugal was riven by the Liberal Wars at the time, Miguel I was not forced to abdicate until 26 May 1834.

'[Not dated, but *c.* 1846–7.] Mr. Sturt bets Captain Macdonald £50 that Lord Stanley is never Prime Minister.

J. B. Macdonald

Gerard Sturt. paid.' – White's.

Lord Stanley, as the 14th Earl of Derby, would go on to become prime minister three times between 1852 and 1868.

'[Not dated, but *c.* April 1851.] Lord Adolphus FitzClarence bets Mr. George Bentinck £10 that there is not a shot fired in anger in London during the year 1851.' – White's.

'March 20th, 1853. Lord Bath bets Lord George Paget £500/10, that there is no uninterrupted communication by Electric Telegraph between England and India ten years from this date.

Bath.

George Paget.' – White's.

'July 17, 1856. Mr. F. Cavendish bets Mr. H. Brownrigg 2/1 that he does not kill the bluebottle fly before he goes to bed.

Selected Betting Book Entries

W. Frederick Cavendish.

Henry M. Brownrigg. Recd. H. B.' – White's.

'6th June 1857. Lord Colville bets Lord Clifden £5 that there will be a larger majority against the Jews in the House of Lords this year than there was last.

Colville.

Clifden.' – White's.

In the event, after several more rejections in the Lords, the Jewish Disabilities Bill eventually passed both Houses of Parliament the following spring, as the Jews Relief Act 1858, permitting Jews to sit in the House of Commons, but giving the Lords a right to administer its own ban, effectively continuing the ban in the Upper Chamber.

'March 22, 1878. Lord Rivers bets Lord Arlington £25 that this country is at war with some European power on or before this day six months.' – White's.

It wasn't.

'June 1913. Lord Osborne Beauclerk bets Lord Howick £1 that some women will be enfranchised before January 1st 1920.' – Brooks's.

'1st August 1914. Lord Murray bets Captain Murray Ten Guineas that if, arising out of the Austro-Serbian crisis, there is a general European War, there will be no crowned head in Europe except the King of England ten years from the date upon which the war breaks out.' – Brooks's.

'12th October 1914. Mr. Arthur Pollen bets Col. Le Roy-Lewis that no shot will be fired by the Allied Forces against the allied enemy in the present European War on or after the 31st December 1915. £1 even.' – Brooks's.

'28th October 1918. Mr. Oswald Partington bets Col. Arthur Murray £5 that by 1st December 1918 there will have been an official cessation of hostilities on the Western Front ... 30th October 1918. The above bet between Mr. Partington and Colonel Murray is doubled.' – Brooks's.

GAMES PLAYED INSIDE CLUBHOUSES

Card games are the mainstay of many of the older, Georgian-era clubs; those games traditionally found in clubs include baccarat (and its historic variant, chemin de fer), bezique, bridge, canasta, cribbage, faro, poker and whist.

Indeed, whist – a game often identified with Phileas Fogg, of Reform Club fame – is a product of Clubland, with the *Laws of Short Whist* having been published in 1865 by members of the Arlington Club on Grafton Street (now the Turf Club, relocated to Carlton House Terrace), seven years before the events of *Around the World in Eighty Days*. Those rules superseded earlier conventions practised since the 1810s by the Stratford Club (later the Portland Club), and were in turn ratified by a string of London clubs in the Victorian era, including the Army and Navy, Arthur's, Boodle's, Brooks's, the Carlton, the Conservative, the Garrick, the Guards, the Junior Carlton, the Portland, the Oxford and Cambridge, the Reform, the St James's and White's.

Bridge remains a particularly popular card game in Clubland, with an Inter-Club Duplicate Bridge tournament between the Athenæum, House of Lords, Hurlingham, In and Out, Lansdowne, MCC, Oxford and Cambridge, RAC, Reform, Roehampton and Savile.

Clubs had a wider **gambling culture** spread beyond card games, however – almost anything could be the subject of a bet. As the preceding section shows, betting books recorded a baffling array of bets on topics, on everything from the who's-in-and-who's-out gossip of politics, to the conduct of public affairs.

Games Played Inside Clubhouses

Gambling was essentially illegal under English law prior to the mid-nineteenth century. This did not stop gambling from being enormously fashionable – and added to the cachet of clubs as a discreet place where members could gamble out of sight. The Gaming Act 1845 legalised what were categorised as games of skill. It also rendered wagers unenforceable as matters of contract – which contributed to their slowly dying out, while also emphasising the importance of honour. The Betting Act 1853 essentially clamped down on proprietorial clubs that hosted gambling, while the Gaming-Houses Act 1854 enacted stiffer penalties.

However, the 1949–51 Royal Commission on Betting, Lotteries and Gaming eventually resulted in the Betting and Gaming Act 1960, which legalised a range of forms of gambling, and created the modern casino. From 1962, John Aspinall's Clermont Club was the first of a wave of legal casinos structured as private members' clubs, which operated under the legislation. London saw a crackdown on a wave of irregularities in these casinos in the late 1970s and early 1980s, but the Gambling Act 2005 has further liberalised the regime, under the regulation of the Gambling Commission.

Board games including **checkers** have long been very popular, and **backgammon** has been played in London clubs since the nineteenth century – though is far more popular today in the clubs of Boston, New York and Philadelphia than in London.

Chess is a far older game, dating back 1,500 years to antecedents in India and Persia, but arrived in Clubland somewhat later, becoming very fashionable in the Edwardian era. There remains today a London Clubs Social Chess Network, which plays both friendly and tournament matches against other clubs, nationally and internationally, combined with dinners. The premier tournament is the Hamilton-Russell Cup. Participating clubs include the Army and Navy, Athenæum, Chelsea Arts, East India, Hurlingham, In and Out, Lansdowne, MCC, NLC, Oriental, Oxford and Cambridge, RAC, Reform and Travellers Clubs. Some clubs produce so many chess players as to field multiple teams, others combine to produce joint teams. Recent international matches have included sorties against the Cercle de l'Union Interalliée in Paris, and the Real Casino the Madrid, as well as hosting in London the Cosmos Club of Washington, DC.

Snooker: born out of Clubland

Snooker first became an official game in a club. The Ootacamund Club, founded in 1841 in Ootacamund (or 'Ooty'), now Udhagamandalam, southern India, was the birthplace of this game. Ooty's cool climate at high altitude made it a popular British hill station in the nineteenth century, and British officers who were stationed elsewhere often diverted there in the summer months. A group of army officers who had first tried a version of snooker in an officer's mess in Jabalpur, central India, brought the game with them to the Ootacamund Club in 1875. One of the officers, Sir Neville Chamberlain (no relation to the later prime minister) then posted the first set of rules in the Club's billiard room, where they are still found today.

Billiards, snooker or pool?

Many traditional clubs have a 'billiard room', yet it is almost unheard of for any of the London clubs to now play billiards in them. Smaller snooker tables suffice. Boodle's, the Chelsea Arts Club, the East India Club, the Garrick Club, the Groucho Club, the National Liberal Club, the Oriental Club, the Oxford and Cambridge Club, Quo Vadis, the Reform Club, the Royal Automobile Club, the Savile Club and White's all have snooker tables. However, there are clubs in Australia and North America where billiards is still played.

Billiards, a French game that had evolved by the 1770s (otherwise known as Carom billiards) involves just three balls, and a table with no pockets which is typically 10 feet x 5 feet. Variants include English billiards, which fell into disuse by the late twentieth century, and American four-ball billiards.

Games Played Inside Clubhouses

Snooker involves up to twenty-two balls (including the white), and a table with six pockets that is typically 12 feet x 6 feet.

Pool also involves a six-pocket table – though generally with larger pockets than a snooker table – but the measurements can vary from 7 feet x 3.5 feet to 9 feet x 4.5 feet. The number of balls in pool can vary considerably, as can the rules.

One particular variant found in Clubland is Savile Snooker, which has been played at the Savile Club since around 1900. Its rules were first set down by Stephen Potter, author of the 'Lifemanship' books.

THE RULES OF SAVILE SNOOKER,*
as compiled by the 'Oldest Regular Player',
Stephen Potter, in 1968

What follows is a direct transcript from Stephen Potter's rules. At the time of transcription, it is believed that the game had already been played by Savilians since at least the dawn of the century.

The rules of Savile Snooker have never been written down. They represent the accumulation of civilised custom and word-of-mouth agreement. These suggestions, made by Oldest Regular Player (sic), are, it must be remembered, a first rough attempt only, although I [Potter] have had the advantage of help and criticism.

<u>1) Value and placing of balls</u>
Savile Snooker is basically 'volunteer', i.e. a colour may be attempted without first potting a red; but if no red is potted and the ball is missed, the value of the ball goes to the opponent.

The game is played with the normal number of reds. The spots for black, pink and blue are the ordinary snooker spots and the

---

* With thanks to the Savile Club for granting permission to reproduce these rules.

value – 7, 6 and 5 respectively are the same as the snooker values. But here the similarity ends; for the yellow and green are not used and the brown is put on a spot peculiar to this game – a point at the bottom of the table corresponding to the black spot at the top. The value of this Savile brown is not 4, as in other snooker games, but 8.

2) When and when not to volunteer

In the Savile game each player must at the start of the match hit a red. Once he has made contact with a red, he may volunteer whenever he wishes.

But remember:

(a) Although a red in baulk can be struck 'from hand' - i.e. from the D, <u>no colour lying in baulk</u> can be volunteered from hand.

(b) After three successive pots, from its spot, of the same colour, for the next shot the ball 'stays down'. And for this next shot, 'any ball free', e.g. no penalty for a missed colour. Ball is then replaced. Penalty for failure to replace: nil. ('Fault of Marker')

3) Last Stages of the Game

When a player pots the last red, any colour is free to him. If he chooses to pot the blue, the blue comes up once more ('blue immediately succeeding the last red' rule). But for the next shot in this same break, only the blue is free.

When the four colours only are left, blue is the 'free' ball, but the other colours may still be volunteered. When the blue is gone, pink is free, then black, then only brown will remain, and if the difference between the players is more than 8 points the game is over. ('One shot each at the brown', with farthing points involved, is a slightly tedious custom but not a rule).

'All on the brown'
If during the crucial moment the brown is missed, the game is over (penalty 8 points).

'Avoiding a draw'
If, after the last colour has been potted, the game is level, the brown is placed on the black spot and the white is played from hand. (This procedure is usually confined to competitions).

4) Additional Rules Peculiar to Savile Snooker
It is uniquely typical of the Savile that certain rules have been accepted because they make things more, not less, agreeable for the player. For instance: –

(i) Pushing
The push shot is allowed, partly because it seldom helps, and partly to avoid long wrangling arguments.

(ii) Nomination
The Player is under no obligation to nominate the colour at which he believes himself to be aiming.

(iii) Alternative Spots
If a colour's own spot is already covered by another ball, colour must be placed on nearest unoccupied spot (not on the next below in value). If all spots are covered, then the brown spot of orthodox snooker must be used – failing that the green spot, then yellow.

(iv) Balls Touching
If red is the 'on' ball and white is touching a colour, player may either volunteer or hit a red. But if white is touching a red, player is deemed to have hit a red. He can (a) play away, not necessarily hitting another red without penalty or (b) pot a red or (c) volunteer.

5) Fouls and Penalties

(a) Some of these have been dealt with under separate headings. Basically, the rule of orthodox snooker is followed; e.g. if the white is pocketed after first striking a red, penalty 4; after first striking a blue, penalty 5, and so on. It is the ball struck first which counts. Note: If a colour should have been played after a red, but a red is struck instead, the penalty is 5, the Player having been assumed to have aimed at the blue however preposterous the shot might have in fact been.

If a red is inadvertently potted when a blue is struck first, penalty 5. If a black is potted when a red is attempted, penalty 7. Here is the 'highest value ball involved' which determines the amount.

(b) Some typical penalties:
White, having hit red first, goes into pocket ... 4
White, having hit colour, goes into pocket ... value of first colour hit.
Blue is potted, but so is black ... 7 (highest value same stroke involved in foul).
Blue is potted but so is black and pink in same stroke ('Lawrence Gilliam Treble') ... 7
White, on a colour (pink) misses it. If no other ball is touched, player is 'deemed to have been on blue' because of the No Nomination rule.
Pink is potted, but red goes in on same stroke ... 6 (value of highest ball involved).

(c) Touching the ball

Fouls involving the inadvertent touching of the ball with any part of the body, clothes, cue or rest bring a break to an end and involve a penalty according to the value of the ball touched (red to count 4). Savile here follows orthodox snooker. The difference lies in procedure. In the (almost invariable) absence of a referee or marker, the player does not declare a foul: his opponent, if he sees it, claims it. This is his responsibility and traditional right.

If, in removing a rest, a ball is inadvertently touched, no penalty is involved <u>if the balls have stopped rolling</u>. Moved ball should be replaced.

Snookers

(a) As in orthodox snooker, a player is 'snookered' from the next ball 'on' if he is unable to hit directly any part he wishes of the hemisphere. But if he is snookered after a foul, and no reds ore 'on', <u>the nearest coloured ball only is free</u>. This rule is peculiar to Savile.

(b) If after this 'nearest coloured ball' shot there is no score, and the ball hit snookers the player's opponent, this ball is free for the opponent's next shot.

(c) A fairly recent new rule could and should be adapted for Savile Snooker. It is worded thus:

After a foul stroke by his opponent, a player may play from the position left (with a free ball, if snookered) <u>or ask his opponent to play the next stroke</u>.

The notion here is to stop a player receiving benefit from his own foul, e.g. his opponent may not only be snookered but angled as well. Or competitor may purposely play for a miss and players are reminded that this stroke, useful and honourable in billiards, is not allowed in any form of snooker.

Etiquette

Feelings about Etiquette are particularly vague among players of this game. Everybody knows that no one should actually place his hand or foot on the table while his opponent is playing, should not stand in his line of sight, and should not dance up and down during the few seconds while his opponent is actually making his shot.

Most of the customs are concerned with fouls.

(a) 'No tie fouls' means that no penalty is involved if the player's tie touches or moves a ball.

(b) Claiming. It seems now to be the custom not to claim a foul unless the ball is actually seen to move.

(c) It is not considered a decent act or necessary evidence of sportsmanship if, in normal circumstances, a player overlooks a foul by his opponent.

Safety Play

No kind of stigma attaches to safety play – a special art of this game. For various reasons, unless on a very 'dangerous' table, no other safety shot is possible, it is not considered good Savile play to put the white repeatedly in the middle of the reds.

Slow Play

One or two attempts have been made over the past 10 years to legislate against a modern tendency to quite unreasonably slow play. 'Not more than 45 minutes for a game if other members want to play', etc., but that is not really the point, for allowance must be made for the fact that the end game is one of the beauties of Savile Snooker. Speed between turns on the other hand is easy to maintain, and those who dwell too long on the stroke, or change their minds on the direction after they have assumed position, are never best strikers of the ball. It can also be remembered that when a game is lost beyond reasonable hope of recall, the phrase 'I retire' involves <u>no loss of face whatever</u> in the eyes of members waiting to play.

Slow play is catching. Beginners should try to model tempo on the brisker styles, not on the over deliberate.

The Reynolds System of Scoring*

Savile Snooker should be played for money – even if the money is as small as farthing points instituted when the game started 50 years ago. Those who find farthing points rather fiddling prefer another method which commemorates a former member of the club, William Ellis Reynolds, a great student and spectator of the game. Namely, if point difference at one game is fifty or less, loser pays for the table.

If point difference is more than 50, loser for the table plus one penny for every point over 50.

The Three Ball Game

There are a few rules which are or should be peculiar to this excellent threesome game, all against all:

1) Handicap difference should not be doubled, as in singles, but increased by one third.
2) Half-way through the game, the order of play should be reversed.
3) If a player leaves a complete snooker, he should be the sole beneficiary of any miss or foul which follows.

This ends the Rules of Savile Snooker. Their status is as always: in draft, for comment and discussion. There is no deadline.

QUEENSBERRY RULES OF BOXING, 1864

Devised by the 9th Marquess of Queensberry for the National Sporting Club in Covent Garden. Until then, boxing had been considered an uncouth sport, but the National Sporting Club's rules were intended to make it a sport fit for gentlemen.

---

* Note that the habit of playing for money at the Savile has since fallen into disuse.

1. To be a fair stand-up boxing match in a twenty-four-foot ring, or as near that size as possible.
2. No wrestling or hugging allowed.
3. The rounds to be of three minutes' duration, and one minute's time between rounds.
4. If either man falls through weakness or otherwise, he must get up unassisted, ten seconds to be allowed to him to do so, the other man meanwhile to return to his corner, and when the fallen man is on his legs the round to be resumed and continued till the three minutes have expired. If one man fails to come to the scratch in the ten seconds allowed, it shall be in the power of the referee to give his award in favour of the other man.
5. A man hanging on the ropes in a helpless state, with his toes off the ground, shall be considered down.
6. No seconds or any other person to be allowed in the ring during the rounds.
7. Should the contest be stopped by any unavoidable interference, the referee to name the time and place as soon as possible for finishing the contest, so that the match must be won and lost, unless the backers of the men agree to draw the stakes.
8. The gloves to be fair-sized boxing gloves of the best quality and new.
9. Should a glove burst, or come off, it must be replaced to the referee's satisfaction.
10. A man on his knees is considered down, and if struck is entitled to the stakes.
11. That no shoes or boots with springs allowed.
12. The contest in all other respects to be governed by the Revised Rules of the London Prize Ring.

GAMES PLAYED OUTSIDE CLUBHOUSES

Apart from the dedicated sports clubs with sprawling suburban grounds, most of the city clubs of central London do not have the capacity to play outdoor games on-site. This does not prevent a profusion of societies including **archery, cricket, fishing, golf** and **shooting** (anything from clay pigeons to grouse). However, these are typically organised as club outings off-site, often at the weekend. Aside from the handful of clubs maintaining a country clubhouse (see p. 170), most of these are organised privately.

Buck's is an exception to this, in that cricket has long been played indoors there, at the bar, with a wicket marked on the bar counter for that purpose.

One of the more eccentric attempts to combine outdoor sports with traditional London clubs was the **Clubland Handicap** of the early twentieth century. This was an underground golf tournament of questionable legality, sometimes played at night, which teed off outside White's at the top of St James's Street, and followed an L-shaped route down Pall Mall, passing all the clubhouses along the way, ending up in front of the Union Club in Trafalgar Square. The game had to be played with great swiftness, as one of the main objectives was to avoid being arrested by passing policemen. Points were deducted for smashed windows.

CLUBS THAT STEPHEN FRY HAS APOLOGISED TO FOR TAKING DRUGS IN

In his 2014 memoir, actor and writer Stephen Fry offers an unreserved apology 'to the owners, managers and representatives' of a number of venues where he claims to have taken drugs during a fifteen-year cocaine addiction from 1986 to 2001. He lists the following London clubs in his 'line-up':*

Army and Navy Club; Arts Club; Beefsteak Club; Boodle's; Brooks's; Carlton Club; Chelsea Arts Club; East India Club; Garrick Club; Groucho Club; House of Commons; House of Lords; National Liberal Club; Naval and Military ('In and Out') Club; Oxford and Cambridge Club; Reform Club; Royal Air Force Club; Royal Automobile Club; Savage Club; Savile Club; Soho House – 40 Greek Street; Travellers Club; White's. (Fry also lists the old BBC Television Centre, prior to the conversion of one of its wings into White City House.)

Needless to say, none of the clubs listed above has ever condoned the drug-taking (quite the reverse); and shortly after the memoir was published, at least one of them circulated a memo to members stressing that illegal drug-taking on the premises would not be tolerated.

---

* Stephen Fry, *More Fool Me: A Memoir* (London: Penguin/Michael Joseph, 2014), pp. 69–71.

TAXES PAST AND PRESENT THAT HAVE BEEN PAID BY CLUBS

Past – no longer paid

Card tax – from 1711 until 1960, all packs of playing cards were subject to a card tax, which oscillated between sixpence, and two shillings and sixpence, until the tax was slashed to threepence in 1862, remaining at that level until its abolition ninety-eight years later.

Window tax – from 1696 until 1851, this was intended to tax households relative to their affluence, by counting the number of windows on a building. Notoriously, some houses had their windows bricked up to reduce their owners' tax liabilities. Examples of this can be seen in surviving period buildings, such as the Buck's clubhouse.

Coal tax – duties on coal had been payable to the Corporation of London in various forms since the Middle Ages, affecting consumers and businesses for dozens of miles around London. In 1861, the boundary was shortened to the Metropolitan Postal District (the area then covered by London), and in 1890 the tax was abolished altogether by the new London County Council.

--- Present ---

Business rates – levied by the local authority, these have seen hefty increases in recent years, especially in Westminster, which covers most of 'Clubland', although some other central London clubs are covered by Bermondsey, Camden, the City of London, Hackney, Hammersmith and Fulham, Kensington and Chelsea, and Richmond. These have increased significantly both before and after the Covid-19 pandemic.

Value Added Tax (VAT) – generally fixed at 20 per cent on goods and services, though some items, such as books and magazines, are zero-rated. Some member-owned clubs are mutuals, and are exempt from taxes like VAT on some transactions, as they would otherwise effectively be trading with themselves. (So, a club will always pay VAT when buying alcohol. But it may not charge VAT on members' drinks purchases, even though it will always have to charge VAT on guests' drink purchases.) Others – particularly proprietary clubs – enjoy no such relief.

Corporation tax – depends on the scope of their trade, and whether they make a taxable profit.

Income tax – this is paid by all club staff, whether as employees or as workers.

National Insurance – again, this is paid by all employers and club staff.

Alcohol duty – this is often paid further up the supply chain, not necessarily directly by the Club, but with the costs passed down to them.

Stamp Duty Land Tax – which is only payable when moving or varying premises; though some clubs have performed complicated manoeuvres to be exempt from this.

RECIPROCATION

One of the perks of membership of a club is the use of reciprocal clubs. By and large, this is highly valued by the members, but it can also be the cause of some despair and anguish for committees and staff.

Club members love exploring reciprocal clubs. It's an adventure; an opportunity to see 'how the other half lives'; or, at least, how other clubs exist, and how things might be done differently. In particular, they can be a godsend to members travelling abroad: they provide a quirky way to get to know another city, and can offer a safe, central, inexpensive and reputable place to stay.

By contrast, those engaged in club management can regard reciprocal clubs more warily. Reciprocation can mean outsiders coming in – some clubs welcome this, while others seem positively terrified of it. This can depend on many things, from a five-hundred-member club fearing being overwhelmed by hordes from a fifty-thousand-member club, to resenting being gawked at by 'smoking-room tourists'. There is also the sheer logistical feat of explaining the hosting club to a reciprocal member, showing newcomers around, and holding them to the rules: this can be a doddle if there are two reciprocal visitors a day, but a trial if there are two hundred. And of course, it depends in no small part on the size and capacity of the hosting club.

A trade-off is usually found around shared interests and shared culture – this is why the grander yacht clubs of the world tend to reciprocate with one another; or the automobile clubs of Dublin, Melbourne, Monte Carlo, Paris and Sydney being a natural fit for the Royal Automobile Club. It is also likely that internationally themed clubs like the Travellers, and cosmopolitan clubs like the National Liberal, are naturally more predisposed towards extensive reciprocal lists, with their emphasis on travel and global connections.

The men-only aristocratic clubs of London have a surprisingly wide range of 'old money' men-only counterparts around the world. These include the Sällskapet of Stockholm; the Wiener Renn-Verein and St Johann's Club of Vienna; Le Cercle Royal du Parc of Brussels; Le Jockey Club and Nouveau Cercle de l'Union of Paris; Le Cercle de la Terrasse of Geneva; Le Cercle de la Grand Société de Berne; La Gran Peña of Madrid; the Turf Club and Real Clube Tauromáquico Português of Lisbon; the Circolo della Caccia and Circolo Antico Tiro a Volo of Rome; the Domino Club of Bologna; the Societa del Giardino of Milan; the Bohemian Club and Pacific-Union Club of San Francisco; the Club of Odd Volumes of Boston; the Boston Club of New Orleans; the Knickerbocker Club, Union Club and the Brook of New York; the Philadelphia Club; the Jockey Club Brasileiro of Rio de Janeiro; the Jockey Club of Buenos Aires; the (unrelated) Australian Clubs of Melbourne and Sydney; the Melbourne Club and Melbourne Savage Club; the Weld Club of Perth; Kasumi Kaikan of Tokyo; and the Sind Club of Karachi. They have their own counterparts in 'old money' women-only clubs around the world, like the St Rule Club of St Andrews; the Colony Club and Cosmopolitan Club of New York; the Acorn Club and Cosmopolitan Club of Philadelphia; the Mount Vernon Club of Baltimore; the Sulgrave Club of Washington, DC; the Metropolitan Club and the Town and Country Club of San Francisco; the Alexandra Club of Melbourne; the Lyceum Clubs of Adelaide, Brisbane and Melbourne; and the Helena May Club of Hong Kong.

The size and scope of a club's reciprocals list can be down to many conflicting pressures. Members often regard an extensive list as highly desirable, maximising their own choice, and affirming their own club as being esteemed by its peers. Managers often prefer a smaller, more tightly managed list. Some club managers encourage their peers to keep a club's reciprocals lists select. However, it is not always the case that a large list is in any way diluted in quality, or that a small list is

Reciprocation

necessarily well-managed. In truth, the contents of the list often owes a great deal to coincidence, personal acquaintance and luck – for instance, a London club may happen to approach a Buenos Aires club, which has been consistently refusing all approaches for thirty years, during the two-year reign of a chairman who is open to forging new arrangements, before his replacement by another officeholder who is averse to adding any further clubs to the list.

There are thousands of clubs worldwide of the type covered in this book, but no club reciprocates with all of them, or anything more than a fraction of them. Members are often surprised to hear that ignorance is one of the biggest determinants of a reciprocals list: 'We tried looking for something there, but there just aren't any clubs in that place' is a common insistence, often blissfully unaware of some small, low-profile gems found in many a city.

Reciprocal clubs can offer wildly differing welcomes. At one end of the scale, the porter may be frightfully excited that someone has come all the way from London, and from such a prestigious club as yours to boot, and breathlessly summon the chairman and the secretary to show you around. At the other end, you may be regarded with cool disdain and a raised eyebrow, met with a blank stare when you say which club you have come from ('Is that even on our reciprocals list? I shall have to check, sir'), or simply waved on, to find your own way in. Club bedrooms are a mecca for the cognoscenti; if the establishment has over two hundred of them, you can usually ring up at a week's notice to book a room. If the Club only has half a dozen bedrooms, then pre-booking at least six months in advance is essential.

There is also a more low-key form of reciprocation across London, found in the annual August exchange. August is usually the quietest month for London clubs – in the nineteenth century, it saw 'the Great Stink', and while modern sanitation means that central London is no longer to be avoided in the summer months, it can still be unpleasantly hot and humid. This is particularly the case in many clubs occupying older listed buildings, which do not offer effective air conditioning. And many members holiday in August, while their children are back from school. Accordingly, some clubs still carry over a traditional exchange dating to the days of partial or complete closure in the month of August. These are, however, ad hoc arrangements year by year, with no guarantee of renewal from one year to the next, and a certain amount of annual bartering going on. And it is not unheard of for members of even the most august establishments to go wild at the range of choice suddenly available to them, only to find that their exuberant antics have resulted in the overnight termination of the agreement by an unimpressed management at the reciprocal club, drawing undying animosity from their fellow members in their own club. The question clubs have reluctantly to engage with, when setting up a reciprocal agreement, is often, 'Can all of our members behave when they're off-site?'

CLUB ANNIVERSARIES

Clubs love an anniversary. The below shows which anniversaries have been celebrated by clubs:

Tercentennial (300 years): White's.
Semiquincentennial (250 years): Boodle's; Brooks's; Royal Thames Yacht.
Bicentennial (200 years): Athenæum; Cavalry and Guards; Oriental; Oxford and Cambridge; Travellers.
Terquasquicentennial (175 years): Carlton; City of London; East India; Farmers; Garrick; Reform.
Sesquicentennial (150 years): Arts; Hurlingham; Naval and Military ('In and Out'); Pratt's; Royal Kennel; Savage; Savile; Turf.
Quasquicentennial (125 years): Beefsteak; Caledonian; Chelsea Arts; City University; Den Norske Klub; Guildhall; London Sketch; National Liberal; Queen's; RAC; University Women's; Winchester House.
Centennial (100 years): Buck's; RAF; Roehampton; Royal Over-Seas League; Union Jack; Victory Services.
Nonaginetennial (90 years): Royal Ocean Racing.
Octogintennial (80 years): Lansdowne.
Semisesquicentennial (75 years): New Evaristo; Special Forces.
Septuagennial (70 years): Civil Service; Gerry's.
Sexagennial (60 years): Annabel's; Aspinall's.
Semicentennial (50 years): Le Beaujolais; Mark's; Tramp.
Quadragennial (40 years): Academy; Brydges Place; Harry's Bar; Sloane; St. James's.
Tricennial (30 years): 40 Greek Street; Bath and Racquets; Groucho; Mosimann's; Union.
Vigintennial (20 years): Century; Electric House; Frontline; George; Home House; Walbrook.
Decennial (10 years): 5 Hertford Street; 12 Hay Hill; 76 Dean Street; Eight; High Road House; Ivy; Little House, Mayfair; Purple Dragon; Quo Vadis; Shoreditch House; Vout-O-Reenee's.

THE COMMITTEE

The time has come, apparently. A member sidles up, and says, 'You've been a member for a while now...', or else observes that you have some talents that the Club could use, typically around finance. And so they suggest that you might throw your hat into the ring for the next round of elections to the Club's committee, or board, or council, or whatever they call their governing body.

This is to be approached with the greatest scepticism and trepidation. If you were to acquiesce, you can expect nothing but months or years on end of misery and heartache. And yet it is the committee which keeps so much of the Club going; and without selfless, philanthropic members fulfilling this thankless task, the Club as we know it would not exist.

People often imagine being on the governing body is a cushy existence. Yet committee members have higher blood pressure than most club members. They often surrender at least two or three full working days a week, and much of their weekends. They also have the broader waistlines that come with entertaining large numbers of people – almost invariably at their own considerable expense, for they can easily spend several thousand pounds a year (or even tens of thousands) in oiling the wheels of the Club.

Club committees are often rife with all manner of intrigue, factionalism, gossip, supposition, amateurishness, incompetence and high-handedness. The cream does not always rise to the top – it is just as often the personally ambitious, the self-serving and those with the most time on their hands who end up chairing a club. Since holding one of the senior posts can be close to a full-time job, it naturally favours the retired or those with an independent income. This is a pity, as some of the most able chairs of clubs have busy working lives, but are able to bring considerable current expertise, rather than skill sets which peaked several decades ago.

There is also a recurring sense of impotence on many club committees. Members are often elected on the assumption that they are going to wield some executive function, only to find on taking office that their powers are quite limited. For one thing, there can be decades of governance past practice to navigate, never set down in writing but virtually set in stone as 'the way we do things around here'. This often involves divided responsibilities between rival committees, jealously feuding for control over matters such as food, wine, membership, reciprocation and licensing arrangements.

Club committees also exist in a state of permanent creative and administrative tension with the full-time staff. The committee is transient – its members will be gone in three or five years. But the Club's chief executive or dining room manager may be there for over a decade. And as they are ultimately responsible for balancing the books, they can decide whether to adjust their strategies to the committee's whims, or quietly undermine and ignore them. This is even more the case in a proprietary club, where the committee may be little more than a talking shop, and the staff are only answerable to the proprietor – not the members. In a member-owned club, personal and professional relationships are more complicated.

Serving on a club committee can be one of the most stretching, rewarding and worthwhile things for which to volunteer. Individual members can and do make a difference in saving a club and in steering its future. But it is fraught with peril and often ends in tears.

THE BATTLE OF THE SEXES

The below lists when single-sex clubs admitted members of the opposite sex as *full* members:*

1900: The Club for Acts and Actors.
1918: House of Commons.
1927: Little Ship Club.
1946: Hurlingham Club.
1958: House of Lords.
1966: Chelsea Arts Club; Guildhall Club; Royal Air Force Club.
1975: Farmers Club.
1976: National Liberal Club; Sloane Club.
1979: Royal Kennel Club.
1981: Reform Club.
1991: Magic Circle.
1994: Cavalry and Guards Club; City University Club.
1995: Army and Navy Club.
1996: Arts Club; Oxford and Cambridge Club.
1998: Marylebone Cricket Club; Royal Automobile Club.
1999: Naval and Military ('In and Out') Club.
2002: Athenæum.
2007: Yeoman Warders Club.
2008: Carlton Club.
2010: Oriental Club.

---

* List does not include forms of associate membership, giving only partial access to the Club, or one-off instances of honorary membership; but routine processing of applications on an equal basis.

The Battle of the Sexes

2011: Caledonian Club; City of London Club.
2014: Royal Thames Yacht Club.
2018: Langham Sketch Club.
2022: London Sketch Club.
2023: Pratt's.
2024: Flyfishers' Club; Garrick Club.

Clubs that have always been men only for full membership: Bath and Racquets Club; Beefsteak Club; Boodle's; Brooks's; Buck's; East India Club; National Club; Portland Club; Savage Club; Savile Club; Turf Club; Travellers Club; White's.

Club that has always been women only: University Women's Club.

Clubs that have always been mixed sex: 1 Warwick; 5 Hertford Street; 12 Hay Hill; 67 Pall Mall; Academicians' Room; Academy Club; Admiralty Arch Club; Annabel's; Apollo's Muse; Arboretum; Aspinall's; BAFTA; BBC Club; Le Beaujolais Club; Brydges Place Club; Cambridge House; Century; Civil Service Club; Cloud Twelve; The Clubhouse; The Conduit; Curtain Club; The Dally; Eight; Frontline Club; George; Gerry's; Groucho Club; Harry's Bar; Home Grown; Home House; The House of KOKO; Ivy Club; Keystone Crescent; Lansdowne Club; Maison Estelle; Mark's Club; The Ministry; Mortimer House; Mosimann's; New Evaristo Club; NEXUS Club; Ognisko Polskie; Oswald's; Pasley Tyler; Purple Dragon; Roehampton Club; The Roof Gardens; Royal Ocean Racing Club; Royal Over-Seas League; Shoreditch Arts Club; Snail Club; Soho House; Special Forces Club; Ten Trinity Square; The Twenty Two; Union Club; Upstairs at the Department Store; Vout-O-Reenee's; Walbrook Club.

THE CLUBS OF UK PRIME MINISTERS

The list only includes London clubs – for instance, Winston Churchill's first club was the Bangalore United Service Club (now the Bangalore Club), which he joined as a young subaltern in India in the 1890s; and after the Second World War, Churchill continued to accept a flurry of honour memberships from around the globe, up to and including the Salmagundi Club of New York, whose invitation he accepted in January 1965, just a few days before his death.

The list does not include instances where a prime minister declined an offer of honorary membership – as with Margaret Thatcher and the Athenæum in 1979.

Robert Walpole (Whig, 1721–42): Kit-Cat Club; White's.

1st Earl of Wilmington (Whig, 1742–3): Kit-Cat Club.

Henry Pelham (Whig, 1743–54): White's.

1st Duke of Newcastle (Whig, 1754–6, 1757–62): Kit-Cat Club; White's.

4th Duke of Devonshire (Whig, 1756–7): White's.

3rd Earl of Bute (Tory, 1762–3): *None known.*

George Grenville (Whig, 1763–5): White's.

2nd Marquess of Rockingham (Whig, 1765–6, 1782): White's.

William Pitt the Elder, 1st Earl of Chatham (Whig, 1766–8): White's.

3rd Duke of Grafton (Whig, 1768–70): Brooks's; White's.

Lord North (Tory, 1770–82): Brooks's; White's.

2nd Earl of Shelburne (Whig, 1782–3): Boodle's.

The Clubs of UK Prime Ministers

3rd Duke of Portland (Whig, later Tory, 1783, 1807–9): Brooks's; White's.

William Pitt the Younger (Tory, 1783–1801, 1804–6): Brooks's; White's.

Henry Addington (Tory, 1801–4): White's.

1st Baron Grenville (Whig, 1806–7): White's.

Spencer Perceval (Tory, 1809–12): White's.

2nd Earl of Liverpool (Tory, 1812–27): Athenæum; White's.

George Canning (Tory, 1827): Athenæum; White's.

1st Viscount Goderich (Tory, 1827–8): White's.

1st Duke of Wellington (Tory, 1828–30, 1834): Army and Navy Club; Athenæum; Carlton Club; City of London Club; Crockford's; Oriental Club; Oxford and Cambridge Club; Travellers Club; Union Club; United Service Club; United University Club; White's.

2nd Earl Grey (Whig, 1830–4): Brooks's; Travellers Club.

2nd Viscount Melbourne (Whig, 1834, 1835–41): Brooks's; Reform Club.

Sir Robert Peel (Conservative, 1834–5, 1841–6): Athenæum; Carlton Club; Union Club.

Lord John Russell, later 1st Earl Russell (Whig, later Liberal, 1846–52, 1865–6): Athenæum; Brooks's; Reform Club; Travellers Club.

14th Earl of Derby (Conservative, 1852, 1858–9, 1866–8): Athenæum; Carlton Club; Travellers Club.

4th Earl of Aberdeen (Peelite, 1852–5): Athenæum; White's.

3rd Viscount Palmerston (Liberal, 1855–8, 1859–65): Athenæum; Brooks's; Oxford and Cambridge Club; Reform Club; Travellers Club.

Benjamin Disraeli, later 1st Earl of Beaconsfield (Conservative, 1868, 1874–80): Athenæum; Carlton Club; Crockford's; Grillion's; Junior Carlton Club; St Stephen's Club; Westminster Reform Club.

William Ewart Gladstone (Liberal, 1868–74, 1880–5, 1886, 1892–4): Carlton Club; National Liberal Club; Oxford and Cambridge Club; Reform Club; United University Club.

3rd Marquess of Salisbury (Conservative, 1885–6, 1886–92, 1895–1902): Carlton Club; White's.

5th Earl of Rosebery (Liberal, 1894–5): Athenæum; Brooks's; National Liberal Club; Reform Club.

Arthur Balfour (Conservative, 1902–5): Athenæum; Carlton Club; Royal Automobile Club; Savile Club; Travellers Club; White's.

Sir Henry Campbell-Bannerman (Liberal, 1905–8): Athenæum; Brooks's; National Liberal Club; Oxford and Cambridge Club; Reform Club.

H. H. Asquith (Liberal, 1908–16): Athenæum; Brooks's; National Liberal Club; Reform Club.

David Lloyd George (Liberal, later National Liberal, 1916–22): 1920 Club; Athenæum; National Liberal Club; Reform Club.

Andrew Bonar Law (Conservative, 1922–3): Carlton Club.

Stanley Baldwin (Conservative, 1923–4, 1924–9, 1935–7): Athenæum; Carlton Club; MCC; Travellers Club; United University Club.

Ramsay MacDonald (Labour, later National Labour, 1924, 1929–35): Athenæum; National Labour Club; National Liberal Club; Parliamentary Labour Club.

Neville Chamberlain (Conservative, 1937–40): Athenæum; Carlton Club.

Sir Winston Churchill (Conservative, 1940–5, 1951–5): 1920 Club; Athenæum; Boodle's; Buck's; Carlton Club; Cavalry Club; City of London Club; Constitutional Club; Devonshire Club; Hurlingham Club; Junior Carlton Club; National Liberal Club; Reform Club; Roehampton Club; Royal Automobile Club; Turf Club.

Clement Attlee (Labour, 1945–51): Athenæum; Oxford and Cambridge Club.

Sir Anthony Eden (Conservative, 1955–7): Buck's; Carlton Club; MCC.

Harold Macmillan (Conservative, 1957–63): Athenæum; Beefsteak Club; Buck's; Carlton Club; Guards (later Cavalry and Guards) Club; Junior Carlton Club; MCC; Oxford and Cambridge Club; Pratt's; Turf Club.

Sir Alec Douglas-Home (Conservative, 1963–4): Carlton Club; MCC; Travellers Club.

Harold Wilson (Labour, 1964–70, 1974–6): Athenæum.

Edward Heath (Conservative, 1970–4): Athenæum; Buck's; Carlton Club; MCC; Royal Ocean Racing Club; Royal Thames Yacht Club; St Stephen's Club.

James Callaghan (Labour, 1976–9): Athenæum.

The Clubs of UK Prime Ministers

Margaret Thatcher (Conservative, 1979–90): Buck's; Carlton Club; St Stephen's Club.

John Major (Conservative, 1990–7): Athenæum; Buck's; Carlton Club; Farmers Club; MCC; Pratt's.

Tony Blair (Labour, 1997–2007): 5 Hertford Street; Commonwealth Club.

Gordon Brown (Labour, 2007–10): Caledonian Club.

David Cameron (Conservative, 2010–16): 5 Hertford Street; Carlton Club; Mark's; Pratt's; St Stephen's Club; White's.

Theresa May (Conservative, 2016–19): Athenæum; Carlton Club; MCC.

Boris Johnson (Conservative, 2019–22): 5 Hertford Street; Beefsteak Club; Carlton Club; Garrick Club.

Liz Truss (Conservative, 2022): 5 Hertford Street; Carlton Club.

Rishi Sunak (Conservative, 2022–4): Carlton Club; Conduit.

Sir Keir Starmer (Labour, 2024–): *None known.*

PERCENTAGE OF A CLUB'S MEMBERS LISTING THEIR CLUB MEMBERSHIP IN AN ENTRY IN THE LATEST (2024) EDITION OF *WHO'S WHO*

Club(s)	Share
House of Commons; House of Lords	100%
Garrick	37%
Athenæum; Beefsteak	36%
Pratt's	24%
Brooks's	18%
Travellers	16%
White's	15%
Reform	12%
All England Lawn Tennis; Boodle's	11%
Carlton	10%
Guildhall; Turf	7%
Caledonian; Savage; Savile	6%
Army and Navy; Oxford and Cambridge; Walbrook	5%
Buck's; Cavalry and Guards; Chelsea Arts; Groucho	4%
Arts; East India; Farmers; MCC; National Liberal; Royal Thames Yacht	3%
Brydges Place; City of London; Frontline; Lansdowne; Naval and Military; Oriental; Queen's; Royal Automobile; Royal Over-Seas League; Special Forces; University Women's	2%
67 Pall Mall; Academicians' Room; Bath and Racquets; Century; City University; Hurlingham; Little Ship; London Sketch; Mark's; Oswald's; Roehampton; Royal Air Force; Sloane	1%

Percentage Listing Their Club Membership in Who's Who *(2024)*

Figures are rounded to the nearest per cent. Not listed are clubs that either averaged 0 per cent or else declined to disclose a total membership figure (which made it impossible to calculate a percentage). Since *Who's Who* depends on self-declaration – and not all entries are necessarily accurate or up-to-date – it remains a matter of interpretation as to whether the above signifies distinction (from a club member qualifying for a *Who's Who* entry in the first place), self-promotion or transparency.

SOME ANIMALS ARE MORE EQUAL THAN OTHERS

Clubland may not seem like much of a menagerie, but a surprising amount of wildlife has been known to crop up.

Dogs

A smattering of modern clubs welcome dogs: the George in Mayfair (which was named after the late Mark Birley's dachshund) and the Snail Club in Soho both proclaim themselves to be 'dog-friendly clubs', as did the now-departed Black's. These clubs are very much the exception to the rule, however. Many clubs have an explicit 'no dogs' rule; indeed, the standard form of words copied-and-pasted by many older clubs singles out dogs as being banned, rather than pets more generally.

Cats

Cats are even rarer than dogs in Clubland, save for where they are gainfully employed on staff, in the exalted position of chief mouser, originally a government role dating back to the reign of Henry VIII. The speaker of the House of Commons keeps two cats, Clem and Attlee, while the Oriental Club has Fliss the Club Cat.

Some Animals Are More Equal Than Others

Puppets

Clubs have been known to appoint non-humans as members. The Magic Circle's only non-human member, Sooty (the original glove puppet owned and operated by the late magician Harry Corbett), 'lives' in the Club's museum.

Foxes

Foxes are a surprisingly common sight in Clubland. It is not only the sporting establishments with capacious grounds like the Hurlingham and the Roehampton which have harboured foxes. St James's Park alone is home to an estimated several hundred foxes, so that it is not unusual to see them wandering in broad daylight, along nearby patches of greenery like Waterloo Gardens, running alongside the Athenæum, Travellers, Reform and Turf clubs.

Vermin

The inevitable by-product of a city filled with old buildings is the occasional appearance of vermin. The former secretary of the Cavalry Club noted of their premises on Piccadilly in the 1970s that his colleagues were, 'always fighting a losing battle with the ubiquitous cockroach and the odd sewer rat who loses his way in the underworld of drainpipes ... despite repeated assaults by D.D.T. experts, Rentokill and other battlers against the pest.'[*] In recent years, extermination methods have become more robust, but have never eliminated this peril altogether. Mice remain a surprisingly popular sight in a number of clubs, with a recent cartoon joking that it was hoped they were members.[†]

---

[*] Anthony O'Connor, *Clubland: The Wrong Side of the Right People* (London: Martin Brian & O'Keefe, 1976), p. 108.
[†] Annie Tempest, 'Tottering-by-gently', *Country Life*, 12 June 2024.

WHERE CLUBS ARE FOUND TODAY:
THE LONDON DISTRICTS WITH MOST CLUBS

District	Total number of clubs	'Old' clubs	'New' clubs
Mayfair	27	7	20
St James's	24	17	7
Soho	13	1	12
City of London	10	4	6
Covent Garden	8	3	5
Chelsea	5	2	3
Marylebone	4	1	3
Covent Garden		4	0
Knightsbridge	3	2	1
Westminster		2	1
Whitehall		3	0
Belgravia	2	1	1
Fulham		1	1
Kensington		0	2
Notting Hill		0	2
Shoreditch		0	2
South Kensington		1	1
Tyburnia		1	1

Where Clubs are Found Today

District	Total number of clubs	'Old' clubs	'New' clubs
Balham	1	0	1
Bermondsey	1	0	1
Brixton	1	0	1
Chiswick	1	0	1
Euston	1	1	0
Fitzrovia	1	0	1
Islington	1	0	1
Kensal Green	1	0	1
King's Cross	1	0	1
Mornington Crescent	1	0	1
Parson's Green	1	0	1
Putney	1	1	0
Richmond	1	1	0
Roehampton	1	1	0
St John's Wood	1	1	0
Strand Embankment	1	0	1
Tower of London	1	1	0
Waterloo	1	1	0
West Kensington	1	1	0
White City	1	0	1
Whitechapel	1	0	1
Wimbledon	1	1	0

307

DRESS CODES:
A SHORT HISTORY AND GUIDE

Despite the widespread perception of London clubs upholding stuffy and rigid dress codes, this state of affairs has not been the norm for most of their history. In fact, London clubs did not really have any meaningful dress codes at all until well after the Second World War, only belatedly acquiring them as something of a *petit-bourgeois* affectation.

The original clubs of the eighteenth and nineteenth centuries had no dress requirements – their origins were heavily informal, in the pubs and taverns. As clubs became more fashionable, from the society balls thrown by Boodle's, to the young rakes around Beau Brummell, the emphasis was on innovation and creativity. Indeed, the modern-day necktie is a product of innovation in Clubland: Brummell, a keen trend-setter, rebelled against the contemporary society conventions for cravats and ascots, and instead devised a singular form of neckwear to bring colour and gaiety to austere late-Georgian attire.

It is sometimes suggested that early club members were so well-bred and immaculately dressed that they did not *need* to be told what to wear, unlike their modern counterparts – but there is little evidence to support this. Surviving diaries, letters, minute books and prints all suggest that members typically dressed down in their club for much of the day, donning an assortment of tweeds, smoking wear and even shirtsleeves – whatever was most convenient. Indeed, after an outbreak of members descending from club bedrooms in their pyjamas, one club byelaw dating from 1888 gave its first and only stipulation on dress:

'No member shall appear in any public rooms of the Club in a dressing gown, slippers, or other *deshabillé*.'*

More generally, casual dress was a staple of London club life at the height of Clubland in the Edwardian era – as was evidenced by the sheer number of contemporary illustrations of jacket-less clubmen in shirtsleeves, not to mention prolific Clubland writings by the likes of John Buchan, Sax Rohmer, 'Sapper', P. G. Wodehouse, Dornford Yates et al., which emphasised the informality of dress. And while there was a widespread convention for dressing for dinner in white tie and tails by the late nineteenth century, this too was waived across many clubs that were keen to involve members in the professions; a 1925 club history noted, 'the practical tabooing of evening dress, which assisted in securing the attendance of the House of Commons and Press Gallery men for at least part of the social evening'.†

London clubs first began to adopt 'jacket and tie' dress codes in the 1950s, copying them from the colonial clubs of India and South Africa, where they had been in operation since the turn of the last century. In the context of these original colonial clubs, the introduction of a jacket-and-tie requirement had been used as a device by white members to keep out non-white members and guests. Colonial-era clubs often had what was called a 'colour bar'; and the introduction of a jacket-and-tie rule was just one of a number of euphemistic alternatives introduced by clubs (including higher subscriptions and literacy tests) when they did not want to be *seen* to have an explicit 'colour bar', but nonetheless wanted to engineer the same effect of an all-white European club that excluded other ethnicities.‡

The Second World War was instrumental in the colonial dress codes being exported to London clubs. Members of London clubs serving

---

* 'Regulations & Bye-Laws: Bedrooms', *National Liberal Club: Rules, Regulations, Bye-Laws, List of Members, etc, 1888* (London: National Liberal Club, 1888).
† Robert Steven, *The National Liberal Club: Politics and Persons* (London: Robert Steven, 1925).
‡ See Benjamin B. Cohen, *In the Club: Associational Life in South Asia* (Oxford: Oxford University Press, 2015); Purshottam Bagheria and Pavan Malhotra (eds), *Elite Clubs of India* (New Delhi: Bagheria Foundation, 2005).

abroad were impressed by the visibly higher standards of dress they found in these colonial clubs – and were presumably unaware of the origins of these dress codes. Upon demobilisation, they brought about both a popularisation of reciprocal clubs (to foster links with these overseas clubs) and the introduction of prescriptive dress codes, emphasising jackets and ties. Brooks's was at the forefront of the introduction of compulsory dress codes, in 1947, and most of the major clubs of London followed through the 1950s. Today, the strictest dress code is found in Boodle's, which insists upon a dark suit for gentlemen.

Dress codes could vary from the vague ('jacket and tie') to the incredibly prescriptive micro-management of individual items, such as the colour of the shirt or the type of collar. Since they were rolled out in men's clubs, they were not devised with women in mind, and so often did not have any provision for ladieswear – a factor that would further complicate the arguments over women's admission in the late twentieth century. The dress codes came in just as London clubs entered a period of post-war fossilisation and decline, and because of their ageing memberships at the time, the dress codes often reflected dress norms from the members' own youths – which were already anachronistic by the 1950s. Consequently, they contributed to the poor image of Clubland. Once introduced and embedded in the bureaucracy of club rules, they also became extremely difficult to amend, further contributing to the sense of anachronism – and prompting often-heated debates, as much about the ethics and practicality of rigid enforcement as about the specific content of the dress codes, or the ethos of each individual club. Some clubs always abstained from dress codes – artistic clubs like the London Sketch Club never had a dress code at all.

Recent years have seen a number of London clubs move towards the relaxation of their dress regulations, in no small part due to the ever-diminishing number of workplaces requiring suits and ties (and indeed the ever-growing number of workplaces banning them). There are also practicalities around heat – with London now regularly topping 30°C for long spells of each summer, there is a point at which affectation becomes impractical. Other clubs have responded by installing elaborate air-conditioning systems in some rooms (no mean feat in a listed building, often with high ceilings), to preserve the dress code in summer. In certain cases, the previous regime required the Club's chief executive to be located, to personally sign off on a request for a member to remove their jacket in 35°C heat. Unsurprisingly under such restrictions, members voted with their feet, and clubhouses would be virtually empty in summer heatwaves – save for the long-suffering staff.

The effect of these dress-code relaxations has not been as marked as many members feared. The Savile Club never had a tie requirement in the first place, at any point in its history, while the Reform Club dropped its tie requirement in 2018. Yet if you wander into either of these clubs, you routinely find that well over 90 per cent of the men there are wearing ties. Why?

Any kind of rigidly enforced rule is bound to generate friction, from the unpleasantness on the front door ('You can't come in here dressed like that'), to the accompanying value judgements (such as members being ridiculed for the design of their tie or the cut of their suit). Unsurprisingly, many members have asked themselves what any of this has to do with joining a club, and whether it makes them more of a tie-fixated sect.

The answer lies in something far more powerful than byelaws, rules, regulations, memoranda and other diktats: normative behaviour. Clubs are an environment where smart dress is still widely expected. Although interpretations of what constitutes smart dress may differ, there is a general consensus on what this entails. Furthermore, members tend to be drawn from – or at least mix in – the same social and economic backgrounds as one another. By and large, they do not need to be told how to dress in a manner acceptable to their peers; at the very least, their guests simply ask for informal guidance, so that they may not embarrass their hosts. Clubs that fall back on overly prescriptive dress rules invariably find pushback from any number of members and guests who enjoy mounting their own subtle (or sometimes not-so-subtle) rebellions. Clubs that trust their members generally find greater long-term harmony. And while many members may object to the content and enforcement of a dress code, few will seriously object to simple guidance on what is *expected*. And the most effective clubs manage those expectations with the greatest of tact ('I'm not sure that's completely in the spirit of things, sir, don't you think? Would you like to borrow this spare jacket?', as opposed to, 'You can't come in here').

And it is for that reason that some of the basic Dos and Don'ts are outlined below – these are not to be rigidly adhered to as matters of doctrine, but knowing the rules allows one to be all the more confident when stretching or even breaking the rules.

Dress codes for individual events

Even if a club has a set dress code (or none at all), individual events often have dress codes of their own. The below tables summarise what they entail. They should be a guide rather than an inflexible set of rules; not least as even clubs with the most rigorous dress requirements typically allow broad latitude for national dress, court dress and military uniforms – though the formality of a specific uniform or dress uniform should relate to the formality of the event. There are local variations worldwide – for instance, in Hawaii the norm is 'Island Casual', requiring a Hawaiian shirt; and the venerable Outrigger Canoe Club of Honolulu simply asks that members wear *some* kind of a shirt after 6 p.m. Scottish equivalents have a whole etiquette of their own – for instance, with Highland wear including kilts, the Montrose doublet is worn (with lace jabot and possibly fly plaid) as a rough equivalent to white tie, the Prince Charlie jacket as an approximation to black tie, and the Argyll jacket as a counterpart to daywear; while Lowland dress substitutes trews (tartan trousers) for a kilt.

Dress Codes

Menswear chart

Type	Garment	Standard
	Attire type	**White tie**
Formal (*evening*) *(Typically worn at a ball.)*	Shirt	White piqué (or marcella) shirt, with double cuffs with buttonholes, and detachable wing collar. *(Mandatory.)*
		Common faux pas to avoid: Standard pleated dress shirt for black tie.
	Tie	White piqué (or marcella) bow tie, matching the shirt. *(Mandatory.)*
		Common faux pas to avoid: 'Colourful' bow ties; pre-tied ties.
	Waistcoat	White piqué (or marcella) waistcoat, matching the shirt. *(Mandatory.)* A backless waistcoat will give a better fit.
		Common faux pas to avoid: Coloured waistcoats.
	Trousers	High-waisted/fishtail-waisted black trousers in barathea wool, with twin silk braids running down the side. No turnups. *(Mandatory.)*
		Common faux pas to avoid: Lower-waisted black-tie trousers, with only one silk braid running down the side; trousers with turnups.
	Jacket	Black tailcoat in barathea wool with silk-faced peaked lapels and no pockets. Four cuff buttons. *(Mandatory.)*
	Shoes	Patent leather black lace-up Oxford or Derby shoes, or else formal slip-on dress shoes; worn with black socks. *(Mandatory.)*
		Common faux pas to avoid: Normal black leather shoes; or shoes in any colour other than black.
	Hat	Black (collapsible) silk or (stiff) felt top hat. *(Outdoors only.)*
		Common faux pas to avoid: Wearing any other kind of hat.
	Accessories	White pocket square; mother-of-pearl cufflinks. *(Mandatory).* Mother-of-pearl studs in place of waistcoat buttons; buttonhole flower on left lapel, typically a carnation; white cotton or silk gloves; silver-topped black wooden cane; full decorations and ribbons (if any). *(Optional)*
		Common faux pas to avoid: Wearing a wristwatch with white tie

Type	Garment	Standard
Formal *(daytime)* *(Typically worn at a formal sporting event.)*	Attire type	**Morning dress**
	Shirt	Cotton dress shirt with turndown collar, and either French cuffs or barrel cuffs. *(Mandatory.)* Shirt is typically white; though a coloured shirt with a white collar can be an acceptable variant.
		Common faux pas to avoid: Coloured shirts.
	Tie	Typically of silk. May occasionally be substituted with an Ascot tie. Pattern and colour at wearer's discretion.
		Common faux pas to avoid: Scrunch ties.
	Waistcoat	Single-breasted or double-breasted. May be full-backed or backless. *(Mandatory.)* Pattern and colour at wearer's discretion, but the most popular colours are pale yellow, sky blue, grey or bottle green. If a grey morning coat is worn, then matching grey waistcoat may be worn.
	Trousers	High-waisted grey striped drainpipe trousers, without turnups. If a grey morning coat is worn, then matching grey trousers without stripes may be substituted. *(Mandatory.)*
		Common faux pas to avoid: Trousers with turnups; pinstripe trousers.
	Jacket	Black or grey one-button cutaway morning coat. Four cuff buttons. *(Mandatory.)*
		Common faux pas to avoid: Tailcoat from white tie.
	Shoes	Black leather lace-up Oxford or Derby shoes, or else formal slip-on dress shoes; worn with black socks. *(Mandatory.)*
		Common faux pas to avoid: Brown shoes; brogues.
	Hat	Solid felt top hat in either black or grey; or collapsible silk top hat in black. *(Mandatory.)*
		Common faux pas to avoid: Any other hat.
	Accessories	Cufflinks. *(Mandatory.)* Pocket square in any colour or design; gloves in either cotton or white chamois leather; buttonhole flower on left lapel, typically a carnation; medals and one neck decoration (if any – but increasingly rare with morning dress). *(Optional.)*

Dress Codes

Type	Garment	Standard
Semi-formal (evening) (Typically worn at a sit-down dinner for a special occasion.)	Attire type	**Black tie**
	Shirt	White dress shirt, either with pleated front, or a white marcella front. Turndown collar. *(Mandatory.)*
		Common faux pas to avoid: Wing-collared shirt; standard shirt; button-down collar.
	Tie	Black silk bow tie *(typical)*; or else in striped colours denoting some affiliation *(optional)*.
		Common faux pas to avoid: Pre-tied ties; leaving the untied tie hanging around the neck.
	Waistcoat	Optional; typically in either matching black barathea to the jacket, or else in black silk.
		Common faux pas to avoid: 'Colourful' waistcoats.
	Trousers	Black trousers in barathea wool, with a single line of silk braid running down the side.
		Common faux pas to avoid: Trousers with turnups.
	Jacket	Black dinner jacket in barathea wool with silk-faced peaked lapels, (typically) single-breasted or (if the wearer is exceptionally slim) double-breasted. Three cuff buttons. In summer weather, a white or off-white dinner jacket with shawl collar may be substituted. Jetted pockets (aka besom or welted pockets) at all times.
		Common faux pas to avoid: Flap pockets; notched lapels.
	Shoes	Highly polished black leather Oxford or Derby shoes, or black patent-leather shoes; worn with black socks.
		Common faux pas to avoid: Hats in colours other than black.
	Hat	Black trilby or fedora. *(Optional.)*
	Accessories	Cufflinks in silver colours; cummerbund to cover your waistline. *(Mandatory.)* Pocket square, typically white (but also coloured); buttonhole flower. Miniature decorations and ribbons (if any). *(Optional.)*
		Common faux pas to avoid: Absence of cummerbund; or having the cummerbund pleats face-down rather than face-up.

Type	Garment	Standard
Lounge wear *(Default for many – though not all – older clubs.)*	Attire type	Lounge suit
	Shirt	Cotton or silk shirt with turndown collar, and regular or French cuffs; colour optional. *(Mandatory.)*
		Common faux pas to avoid: Button-down collar.
	Tie	Pattern and colour at wearer's discretion.
	Waistcoat	Optional. Either a matching full-backed waistcoat to the rest of the suit; or else a contrasting full-backed waistcoat, typically a moleskin waistcoat with popular colours being mustard, bottle green, dark red or dark blue; some checked patterns also worn.
	Trousers	Suit trousers that match the suit jacket, without turnups; although 'casual separates' in a contrasting colour (which can have turnups) are acceptable, but less formal.
	Jacket	Suit jacket that matches the suit trousers, either single-breasted or (if the wearer is exceptionally thin) double-breasted, with flap pockets. Three or four cuff buttons. Pattern and colour at wearer's discretion, though as a general rule of thumb, the darker the colour, the more formal the suit – though with considerable relaxation in the summer months, as pale linen suits and seersucker become preferable.
	Shoes	Black or brown leather shoes; precise style at wearer's discretion, but Oxfords, Derbys, brogues and wingtips are all common. Sock colour and pattern at the wearer's discretion, though dark colours are more formal.
		Common faux pas to avoid: Deck shoes; boat shoes; loafers; red socks.
	Hat	Trilby, fedora or homburg. *(Optional.)*
	Accessories	Pocket square in any pattern or colour; watch (whether wristwatch or fob watch); tie pin; tie clip; cufflinks. *(Optional.)*

Type	Garment	Standard
Informal *(Default for most newer clubs. Permitted by some older clubs, in some areas.)*	Attire type	Smart-casual
	Shirt	Design and colour at wearer's discretion.
	Tie	Very much optional, and most likely absent.
	Waistcoat	None.
	Trousers	Design and colour at wearer's discretion; may match the jacket; or may be 'casual separates'.
		Common faux pas to avoid: Jeans are considered inappropriate – as are red trousers (especially red corduroys), which are only worn by onanists.
	Jacket	Most likely to be of a paler colour, with flap pockets or patch pockets. Cuff buttons variable in number.
	Shoes	Design and colour at wearer's discretion.
	Hat	Optional. Common styles include a trilby, fedora, homburg, Panama hat, cloth cap.
	Accessories	Pocket square in any pattern or colour; watch (whether wristwatch or fob watch); tie pin; tie clip; cufflinks. *(Optional.)*

Ladieswear chart

As noted, because most of today's surviving traditional clubs started out as men-only clubs, ladieswear has in many cases been regarded as an afterthought; and a number of the older clubs grant women far more latitude in their choice of dress, simply stipulating something along the lines of 'equivalent formality'. And as can be inferred from the relative sizes of the men's and women's charts, formal ladieswear has always granted far more discretion to the wearer's personal taste, compared to menswear. Yet again, there are certain broad guidelines:

Type	Garment	Standard
	Attire type	White tie
Formal *(evening)* *(Typically worn at a ball.)*	Dress	Full, floor-length ball gown. *(Mandatory.)* Design, pattern and colour at wearer's discretion. Dresses are generally a tailored fit with a form-fitting bodice and more volume or detailing in the skirt. Choice of colour is generally open, though darker hues and classic colours such as black, navy, or jewel tones are usually preferred.
		Common faux pas to avoid: Dress too high off the ground (ankle-length or above). Dress too risqué (no sheer/illusion panels, no slits or cut-outs; all hemlines expected to be cut straight, so no asymmetric hemlines, no revealing necklines, no garish colour or print dress fabrics). The convention of a conservative neckline is more optional than mandatory – but low-cut would probably be considered vulgar.
	Shoes	Formal heels with a closed toe. Design and colour at wearer's discretion. Generally, neutral colour preferred.
	Handbag	Small clutch, or clutch-sized evening purse such as a minaudière. *(Optional.)*
	Hat	Tiara traditionally only worn by married women. *(Optional.)* Hairstyle should be formal and polished, such as an updo, or a sleek, low bun.
	Accessories	Elbow-length silk opera gloves if the gown is sleeveless. Gloves are worn in white, ivory or taupe, a black pair should be paired with dark-coloured or bright clothing. Jewellery, including a necklace, earrings and/or no more than one bracelet over gloves. *(Optional.)* Opera gloves are longer – they traditionally cover the mid-upper arm (16–23 inches measured from the widest part of the palm). **Sashes** Ribands not covered. Sash-wearing at Scottish white-tie balls (clan tartan over single-coloured dresses) – also worn by Scottish women at English events. Cover ups – a matching stole preferred, rather than a formal cover up such as bolero.
		Common faux pas to avoid: Wearing a wristwatch with white tie; Rings over gloves, although Cornelia James says individual, important rings can be worn over gloves. Gloves should be kept on when shaking hands (e.g., in a reception line) or when dancing, though never when dining. Once removed, opera gloves should be folded in half and placed under the lap napkin, unless mousquetaire style.

Dress Codes

Type	Garment	Standard
Formal (*daytime*) *(Typically worn at a formal sporting event or a church wedding.)*	Attire type	**Morning dress**
	Dress	Formal dress, whose hem is below the knee. *(Mandatory.)*
		Common faux pas to avoid: Considered good etiquette to keep shoulders covered in certain situations (e.g. church weddings and some sporting events). Avoid materials that crease easily.
	Jacket	Jacket or blazer over dress. *(Optional.)*
	Shoes	Formal shoes with a closed toe, with or without heels. Design and colour at wearer's discretion.
	Handbag	Clutch, or clutch-sized purse. *(Optional.)*
	Hat	Broad-brimmed hat or fascinator. *(Optional.)*
		Common faux pas to avoid: Specific rules for different sporting events: fascinators are not permitted, but a headpiece that has a solid base of 4 inches is acceptable as an alternative to a hat in Royal Enclosure.
	Accessories	Wrist-length gloves; plus jewellery, including a necklace, earrings and/or bracelet. *(Optional.)*
Semi-formal (*evening*) *(Typically worn at a sit-down dinner for a special occasion.)*	Attire type	**Black tie**
	Dress	Full-length dress, whose hem is below the knee *(mandatory)* but more typically reaches the ankle *(preferred)*.
		Common faux pas to avoid: Avoid anything short, revealing, or bright and bold colours.
	Shoes	Formal shoes, with or without heels. Design and colour at wearer's discretion.
	Handbag	Small clutch or clutch-sized purse; small clutch, or clutch-sized evening bag such as a minaudiere. *(Optional.)*
	Hat	Generally, no; though a small decorative headpiece is acceptable.
	Accessories	Jewellery, including a necklace, earrings, cocktail watch and/or bracelet. *(Optional.)*

Type	Garment	Standard
Semi-formal (*daytime*) *(Typically worn at a garden party.)*	Attire type	Semi-formal daytime
	Dress	Cocktail dress, with a hem just above or just below the knee. *(Mandatory.)*
	Blazer	Jacket or blazer over dress, or worn with a skirt; alternatively a trouser suit. *(Optional.)*
	Shoes	Formal shoes, with or without heels. Design and colour at wearer's discretion.
	Handbag	Handbag.
	Hat	Broad-brimmed hat or fascinator.
		Common faux pas to avoid: Not a faux pas, but trends are increasingly favouring fascinators over broad hats.
	Accessories	Jewellery, including a necklace, earrings, cocktail watch and/or bracelet. *(Optional)*
Lounge wear *(Default for many – though not all – older clubs.)*	Attire type	Lounge suit
	Principal item	Relatively broad, but still formal: dresses of different length, trouser suits, jumpsuits, jackets, blazers and skirts. Lighter colours and lightweight fabrics, such as cotton and linen.
	Shoes	Formal shoes, with or without heels. Design and colour at wearer's discretion.
	Handbag	Handbag.
	Hat	Optional.
		Common faux pas to avoid: As noted, not a faux pas, but trends are increasingly favouring small hats – dress codes are becoming less formal generally, and hats are the next victim after gloves – so that at most, a small perch or pillbox hat (at most) is preferred for a specific event.
	Accessories	Wristwatch.

Dress Codes

Type	Garment	Standard
Informal *(Default for most newer clubs. Permitted by some older clubs, in some areas.)*	**Attire type**	**Smart-casual**
	Principal item	Slightly more relaxed than 'lounge suit': midi dresses, trouser suits, jumpsuits, jackets, blazers, cardigans and skirts.
		Common faux pas to avoid: Jeans are considered inappropriate.
	Shoes	Shoes or sandals, with or without heels. Design and colour at wearer's discretion.
	Handbag	Handbag.
	Hat	Optional.
	Accessories	Wristwatch.

The growth in recent years of openly non-binary members means that the above guidelines will inevitably be subject to further flexibility, not only due to members choosing to align with one gender or another, but also due to non-binary members choosing their own blend of the two. This is to be welcomed, in line with the original spirit of Beau Brummell in finding new levels of elegance that did not conform to established rules. Nonetheless, for the less adventurous members who prefer a reliable fallback, the above guidelines offer a template.

MERGERS AND ACQUISITIONS

Clubs have often merged – typically, when one runs into financial trouble, and agrees to move into another. It is a preferable alternative to closing down altogether. Below are some of the notable mergers over the years.

1781: White's 'Old' Club ('White's') + White's 'New' Club ('Arthur's') → White's.
1799: Weltje's → Cocoa Tree Club.
1816: General Military Club + Naval Club → United Service Club.
1828: Bombay Club → Oriental Club.
1854: Alfred Club → Oriental Club.
1876: Egerton Club → Graham's.
1882: Century Club → National Liberal Club.
1896: Hogarth Club → Arts Club.
1902: Cosmopolitan Club → Alpine Club.
1920: Whitehall Club → St Stephen's Club.
1923: 1920 Club → National Liberal Club.
1927: Half-Circle Club + Parliamentary Labour Club → National Labour Club.
1928: Ladies' Imperial Club → Pioneer Club.
1931: Junior Athenæum → Athenæum.
1933: New Oxford and Cambridge Club → New University Club.
1935: Bruton Club → Lansdowne Club.
1938: New University Club → United University Club.
Sports Club → East India Club.
1939: Albemarle Club → Naval and Military ('In and Out') Club.
Junior Naval and Military Club → Naval and Military ('In and Out') Club.
Pioneer Club → Sesame Club.
St Andrew's Club → Golfers' Club.
1941: Bachelors' Club → St James's Club.
Royal Societies' Club + Empress

Mergers and Acquisitions

Club → Empress and Royal Societies' Club.
1945: Marlborough Club + Windham Club + Orleans Club → Marlborough-Windham Club.
1949: Thatched House Club → Junior Carlton Club.
1950: Conservative Club → Bath Club.
1953: Junior United Service Club → United Service Club.
1955: Empress and Royal Societies' Club → Public Schools Club.
1956: Pathfinder Club → Sesame Club.
1957: Ladies' Empire Club → Ladies' Carlton Club.
1958: Ladies' Carlton Club → Naval and Military ('In and Out') Club.
1959: Royal Cruising Club → Naval and Military ('In and Out') Club.
1962: Lady Golfers' Club → Golfers' Club.
1963: Cowdray Club → Naval and Military ('In and Out') Club.
1964: Union Club → United Service Club.
1968: Goat Club → Naval and Military ('In and Out') Club.
Junior Army and Navy Club → Army and Navy Club.
1971: United University Club + Oxford and Cambridge Club → United Oxford and Cambridge Club.
1972: Public Schools Club → East India Club.
1975: Dutch Club → Royal Thames Yacht Club.
Ladies' Alpine Club → Alpine Club.
United Service Club → Naval and Military ('In and Out') Club.
1976: Devonshire Club → East India Club.
Guards Club + Cavalry Club → Cavalry and Guards Club.
1977: Junior Carlton Club → Carlton Club.
1978: St James's Club → Brooks's *(informal)*.
1979: Constitutional Club → St Stephen's Club.
1984: Eccentric Club → East India Club *(informal)*.
2012: St Stephen's Club → Carlton Club *(informal)*.
2014: New Cavendish Club → Naval and Military ('In and Out') Club.
2018: Lloyds Club → City University Club.
2021: Naval Club → Army and Navy Club.

323

CLUBS WITHIN CLUBS

Sometimes, club mergers are on rather more favourable terms for the dissolved club, so that instead of being absorbed entirely into the membership of another club, they retain a demarcated space of their own within the new club – typically a 'clubroom'. Here are some examples from over the centuries. This list can be read in conjunction with Section 4 of the book, to see where 'vanished' clubs were hosted over the years.

Authors Club → National Liberal Club (1966–76; 2014–present); Arts Club (1976–2011); Black's (2011–14).

Canning Club → Naval and Military ('In and Out') Club (1970–present).

City Livery Club → Little Ship Club (2010–present).

Constitutional Club → Junior Carlton Club (1962–4); United Service Club (1964–9).

Danish Club → Arts Club (1998–2010); St Stephen's Club (2010–11); Naval Club (2011–18).

Europe House Club → National Liberal Club (1975–90).

Flyfishers' Club → Garrick Club (1941–5); Junior Carlton Club (1945–51); Bath Club (1970–81); Savile Club (1995–present).

Guards Club → Travellers Club (1919); Junior Carlton Club (1919–21).

Junior Carlton Club → Carlton Club (1963–8).

National Club → Junior Carlton Club (1913–63; 1968–77); Carlton Club (1963–8).

Den Norske Klub → Danish Club (1997–8); Arts Club (1998–9); Naval and Military ('In and Out') Club (1999–present).

Portland Club → Naval and Military ('In and Out') Club

(1969–95); Army and Navy Club (1995–present).

Royal Aero Club → Lansdowne Club (1961–8); Junior Carlton Club (1968–71); United Service Club (1971–5).

Royal Anglo-Belgian Club → Royal Thames Yacht Club (1978–2010).

Royal Thames Yacht Club → Naval and Military ('In and Out') Club (1961–3).

Savage Club → National Liberal Club (1963–5; 1990–2021); Constitutional Club (1968–75); Lansdowne Club (1975–90).

United Clergy and Laity Club → United Club and Hotel (1865–78).

Windham Club → Travellers Club (1941–5).

WARTIME LODGINGS, DUE TO BOMBINGS

A number of clubs were 'bombed out' during the Second World War, mainly during the Blitz of 1940–1 and the V-weapons bombardment of 1944–5. Some were merely damaged, while others suffered direct hits that devastated their clubhouses. In the months and years following bombings, these clubs enjoyed the hospitality of other clubs rallying round and accommodating their members.

- Arts Club → Devonshire Club, 1941–3.
- Bath Club → Lansdowne Club, 1941–50.
- Caledonian Club → East India Club, 1940–3; Devonshire Club, 1943–6.
- Carlton Club → Reform Club and Travellers Club, 1940–3.
- Flyfishers' Club → Garrick Club, 1941–5.
- Orleans Club → Marlborough Club, 1944–5, prior to full merger.
- Savage Club → East India Club, 1940–6.
- Windham Club → Marlborough Club, 1941–5, prior to full merger.

Wartime Lodgings, Due to Bombings

CLUBLAND BOMBINGS BY THE IRA

'The Troubles' saw terrorist bombings of civilian targets across the United Kingdom between 1969 and 1998, either claimed by or attributed to the Provisional Irish Republican Army (IRA). A number of clubs were targeted, ostensibly due to their links to the political and military establishment. The following Clubland bombings occurred.

8 March 1973: **Civil Service Club** car bombing from a car parked in front of the clubhouse, with a telephone call warning of the imminent explosion just ahead of detonation. There was extensive damage to the building, but thanks to a swift evacuation, no one was injured.

21 August 1973: **Union Jack Club** received a book bomb, but it did not explode.

11 December 1973: A suitcase bomb destroyed the front entrance of the **National Liberal Club**, and one porter was injured.

11 October 1974: **Victory Services Club** explosion after a small, short-fuse bomb was thrown in through a basement window at 10.30 p.m., but no one was injured; a few minutes later, the **Army and Navy Club** suffered an identical bomb thrown in through a ground-floor window, and one person was injured.

22 October 1974: A 5-lb bomb was thrown into the empty ground-floor coffee room of **Brooks's** out of hours, and three staff were injured – two of them severely.

11 December 1974: **Naval and Military Club** on Piccadilly – a 30-lb bomb was thrown into the Long Bar at 7.34 p.m.; members and staff were shaken but uninjured. Almost simultaneously, there was a gun attack on the **Cavalry Club** further along Piccadilly, but no one was injured.

26 June 1990: A 15-lb Semtex bomb in the **Carlton Club** injured twenty people; and one member, Tory peer Lord Kaberry, later died of complications from his injuries. There was heavy damage to the ground floor, which necessitated extensive rebuilding, while the Royal Over-Seas League offered hospitality to the Carlton's members.

10 January 1992: A 5-lb suitcase bomb wedged between two parked cars exploded by the **National Liberal Club**, shattering all the windows facing Whitehall Place. Several passers-by were injured.

As will be noted, most of the attacks came during two peaks of IRA activity, in the early 1970s and the early 1990s.

LOST PROPERTY

All manner of things go missing in clubs. Guests, staff and members alike have been known to keep 'souvenirs', whether they are casual visitors looking for a trophy, an underpaid staffer looking to be compensated for their poor remuneration, or lifelong habitués looking for a comforting reminder of their favourite place. Even more awkward is the phenomenon of 'tit for tat' thefts – typically by a member who has lost several hats and coats from the cloakroom over the years, and has now decided they are owed some replacements. One club secretary recalled accompanying a retired colonel to Bow Street Magistrates' Court to retrieve some items that had been burgled from the colonel's flat, and were later seized by the police when the burglar was arrested. Most of the items turned out to have been the property of fellow club members, stolen by the colonel from the cloakroom.*

Among the range of items 'liberated' from clubs over the years:

Armchairs, bedding and blankets, books and pamphlets, brushes and combs, candlesticks, carpets, coasters, colostomy bags, complete sets of clothing (from changing-room lockers), crockery, cutlery, diaries, dresses and skirts, dressing gowns, false teeth, glass eyes, glasses, golf balls, hats, hearing aids, illegal drugs of assorted classes, jackets, jewellery, laptops, light fittings from the wall, lighters, mobile phones, monocles, napkins, neckties and cravats, newspapers and magazines, overcoats, paintings, placemats, potties, racquets, razors (both manual and electric), salt and pepper shakers, scarves, sculptures

---

* Anthony O'Connor, *Clubland*, pp. 137–9.

and busts, shaving brushes, shirts, soap and other toiletries, staff uniforms, stationery, stuffed animal heads, swimsuits, tables, telephones (even when fitted to the wall), tights and stockings, toilet seats, toupees, trousers, umbrellas, underwear, waistcoats, wastepaper baskets, watches, weighing scales, wigs, wines and spirits, and wooden legs.

In other words, in an adaptation of Murphy's law, anything that can go missing, will. Prescient is the member who is fully insured against theft.

The theft of club-crested crockery and cutlery can be particularly debilitating to the Club when it needs to cater to larger gatherings. The wiser clubs head off some of these thefts by offering crested items for sale, minimising the excuse for purloining, and the need to pay for any replacements.

HOME IMPROVEMENTS

One telltale sign that someone has been spending a great deal of time in clubs is that visitors to their home begin noticing redecorations that increasingly look quite clublike. Even modest student digs may start to be adorned with a range of regularly stocked (and depleted) decanters, and wingback leather armchairs from the local flea market. More ambitiously, features such as heaving bookcases, old prints and paintings, an extensive wine cellar, assorted Chesterfields, and even a billiard table, may all be found. These are signs that the member pines for their club. The key ingredient missing, however, is other members popping in by right. Unless one opens a literary salon with plenty of regular drop-ins, the home club can only be an echo of the real thing.

CLUB-CRASHERS: WHY THEY FAIL

As long as there have been members-only clubs, non-members have attempted to access them, for reasons ranging from mild curiosity to determined social climbing. And a great many gatecrashers have used a combination of techniques to gain entry. Over a decade ago, the *Evening Standard* attempted to lift the lid on some of the favoured methods used, with its guide by hardened club-crasher Nimrod Kamer.* However, many of these techniques are now easily rumbled. What follows is an overview of the principal techniques that have been used by non-members to gain entry in the past – and how they have been foiled. And the foiling of such attempts can make for a popular spectator sport among members in the lobby, as well as providing fodder for gossip in the bar.

The hardest clubs to gatecrash are the aristocratic citadels, such as White's, Boodle's, Brooks's, the Turf or the Beefsteak. That is not to say that it is impossible. But their memberships are smaller than average, meaning that there is a much greater chance that the porters will personally know most of their members by sight. They are also demographically much older clubs (with a small sprinkling of younger-to-middle-aged members thoroughly standing out), so if you are anything other than an old, white male, you will be extremely conspicuous. So, if you are not an old, white male, then your gatecrashing

---

* Nimrod Kamer, 'The Gateleaper: How to Get in to London's Private Members' Clubs', *Evening Standard*, 19 December 2013.

companion would typically be, to lend plausibility to the proceedings. At the larger clubs, by contrast, there is 'safety in numbers', with gatecrashers merging into crowds and events. A club the size of the RAC, with its vast clubhouse, is incredibly easy to wander into – though it is also near-impossible to purchase anything without the correct club membership card, which will be asked for at every transaction. If (usually when) a gatecrasher is discovered, it is highly likely that the porter will make a point of remembering their face. Since porters work long hours and can remain in post for decades, this makes repeat expeditions all but impossible (not to mention awkward, if the club-crasher later attempts to revisit the Club as a bona fide guest).

There have long been a few background dos and don'ts for all gatecrashers. Firstly, it is important to remember the difference between trespass and fraud. Trespass may well be the bane of a club's life, but it is not a criminal offence, it is a tort. And unless someone is a repeat offender, a club is highly unlikely to go to the inconvenience and expense of suing an individual over an isolated incident of trespass. By contrast, fraud is very much a criminal offence, and it has always been important for the mischievous gatecrasher to ensure that a harmless spree to have a nose around does not escalate into securing goods or services under false pretences, or gaining some pecuniary advantage.

Other basic precautions taken include never wearing an overcoat on a gatecrashing expedition (as a befuddled search for the cloakroom is always a dead giveaway that someone does not know their way around), and doing some basic research on the names of existing members, to claim as friends. Which leads us onto:

THE GOLDEN RULE OF GATECRASHING

which has been to: 'Always move in pairs.' Three or more people would instantly constitute a crowd, and would immediately draw the eye, with accompanying suspicion. Conversely, solitary gatecrashers are all too easy to overwhelm with questions: 'Who are you? What are you doing here?' You'd better have an almightily plausible – and well-delivered – response up your sleeve if such simple questions are thrown at you.

By contrast, a pair embroiled in deep conversation, their voices in a low murmur, can all too easily feign ignorance of such obvious questions, pretending not to hear, and passing on unobserved.

And now to the favoured feints and approaches of the gatecrasher – and their undoing:

1. **Tail-gating**

    A well-worn trick, wandering in on the heels of actual members being waved through. It has worked best when a conversation has been struck up with an entourage of members – even if just asking them for the time, the gatecrasher then appeared to be part of the crowd of recognised figures. Altogether less competent was one notorious gatecrasher of London clubs, who would stand outside the front door, offering cash bribes to any members letting him in with them.

    Achilles heel: Club porters are routinely trained to spot tail-gaters, and even if you get past the front desk, many clubs have a second layer of staff inside, waiting to pounce on anyone who may be an intruder.

2. **The events list**

    Another old favourite, this simply involved a would-be gatecrasher monitoring the events list posted to the Club website, and turning up on the dot at the appointed hour, saying, 'Sorry, I'm late for X event, must dash to make it!'

    Achilles heel: For this reason, most clubs no longer post their events list to their website, typically restricting it to a members-only area.

3. **'I'm with a function'**

    This only worked at the larger clubs, but it was a reliable variant on the events-list technique – simply claiming to be with a private party. Such events are now much more common in clubs than they were thirty years ago, happening most nights. Private functions often have guest lists of their own, so the staff have been more likely to shrug their shoulders.

Achilles heel: You will have a very hard time persuading anyone that you're part of any function unless you can name the host, room name and reason for the event.

4. **Instagram and Foursquare**
Another variant on 'the events list', this depended upon following the online posts of known members of a particular club, and dropping everything at the first sign that they were in the Club, typically turning up to tell the porter that you were a guest of this named member, who was definitely on the premises.

Achilles heel: The more discreet clubs resolutely refuse to permit photography and/or social media posts on their premises, making this all but impossible; and the handful of people posting online about being in the Club are likely to be in breach of the Club's rules, and so their 'guests' are treated with some suspicion.

5. **Brazenly wandering in**
There have traditionally been rich pickings for the gatecrasher endowed with supreme chutzpah, who simply sauntered in as if the place belonged to them. Indeed, even though the actor Stephen Fry belonged to no fewer than seven clubs, he boasted in the early 2000s that he was a devotee of this technique at scores more clubs, typically striding purposefully towards the nearest staircase.

Achilles heel: While the days are long gone of porters personally remembering the names of every single member, they will routinely ask any non-familiar face their business, and the slightest uncorroborated detail is likely to result in the gatecrasher being asked to produce their membership card, or else proof of ID while pointing to a matching name on the membership list.

6. **Having food or a glass in hand**
   Otherwise known as 'The Dempster', having been a preferred technique of the late gossip columnist Nigel Dempster. He would typically secrete a champagne flute on his person, pulling it out to make it look like he'd come from within the Club, and just momentarily slipped out for a smoke. Other variants of this technique included holding aloft a bar snack on a small plate.

   Achilles heel: Clubs often have highly distinctive glassware and crockery. Unless you have precisely matched their own brand, right down to the Club seal, you won't be fooling anybody. Furthermore, clubs are now much more likely to have a designated smoking terrace within.

7. **Changing into sportswear**
   Not a means of entry, but an excellent way of staying within the Club, this worked particularly well within sporting clubs. Once you were inside, you would change into a club-branded garment, from a polo shirt to a dressing gown, making it look like you belong there.

   Achilles heel: It still won't get you into the Club; and most London clubs do not have any athletic facilities that call for sportswear. There is a toned-down version of this technique, involving wearing a club tie, but (a) most London clubs do not have a club tie, and (b) those that do often check membership credentials before selling one.

8. **Walk in backwards during a commotion**
   This only worked at busier times, for instance, when a showy, glitzy modern club was hosting a paparazzi-laden event, with a large crowd thronging at the door – but Kamer still swears by this technique of simply walking backwards, as if you belong inside and had just popped out.

   Achilles heel: You're walking backwards. Of course you're going to be noticed.

9. **The name mumble**

   Sometimes – particularly if the porter was new – they would resort to checking the members' list for your name. Never make the rookie error of saying something bland like 'John Smith' – it may well be that the Club does not have a single John Smith on its books. Instead, an incoherent mumble may encourage the porter to check the book. Then, quick as a flash, reading upside-down allows you to point to a suitably improbable and specific name in the book.

   Achilles heel: It's not very likely to work, is it?

10. **Fake delivery – tradesman's entrance**

    One of the more reliable means of gaining admission, this was the tried-and-tested route of finding the tradesman's entrance, and rocking up in an orange boiler suit and clipboard, brandishing a cardboard box which you claimed was a delivery.

    Achilles heel: Congratulations, you've made it as far as the kitchen loading bay. Now what? Yes, you might be wearing a suit under the boiler suit. But where are you going to change, unobserved? This scheme appeals most to those who have watched too many James Bond films. You might as well scale the building with a grappling hook, and hope nobody notices in the middle of London …

11. **Cloakroom ticket**

    Not a means of initially gaining admission; but historically, it was a reliable way of ensuring repeat visits once you had already breached the perimeter. Simply leaving an item in the cloakroom would allow you have a cloakroom ticket – 'as good as a membership card', Kamer assures us – which you could then brandish at the front desk on repeat visits, saying, 'I need to fetch my coat.'

    Achilles heel: Most establishments have a periodic clear-out of their cloakrooms. Besides which, while this may have worked at some of the newer clubs emulating the layout of a nightclub, it is unlikely to work in the older clubs, where the cloakroom regime varies from operating on a 'trust' basis (without tickets), to the porter's front desk doubling as a check-in for valuables, so that the very person guarding the entrance will want to know precisely which item you wish to retrieve, without proceeding any further.

12. **High-visibility construction jacket and clipboard**
There are, broadly speaking, two approaches to camouflage – blending seamlessly into the background, or else choosing something so utterly conspicuous that attracts so much attention that nobody would ever suspect you of being a gatecrasher. This latter approach has tended to evade scrutiny over the years – and it is why Kamer has not tended to gatecrash in three-piece pinstripe suits, but in loud plaid jackets with flowery shirts and bright red corduroys. It is also why the gatecrasher's ultimate friend has long been the high-visibility construction jacket. This was typically used claiming to be doing some survey work from 'next door' or 'across the street', with the gatecrasher being shooed in, and then disposing of the construction jacket in the nearest bathroom.

Achilles heel: You will have been so conspicuous at the front entrance that, when you don't return for five minutes, a search party is likely to be sent out for you – assuming the Club didn't accompany you with a porter in the first place. Even if it works, it will only do so for a few minutes at a time.

13. **Mobile phone ploy**
An old ploy, dependent upon knowing the name of a real member. You might have set up a fake email from this member to you, and shown a copy on your phone, of 'them' apparently saying 'I'll be there in 20 minutes.' Or you might even have arranged a friend to call you on your phone, claiming to be them,

so you could offer to hand the phone to the porter – again, with an assurance of 'I'll be there in 20 minutes.'

Achilles heel: Many clubs won't let you into the main building without the hosting member being on the premises. They'll shoo you into a broom cupboard-sized side room, explicitly designed for guests without a host, and make you wait there until this magical member appears. You may be there for some time.

14. **Open bar tab**

    Kamer's favoured technique for ensuring repeat visits. You would turn up at the Club, claiming to have spent £500 at the bar the night before, but only just having remembered that you didn't pay your tab. Pandemonium would ensue. During the mounting chaos of searching for such a high-value tab, you would slip away to the bar and order a drink – this time setting up an *actual* tab, which you would leave unpaid. On future visits, you could then say you have come to pay your tab, showing them the chit for the actual tab set up.

    Achilles heel: This won't work in most clubs. A great many have a monthly account paired with the membership list, where any outstanding bar tabs are automatically charged back to the member's bank account. Besides, they are unlikely to forget that you once showed up owing them £500 – you will be speaking to the very same bar staff.

In short: gatecrashers, don't do it. It can sound like great fun, and the whimsy of it makes for some fabulous copy. But the reality is that gatecrashers can often find themselves out of their depth, with the constabulary swiftly brought in.

GLOBAL CLUB STATISTICS

Several thousand clubs may be found globally. The following cities have the largest concentrations of them in the world — as can be seen, outside of the United States, former British imperial cities tend to dominate much of the list:

No. of clubs in 2025	Cities
133	London, UK.
53	New York, USA.
37	Mumbai/Bombay, India.
26	San Francisco, USA.
25	Hong Kong, China.
22	Kolkata/Calcutta, India; Singapore.
21	Buenos Aires, Argentina; Delhi (New and Old), India; Toronto, Canada.
20	Karachi, Pakistan.
18	Bengaluru/Bangalore, India.
17	Los Angeles, USA.
16	Boston, USA.
15	Philadelphia, USA; Paris, France.
14	New Orleans, USA; Washington, DC, USA.
13	Melbourne, Australia; Vancouver, Canada.
12	Sydney, Australia.
11	Chennai/Madras, India; Chicago, USA; Lagos, Nigeria; Nairobi, Kenya.
10	Atlanta, USA.

Other countries such as Italy and Spain have extremely high concentrations of clubs, but they tend to be much more evenly dispersed around different regions, with between one and three clubs in each major town or city, rather than with ten or more clubs in the same city. Other cities with half a dozen or more clubs are Brisbane, Australia; Brussels, Belgium; São Paulo, Brazil; Beijing and Shanghai, China; Hamburg, Germany; Coimbatore, Hyderabad, Jaipur, Kochi/Cochin and Lucknow, India; Jakarta, Indonesia; Dublin, Ireland; Rome, Italy; Kuala Lumpur, Malaysia; Lahore, Pakistan; Lima, Peru; Manila, the Philippines; Lisbon and Porto, Portugal; Barcelona, Madrid and Seville, Spain; Colombo, Sri Lanka; Bangkok, Thailand; and Austin, Baltimore, Cincinnati, Dallas, Denver, Palm Beach and Seattle, USA.

Largest concentration of country clubs in the world: the southern Florida coast, between Miami, Palm Beach and Fort Lauderdale, where there are over a thousand golf and country clubs.

WORLD OF SUPERLATIVES
INTERNATIONAL VITAL STATISTICS

Highest club (altitude) ... Círculo de la Unión, La Paz, Bolivia (3,650 metres above sea level).

Largest club (area, including grounds) ... Mission Hills Golf Club, Shenzhen, China (40 km²).

Largest club (internal volume) ... Yale Club of New York City (174,895 square feet).

Largest club (membership) ... Soho House (250,000 members worldwide).

Lowest club ... Dhaka Club, Dhaka, Bangladesh (32 metres below sea level).

Tallest club structure ... 10 Cubed, New York, USA (altitude of 1,550 feet, on the 100th floor of the Central Park Tower).

Northernmost club ... Petroleum

Global Club Statistics

Club, Anchorage, Alaska (61.19064626357343, -149.8853716).

Southernmost club ... Club de la Unión, Punta Arenas, Argentina (-53.161757151419, -70.90776097412228).

Smallest club (internal volume) ... Ovalau Club, Levuka, Fiji.

Smallest club (membership) ... Factory House, Porto, Portugal – 25 members. (To qualify for membership, members must be involved in the running of one of seven British-owned port houses.)

Warmest club location ... Library Club, Riyadh, Saudi Arabia (average temperature of 36°C in July and August).

Coolest club location ... Edmonton Petroleum Club, Edmonton, Alberta (average temperature of -11°C in January).

Oldest club in the world ... South River Club, Maryland, USA (already up and running as a recognisable club by 1690, and possibly older).

Club with the oldest roots in the world ... Gesellschaft der Schildner zum Schneggen, Zurich, Switzerland. (Although not reconstituted as a club until 1866, its roots were as a guild founded in 1380.)

CITY OF SUPERLATIVES
LONDON CLUB VITAL STATISTICS

Highest club (altitude) ... Home House (37 metres above sea level).

Largest club (area, including grounds) ... Roehampton Club (100 acres).

Largest club (internal volume) ... Royal Automobile Club (floorplan of 31,920 square feet).

Largest club (membership) ... Victory Services Club (60,000 members).

Lowest club (altitude) ... National Liberal Club (28 metres above sea level).

Tallest club structure ... National Liberal Club (9th floor tower).

Smallest club (internal volume) ... New Evaristo Club/Trisha's (floorplan of approximately 180 square feet).

Smallest club (membership) ... Yeoman Warders Club (37 members).

Oldest club in London ... White's (opened as a club in 1736; previously a chocolate house with private rooms since 1693).

Newest club in London (at the time of going to press) ... Surrenne in Knightsbridge (due to open in 2025).

SELECT FILM APPEARANCES OF LONDON CLUBS

Clubs often find that hiring themselves out for filming locations is a handy way to balance the books, as well as a nifty spot of free advertising, if the film should turn out to be a particularly prestigious production. (Of course, if it's a box-office bomb, it's best forgotten about.) An exhaustive list of all the film and television appearances of London clubs would fill a hefty volume, but the following indicative list gives an idea of the range of establishments used as locations.

Army and Navy Club

Rocketman (2019) – doubles for assorted hotels and offices in this Elton John biopic.

The Athenæum

Wilde (1997) – doubles for Oscar Wilde's club, the Albemarle, with Stephen Fry as Wilde discovering a fateful note.

A Very English Scandal (2018) – the morning room doubles for the Carlton Club, with Hugh Grant as Jeremy Thorpe meeting the home secretary.

Brooks's

Sebastian (1968) – doubles for the exterior of Dirk Bogarde's unnamed club, where Susannah York follows him.

Garrick Club

Brannigan (1975) – an improbable John Wayne appearance in Clubland, complete with some argy-bargy on the front desk over his not wearing a tie. Richard Attenborough put in a word, to allow filming at his club.

Home House

Some of the better-known uses of the Home House building – particularly the grand staircase – predate its conversion into a club in 1998. These include doubling for Mayfair townhouses in *Jeeves and Wooster* (1990), and in the Dora Carrington and Lytton Strachey biopic *Carrington* (1995).

National Liberal Club

The Elephant Man (1980) – the Club doubles for the administrative parts of the London Hospital in this David Lynch film, in scenes featuring Anthony Hopkins and John Gielgud.

Brazil (1985) – a particularly oddball use of the building in this futuristic Terry Gilliam science-fantasy epic, covered in steampunk ephemera.

The Crown, season 3, episode 8, 'Dangling Man' (2019) – Andrew Buchan's Andrew Parker-Bowles is introduced to Erin Doherty's Princess Anne at a ball in 1970.

Select Film Appearances of London Clubs

Queen's Club

Match Point (2005) – much of this Woody Allen thriller set at an unnamed London tennis club was filmed around the building and its grounds.

Reform Club

The Seven-Per-Cent Solution (1976) – doubles for Mycroft Holmes's club, the Diogenes. Charles Gray plays Mycroft.
Around the World in 80 Days with Michael Palin (1989) – Palin sets off from the main atrium, although he is denied entry at the end of his journey, as he is not wearing a tie.
The Avengers (1998) – doubles for Boodle's, where John Steed is a member, and where Emma Peel (Uma Thurman) wanders in, despite the porter's (Richard Lumsden) best efforts.
Die Another Day (2002) – the swordfight between James Bond (Pierce Brosnan) and Gustav Graves (Toby Stephens) in Blades club is filmed both on a set and in the real-life Reform Club.
Quantum of Solace (2008) – government offices, with Judy Dench as 'M'.

Royal Automobile Club

Brannigan (1975) – the Club's Victorian Turkish baths are the scene of a kidnapping.
Downton Abbey (2015) – the Great Gallery doubles as the dining room of an unnamed London club, 'a temple for car lovers'.

Savile Club

Jeeves and Wooster, throughout season 1 (1990) – the exterior and front hall were used for the fictional Drones Club, but not for subsequent seasons, when the location switched to the (now-defunct) Naval Club.
Finding Neverland (2004) – used for the bedroom interiors of Kate Winslet's scenes as the bed-bound Sylvia Llewelyn Davies in this J. M. Barrie biopic.
Poirot, season 10, episode 4, 'Taken at the Flood' (2006) – the bar and ballroom portray a club where David Suchet's Hercule Poirot is taken to dinner in the opening.
Downton Abbey (2013) – doubles as two clubs, one called the Embassy Club, the other the Lotus Club.

Travellers Club

All Passion Spent (1986) – portrays the members' club in this BBC adaptation of the Vita Sackville-West novel.
Around the World in 80 Days (1989) – with Pierce Brosnan as Phileas Fogg, and the Travellers doubling for the Reform Club next door.

CONVERSATIONS THAT BORE ME

People tend to imagine that clubs are filled with momentous, informed conversations. Sadly, this is not the case. Club members are capable of being just as frivolous, parochial, ignorant and ill-informed as anyone else.

WhatsApp groups are rife (no, really – even in the fustiest and most traditional clubs), and they are no better than WhatsApp groups found anywhere else; as is the case across society post-pandemic, they can bring out the worst in members. One dedicated club WhatsApp group, given over to discussing topical news and current affairs, is known among its members as the 'Three Hours to Five Days Group', on account of the typical lag time between the more informed members being made aware of some recent development, and someone first breathlessly posting to the unimpressed group about the 'breaking news'. But the following gives a sense of some of the duller in-person conversations I have found across Clubland:

'Honestly, last night I got so drunk here. I don't think I'd been that drunk since ... the night before. Every day's a party, eh? Can I tell you how drunk I got?'

'I've never really thought about it before. But this is what I think ...'

'I've just been elected to this club. It's a step up from my last club. What I really want to know is ... how I can join a club on the next tier up? How quickly can I get in over there? This club will do for the time being.'

'No, I'm not an actual lord, I just put that on my business cards. But the title's all above board, I bought it on the internet, and it comes with a real plot of land in Scotland, and I printed out a certificate and everything.'

'Of course, I can't actually stand the things this club was set up for, I just come here for the food/wine list.'

'What's the very best brand of champagne/cigar? And how can I get it at a discount?'

'Who's your favourite James Bond?'

'You're a member of this club, you must also be interested in Freemasonry...'

Texted to fellow members, several times a day, with increasing desperation:
'Let me know if you know anyone in private equity. Or banking. Or private credit. Or general finance. Or who has contacts in these areas. I have unique opportunities in these areas, for the right person.'

The following, repeated ad nauseam:
Person A: 'What/Where is the In and Out Club?'
Person B: 'It's not actually called the In and Out Club, it's the Naval and Military Club. It's just known as—'
A: 'But I thought there was an In and Out Club?'
B: 'No, the old building of the Naval and Military Club had the words "In" and "Out" written on the two driveways into it.'
A: 'Oh. So it wasn't called the In and Out Club?'
B: 'No. Just known as that.'
A: 'So does this club have anything to do with going in and out?'
B: 'No.'
A: 'Is it *really* called the In and Out Club?'
B: 'No.'
A: 'But where's the *real* In and Out Club?'
B: 'That's it.'
A: 'No, come on, I read about an In and Out Club...'

And of course...
A: 'What's the best club?'
B: 'What do you mean by best?'
A: 'You know, the very best. The top one. The best of all.'
B: 'Lots of clubs have different things going for them... it's very hard to compare...'
A: 'Yes, but there's got to be a best. The one that *everyone* knows is best.'
B: 'If that's true, then why don't you already know it?'

READING LIST

The bibliography of Clubland is extensive: I maintain one on my website which runs to some twenty-one A4 pages just on London alone, and would surely run to several hundred pages for clubs worldwide. Yet a few highlights are mentioned here . . .

―――――――――――― Required ――――――――――――

- Anthony O'Connor, *Clubland: The Wrong Side of the Right People* (London: Martin Brian and O'Keefe, 1976) remains one of the very best books on the topic. It is the knowing and indiscreet memoir of a somewhat jaded club secretary of thirty years' standing, who had seen all manner of misbehaviour from members, staff and guests alike.
- At the risk of shameless self-promotion, my book *Behind Closed Doors: The Secret Life of London Private Members' Clubs* (London: Robinson, 2022) was the most recent full-length Clubland history.
- I have already mentioned my debt to Charles Graves, *Leather Armchairs: The Chivas Regal Book of London Clubs* (London: Cassell, 1963), which gently guides the reader through early 1960s London, club by club. Just as compelling is its forebear, John Timbs, *Clubs and Club Life of London*, which passed through multiple editions between 1853 and 1872.
- Of the many academic monographs around clubs, perhaps the most far-reaching is Erika Diane Rappaport, *Shopping for Pleasure: Women in the Making of London's West End* (Princeton, NJ:

Princeton University Press, 2000), which played a central role in the reassessment of the many women's clubs found in Victorian Britain.
- Since the Victorian era, there have been numerous relevant legal textbooks. The most comprehensive and recent is David Ashton, Paul Reid and Ian Snaith, *Ashton & Reid on Clubs and Associations*, 3rd ed. (London: Bloomsbury Professional, 2020), giving a good sense of the full range of activities and responsibilities of any club.

Additional

- It is impossible to summarise the field of single-club histories here; there are hundreds of them. Traditionally, these could often be rather lightweight affairs, but recent efforts have often combined serious, substantive history with attractive coffee-table book production. Examples include the recent histories of Boodle's by Marcus Binney and David Mann (2013), Brooks's by J. Mordaunt Crook and Charles Sebag-Montefiore (2014), the In and Out by Tim Newark (2015), and the Travellers by John Martin Robinson (2018), which are listed in those clubs' respective entries in Section 1. Also worthy of mention is the recent history of the Athenæum (2020) by Michael Wheeler, which is not in the 'coffee-table book' mould, but is as scholarly and comprehensive as you would expect of its subject.
- Many of the antiquarian guides to Victorian and Edwardian Clubland remain highly readable, including Joseph Hatton, *Club-Land, London and Provincial* (London: J. S. Virtue, 1890), Arthur Griffiths, *Clubs and Clubmen* (London: Hutchinson, 1907), Ralph Nevill, *London Clubs* (London: Chatto & Windus, 1912), and T. H. S. Escott, *Club Makers and Club Members* (London: T. F. Unwin, 1914). These were written when Clubland was at its height, with a strong sense of identity.

Reading List

- Lovers of the niche and arcane are well-served by Robin McDouall, *Clubland Cooking* (London: Phaidon, 1974), penned by a former secretary of the Travellers Club, and containing some beautifully bizarre recipes.
- Long popular for its pictures is Anthony Lejeune, *The Gentlemen's Clubs of London*, which passed through successive editions from 1979 to 2012. The more recent Charles-Louis de Noüe (with Serge Gleizes), *Clubs & Cercles en Europe* (Paris: Éditions du Palais, 2020) focuses on a selection of highly aristocratic (and mostly, though not exclusively, male-only) clubs across Europe, with an English translation published in 2022 as *Gentlemen's Clubs in Europe*. A forthcoming book by Andrew Jones on Clubland architecture will provide even more up-to-date interiors for the London clubs.
- For lovers of fiction, Clubland has long proved an irresistible target of satire. Two particularly acerbic novels, each sharing a title with the other, are Andrew Graham, *The Club* (London: Macmillan, 1957), and A. D. Wintle, *The Club* (London: Cassell, 1961). Of course, the undisputed master of club fiction remains P. G. Wodehouse. Clubs suffused much of his work – especially his Drones Club story collections, such as *Young Men in Spats*, and *Eggs, Beans and Crumpets* (London: Herbert Jenkins, 1936/1940).

RESIGNATIONS

[There is a] tendency of weak-minded people like myself to join clubs ... You know how it is. You lunch with a friend at his club and in the course of the meal he says, 'You ought to be a member here'. It is impossible to reply that you would consider it the fate that is worse than death, so you make polite noises and the next thing you know you have been elected and all the weary work of resigning to be done ... How to word the letter of resignation. What you will want is something that will not hurt anybody's feelings but at the same time will make it quite clear that the twenty pounds a year you have been paying for never going into the place has got to stop. 'Kindly accept my resignation' seems so abrupt, and one feels one ought to edge into the thing with a few preliminary words on the weather, the crops and any good books one may have been reading lately, springing the bad news in a postscript. (P. S. Oh, by the way ...)

P. G. Wodehouse, in Charles Graves,
Leather Armchairs: The Chivas Regal Book of London Clubs
(London: Cassell, 1963)

Resignations are not always tendered with so much charm, although Wodehouse was correct that the single most common reason for resignation through the ages has simply been underuse of the building.

Resignation can also involve a game of intrigue. Members dissatisfied with the way things are going at their club often threaten to resign. This is not a threat to make lightly, as the bluff can and will be called. Even after resignation is offered, it may not be fully believed or accepted.

Resignations

Conversely, a less-than-popular member may find a passing offer of resignation accepted with the greatest possible haste and enthusiasm. One of the more dramatic examples of this was the double resignation of Winston Churchill and David Lloyd George from the Reform Club, in 1913.

The prompt for this dual resignation – one of the most notorious in Clubland – was the blackballing of one of Churchill's closest friends, the Liberal MP Baron de Forest. De Forest already had to contend with antisemitism and antipathy towards his Austrian title, but it was in 1911 that he embarked on an ill-advised course of litigation, suing his mother-in-law for slander. The case collapsed on the opening morning of the trial, resulting in a cause célèbre that saw de Forest ostracised in polite society. Churchill's attempt to sponsor him for the Reform Club in 1913 was then a bid to see de Forest rehabilitated – only to see him blackballed. Churchill, then the president of the Board of Trade, responded as follows:

Jan 29th 1913

Dear Sir,

I learn with great regret that a Liberal Member of Parliament, proposed by me for election to the Club, has been rejected at the recent ballot. In these circumstances I must request you to take the necessary steps to remove my name from the list of members. The Chancellor of the Exchequer [David Lloyd George] authorises me on his behalf to ask you to take similar steps in regard to his membership, & to arrange with as little delay as possible to remove his name with mine from the Club list. I should be glad if you would bring the reason for my resignation to the notice of the Committee, and express to them my regret at being unable to continue a member of the Club to which I had been by their kindness unanimously elected.

Yours very truly
Winston S. Churchill

---

* Quoted in Russell Burlingham and Roger Billis (eds), *Reformed Characters: The Reform Club in History and Literature* (London: Reform Club, 2002), p. 202.

It appears likely that Churchill's letter was intended as a double bluff, offering up the double whammy of two senior members of the cabinet resigning from the foremost Liberal club of the day; and bringing the matter to the attention of the committee, to check whether they did not wish to reconsider their blackballing of de Forest. The bluff was called, and after the committee first confirmed that Lloyd George had indeed authorised Churchill to make this threat, both resignations were promptly accepted.

How to resign

Is there such a thing as a 'good' resignation? Absolutely. For one thing, whatever your reasons, you will want to withdraw without a stain on your character – no hint of any unpaid bar tabs, for instance.

Successfully resigning from a club is more difficult than it may seem. Just as joining a club can take months or even years to realise, resignation is seldom a swift matter.

This is partly down to the contractual nature of club membership, and people leaving it too late. At the start of the calendar year, you will have paid your subscription, either in whole or in instalments. Paying any part of that subscription immediately signals your acceptance of the terms and conditions of membership. Most clubs will have the standard clause that you are renewing for another calendar year. But there's a catch. There is usually a deadline for confirming that you will *not* be renewing your membership next year. This can be as late as 1 December, or it can be as early as 1 July. It is almost unheard of for it to be 31 December. Suffice to say, the member who winces at the state of their bank balance going into Christmas, and decides to relinquish their club membership as a cost-cutting measure, will be pained to receive a stiff reminder that they have left it too late, and are still liable for the whole of the next year's subscription.

Clubs are not gyms. (Although paradoxically, the membership structure of gyms first came out of clubs.) This means that you cannot resign and then re-join seasonally, in line with whether or not you use the facilities; the Club's subscriptions are calculated on the basis of year-round contributions, and they would be much more expensive for everyone if there were a drop-out, drop-in-again culture. This means that if you *do* resign, you are unlikely to be able to re-join anytime soon; and indeed, outside of some dramatic extenuating circumstances, any application to re-join within the next few years is likely to be regarded with extreme suspicion.

Why do people resign? The single most common reason, by far, is underuse of the Club, which can make it poor value for money. If the Club has a hefty subscription, then this is thrown sharply into focus. Another complicating factor is if the member moves, and anticipates their use of the Club dropping (although most clubs have some form of discount for country and overseas members).

Yet there is a multiplicity of other reasons why people quit clubs: personal feuds with other members or staff; disapproval of the Club's direction; change in personal circumstances.

Of course, the most dignified method of resignation of all is death. This is best done swiftly, with a quiet notice in *The Times*.

SECTION 3

FOOD AND DRINK

BACKGROUND

Clubs were founded on refreshment. They began by dispensing drinks in the eighteenth century. As members engaged in all-night gambling sessions, there grew a demand for solid sustenance – initially, for hearty fare rather than *haute cuisine*. This was very much part of the Enlightenment dash towards greater informality in mealtimes, with members snacking or else picking at a joint of meat for hours or days on end.

All this changed in the nineteenth century, with the growth of more palatial clubs aimed at middle-class professionals. These saw themselves as pushing the boundaries of culinary innovation, competing with the leading restaurants and hotels. Several major London clubs hired celebrity European chefs, and they were at the forefront in innovation and experimentation in cuisine.

For much of the twentieth century, London clubs lapsed into a long, slow decline – and this was reflected in the choice of foods. The privations of wartime rationing left a shadow for many decades afterwards, with members often favouring food 'just how it used to be'. Clubs were seldom synonymous with culinary excellence in these years.

Since the 1980s, however, clubs have had something of a rebirth, and this has been reflected in the selection of food. As trendy new clubs often traded on the quality of their meals, the traditional clubs have had to compete, revitalising their kitchens.

What is presented here is not the 'best' food or drink. I am not a food critic, and I would not know where to begin. What this section does is give the reader an introduction to quintessential Clubland recipes, not to mention equipping the reader with the confidence to select food and

Food and Drink: Background

drink, free of snobbery or embarrassment. Collectively, they present a culinary tradition, of food and drink to argue and discuss over.

One of the most common questions I get about my work on Clubland is on 'research trips' – people imagine these are bacchanalian affairs, but I do take them very seriously indeed. This section has been scrupulously researched: every recipe has been tried out (and sometimes lightly modified) in my own kitchen. Some are more dangerous than others: you can get alarmingly drunk on even the smallest serving of the Byculla Soufflé.

BEVERAGES IN CLUBS

Beverages are the beating heart of London clubs, even among non-drinkers. Since their very beginnings, clubs have been synonymous with serving up stimulants to encourage candid and convivial conversation among the members.

Coffee

Clubs have their roots in the informal gatherings in the earliest coffee houses, so a strong coffee offering clearly goes back to first principles. Despite this, during the years of Clubland decline in the late twentieth century, the quality of coffee served up in clubs could leave a great deal to be desired – one long-standing member strongly opposed the bar's acquisition of an espresso machine, on the grounds that he, 'quite liked the coffee nice and weak here, not like everywhere else'. These days, clubs take matters rather more seriously, and many offer up a choice of different coffee beans.

Hot chocolate

This has almost entirely died out in Clubland. Which is odd. When we speak of White's having started as a chocolate shop, it was the then-new luxury of drinking chocolate which they served. With the importation of cocoa beans from Ecuador, New Spain (Mexico) and Venezuela in the seventeenth century, hot chocolate skyrocketed in popularity. It was originally seen as a genteel alternative to alcohol, at a time when a series of moral panics looked down upon many forms of alcohol as coarse drinks. By the late eighteenth century, however, coffee and hot chocolate had been eclipsed by alcoholic drinks.

Tea

Although afternoon tea is often thought of as quintessentially British, London clubs were slow to adopt tea as a major ritual in the eighteenth and nineteenth centuries. Around-the-clock gambling, found in the older clubs, called for stiffer stimulants than a cup of tea. It was only with the popularisation of department stores and luxury hotels at the end of the nineteenth century that tea began to take its place in the clubs – initially in women's clubs, as a respectable drink that could be enjoyed without reproach.

Clubs today, heavily influenced by the 'high teas' of West End hotels, typically offer some of the biggest, best and most elaborate (not to mention cheapest) afternoon teas in London. Loose leaf is always preferable to teabags – the tea comes unfiltered – and the quantity of milk (if any) is a matter of deeply personal preference, which the hosting member should leave to the individual.

Soft drinks

The old Cavalry Club once had a pair of members enquire whether they might be able to get hold of a Coca-Cola. The wine waiter regarded them coolly, and raised an eyebrow: 'For drinking purposes, sir?'

Today's clubs are rather more understanding, not only reliably serving up any number of soft drinks, but also non-alcoholic wines.

CLUB COCKTAILS

Cocktails have been warmly embraced by London clubs – but they are not a British innovation. The cocktail was a nineteenth-century American novelty, which caught on in early-twentieth-century Britain. Consequently, several of the most prominent Clubland cocktails are synonymous with international clubs.

Bellini (Harry's Bar)

First developed in Harry's Bar in Venice; and so emulated by the London club that takes its name. Peach purée is shaken on ice, and then poured into a glass, where it is matched with an equal quantity of champagne.[*]

Black Velvet (Brooks's)

Attributed to a waiter at Brooks's, who first served this drink in 1861 during the period of official mourning for Prince Albert, it was intended to convey the black armbands that were widely worn among members and staff. The cocktail is a simple one: an equal mixture of champagne and Guinness stout, mixed together and served in a champagne flute.[†]

---

[*] Traditional.
[†] Traditional.

Club Cocktails

Boston Club Punch (Boston Club)

A recipe from the Boston Club of New Orleans, the oldest club in the Deep South of the United States, founded in 1841. The cocktail is mixed in an Old Fashioned glass, and consists of:

30 ml water	4 or 5 dashes of orange-flower water
1 bar-spoon sugar	
Juice of half a lemon	45 ml bourbon whiskey

Place into a shaker with lumped ice and shake well. Then pour into a chilled Old Fashioned glass, adding two bar-spoons full of cherry juice, one cherry and a slice of lemon before serving.*

Buck's Fizz (Buck's)

The most famous of London club cocktails, taking its name from the establishment that bred it, in the early 1920s. The basic champagne-and-orange juice recipe is rudimentary, and often mistaken for a Mimosa. Yet the quantities differ. Whereas a Mimosa is a half-and-half combination of the two, Buck's Fizz has two parts champagne to one part orange juice.

In addition, there is a long-standing 'secret ingredient', known only to the barmen of Buck's. Those hoping to gain an insight, through assiduously watching a Buck's Fizz being made on-site, are in no such luck: the ingredient is poured from a darkened, unmarked bottle stored securely behind the bar.†

Club Cocktail

Not actually a product of Clubland, but named in its honour, this recipe from the Savoy Hotel's barman Harry Craddock is a variation on a

---

* Jim Iorio, in Kendall Hamilton (ed.), *The Leash Cocktails* (New York: Leash Club, 2023), p. 18.
† Imparted at the bar of Buck's.

Martini. It consists of two-thirds dry gin, one-third vermouth, and a dash of yellow Chartreuse. Shake well and strain into a cocktail glass.[*]

Fish House Punch (Schuylkill Fishing Company)

One of the oldest clubs in the world, founded in 1732 and located in Andalusia outside Philadelphia, the Schuylkill Fishing Company originated this cocktail.

1 part simple syrup, made with brown sugar and English breakfast tea
1 part dark rum

1 part an equal mix of cognac and peach brandy, cut with fresh lemon juice

Serve in a large punch bowl with a ladle and add sliced lemon wheels as a garnish. Keep away from any open flame.[†]

Jockey Club Cocktail

A Clubland classic, from the one-time London clubhouse of the Jockey Club:

1 dash Angostura bitters
1 dash orange bitters
2 dashes Crème de Noyaux

4 dashes lemon juice
¾ glass of dry gin

Shake well, and strain into a cocktail glass.[‡]

---

[*] Harry Craddock, *The Savoy Cocktail Book* (London: Constable, 1930), p. 48.
[†] Charles Keates, in Hamilton, *Leash Cocktails*, p. 27.
[‡] Craddock, *Savoy Cocktail Book*, p. 89.

Club Cocktails

Pegu Club Cocktail (Pegu Club)

This cocktail takes its name from the now-defunct club in Rangoon during the years of British imperial rule.

- 1 dash Angostura bitters
- 1 dash orange bitters
- 1 teaspoonful lime juice
- ⅓ glass Curaçao
- ⅔ glass dry gin

Shake well and strain into a cocktail glass.[*]

RAC Special Cocktail (Royal Automobile Club)

One of the earlier Clubland cocktails, from the bar of the RAC:

- 2 dashes orange bitters
- ¼ glass French vermouth
- ¼ glass Italian vermouth
- ½ glass dry gin

Shake well and strain into a cocktail glass. Squeeze orange peel on top.[†]

Rum Dum (Lyford Cay Club)

Invented by Wilfred Sands, the barman of the Lyford Cay Club in the Bahamas:

- 45 ml Mount Gay rum (or similar amber or light rum)
- 15 ml Myers's rum (or similar dark rum)
- 40 ml lemon juice
- 1 splash simple syrup
- 1 raw egg white

Stir the sour mix (lemon juice, simple syrup and egg white) and add the amber or light rum into a shaker, shaking vigorously. Pour over ice in an Old Fashioned glass; and then top with the dark rum as a float.[‡]

---

[*] Ibid., p. 120.
[†] Ibid., p. 131.
[‡] Bill Hobbs, in Hamilton, *Leash Cocktails*, p. 70.

London Clubland

Sidecar (Buck's)

Often claimed by the Ritz in Paris as one of their innovations, the Sidecar owes its origins to McGarry, the enterprising pioneer barman of Buck's club. The ingredients are relatively straightforward:

- 50 ml cognac
- 25 ml Cointreau or other orange liqueur
- 25 ml freshly squeezed lemon juice

Garnish with an orange twist.*

---

* Traditional.

WINE

Club wine lists differ considerably. This depends as much upon the physical limitations of a club's cellaring arrangements as the expertise of its sommelier and wine committee. Some wine lists focus on as extensive and varied a list as possible, mindful that this risks a considerable quantity of waste, with many wines going untasted over time. Others prefer a slimmer, more focused wine list where the emphasis is on quality, not quantity. The enemy of the latter is the opinionated whataboutery of the persistent, brow-beating member who *insists* that the Club must serve up their favourite wine, which no one else seems to ever drink.

Newer clubs tend not to be as good value for money as older clubs; by definition, they will have had to purchase their whole wine list relatively recently, fully bottled and aged and matured. Longer-established clubs with extensive cellar space, by contrast, are well-placed to buy wine in bulk *en primeur*, and reap the dividends for decades to come – subject to having made the right call when selecting new wines for laying down.

Much attention goes to the more exotic vintages on a wine list, but many club members can be remarkably unadventurous, sticking to the Club Claret or the Club Burgundy. This is not a solely financially motivated decision (although it can be cost-effective, too). Inertia can be a powerful force in Clubland, and members tend to assume that the Club's own-brand wines come with the warm recommendation of the wine committee. While this may be the case, there is the world of difference between an alert wine committee, which regularly monitors the scope for replacing Club-branded wines with improved selections; and the complacency of a committee that has not reviewed the Club wines for over twenty years. Accordingly, it can be rewarding to be adventurous with the wine list selections.

Fortified wine

This comes in three principal varieties: port, sherry and madeira.

'All wine would be port, if it could', goes the saying. A port is a thing of beauty, traditionally served up after dinner; although in truth, a good, light port such as an aged tawny can be served up at any hour. Chilled white port makes an especially good pre-meal aperitif before lunch or dinner.

Ports were some of the earliest wines to be served in London clubs. Portugal is England's oldest continuous ally, with treaties stretching back to the fourteenth century, and supply chains remained consistent, whereas serving continental alternatives like French wine were apt over the centuries to be affected by variations in the relations between the two often-warring nations. Besides, the port-wine industry, which stretches back to the seventeenth century in northern Portugal's Douro Valley, remains very reflective of evolving British tastes, and has long been dominated by a series of expatriate English and Scottish families.

Vintages tend to occupy a disproportionate amount of attention with ports. Avoid like the plague any establishment that sells vintage port by the glass. Most port is very sturdy and versatile, with bottles not going off for weeks or even months on end. But vintage port is a highly volatile drink, with a chemical reaction triggered by being opened, and it reacts with oxygen, going off within hours. Bars that sell this by the glass, for the cachet of having something marked 'vintage' on offer, clearly do not know how to serve it. Vintage port should always be served by the bottle, with the decanting process performed in front of you. If the Club has a flair for the dramatic, the bottle-top can be removed by port tongs, or sabre, but these are merely for show. Leave to air for at least an hour, and make sure the whole bottle has been drunk within four to six hours of opening, or it will spoil.

Wine

As with all wines, optimal choices are a deeply personal matter of taste. Personally, as one who spends a lot of time visiting Portuguese vineyards and port lodges, I currently favour a Quevedo for a simple ruby port; Fonseca Bin 27 for a 'super-ruby'; Churchill's for an aged white port; Ramos Pinto's Lágrima for a sweet white port; Quinta de Noval for a tawny port (and a 40-year-old tawny); Niepoort for a 10-year-old tawny; Bulas (a small family vineyard) for a 20-year-old tawny; Ramos Pinto for a 30-year-old tawny, and for an LBV (Late Bottled Vintage). Vintages peak around the forty-five-year mark, and Fonseca 1977 is still currently my favourite, but the stellar Churchill's 1991 continues to improve and I think will soon overtake it. The much-vaunted 1963 vintage port is generally well past its prime from most houses, often showing signs of degradation, though still packs a punch. *Anything* by Niepoort is sublime, and is to be savoured. Colheita ports are a magnificent collectors' item, and certainly a curio to serve up at organised tastings, but they make a poor choice for a club to stock: their whole value lies in the considerable variation from bottle to bottle, which may make for exciting tastings, but also makes for poor consistency. Pink port also exists – a kind of port rosé – but I've never tasted one I didn't promptly want to throw up. And crusted port is shockingly overlooked, still only produced by a handful of wineries, yet one of the most divine drinks, which can be drunk as table wine as well as a dessert wine – it is the perfect wine to introduce to anyone who says, 'I don't like port, because I normally find it too sweet.' Niepoort makes a particularly powerful crusted port.

Recent years have seen port cocktails grow in popularity. Personally, I think they are an abomination – a waste of three-to-forty years of maturing a very resource-intensive wine in a barrel, only to see it diluted. For that reason, I'd avoid a port-and-tonic as an affectation. That said, serving white port in a tumbler filled with crushed ice and a sprig of fresh mint can be supremely refreshing on a hot day.

Sherry has never fully challenged the domination of port as the drink of choice in clubs – the 1930s saw the marketing of a 'Clubland Port' brand, but never a Clubland sherry. Nevertheless, it offers a rich range of flavours. Expert opinion in Spain is somewhat at odds with British tastes. Discerning Spanish palettes favour the Fino sherries (such as the estimable Bodegas Tradición) with a dry, even salty flavour (typical of a Manzanilla), which makes them perfect *aperitifs*, or else a summer pairing with seafood; while looking down with disdain at the sweeter sherries. Nevertheless, British palettes tend to strongly favour the sweeter sherries, with Pedro Ximénez being particularly popular across London clubs; I find Bodegas Valdespino's El Candado PX an especially powerful and invigorating drink to sip at all hours. For a middle course, Amontillado and Oloroso are popular, with Tio Diego from Valdespino being a solid example of the former (especially if you like a strong dose of Fino flavour). Olorosos, being at the sweeter end of the middle range, are favoured in London clubs – my taste runs to the estimable Oloroso Tradición VORS, from Bodegas Tradición, which blends sherries typically fifty-five to sixty years old.

But then, you may regard my tastes in sherry as highly suspect, and to be ignored; I have high-end tastes in port, but low-end tastes in sherry, and am also quite contented with a glass of Harvey's Bristol Cream, an affordable supermarket staple that blends thirty different varieties of the Fino, Oloroso, Amontillado and Pedro Ximénez grapes. A slightly richer and more upmarket variety is the Lustau Solera East India Sherry, blended from Oloroso and aged Pedro Ximénez.

Madeira is a somewhat more niche category of fortified wine. Whereas there are over four hundred port wine producers dotted around the Douro Valley (most of them small producers, but with over thirty major companies), and fifty-three sherry shipping bodegas (twenty-eight in the spiritual home of Jerez, five in El Puerto, and twenty in nearby Sanlúcar de Barrameda), the island of Madeira hosts just eight firms making the eponymous wine. While sherry's taste owes much to the blazing sun of Andalucia, and port traditionally contrasts the heat of upland Douro summers with being cooled downstream in underground lodges by coastal Porto, Madeira is the product of a remarkably consistent Atlantic climate, with minimal temperature changes all year around. Blandy's and Henriques & Henriques are the most celebrated brands, but it is well worth trying the other houses of Barbeito, Borges, J. Faria & Filhos, Justino's, Madeira Vintners and Pereira D'Oliveiras as well. The leap in quality with the aged varieties is seminal, so that they are practically a different wine.

ORDERING IN CLUBS

In the older clubs, ordering is quite unlike most restaurants – it is all done in writing, on little slips of paper. This stems from the long-standing practice of members having an account for the settling of bills (typically monthly). Putting everything in writing makes it easier to track whom has ordered what, and when. Excessively neat handwriting on these forms is strongly recommended, to prevent all manner of comical mix-ups from occurring.

BEEFSTEAK SURPRISE

There is a story told of the Beefsteak Club in the early 1900s:[*]

The police, seeing old men emerging happily every evening, assumed it was a brothel and began watching the club; one night they raided it, and found four men sitting round the long table. The conversation went something like this:

'And who might you be?' asked the policeman of one old gentleman.

'I am the Lord Chancellor.'

'Aha! And you, sir?'

'The Archbishop of Canterbury.'

'Oh yes! And the next?'

'I am the Governor of the Bank of England.'

'And I suppose,' said the policeman to the fourth, 'that you're the Prime Minister.'

'As a matter of fact, I am,' said Arthur Balfour.

---

[*](From, Anthony Sampson, *Anatomy of Britain* (London: Hodder & Stoughton, 1962), p. 72.)

CLUB SIGNATURE DISHES

'You should only ever eat in a club what you wouldn't cook at home.' This was the view of one long-term club member, and she had a point. Certainly, the signature dishes presented here are items that you would not typically expect to find out of a club, but which are an integral part of the experience of dining in a club, as much as the conversation or the candlelight.

Breakfast

My own favourite Clubland breakfast is not from London at all: the Metropolitan Club of the City of Washington, DC does an invigorating and zesty corned beef hash with finely diced onions and bell peppers that have all been stir-fried together until lightly crisp, topped with a helping of poached egg and asparagus. (There are no potatoes, unlike most hash recipes.) Take the dining room's rear window table overlooking the Old Executive Building and Washington Monument, and enjoy the view. But then, DC is an early-to-bed, early-to-rise kind of a city, where breakfast is much more of an event. London clubs, by contrast, have no shortage of characters carousing into the small hours, unlikely to be up at the crack of dawn. Nevertheless, a steady stream of country members and reciprocal members means that London club breakfast tables are usually fairly busy. London Clubland breakfasts do not, however, differ that much from other breakfasts – full English and continental breakfasts tend to be the order of the day.

London Clubland

Soup

Mulligatawny Soup (Oriental Club)

1 x fowl (10–15 lb)	2 sprigs thyme
7 lb/3 kg lean veal	4 oz/110 g butter
3 oz/85 g lean ham	5 tbsp curry powder
2 x large carrots	1 oz/28 g curry paste
2 x turnips (4 lb)	4 oz/110 g potato flour
7 x cloves	2 oz arrowroot
2 x teaspoons allspice	¾ lb/340 g flour
Teaspoon of mace	1 clove garlic
2 x teaspoons of mixed herbs	1 tbsp salt
1 x small carrot	½ tbsp sugar
2 x medium onions	Cooked chicken pieces
Bay leaf	Rice, to serve
4 oz/110 g celery	

A historic recipe, from 1861. Cut into small pieces the fowl and the veal. Place into a stewpan with 1 oz of lean ham, along with the large carrots, turnips, 4 of the cloves, allspice, 1 blade of mace and mixed herbs.

Reduce the mix over the fire, then fill the stewpan up with water, and let the stock boil gently for 4 hours, before straining it off into a pan.

Have ready in another stewpan the small carrot, onions, 2 oz of lean ham, bay leaf, celery, thyme, 3 cloves, 1 blade of mace and the butter. Stir the whole over a low heat for 10 minutes. Then add 5 tablespoons of curry powder, and the curry paste.

Stir this again over the heat for 2 minutes, adding the potato flour, arrowroot and flour. Stir all this well together, then add the stock, and stir over a high heat until boiling. Add a clove of garlic and let it all boil for 2 hours. If this should be too thick, add some more stock – any kind will do.

The soup should then be strained with a tammy cloth and placed again in a stewpan. Add a little more stock, and stir again until boiling gently, leaving it boiling for 1 hour, but keeping it well skimmed.

Season with a tablespoonful of salt, and half a tablespoonful of sugar. If the soup is too spicy in flavour, you can add more potato flour. When finished, the soup should not be too thick. Serve with small pieces of chicken in the soup, and rice in a separate dish.*

---

* Richard Terry, *Indian Cookery* (London: F. K. Gurney, 1861), pp. 5–7.

Club Signature Dishes

Starters

Oeufs sur le Plat Jockey Club

A favourite appetiser of Winston Churchill's, from the Jockey Club in Newmarket, this serves six people:

6 chicken livers	¼ lb/450 g veal kidney
6 slices fried bread	6 oz/170 g mushrooms
Butter	Seasoning
6 eggs	

Cook the chicken livers, and then mash them into a purée. Coat each slice of fried bread with the purée. Place these in a dish, and keep warm. Melt some butter in an omelette pan, and then fry on a medium heat 6 eggs until the whites set. Trim with a round cutter, placing one on each slice of bread.

Slice and sauté the veal kidney. Garnish the centre of each dish with the sautéed kidney, and a julienne of cooked mushrooms. Season to taste.[*]

Potted Grouse (Annabel's)

This pâté was introduced to Annabel's by Mark Birley in the 1960s, adapted from an old family recipe.

4 grouse	Pepper, to taste
4¼ oz/120 g streaky bacon, diced	4 bay leaves
6 oz/180 g butter	Thyme, to taste
Salt, to taste	Bread (toasted)

Skin, bone and dice the grouse, and then lightly fry it with the diced bacon in 2 oz/60 g of butter, adding the herbs. Place this into a blender, slowly adding 4 oz/120 g of butter, until the consistency of smooth paste is achieved. Decant this into a serving dish, placing some bay leaves on top, and leave to chill in the fridge. Serve with toast.[†]

---

[*] Georgina Landemare, *Churchill's Cookbook* (London: Imperial War Museums, 2015), p. 52.
[†] Robin McDouall, *Clubland Cooking* (London: Phaidon, 1974), pp. 43–4.

London Clubland

Potted Shrimp (Boodle's)

A quintessential starter found across Clubland, the Boodle's variant on this serves 40 people:

17.5 fl. oz/500 ml USA sauce (recipe below)	4 lb/2 kg peeled brown shrimp
2 lb/1 kg Normandy butter	2 lb/1 kg salad garnish
1 tsp ground mace	10 lemons, quartered
1 tsp ground nutmeg	2 oz/60 g dill
1 tsp fine sea salt	3 oz/80 g Avruga caviar
½ tsp ground black peppercorns	Melba toast
1¾ fl. oz/50 ml brandy	

40 individual small ramekins

To make the potted shrimp: heat the USA sauce in a heavy-bottom pan. Whisk the butter into sauce, without splitting it. Add the mace and nutmeg. Then add salt and pepper to taste, and then brandy and shrimps. Stir thoroughly, and season as required – extra lemon juice may be needed. Drain the shrimp mixture, but keep the liquid to one side. Pack the shrimp into the small ramekins, and place in the fridge for 10 minutes. Then add enough of the reserved liquid to cap each mould. Return to the fridge. When serving, turn the potted shrimp out of the ramekins, garnishing with salad, a quarter lemon, dill and Avruga caviar. Serve alongside Melba toast.

To make the USA sauce (for 10 litres):

9 lb/4 kg langoustine, size 3	3½ oz/100 g garlic
½ lb/250 g celery head	2 tsp whole white peppercorns
1¼ lb/600 g onions	7 oz/200 g tomato purée
½ lb/250 g fennel	7 fl. oz/200 ml brandy for cooking
½ lb/250 g leeks	34 cups/8 litres chicken stock
14 oz/400 g carrots	5 fl. oz/150 ml white wine (Castelbello Bianco)
1 tsp thyme	
½ tsp bay leaves	

Wash the langoustines and then remove their eyes. Next, smash them in a large mixer. Dice and sweat the celery, onions, fennel, leeks and carrots in a large, heavy-bottom pan, adding the thyme, bay leaves, garlic and

Club Signature Dishes

peppercorns, and then pouring on the wine. Once you have a consistent mix of diced and reduced mirepoix, add the langoustines, tomato purée and brandy, cooking on a high heat for two minutes. Then add the chicken stock, and reduce to a simmer for two hours, skimming the surface to remove any scum. Blend in a food processor, and filter through a fine sieve.[*]

Fish Course

Supreme of Turbot Beau Brummel (White's)

Poached young turbot on a bed of shrimp and lobster purée, coated with a chive soufflé sauce, garnished with truffle and lobster, and glazed.[†]

Entrées

Brooks's Pie (Brooks's)

A 60-year-old recipe from former Brooks's chef Jean-Claude Seraille:

1¾ oz/50 g turkey	1¾ oz/50 g chicken
1¾ oz/50 g beef	10½ oz/300 g shortcrust pastry
1¾ oz/50 g veal	3½ oz/100 g aspic jelly
1¾ oz/50 g lamb	Herbs, to taste

Pre-cook the meats, and cut into cubes. Line a pie dish with the shortcrust pastry, and place the meat on top, adding as much aspic jelly as required to fill the gaps. Cover with shortcrust pastry, and cook for 1½ hours in an oven preheated to 180°C. Once cooked, cut a ½-inch circular hole atop the pie, and pour in more hot aspic jelly, along with the herbs, until the pie has been filled up. Leave in the fridge for at least a day before serving, and serve cold.[‡]

---

[*] Marcus Binney and David Mann (eds), *Boodle's: Celebrating 250 Years, 1762–2012* (London: Boodle's, 2012), p. 217.
[†] Ibid., p. 216.
[‡] McDouall, *Clubland Cooking*, p. 79.

London Clubland

Lamb Cutlets Reform (Reform Club)

This Clubland staple was improvised from odds and ends in the kitchen by the Reform Club's pioneering chef Alexis Soyer in the 1840s, when a member demanded 'something different' late at night.

For the lamb cutlets:

2 eggs	Salt and pepper to season
8 lamb cutlets, French-trimmed	1¾ oz/50 g breadcrumbs

For the Reform jus:

2 cloves of garlic	1¼ fl. oz/35 ml tarragon vinegar
1 shallot	5 fl. oz/150 ml lamb stock
1¼ oz/35 g unsalted butter	2 tbsp redcurrant jelly
1 tsp tomato purée	1¾ oz/50 g cooked beetroot
1¾ fl. oz/50 ml red wine	¾ oz/25 g gherkins
3½ oz/100 g flour	2¾ oz/75 g ham batons
2 peppercorns	1¾ oz/50 g cooked ox tongue

Separate the egg yolks and egg whites. The egg whites should be wrapped in clingfilm and steamed over boiling water until firm, and then left to cool. The egg yolks should be beaten. The lamb cutlets should be seasoned in salt and pepper, and then a covering of flour, and dipped into the egg yolks, before being covered in breadcrumbs. They can then be pan-fried on each side until golden, and then placed in a 180°C oven for six minutes.

Chop the garlic and shallot extremely finely, then add to a pan on medium heat with the butter until lightly brown; then add the tomato purée and stir for 1 minute before adding the red wine, peppercorns and vinegar. Leave to reduce in volume by a third, before adding the lamb stock with redcurrant jelly; and then further reduce by half. Add the beetroot, egg white, gherkins, ham batons and ox tongue, and stir lightly.

When serving, pour the Reform jus into the bottom of the bowl, placing the batons in a pile in the middle of the bowl. The lamb cutlets should then be placed to one side, leaning against the batons.[*]

---

[*] Craig MacDonald Marshall, Alex Fulluck and Amy Crangle, *Recipes from the Reform* (London: Reform Club, 2014), pp. 62–3.

Club Signature Dishes

Mutton curry (Oriental Club)

For the curry powder:

- 1 lb/450 g best turmeric
- ¾ lb/330 g coriander seeds
- 3 oz/85 g powdered ginger
- 3 oz/85 g cayenne
- 2 oz/55 g black pepper
- 3½ tsp cardamon seeds, pounded
- 3½ tsp carraway seeds
- 3½ tsp cloves, pounded

The whole must be reduced to a fine powder, well mixed, and kept in a bottle tightly corked.

For the curry:

- 5 x medium onions
- 4 oz/110 g butter
- 3 oz/85 g curry powder (as above)
- 1½ oz/42 g curry paste
- Juice of 1 lemon
- ½ tsp salt
- 3 lb/1.4 kg lean mutton, deboned
- Patna rice (prepared as below)

A historic recipe, from 1861. Cut the onions into small slices, place them into a stewpan with the butter, and fry over a low-medium heat until light brown. Then add 4 tablespoons of curry powder and 2 of curry paste. Stir well over the heat for 10 minutes.

Next, add the juice of 1 lemon and ½ a teaspoonful of salt, plus 3 lb of lean mutton, without bone (leg or chumps will make the best curry).

Then turn up to a high heat and fry for five minutes, cover it with water, and place it in a slow oven at 150°C for 3 hours, or until done and quite tender. By this time, it should be almost dry, so skim off the fat, and serve the curry with rice in a separate dish.

For the rice:

Wash one pound of Patna rice in cold water; have a large stewpan of boiling water ready, in which to add the rice. Let it simmer for 20 minutes, stirring occasionally, but not too often lest it breaks the rice.

When it is done, strain through a large colander or sieve, and pour 8 quarts of cold water over it. Leave it to drain for 5 minutes, then pour on 6 quarts of cold water, leaving to dry for another 10 minutes. Although this may sound simple, it requires great care to be served dry.

If the rice needs to be kept warm for any length of time, place it in a napkin and leave it in a warm place until required.[*]

---

[*] Terry, *Indian Cookery*, pp. 12–13, 39–40, 45.

Travellers' Pie (Travellers Club)

A dish invented at the Travellers Club by chef Raymond Serre in the 1960s, which the club secretary Robin McDouall said was necessitated, 'One year, when the grouse ran out and we couldn't make the grouse-and-steak' pie that the Club was then known for. Successive club chefs have since evolved the recipe. Below is one more recent variant.

½ lb/230 g lean veal	Pepper, to taste
1 lb/450 g pork – fat and lean	Nutmeg, to taste
¼ lb/110 g ham	1 large ½ fl. oz/120 ml glass of sherry
1 medium onion	
1 clove garlic	6 rashers of lean bacon
1 oz/30 g chopped parsley	4 rashers of streaky bacon
Marjoram, to taste	½ fl. oz/120 ml stock
Tarragon, to taste	10 oz/300 g short pastry
Salt, to taste	2 eggs

Chop the veal, pork, ham, onion, garlic and parsley, season them with salt, pepper and nutmeg, and leave them to marinate overnight in the sherry. Line a pie dish with the lean bacon rashers, then add the mixture on top. Cover with the rashers of streaky bacon, and then add stock, to soften. Beat the eggs and add water, to make an egg wash. Cover with a pastry lid, glaze the lid with the egg wash, and cook in an oven at 170°C for 75 minutes. Chill overnight in the fridge, and serve cold.*

Savouries

Sweet and savoury dessert courses are typically served 'from the trolley', with it being wheeled out with great ceremony, laden with all manner of cheeses, trifles and cakes. Or there may be separate sweet and savoury trolleys. This does not rule out ordering a hot savoury from the kitchen.

---

* McDouall, *Clubland Cooking*, p. 78, embedding subsequent modifications by the Travellers Club.

Club Signature Dishes

Ale Rarebit

A Clubland staple: most of the older clubs have their own variant.

½ lb/250 g mature Welsh cheddar
30 g/1 oz melted butter, melted
1 tbsp mustard
1 tbsp Worcestershire sauce
1 tbsp plain flour
¼ oz/5 g black peppercorns, freshly crushed
6 tbsp ale (brown or golden)
4 thick-cut slices wholemeal farmhouse bread

Grate the cheese, and melt in a saucepan over a gentle heat, mixed in with the butter, mustard, Worcestershire sauce, flour and pepper. Gradually add the ale, but never too much at once, leaving it a thick mixture. Leave to cool slightly, while grilling the bread until golden brown. Serve promptly on the bread.[*]

Devils on Horseback (Guards Club variant)

Much loved by Edwardian hostesses, and immortalised in the novels of Anthony Powell, 'Devils on Horseback' are prunes wrapped in bacon. But the old Guards Club (before its merger into today's Cavalry and Guards Club) had its own unique variant: grapes wrapped in bacon.[†]

Desserts

Boodle's Orange Fool (Boodle's)

More of a trifle than a fool, this is Boodle's signature dish. The recipe was first disclosed by Dorothy Allhusen – who was married to Henry Allhusen, chairman of Boodle's in 1922–5 – in *A Book of Scents and Dishes* (1926).

4 oranges
2 lemons
2½ cups/570 ml cream
Sponge cakes
Sugar

---

[*] Traditional.
[†] McDouall, *Clubland Cooking*, p. 153.

Take the juice of the four oranges and the two lemons, and the grated rind of one lemon and two oranges. Sweeten to taste, and add the cream. Whip the cream-zest mixture thoroughly.

Fill a bowl with the sponge cakes, cut in four pieces each, and pour the mixture over the cakes. The dish should be made some hours before it is served, to allow the juice of the fruit to penetrate the cakes.

A modern variant of the dish, current served in Boodle's, adds an Orange Italienne to the cakes (typically Aurum liqueur, but another brandy-based orange liqueur like Grand Marnier may be substituted), and involves the liberal use of honey.

The dish is usually silver-served.[*]

Byculla Soufflé (Byculla Club)

Not actually a soufflé, this boozy dessert was the signature dish of the now-defunct Byculla Club in nineteenth-century Bombay.

6 eggs	Chartreuse
3 tbsp sugar	Curaçao
2½ cups/600 g cream	Benedictine
20 ml isinglass	Digestive biscuit crumbs – small sprinkling per serving
Kummel	

Take the yolks of 6 eggs, add 3 tablespoons of white sugar, beat well until dry, and keep to one side. Then take 600 g of cream and also beat until dry. Now take half a packet of isinglass, well soaked, and add one 60 ml liqueur glass each of Kummel, Chartreuse, Curaçao and Benedictine. Mix the whole well together then put each portion into a small bowl, no larger than half a cup in volume.

On the top of the bowl, place crumbs of mixed digestive biscuits, and keep in the fridge until desired.[†]

---

[*] Binney and Mann, *Boodle's*, p. 214.
[†] Samuel T. Sheppard, *The Byculla Club, 1833–1916: A History* (Bombay: Bennett, Coleman, 1916), pp. 153–4.

Club Signature Dishes

Reform Trifle (Reform Club)

For the crème anglaise:

   1 vanilla pod
   2 cups/500 ml double cream
   6 egg yolks
   3½ oz/100 g sugar
   1 oz/25 g corn flour

For the trifle sponge:

   13 oz/375 g butter
   13 oz/375 g sugar
   2 tsp vanilla essence
   6 eggs
   13 oz/375 g self-raising flour

For the fruit compote:

   3½ oz/100 g caster sugar
   4 tbsp water
   12 oz/340 g frozen raspberries

For the Chantilly cream:

   6¾ fl. oz/200 ml whipping cream
   Icing sugar to taste

To serve:

   Sherry to taste – typically Oloroso
   Summer berries
   Chocolate shavings

For the crème anglaise, mix the split vanilla pod in with the cream in a saucepan, and bring to the boil. In a mixing bowl, whisk the egg yolks, sugar and corn flour, and add half of that to the cream once it is boiling, stirring until consistent. Strain and leave to cool.

For the sponge, beat the butter, sugar and vanilla essence together until a light and fluffy consistency is achieved, then beat the eggs and begin adding them slowly. Afterwards, fold in the flour. Bake the sponge mixture at 170°C for 40 minutes, or until golden brown and spongey to the touch. Leave to cool, and then slice into small cubes.

For the compote, mix the sugar, water and raspberries in a small saucepan, bringing to the boil and leaving on a high heat for 5 minutes. Then reduce the heat, and leave to simmer for around 10 minutes, until the compote thickens.

Whip the whipping cream until soft peaks emerge, then add the icing sugar to taste. Pour into a piping bag for serving.

Pour the sponge mix and fruit compote together, and then add a generous dash of sherry to taste. Marinade for 15 minutes. Spoon the mixture into a serving bowl, and cover with a thick layer of crème anglaise. Pipe the Chantilly cream atop that, and add decorative chocolate shavings and summer berries.[*]

Gooseberry Pie (Athenæum)

For the pastry:

- 4 egg yolks
- 4½ oz/125 g softened, unsalted butter
- 2½ oz/70 g icing sugar
- 9oz /250 g plain flour, plus extra for dusting

For the filling:

- 2 lb/900 g gooseberries
- 7 oz/200 g caster sugar, plus extra for sprinkling
- 2 glasses of Prosecco

To serve:

- 150 g single pouring cream

Separate the egg yolks. Mix the butter and icing sugar together, adding 3 of the egg yolks, and then add flour until the texture begins to be crumbly, adding 1–2 tablespoons of water to ensure consistency. Roll into a ball across a floury surface, then flatten. Wrap in clingfilm and place in the fridge for at least half an hour.

Place the gooseberries, caster sugar and Prosecco into a saucepan over a medium heat and simmer for around 10 minutes, until the gooseberries are softened. Add further caster sugar to taste, if required. Pour the mixture into a pie dish. Heat oven to 180°C.

Extract the pastry from the fridge, rolling out to be large enough to cover the pie dish, and add it on top. Make a small incision in the middle of the pie top, and brush it with the remaining egg yolk, sprinkling some caster sugar on top. Bake for 30 minutes, or until the top is golden brown. Leave to cool slightly.

Serve alongside a small serving jug for the cream.[†]

---

[*] MacDonald Marshall et al., *Recipes from the Reform*, pp. 94–5.
[†] Traditional.

HUNTING OPEN SEASONS

London clubs are often renowned for their fresh game. The below tables illustrate the seasons for these. (While clubs will offer vegetarian and vegan options, this is not the speciality of most.)

Game birds and wildfowl	Season start	Season end
Grouse	12 August	10 December
Ptarmigan	12 August	10 December
Snipe	12 August	31 January
Black Game	20 August	10 December
Woodcock (Scotland)	1 September	31 January
Wild Duck and Geese (inland)	1 September	31 January
Partridge	1 September	1 February
Wild Duck and Geese (below high-water mark)	1 September	20 February
Capercaillie	1 October	31 January
Woodcock (England and Wales)	1 October	31 January
Pheasant	1 October	1 February

Deer	England and Wales		Scotland	
	Starts	*Ends*	*Starts*	*Ends*
Roe Buck	1 April	31 October	1 May	20 October
Red Stags	1 August	30 April	1 July	20 October
Fallow Buck	1 August	30 April	1 August	30 March
Sika Stags	1 August	30 April	1 August	30 April
Red Hinds	1 November	28/29 February	21 October	15 February
Fallow Doe	1 November	28/29 February	21 October	15 February
Sika Hinds	1 November	28/29 February	21 October	15 February
Roe Doe	1 November	28/29 February	21 October	28/29 February

TOASTING

Toasting during meals was at the very heart of clubs, from their early beginnings. As Ian Newman argues:

> Toasting formally enacted the central principles of convivial agreement. First a toast was proposed, often a pithy, witty idea or opinion intended to reflect the feelings of all those gathered; then everyone responded, signalling their assent by drinking. Differences were set aside, unanimity was asserted, and indeed unanimity, or 'social harmony', was the precondition for the form.*

A prime example of this can be observed in the Fox Club, a dining society founded in 1813 which is dedicated to the memory of Whig statesman Charles James Fox (1749–1806). It dines twice a year in the Great Subscription Room of Brooks's, every May and November. No speeches are permitted, but the highest-ranking member proposes the following four toasts, which are all taken sitting down:

1. To the Memory of Charles James Fox.
2. Earl Grey and the Reform Bill.
3. The Memory of Lord Holland.
4. To the Memory of Lord John Russell.

---

* Ian Newman, 'The anti-social convivialist: toasting and resistance to sociability', in Valérie Capdeville and Alain Kerhervé (eds), *British Sociability in the Long Eighteenth Century* (London: Boydell Press, 2019), p. 220.

Toasting

(While Fox was in many ways an unsuccessful politician, spending much of his career in opposition, the passage of the First Reform Act in 1832, during the government of Earl Grey, is seen as the apotheosis of Whig influence. Lord Holland, a Whig grandee, owned Holland House, a key social headquarters for the Whigs; while Lord John Russell, who proposed the Reform Bill, was later prime minister. Grey, Holland and Russell were all members of Brooks's and of the Fox Club.)

A more typical Clubland toast would be to the monarch, plus to any founders or key themes of the Club.

WEIGHTY MATTERS

Most historic clubs the world over have a curious item: the weighing chair. They can be found in English-style clubs from Calcutta to California. Each club's chair may be semi-retired to a distant corridor, but it is usually kept within dashing distance of the dining room or lavatories. Its purpose is very simple: members used to weigh themselves before and after a meal, to see how much weight they had gained.

HANGOVER CURES

So you crawled back in from the Club in the small hours, and are feeling decidedly fragile after a night's indulgence in the Club Claret. What you need is a hangover cure.

The Prairie Oyster cocktail

A traditional cure, with numerous regional variants. Crack open one raw egg into a small glass tumbler and beat vigorously, then add in tomato juice to fill the glass half-full, then mix in one teaspoon full of Worcestershire sauce, a few drops of vinegar, a sprinkle of salt and pepper, and finally, a dash of Tabasco sauce. Mix thoroughly, and gulp it down swiftly. It does wonders for relieving you of your hangover. (It shan't make the thing go away entirely, but the drink tastes so foul that your hangover is no longer your biggest problem.)

A full English breakfast

Back to the Club (or perhaps you've never left, having passed out in one of its bedrooms, or even pitched out overnight in an armchair) for a hearty full English breakfast, with sausages, bacon, black pudding, tomatoes, mushrooms, eggs (poached, scrambled or fried) and plenty of toast, all washed down with orange juice and coffee. The bread in particular is good at soaking up alcohol.

Kedgeree

A good kedgeree that's heavy on the smoked haddock flakes, and light on the rice, with plenty of seasoning to clear the sinuses, can do wonders. The Caledonian Club does a particularly good kedgeree.

Ginger tea

A simple cure, as old as time itself. You can fortify your ginger tea with cayenne, turmeric or a dash of squeezed lemon, to taste.

'Hair of the dog that bit me'

Alcohol deadens the nerves. If you're so suffused with industrial quantities of booze that the hangover just won't go away, then one solution may be to keep drinking – lightly – in the morning, to dull the pain, on the understanding that you'll dry out by the mid-afternoon. An early morning glass of champagne every half-hour should do it, reducing the dosage to one glass an hour by 11 a.m., and abstaining by 3 p.m. (Note that if you're suffering from severe alcohol poisoning from the night before, this is not a good idea.)

Water

Water allegedly has some sort of health-giving qualities or other, although these rumours are often treated with significant scepticism across Clubland.

SECTION 4

LONDON CLUBS, PAST AND PRESENT

MAPS OF LONDON CLUBLAND

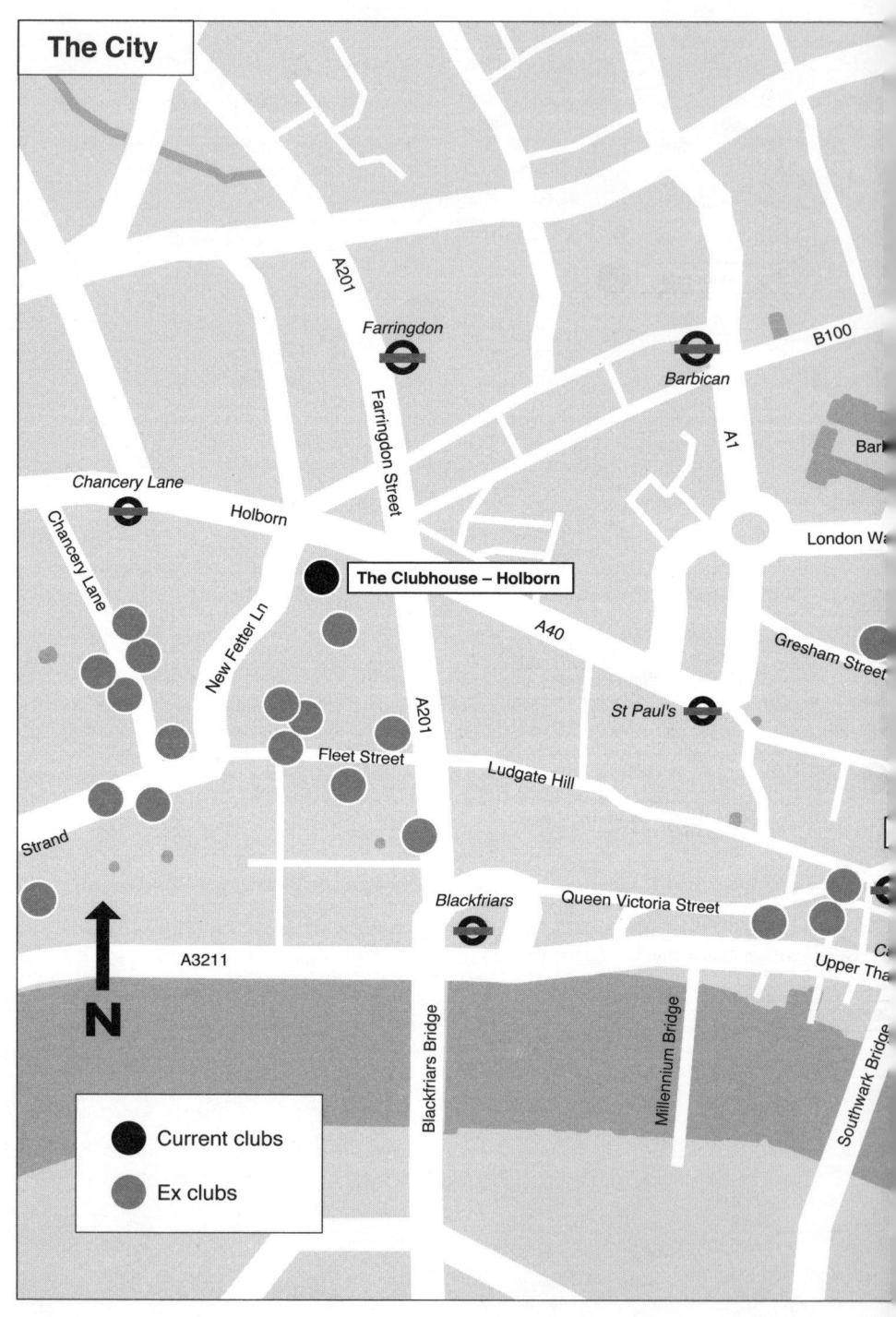

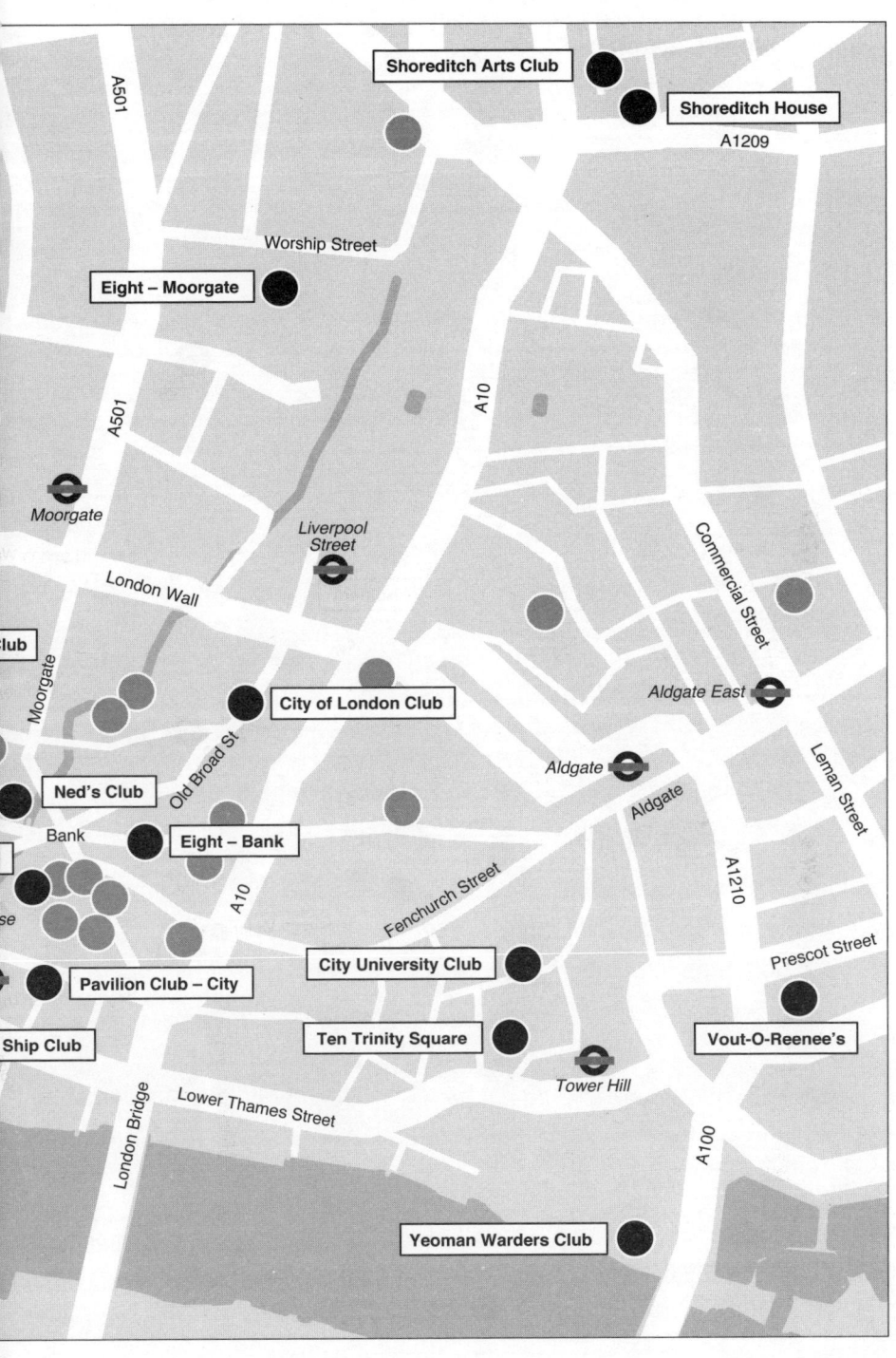

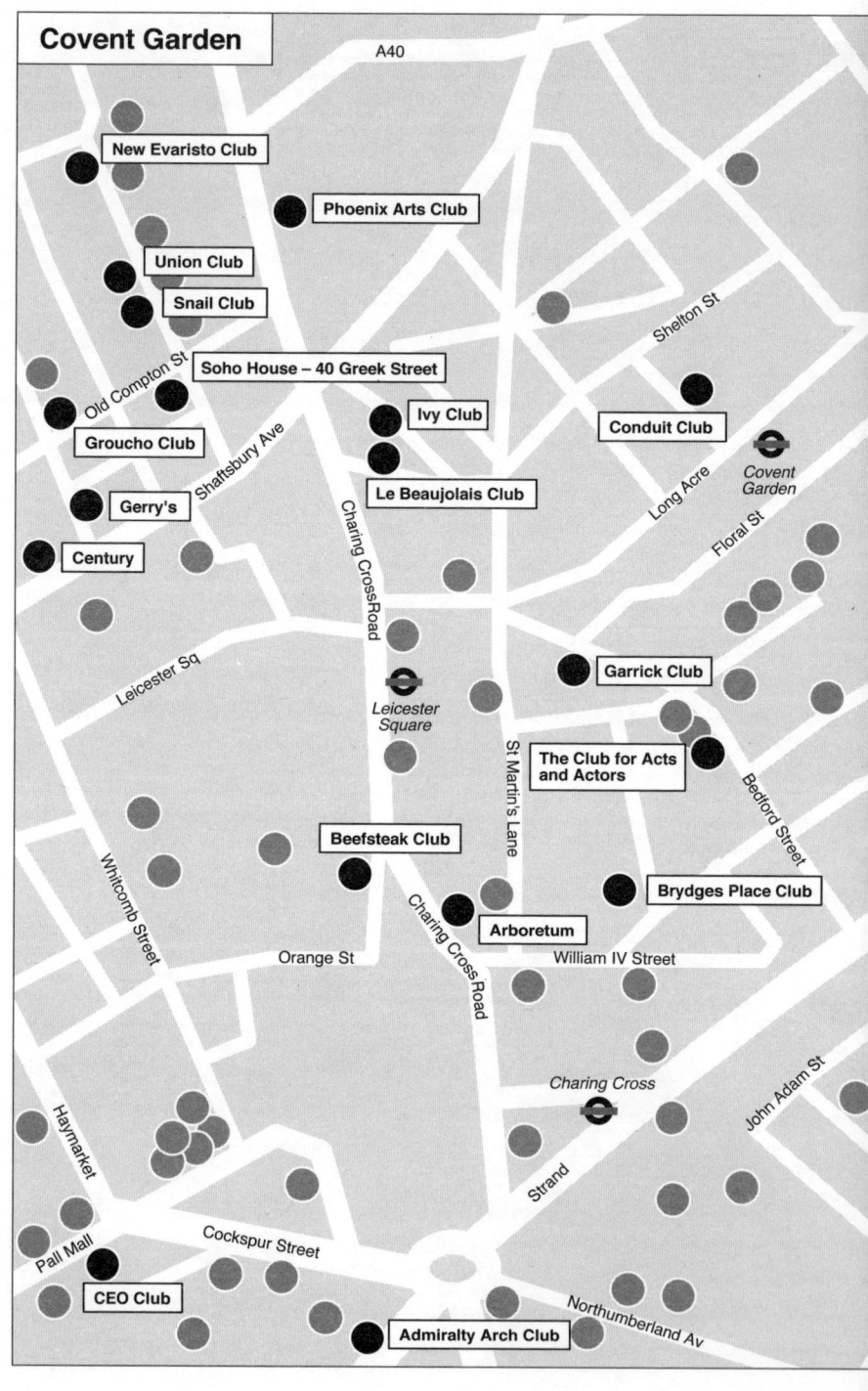

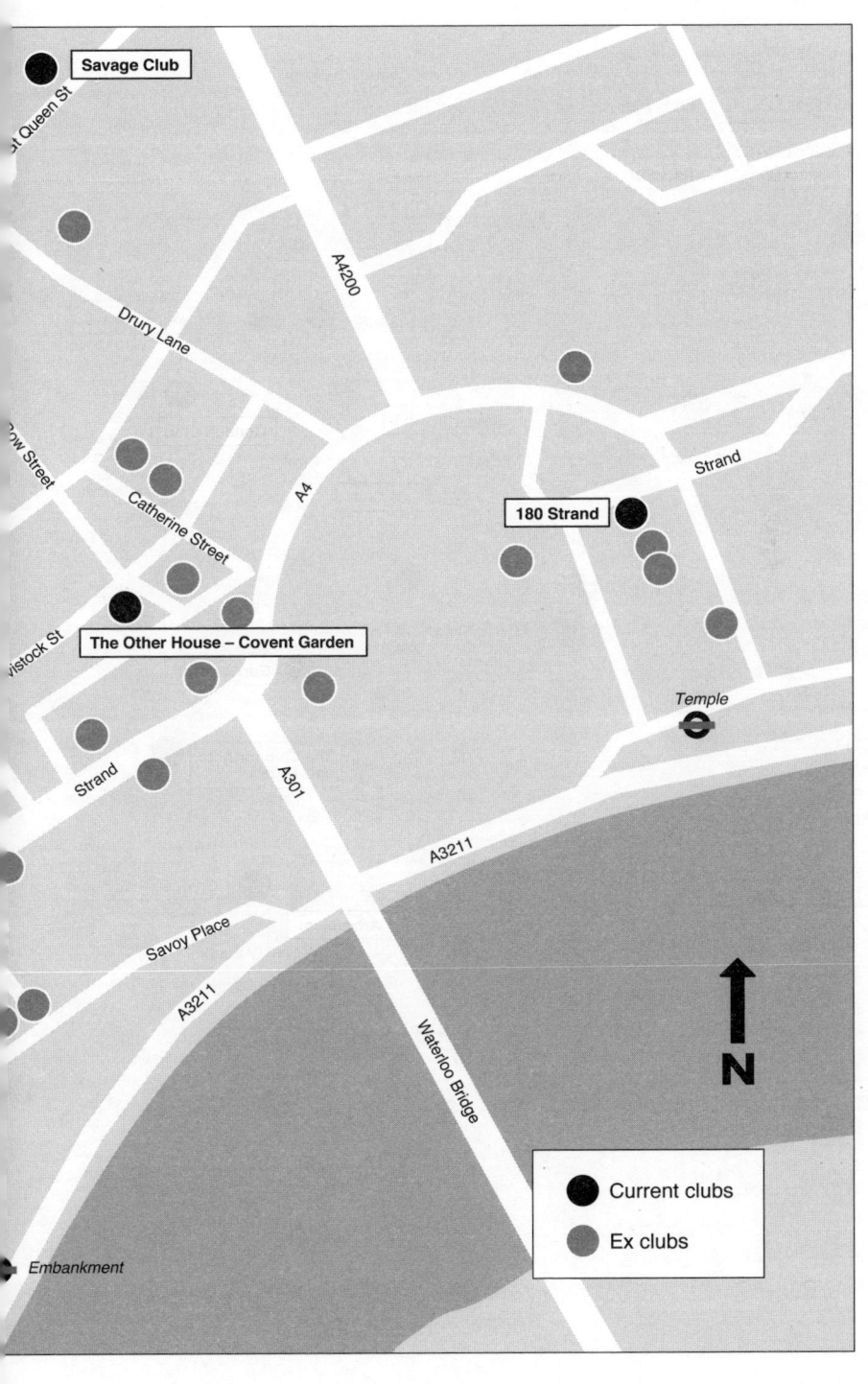

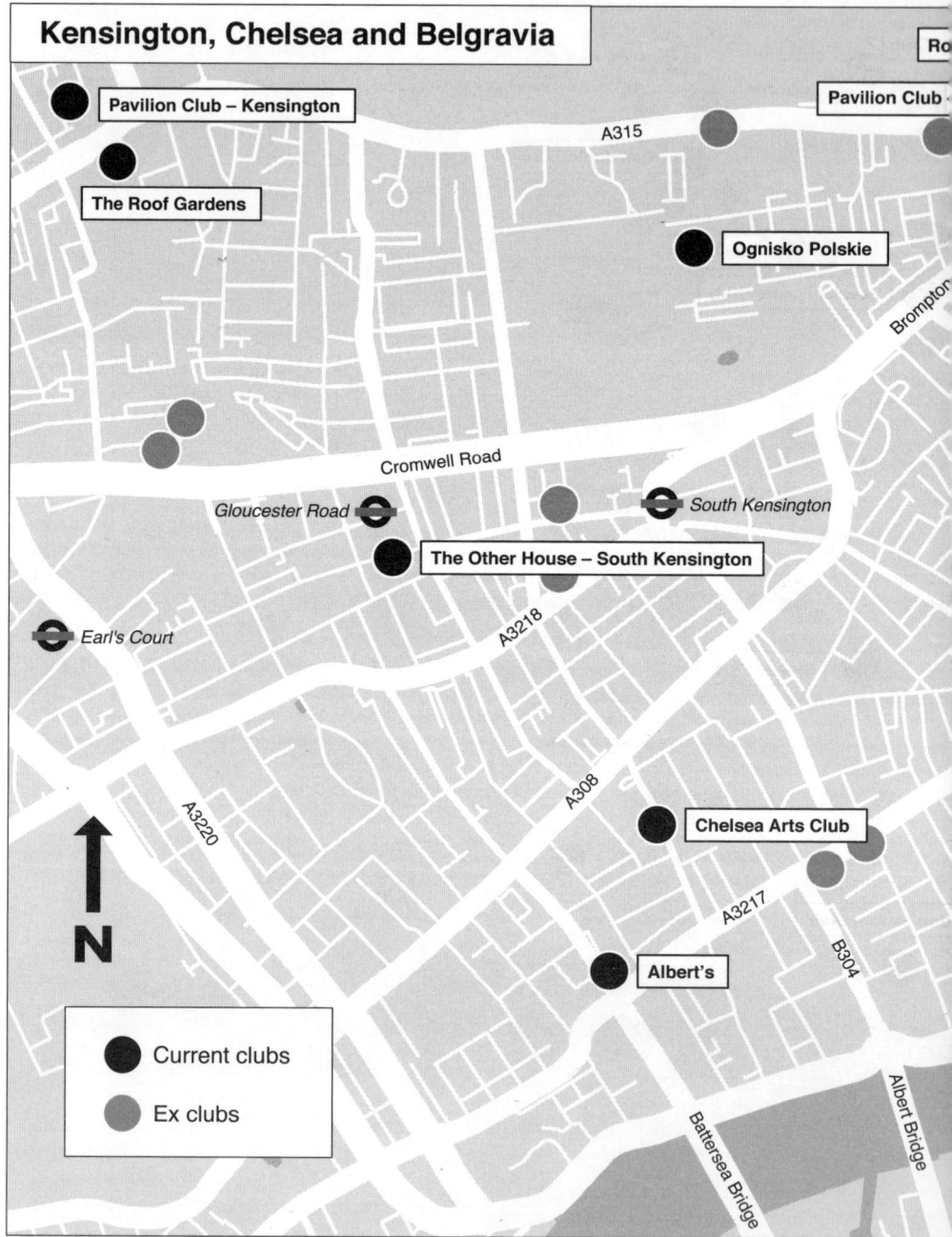

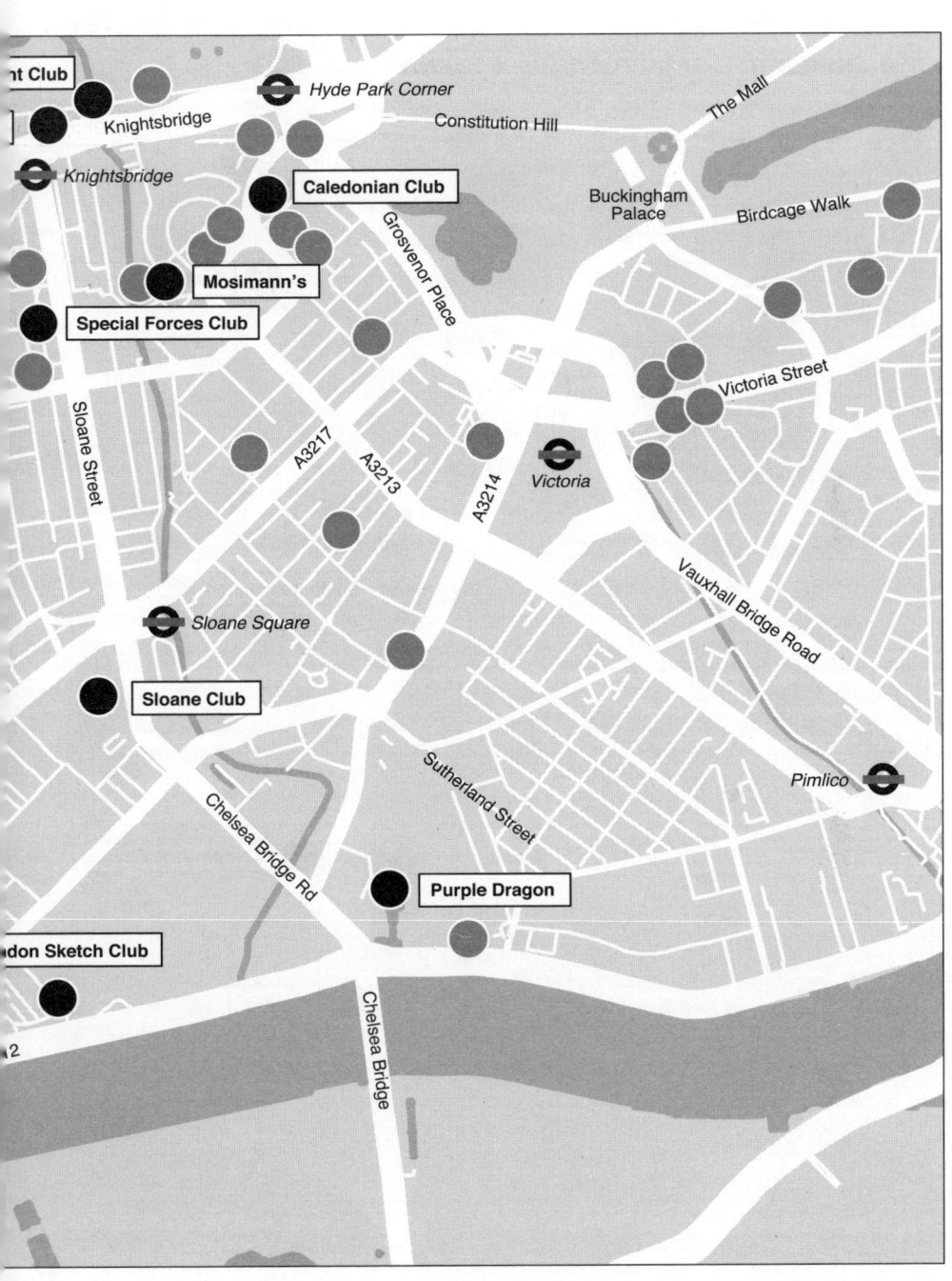

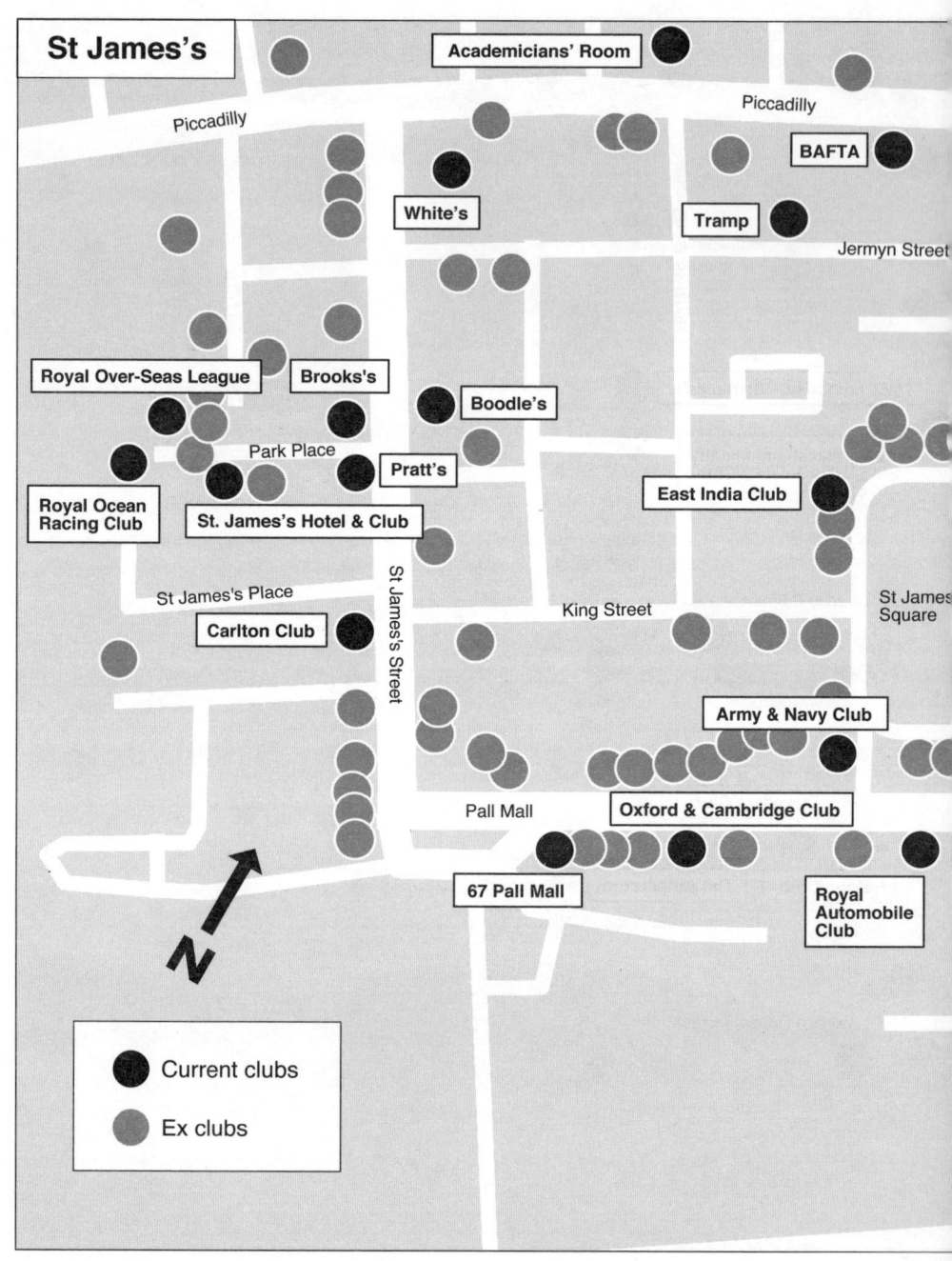

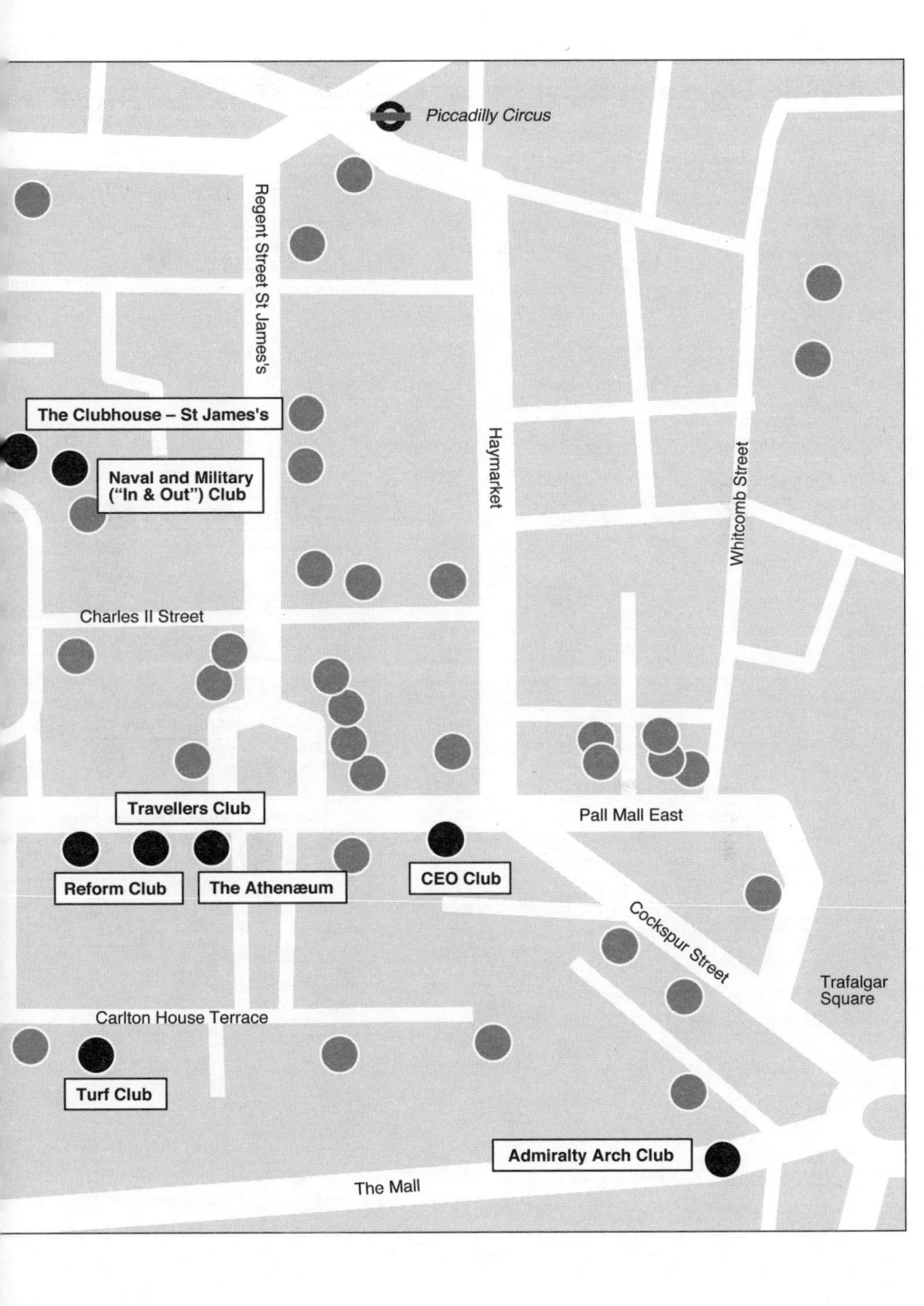

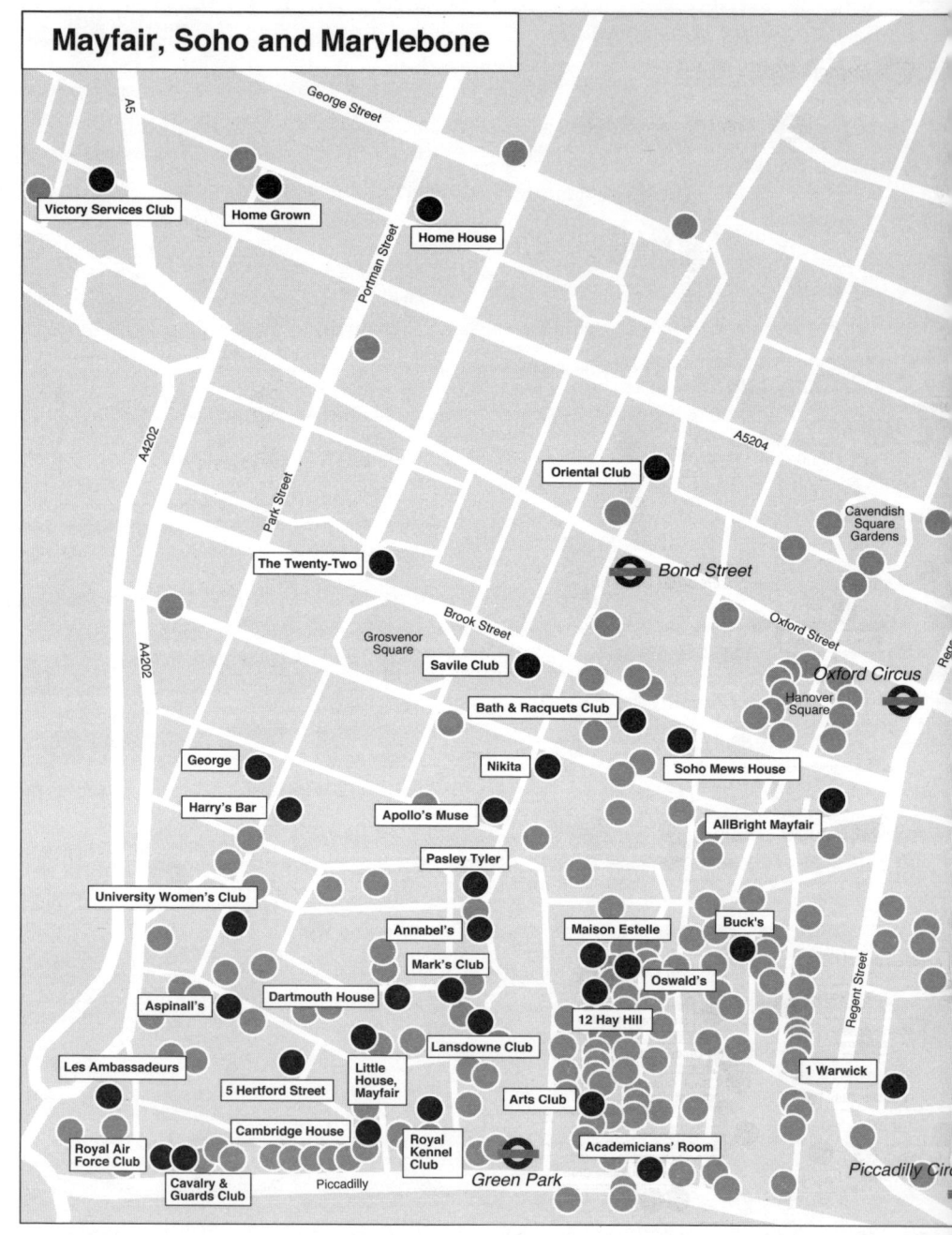

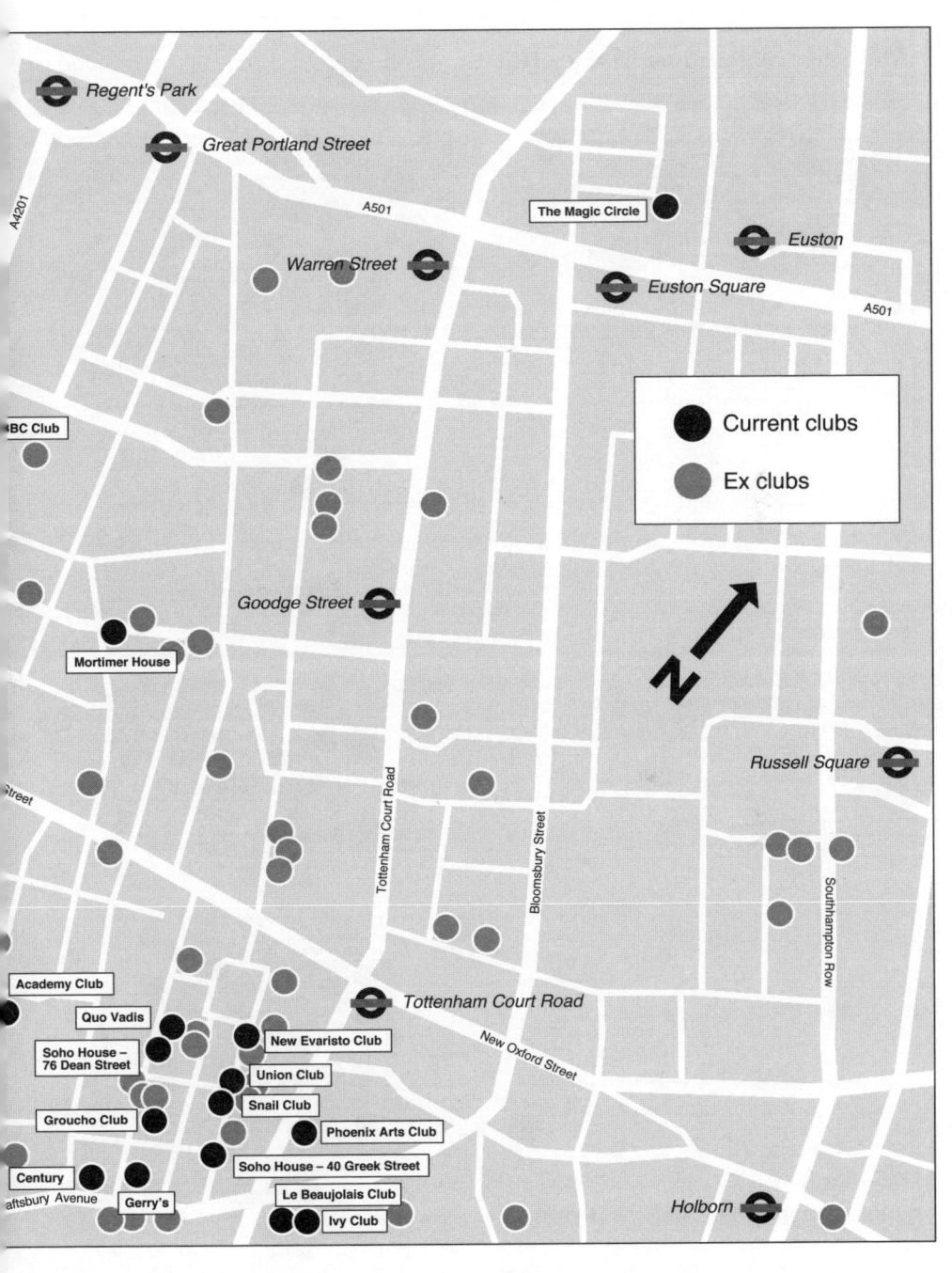

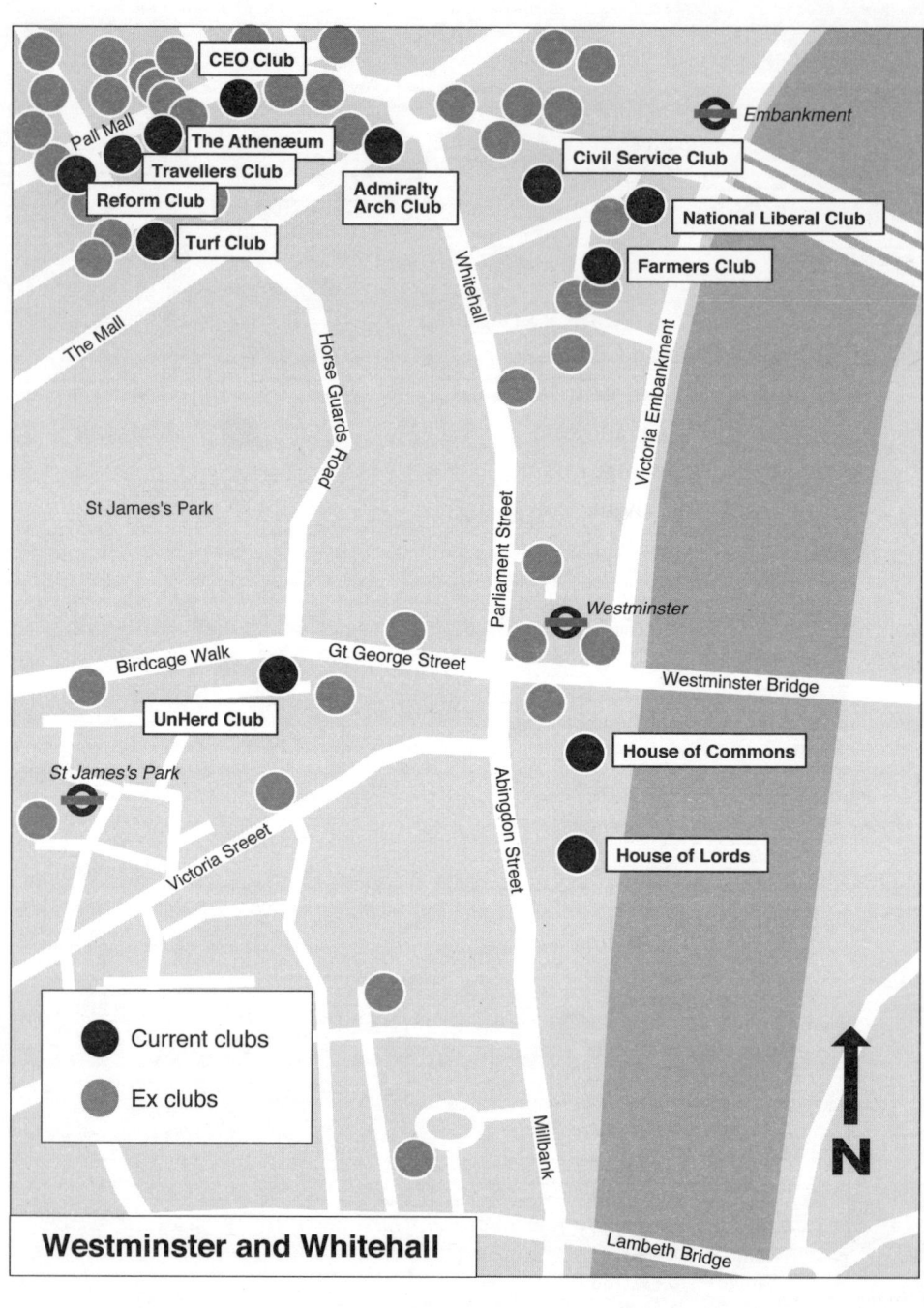

INDEX OF CLUBLAND ADDRESSES, PAST AND PRESENT

Today's Clubland contains many fleeting establishments that are unlikely to still exist in ten or twenty years. It was ever thus. A look at the principal addresses of clubhouses over the last few centuries makes it clear how many clubs have come and gone. It also provides a convenient guide, should you want to undertake a walking tour of the central London streets that have been lined with clubs over the years.

♂ *Men's club.*
♀ *Women's club.*
⚥ *Mixed-sex club.*
♂⚥ *Men's club which became a mixed-sex club.*
♀⚥ *Women's club which became a mixed-sex club.*
† *denotes bomb damage in the Second World War.*
†† *denotes destruction by bombing in the Second World War.*
Numbers denote the street number of the building.

Abchurch Lane, EC4
   15: Gresham Club ♂ (1915–91); London Capital Club ⚥ (1994–2018).
Adam Street, WC2
   8–9: Green Room Club ♂ (1955–99).
   9: Adam Street Club ⚥ (2001–14).
Adelphi Terrace, WC2 *(demolished in 1936 for redevelopment as the Adelphi building)*
   1: French Club ♂ (1883–8); Arundel Club ♂ (1883–1901).
   1A: Junior Garrick Club ♂ (1878–88; 1897–1936).
   6–7: Savage Club ♂ (1889–1936).
   10: Green Room Club ♂ (1877–83); Crichton Club ♂ (1891–6); Liberal Forward Club ⚥ (1899–1901); New Reform Club ⚥ (1901–12).
Albemarle Street, W1
   7: Royal Thames Yacht Club ♂ (1860–1910).
   13: Bombay Club ♂ (1820–4); Albemarle Club ⚥ (1874–1909); Public Schools Club ♂ (1909–13); Players' Theatre Club ⚥ (1940–6).
   20: New Oxford and Cambridge Club ♂ (1885–93).

Albemarle Street, W1 – *continued*
  23: United Service Club ♂ (1816–19); Alfred Club ♂ (1808–54); Westminster Club ♂ (1857–82); Regency Club ♂ (1882–6); National Union Club ♂ (1887–93).
  25: Oswald's ⚧ (2018–present).
  27: Hogarth Club ♂ (1881–7).
  28: Hurst Park Club ♂ (1889–90).
  41: Amphitryon Club ♂ (1870–95).
  43–44: County Club ♂ (1866–85); Junior Conservative Club ♂ (1889–1914).
Aldwych, WC2
  1: Aldwych Club ♂ (1910–53).
  Aldwych House: Old Colony Club ♂ (1923–6).
Alfred Place, WC1
  1: One Alfred Place ⚧ (2008–21).
All Souls' Place, NW1
  1 Langham Chambers: Langham Sketch Club ♂ (1854–1940)††.
Archer Street, W1
  3–4: Rehearsal Club ♀ (1949–68).
Argyll Street, W1
  8: Ladies' Victoria Club ♀ (1878–81).
Arlington Street, SW1
  4: Arlington Club ♂ (1865–75); Golfers' Club ♂ (1968–74).
  9: Ladies' Imperial Club ♀ (1925–8).
  10–11: New University Club – *rear of St James's Street clubhouse* ♂ (1864–1938)
  15A: Primrose Club ♂ (1910–13).
  22: New Travellers Club ♂ (1869–71); Ritz Club ⚧ (1998–2020).
Arundel Street, WC2
  37: Whittington Club ♂ (1846–73); Temple Club ♂ (1873–81).
Baker Street, W1
  Unknown number: Three Arts Club ♀ (1941–9)†.
Beak Street, W1
  16–18: Murray's ⚧ (1913–75).

Bedford Hill, SW12
  15–19: Little House, Balham (2022–present).
Bedford Place, WC1
  20–21: Penn Club ♂⚧ (1920–2021).
Bedford Square, WC1
  22: Chief ♀ (2022–4).
Bedford Street, WC2
  20: Green Room Club ♂ (1883–1903); The Club for Acts and Actors ⚧ (1949–present).
  21: Camera Club ♂ (1885–91).
  30: Yorick Club ♂ (1897–1908).
Belgrave Square, W1
  6: Belgian Institute ⚧ (1942–6); Royal Anglo-Belgian Club ⚧ (1946–78).
  10: Number 10 Club ♂ (1955–77).
  42: Forum Club ♀ (1953–8).
  45: Ognisko Polskie ⚧ (1942–6).
Berkeley Square, W1
  28: Morton's ⚧ (1981–2020).
  42: Pasley Tyler ⚧ (2019–present).
  44: Clermont Club – *above-ground* ♂ (1962–2018); Annabel's – *basement* ⚧ (1963–2018).
  46: Annabel's ⚧ (2018–present).
Berkeley Street, W1
  11: Scottish Club – *rear entrance to clubhouse on Dover Street* ♂ (1879–1927).
  13: National Sporting Club ♂ (1947–51).
  16: Albemarle Club – *ladies' entrance, to main clubhouse on Dover Street* ⚧ (1909–39).
  19: Public Schools Club ♂ (1913–15).
  20: Almack's ⚧ (1904–21).
Berners Street, W1
  9: Berners Club ♀ (1870–2).
  31, Berners Street Mansions: Ladies' Town and Country Club ♀ (1897–1900).
Bishopsgate, EC2
  94–96: Overseas Bankers' Club ♂ (1948–50).
Bolton Street, W1

Index of Clubland Addresses

Unknown number: Baldwin Club
  ♂ (1911–27).
Bridge Street, EC4
  York Hotel: Farmers Club ♂
    (1843–63).
Bridge Street, SW1
  1: St Stephen's Club ♂ (1870–1962).
  9: Palace Club ♂ (1882–1903).
Brompton Road, SW1
  87–135: Harrods Gentlemen's Club
    ♂ (1905–26); Harrods Ladies'
    Club ♀ (1905–39).
Brook Street, W1
  5: Gun Club ♂ (1910–13).
  39: Guards Club – *ladies' annexe* ♀⚥
    (1926–46).
  41–43: Guards Club ♂
    (1921–46).
  43: Bath Club ⚥ (1959–81).
  Claridge's: Ladies' Automobile Club
    ♀ (1904–14).
  69–71: Savile Club ♂
    (1927–present).
Brook's Mews, W1
  49: Bath and Racquets Club ♂
    (1989–present).
Brunswick Square, WC1
  28A: Minerva Club ♀ (1920–62).
Bruton Mews, W1
  Unnumbered: Bruton Club ♀
    (1930–5).
Bruton Street, W1
  13: Royal Flying Corps Club ♂
    (1917–18); Royal Air Force
    Club ♂ (1918–22).
  22: Pioneer Club ♀ (1895–7).
Brydges Place, WC2
  2: Festival Club ♂ (1951–79); Two
    Brydges ⚥ (1982–2018);
    Brydges Place Club ⚥
    (2019–present).
Brydges Street, WC2 *(renamed Catherine Street in 1872)*
  Theatre Royal, Drury Lane: Garrick
    Club ♂ (1831–2).
  Vinegar Yard: Savage Club ♂
    (1857–8).
Buckingham Gate, SW1
  54, 44 St James's Court: Austral Club
    ♀ (1903–6).
Buckingham Palace Road, SW1
  200: Grosvenor Club ♀ (1911–57).
Buckingham Street, W1
  15: Denison Club ⚥ (1886–1905);
    Junior Denison Club ⚥
    (1886–90).
Buckingham Street, WC1
  19: Emerson Club ♀ (1911–24).
Burlington Gardens, W1
  2: Empress Club ♀ (1910–11).
  34: Ladies' Army and Navy Club ♀
    (1903–27).
Bush Lane, EC4
  27: Pavilion Club – City ⚥
    (2017–present).
Caledonian Road, N1
  28, 'Grey Door': Keystone Crescent
    ⚥ (2015–present).
Carey Street, WC2
  62: Women's Press Club ♀
    (1944–72).
Carlton Gardens, SW1
  6: Athenæum – *ladies' annexe* ♀⚥
    (1936–61).
  7: Carlton Club – *annexe* ♂
    (1925–40)†.
Carlton House Terrace, SW1
  1: Savage Club ♂ (1936–63)†.
  2: Carlton Club ♂ (1832–5).
  5: Turf Club ♂ (1965–present).
  10–11: Union Club ♂ (1924–51)†.
  16: Crockford's ♂⚥ (1934–82).
Cavendish Place, W1
  12: Pioneer Club ♀ (1920–39).
Cavendish Square, W1
  20: Cowdray Club ♀ (1922–74).
  28, 'Queen Anne House': V. A. D.
    Ladies' Club ♀ (1920–57).
Caxton Street, SW1
  2, St Ermin's Court: New Reform
    Club ♂ (1899–1901);
    Northumberland and Northern
    Counties Club ♂ (1901–5).
Chancery Lane, WC2
  22: Press Club ♂ (1887–90).
  27: Eldon Club ♂ (1890–3).
  103–109: Law Club, later the Law
    Society Club ♂ (1828–1903).
Change Alley, EC3
  1: Eight – Bank ⚥ (2008–present).

407

Charing Cross Road, WC2
  2A: Arboretum ⚧ (2019–present).
  28: Camera Club ♂ (1891–1905).
Charles Street, SW1 *(renamed Charles II Street in 1939)*
  11–12: United Service Club ♂ (1819–28); Junior United Service Club ♂ (1828–1953).
  19–25, United Hotel: United Club ♂ (1865–89).
  24: United Clergy and Laity Club ♂ (1865–78).
Charles Street, W1
  16: Guards Club ♂ (1946–76).
  30, 'Crewe House': Cosmopolitan Club ♂ (1854–1902); Portland Club ♂ (1943–69).
  37–38: Dartmouth House ⚧ (2023–present).
  46: Mark's Club ♂⚧ (1973–present).
  47–48: Guards Club – *ladies' annexe* ♀⚧ (1946–59).
Charlotte Street, W1
  84: Hogarth Club ♂ (1874–81).
  76, 'Constable Studios': Slade Club ♀ (1900–10).
  110: Cave of Harmony ⚧ (1924–7).
Chesterfield Gardens, W1
  9: Lyceum Club ♀ (1933–6).
Chesterfield Street, W1
  1A: Chess Club ⚧ (2017–18).
Church Road, SW19
  Unnumbered: All England Lawn Tennis and Croquet Club ♂⚧ (1877–present).
Clarges Street, W1
  1–4: Kennel Club ♂⚧ (1957–2015).
  10: Kennel Club ⚧ (2016–23); Royal Kennel Club ⚧ (2023–present).
  46: Fox Club ⚧ (2004–21).
  47: Turf Club ♂ (1876–1965).
Cleveland Row, SW1
  7: London Fencing Club ♂ (1893-1950).
Clifford Street, W1
  3: Royal Aero Club ♂ (1916–33).
  10: Ladies' Grafton Club ♀ (1908–10).
  18: Naval and Military Club ♂ (1862–3); Buck's ♂ (1919–present)†.
Clipstone Street, W1
  21: Langham Sketch Club ♂ (1838–54).
Cockspur Street, SW1
  21–24, 'Norway House': Den Norske Klub ♂⚧ (1924–97).
  27: Junior United Service Club ♂ (1827–8); Royal Thames Yacht Club ♂ (1839–45).
Colville Mews, W11
  2–5: Cloud Twelve ⚧ (2019–present).
Commercial Street, E1
  28, 'Toynbee Hall': Denison Club ♂ (1885–6).
Conduit Street, W1
  9: Aeronautical Club ♂ (1880–3).
  40: Conduit ⚧ (2018–20).
Cork Street, W1
  2, 3, 4 and 4A: Imperial Rifle Club ♂ (1911–14).
  5–6: Hurst Park Club ♂ (1929–39).
  13–14: Halcyon Club ♀ (1918–36).
  22: Pioneer Club ♀ (1893–5).
Cornhill, EC3
  50: City University Club ♂⚧ (1895–2017).
Covent Garden Piazza, WC2
  Evans's Hotel (unnumbered, north–west corner with King Street): Savage Club ♂ (1873–6).
  3, Gordon Hotel: Savage Club ♂ (1869–73).
Cranbourn Street, WC2
  Above the Underground station: Playgoers' Club ⚧ (1912–39); Rehearsal Club ♀ (1930–49).
Craven Street, SW1
  41: India Club ⚧ (1951–64).
Crowndale Road, NW1
  74: The House of KOKO ⚧ (2022–present).
Crutched Friars, EC3
  42: Lloyds Club ⚧ (2009–18); City University Club ⚧ (2018–present).
Curtain Road, EC2
  45: Curtain Club ⚧ (2016–23).

Index of Clubland Addresses

Curzon Street, W1
  5: Ladies' United Service Club ♀ (1872–1920).
  6: Ladies' United Service Club ♀ (1915–20).
  20: Curzon House Club ♂ (1939–79).
  20–22: Aspinall's ⚧ (1984–92).
  21: Albemarle Club ⚧ (1909–39).
  27–28: Aspinall's ⚧ (1992–present).
  30: Crockford's ♂⚧ (1982–2023).
  61: Alliance Club ♀ (1905–13); Public Schools Club ♂ (1919–38).
  67: New Era Club ♀ (1907–12).

Davies Street, W1
  22: Nikita ⚧ (2021–present).
  52–56: Rifles Officers' London Club ♂ (1890–2018).

Dean Street, W1
  8A: West Central Jewish Girls' Club ♀ (1893–1913).
  23: Interval Club ⚧ (1933–64).
  26–29: Quo Vadis ⚧ (2012–present).
  41: Colony Room Club ⚧ (1948–2008).
  45: Groucho Club ⚧ (1985–present).
  52: Gerry's ⚧ (1955–present)
  67: Black's ⚧ (1992–2023).
  69–71: Gargoyle Club ⚧ (1925–55); Soho House – *while 40 Greek Street was being renovated* ⚧ (2016–18).
  76: Soho House – 76 Dean Street ⚧ (2009–present).

Denman Street, W1
  21: Pelican Club ♂ (1853–87); Eccentric Club ♂ (1890–3).

Devonshire Square, EC2
  5: Devonshire Club ⚧ (2016–20).

Dilke Street, SW3
  7: London Sketch Club ♂⚧ (1957–present).

Dorset Fields, NW1 *(subsequently renamed Dorset Square in the 1810s)*
  Unnumbered: Marylebone Cricket Club ♂ (1787–1810).

Dover Street, W1
  1A: Victoria League Club ♂ (1916–19).
  10: United Arts Club ♂ (1905–11).
  17–18: Ladies' Army and Navy Club ♀ (1902–3); Ladies' Imperial Club ♀ (1906–25).
  19: Junior Naval and Military Club ♂ (1870–5).
  25: Sesame Club ⚧ (1895–7).
  27: United Arts Club ♂ (1886–8).
  28–29: Sesame Club ⚧ (1897–1924).
  31–32: Ladies' Athenæum ♀ (1907–27).
  31: Suffrage Club ♀ (1913–27).
  32: Empress Club ♀ (1897–8); Ladies' Field Club ♀ (1902–6).
  34: Bath Club ⚧ (1894–1941)††.
  35: Empress Club ♀ (1898–1941)†; Empress and Royal Societies' Club ⚧ (1941–55).
  36: Hogarth Club ♂ (1887–96).
  37: Albemarle Club ⚧ (1909–39).
  38: Maison Dorée Club ⚧ (1887–93); Sandringham Club ♀ (1899–1903).
  39: Scottish Club ♂ (1879–1927).
  40: Arts Club ♂⚧ (1893–present)†.
  45: Austral Club ♀ (1909–14).
  46: Omega Bridge Club ⚧ (1910–28).

Drury Lane, WC2
  Vinegar Yard: Savage Club ♂ (1857–8).

Dysart Street, EC2
  1: Eight, Moorgate ⚧ (2008–present).

Earlham Street, WC2
  31: Cave of Harmony ⚧ (1927–8).

Eaton Square, SW1
  82: Irish Club ♂⚧ (1950–2003).
  118: Alpine Club ⚧ (1990–1).

Ebor Street, E1
  1: Soho House – Shoreditch House ⚧ (2007–present).

Edgware Road, W2
  357: Ladies' United Club ♀ (1884–1905).

Elizabeth Street, SW1
  44: Fitzdares Club ⚧ (2020–2).

Endell Street, WC2
  24: Hospital Club ⚧ (2002–19); h-Club ⚧ (2019–20).

Fitzmaurice Place, W1
　9, 'Lansdowne House': Lansdowne Club ⚥ (1935–present).
Fitzroy Square, W1
　9: Honor Club ♀ (1892–1910).
　23: Hogarth Club ♂ (1873–4).
Fleet Street, EC4
　1 Bolt Court: Albert Club ♂ (1870–1912).
　3 Hare Court: Eighty Club ♂ (1880–1979).
　7 Wine Office Court: Press Club ♂ (1893–1914).
　63: Press Club ♂ (1882–4).
　190: Women Writers' Club, aka Writers' Club ♀ (1892–4).
　Salisbury Hotel, Salisbury Court *(now Salisbury Square)*: Farmers Club ♂ (1893–63).
Frith Street, W1
　62: Moscow Club ⚥ (1986–92).
　63: Interval Club ⚥ (1964–5).
Fulham High Street, SW6
　69–79: Pavilion Club – Fulham ⚥ (2024–present).
Garrick Street, WC2
　13–15: Garrick Club ♂ (1864–present).
Gate Street, WC2
　12: Little Ship Club ♂♀ (1926–32).
Gatliff Road, SW1
　30: Purple Dragon ⚥ (2012–present).
Gaunt Street, SE1
　103: The Ministry ⚥ (2018–present).
George Street, W1
　4: University Club for Ladies ♀ (1909–21).
　15: Albert Club ♂ (1862–70); New Travellers Club ♂ (1871–8); Junior Travellers Club ♂ (1892–4).
Gerrard Street, W1
　4: 1917 Club ⚥ (1917–32).
　5: Coloured Colonial Social Club ⚥ (1939–48).
　32–35: Pelican Club ♂ (1887–91).
Grafton Street, W1
　4: St James's Club ♂ (1867–8); Berkeley Club ♂ (1870–80).
　5: Pioneer Club ♀ (1897–1913).
　6: Maison Estelle ⚥ (2022–present).
　7: Kennel Club ♂ (1902–10).
　9: International Women's Franchise Club ⚥ (1911–24).
　10: Grafton Club ♂ (1870–80); Green Park Club ♀ (1896–1908).
　12–13: Junior Army and Navy Club ♂ (1879–82); Isthmian Club ♂ (1882–9).
　16: Junior Reform Club ♂ (1866–7).
　24: Northumberland and Northern Counties Club ♂ (1905–7).
Granville Place, W1
　Unknown number: Three Arts Club ♀ (1938–41)†.
Great Coram Street, WC1
　55: Russell Whist Club ♂ (1870–95).
Great Cumberland Place, W1
　35 & 35A: Three Arts Club ♀ (1949–55).
　40–44: V. A. D. Ladies' Club ♀ (1959–74); New Cavendish Club ♀ (1974–2014); Home Grown ⚥ (2019–present).
Great George Street, SW1
　24: Westminster Reform Club ♂ (1834–6).
Great Newport Street, WC2
　6–7: Arts Theatre Club ⚥ (1927–89).
　15–16: Pickwick Club ♂ (1963–71).
Great Portland Street, W1
　20: BBC Club ⚥ (2024–present).
　99, 'Wogan House': BBC Club ⚥ (2013–24).
Great Queen Street, WC2
　27: Savage Club ♂ (2025–present).
　61–65, 'Grand Connaught Rooms': RNVR (Auxiliary Patrol) Club, aka RNVR Club ♂ (1919–46).
Great Russell Street, WC1
　17: Tom's ♂ (1764–1820).
　103: Ladies' Chess Club ♀ (1895–6).
　Unknown number: Doric Club ♂ (1865–80).
Great Scotland Yard, SW1
　13–15: Civil Service Club ⚥ (1953–present).

Index of Clubland Addresses

Greek Street, W1
  1: The House of St Barnabas ⚧ (2013–24).
  15: Italian Co-Operative Club ⚧ (1921–39).
  18: The Establishment ⚧ (1961–4).
  40: Soho House ⚧ (1995–2016; 2018–present).
  48: Upstairs at L'Escargot ⚧ (2013–16); Snail Club ⚧ (2024–present);
  50: Union Club ⚧ (1993–present).
  57: New Evaristo Club ⚧ (1948–present).
  59: Soho Club ♀ (1880–1909).
  Unknown number: Foyer Club ⚧ (1930–5).
Green Street, WC2 – *see Irving Street*.
Gresham Place, EC4 *(now demolished)*
  Unnumbered: Gresham Club ♂ (1911–15).
Grosvenor Crescent, SW1
  15: Grosvenor Crescent Club ♀ (1897–1910); Park Gates Club ♀ (1910–14).
Grosvenor Hill, W1
  50: The Clubhouse, Mayfair ⚧ (2012–19).
Grosvenor Place, W1
  1: Wellington Club ⚧ (1884–1939).
  5: Ladies' Carlton Club ♀ (1910–58).
  6: Forum Club ♀ (1919–52).
Grosvenor Road, SW1
  41: Half-Circle Club ♀ (1920–7).
Grosvenor Square, W1
  22: The Twenty Two ⚧ (2022–present).
  49: Sesame Club ⚧ (1924–64).
Grosvenor Street, W1
  12: Alexandra Club ♀ (1886–1939).
  20: Number Twenty ⚧ (2015–19).
  46: Dominion Officers' Club ♂ (1940–5).
  69: Ladies' Empire Club ♀ (1902–57).
Half-Moon Street, W1
  42: Portland Club ♂ (1969–99).
Halkin Street, SW1
  9: Caledonian Club ♂⚧ (1946–present).
Hamilton Place, W1
  1: Argentine Club ♂ (1910–48)†; Canning Club ♂ (1948–70).
  5: Les Ambassadeurs ⚧ (1950–present).
  11: Bachelors' Club ♂ (1888–1930).
Hanover Square, W1
  9: Hanover Square Club, aka Cercle des Nations ♂ (1876–99).
  12: Smithfield Club ♂ (1880–1901).
  17: International Club ♂ (1862–3); Arts Club ♂ (1863–93).
  18: Oriental Club ♂ (1828–1961)†.
  19A: New Somerville Club ♀ (1888–93).
  20: Quekett Microscopical Club ♂ (1865–1919).
  21: Tea and Shopping Club, aka Ladies' County Club ♀ (1894–1915).
  32: Naval and Military Club ♂ (1863–5).
  Unknown number: Les Ambassadeurs ⚧ (1941–50).
Hans Crescent, SW1
  1, Hans Cresent Hotel: Ladies' Automobile Club ♀ (1903–4).
Hans Place, SW1
  1: Aspinall's ⚧ (1978–84).
  22: Prince's Racquet and Tennis Club ♂ (1853–86).
Harrington Gardens, SW7
  15–17: The Other House, South Kensington ⚧ (2022–present).
Harrington Road, SW7
  38–42: South Kensington Club ⚧ (2015–23); NEXUS Club ♂ (2025–present).
Hay Hill, W1
  12: New Century Club ♀ (1899–1939); 12 Hay Hill ⚧ (2015–present).
Henrietta Street, WC2
  Unknown number: Women Journalists' Club ♀ (1894–1900).
Herbert Crescent, SW1
  8: Special Forces Club ⚧ (1946–present).

Hertford Street, W1
  2–5: 5 Hertford Street ⚧ (2012–present).
  21: Crockford's ⚧ (1928–34).
  23: New Carlton Club ♀ (1910–12).
  28: Shamrock Club ♂ (1943–7).
High Holborn, WC2
  85: National Sporting Club ♂ (1929–30).
  Hand Court: Veterans' Club ♂ (1907–36); Victory Services Club ♂ (1936–48).
Hill Street, W1
  22: Quent's ♂ (1962–7).
  38: RNVR Club ♂ (1946–69); Naval Club ♂⚧ (1969–2021).
Holland Park, W11
  81–82: London and Country Club ♀ (1920–4).
Holles Street, W1
  16–17: Ladies' Victoria Club ♀ (1889–91).
Horse Guards Avenue, SW1
  Unnumbered: Junior Army and Navy Club ♂ (1871–9).
Hyde Park Place, W2
  1: Almack's ⚧ (1921–8).
Ilchester Gardens, W2
  2–3: Ilchester Club ♀ (1897–1900).
Irving Street, WC2 *(previously called Green Street)*
  9: Beefsteak Club ♂ (1896–present).
James Street, W1
  30–34: Harry's Bar ⚧ (1979–present).
Jermyn Street, SW1
  40: Tramp ⚧ (1969–present).
  66: Albert Club ♂ (1840–2).
  71: Universities Club ♂ (1871–94).
Kensington High Street, W8
  96: Dryland Business Members' Club ⚧ (2012–14); Pavilion Club – Kensington ⚧ (2014–present).
  99: The Roof Gardens ⚧ (2024–present.)
King Street, EC2
  44: Enterprise Club ♀ (1911–13).
King Street, SW1
  1: Army and Navy Club – *part of clubhouse on St James's Square* ♂ (1838–46).

20–21: Junior Army and Navy Club ♂ (1882–1904).
29: Junior Conservative Club ♂ (1873–8); Orleans Club ♂ (1878–1944)††.
37: Crichton Club ♂ (1871–91).
43: Pelican Club ♂ (1887–91).
King Street, WC2
  22: Green Room Club ♂ (1883).
  35: Garrick Club ♂ (1832–64).
  37: Savage Club ♂ (1965–8).
  43: National Sporting Club ♂ (1891–1929); Players' Theatre Club ⚧ (1936–40)††.
King William Street, EC4
  1: Gresham Club ♂ (1844–1911).
  83: City Carlton Club ♂ (1868–79).
Kingly Street, W1
  4 Kingly Court: Disrepute ⚧ (2016–20).
  9: The Court ⚧ (2019–23).
King's Road, SW3
  181: Chelsea Arts Club ♂ (1891–1902).
  354: 'Beaufort House': Albert's ⚧ (2018–present).
Knightsbridge, SW1
  32, 'Wilton House': Ladies' Park Club ♀ (1906–40)††.
  60: Royal Thames Yacht Club ♂⚧ (1923–61; 1963–present).
  62–64: Danish Club ♂⚧ (1922–98); Pavilion Club – Knightsbridge ⚧ (2022–present).
  197: New Prince's Club ♂⚧ (1888–1940).
  243: Prince's Skating Club ♂ (1896–1917).
Langham Place, W1
  Unnumbered: Ladies' Institute ♀ (1860–7).
  Unnumbered: Chandos Club ♂ (1879–82).
Langley Street, WC2
  6: Conduit ⚧ (2021–present).
Leadenhall Street, EC3
  57–58: Enterprise Club ♀ (1899–1911).
Leicester Square, W1
  28A: 400 Club ⚧ (1935–60).

Index of Clubland Addresses

29: Rehearsal Club ♀ (1892–1930).
46: Green Room Club ♂ (1903–40)††.
Unknown number: Eccentric Club ♂ (1858–81).
Lexham Gardens, W8
  4, 6 and 8: Ladies' Imperial Club ♀ (1910–11).
  19: Columbia Club ♀ (1892–1901).
Lexington Street, W1
  10: Trouble Club ♀ (2014–15).
  46: Academy Club ⚧ (1985–present).
Lisson Grove, NW8
  Unnumbered: Marylebone Cricket Club ♂ (1810–14).
Litchfield Street, WC2
  25: Le Beaujolais Club ⚧ (1972–present).
Little St George Street, SW1
  1: Emerson Club ♀ (1924–8).
Little Trinity Lane, EC4
  Beaver House: Little Ship Club ⚧ (1932–62).
Lombard Street, EC3
  2 Lombard Court: Overseas Bankers' Club ♂ (1950–7).
  4 George Yard: New City Club ♂ (1864–79); New City Conservative Club ♂ (1884–5).
Lothbury, EC2
  1 Angel Court: The Clubhouse – Bank ⚧ (2017–19).
  7l: Overseas Bankers' Club ♂ (1962–98).
Lower Belgrave Street, SW1
  7C: Dressmaking, Millinery and Plain Needlework Club ♀ (1889–90); Gentlewomen's Employment Club ♀ (1890–9).
Lower Sloane Street, SW1
  52: Service Women's Club ♀ (1922–72); Helena Club ♀ (1972–6); Sloane Club ⚧ (1976–present).
Ludgate Circus, EC4
  418, 'Ludgate House': Press Club ♂ (1890–3).
Maddox Street, W1
  24–26: AllBright Mayfair ♀ (2019–24).
The Mall, SW1
  Admiralty Arch: Admiralty Arch Club ⚧ (2026–present).
Marylebone Road, NW1
  19A: Three Arts Club ♀ (1911–38).
  222, Great Central Hotel: Ladies' Alpine Club ♀ (1907–75).
  246A: London Sketch Club ♂ (1914–57).
Mortimer Street, W1
  31A: St Andrew's House Club ♀ (1908–42).
  41: Mortimer House ⚧ (2017–present).
  73–75: Ladies' Town and Country Club ♀ (1900–24).
  93: German Athenæum ♂ (1868–1907).
Mount Street, W1
  1–3: Apollo's Mews ⚧ (2022–present).
  87–88: George ⚧ (2001–present).
  115: Pathfinder Club ♂ (1944–56).
New Bond Street, W1
  31: University Club for Ladies ♀ (1886–1909).
  37: Austral Club ♀ (1906–9).
  135–137: Grosvenor Club ♀ (1882–97).
  157: London Sketch Club ♂ (1902–3).
  160: Royal Naval Club ♂ (1828–43).
  179: Goat Club ♂ (1936–68).
New Palace Yard, SW1
  Unnumbered: National Club ♂ (1846–52).
Newman Street, W1
  Unknown number: Working Women's Club ♀ (1868–70).
Norfolk Place, W2
  13: Frontline Club ⚧ (2003–present).
Norfolk Street, WC2 *(now demolished)*
  10, 'Hastings House': Writers' Club ♀ (1894–1924).
  12, 'Amberley House': West Indian Club ♂ (1898–1910).

London Clubland

Northumberland Avenue, SW1
  1–3: National Liberal Club ♂ (1883–7).
  8: Royal Anglo–Belgian Club ⚥ (2010–12).
  25: Colonial Club ♂ (1885–1928); Empire Club ♂ (1928–58); Commonwealth Club ♂⚥ (1958–2013).
  28: Constitutional Club ♂ (1886–1959)†.
Oakley Street, SW3
  6: Beechwood Club ♀ (1895–1905).
Old Bond Street, W1
  13: Ladies' International Club ♀ (1896–8); Sandringham Club ♀ (1898–9).
  24: Wells' Club ♂ (1910–22).
  49: Cosmopolitan Club ♂ (1852–4).
  175: London Sketch Club ♂ (1898–1902).
Old Broad Street, EC2
  19: City of London Club ♂⚥ (1832–present).
Old Brompton Road, SW7
  92B: Albert's ⚥ (2016–18).
Old Burlington Street, W1
  3: Royal Ocean Racing Club ⚥ (1934–6).
  10: Golfers' Club ♂ (1974–9).
  24A: Flyfishers' Club ♂ (1981–95).
  24C: Buck's – *ladies' annexe* ♀⚥ (1932–86).
Old Cavendish Street, W1
  3: Ladies' Victoria Club ♀ (1881–9).
Old Church Street, SW3
  143: Chelsea Arts Club ♂⚥ (1902–present).
Old Jewry, EC2
  11: Overseas Bankers' Club ♂ (1957–62).
Oxford Street, W1
  6 Oxford Mansions: Cavendish Club ♂ (1895–1913).
  126: Ladies' Dramatic Club ♀ (1920–5).
  231: Somerville Club ♀ (1878–87); New Somerville Club ♀ (1888).
Pall Mall, SW1
  2: Royal Ocean Racing Club ⚥ (1936–40)††.
  6: Century Club ♂ (1867–82).
  9: Wanderers' Club ♂ (1874–97).
  29: Junior Carlton Club – *ladies' annexe* ♀⚥ (1925–63).
  29A: Kennel Club ♂ (1877–95).
  30–35: Junior Carlton Club ♂ (1869–1963; 1968–77)†.
  36–39: Army and Navy Club ♂ (1851–1962; 1963–present)†.
  46: Cocoa Tree Club ♂ (1787–93).
  46–47: Army and Navy Club ♂ (1962–3).
  48: Ladies' Boodle's ⚥ (1770–9).
  49: Brooks's ♂ (1764–78); Travellers Club ♂ (1821–7).
  50: Boodle's ♂ (1762–83).
  51: Goosetree's ♂ (1773–87).
  52: Marlborough Club ♂ (1868–1945); Marlborough-Windham Club ♂ (1945–1953).
  64: Cocoa Tree Club ♂ (1793–7).
  66–68: Junior Naval and Military Club ♂ (1874–9); Beaconsfield Club ♂ (1880–7); New Oxford and Cambridge Club ♂ (1893–1921).
  67: 67 Pall Mall ⚥ (2015–present).
  69: Guards Club – *annexe* ♂ (1901–19).
  70: Guards Club ♂ (1827–1919).
  71–76: Oxford and Cambridge Club ♂⚥ (1838–present).
  77: Oxford and Cambridge Club – *annexe* ♀⚥ (1952–present).
  79A: Baldwin Club ♂ (1897–1911).
  86, 'Cumberland House': Cocoa Tree Club ♂ (1762–87); Union Club ♂ (1799–1807).
  89–91: Royal Automobile Club ♂⚥ (1913–present)†.
  94: Carlton Club ♂ (1836–1940)††.
  104–105: Reform Club ♂⚥ (1836–8; 1841–present)†.
  106: Guards Club ♂ (1826–7); Travellers Club ♂ (1827–present)†.
  107: Athenæum ♂⚥ (1830–present)†.

Index of Clubland Addresses

116–117: United Service Club ♂
(1828–1975)†.
120: CEO Club ⚧ (2025–present).

Pall Mall East, SW1
3: Eton and Harrow Club ♂
(1873–86); Baldwin Club ♂
(1887–97).
4: United University Club ♂
(1826–1971).
5A: Royal Water Colour Society Art
Club ♂ (1886–1935).

Palliser Road, W14
Unnumbered: Queen's Club ♂⚧
(1886–present).

Park Lane, W1
19, 'Londonderry House': Royal Aero
Club ♂ (1947–61).
45: Playboy Club ♂ (1966–82).

Park Place, SW1
2: Brooks's – *annexe* ♂
(1856–present).
4: Wanderers' Club ♂ (1870–4);
Road Club ♂ (1874–86).
4–5: Primrose Club ♂
(1886–1910).
5: University and Public Schools
Club ♂ (1880–5); Vernon
Club ♂ (1885–6).
6: Over-Seas League ⚧ (1921–2);
Royal Over-Seas League ⚧
(1922–present)†.
7: Park Club, aka Field Club ♂
(1882–90).
7–8: St James's Hotel and Club ⚧
(1980–present).
9: Pioneer Club ♂ (1913–20).
14: Pratt's ♂⚧ (1857–present).

Parliament Square, SW1
Unnumbered: House of Commons
♂⚧ (1852–present); House
of Lords ♂⚧ (1847–present).

Parliament Street, SW1
47: Whitehall Club ♂ (1866–1906).

Pembroke Road, W8
58–60: Maggie and Rose –
Kensington ⚧ (2007–24).

Piccadilly, W1
36: Flyfishers' Club ♂ (1907–41)††.
68A: Grosvenor Club ♀
(1897–1911).
80–81: Royal Thames Yacht Club
♂ (1911–23).
81: Watier's ♂ (1807–19).
83: Hurst Park Club ♂
(1890–1929).
84: Kennel Club ♂ (1916–57).
94, 'Cambridge House': Naval and
Military ('In and Out') Club
♂ (1865–1999)†; Cambridge
House ⚧ (2025–present).
95: American Club ♂ (1919–84).
96–97: Junior Naval and Military
Club ♂ (1879–89);
New Travellers Club ♂
(1890–1906).
100: Badminton Club ♂ (1875–
1938); Public Schools Club ♂
(1938–72).
101–104: Junior Constitutional Club
♂ (1887–1926).
105: Isthmian Club ♂ (1889–1920);
National Sporting Club ♂
(1938–47).
106: Coventry House Club, aka
Ambassadors Club ♂
(1829–54); St James's Club ♂
(1868–1978).
107: Savile Club ♂ (1882–1927).
116: Junior Athenæum ♂
(1864–1931).
117: United Empire Club ♂
(1904–15).
119: Royal Automobile Club ♂
(1902–13); Cavendish Club
♂ (1913–33); Royal Aero
Club ♂ (1933–47)†.
127: Cavalry Club ♂ (1890–1976);
Cavalry and Guards Club
♂⚧ (1976–present).
128: Piccadilly Club ♂ (1892–
1903); Imperial Service Club
♂ (1903–5); Lyceum Club
♀ (1905–19); Royal Air Force
Club ♂ (1922–present).
138: Ladies' County Club, aka New
County Club ♀ (1915–19);
Lyceum Club ♀ (1919–33).
166: Royal Aero Club ♂ (1910–16).
177: Burlington Fine Arts Club ♂
(1866–9).

Piccadilly, W1 – *continued*
   178: Hogarth Club ♂ (1858–9).
   195: BAFTA ⚧ (2022–present).
   213: London Fencing Club ♂ (1848-93).
   224, Criterion: O. P. (Old Playgoers') Club ♂ (1900–39).
   Burlington House: Academicians' Room ⚧ (2022–present).

Poland Street, W1
   61: Milk and Honey ⚧ (2002–20).

Portman Square, W1
   20: Home House ⚧ (1998–present).

Portobello Road, W11
   191: Soho House – Electric House ⚧ (2001–present).

Poultry, EC2
   27: Ned's Club ⚧ (2017–present).

Prescot Street, E1
   30, The Crypt: Vout-O-Reenee's ⚧ (2014–present).

Prince's Gate, SW7
   20: Ognisko Polskie ⚧ (1946–78).
   55: Ognisko Polskie ⚧ (1940–2; 1978–present).

Prince's Square, W2
   74–76: International Ladies' Club ♀ (1922–50).

Prince's Street, Storey's Gate, SW1
   10: Whitehall Club ♂ (1906–20).

Prince's Street, W1
   14A: Ladies' Institute ♀ (1860).

Queen Anne's Gate, SW1
   34: St Stephen's Club ♂⚧ (1962–2012).

Queen Street, EC4
   71: City Liberal Club ♂ (1874–7).

Queen Street, W1
   2: Soho House – Little House, Mayfair ⚧ (2014–present).

Queen Victoria Street, EC4
   1 Fye Foot Lane: Shuttleworth Club ⚧ (1889–1911).

Queen's Square, WC1
   29: Camelot Club ♀ (1898–1903).

Rathbone Place, W1
   7: Beaufort Club ⚧ (1865–8).
   11: AllBright Fitzrovia ♀ (2018–20).
   43: United Scandinavian Club ♂ (1888–93).

Redchurch Street, E2
   6: Shoreditch Arts Club ⚧ (2023–present).

Regent Street, W1
   14: Junior Carlton Club ♂ (1864–9); Constitutional Club ♂ (1883–6).
   16: Parthenon Club ♂ (1836–61); Raleigh Club ♂ (1879–1914); Victoria League Club ♂ (1915–16).
   25: Victoria Ladies' Club ♀ (1875–8).
   68: National Sporting Club ♂ (1951–82); The Club at Café Royal ⚧ (2014–17).
   87: Goat Club ♂ (1916–36).
   168: Ladies' Chess Club ♀ (1898–1904).
   180: Pioneer Club ♀ (1892–3).
   294: Women's Club ♀ (1872–98).
   307: Cavendish Club ♂ (1855–79); Rous Club ♂ (1879–81).
   314: New Lotos Club ⚧ (1882–5).
   316: Russell Club ♀ (1878–80); Lotos Club ⚧ (1880–2).

Roehampton Lane, SW15
   Unnumbered: Roehampton Club ⚧ (1901–present).

Romney Street, SW1
   58: Parliamentary Labour Club ⚧ (1927–8); National Labour Club ♂ (1928–40).

Russell Square, WC1
   52: Arachne Club – *annexe* ♀ (1907–8); Argyll Club ♀ (1908–10).
   55: International Women's Franchise Club ⚧ (1910–11).
   60: Arachne Club ♀ (1904–8).

Ryder Street, SW1:
   9: Eccentric Club ♂ (1914–84).

Sackville Street, W1
   30A: New Victorian Club ♀ (1893–1901); Ladies' Chess Club ♀ (1904–13).
   31: Dutch Club ⚧ (1935–75).
   32: Alexandra Club ♀ (1884–6).

St Andrew's Street, EC4
   20: The Clubhouse – Holborn ⚧ (2018–present).

Index of Clubland Addresses

St James's Place, SW1
  16–17: Stafford Club ♂ (1886–99).
  20: Royal Ocean Racing Club ⚥ (1941–present)†.
  27: Ladies' Army and Navy Club ♀ (1927–40)††.

St James's Square, SW1
  3: Wellington Club ♂ (1853–4); 3 St James's Square ⚥ (2017–18).
  4: Naval and Military ('In and Out') Club ⚥ (1999–present).
  8: Erectheum Club ♂ (1839–54); Junior Oxford and Cambridge Club ♂ (1879–84); Vine Club ♂ (1885); York Club ♂ (1886–8); Junior Travellers Club ♂ (1889–92); Sports Club ♂ (1893–1938); The Clubhouse – St James's ⚥ (2016–present).
  9: Portland Club ♂ (1888–1943).
  10: Windham Club ♂ (1829–36).
  12: Salisbury Club ♂ (1880–92); Nimrod Club ♂ (1894); British Empire Club ♂ (1910–40).
  13: Windham Club ♂ (1836–1941).
  15, 'Lichfield House': Army and Navy Club ♂ (1846–51); Junior United Service Club ♂ (1855).
  16: Prince of Wales Club ♂ (1846); Free Trade Club ♂ (1847–9); East India United Service Club ♂ (1849–present)†.
  17: Colonial Club ♂ (1839–42); East India United Service Club ♂ (1863–present)†.
  18: Oxford and Cambridge Club ♂ (1830–8); Army and Navy Club ♂ (1838–46).
  19: Cleveland Club ♂ (1898–1914).
  21, 'Winchester House': Union Club ♂ (1807–17).
  33: Caledonian Club ♂ (1917–40)††.

St James's Street, SW1
  3: Junior Turf Club ♂ (1882–1910).
  4: Sandown Park Club ♂ (1905–10).
  16: Arthur's ♂ (1811–27).
  28: White's ♂ (1693–8); Savoir Vivre Club ♂ (1775–82); Boodle's ♂ (1783–present)†.
  37–38: White's ♂ (1778–present)†.
  49: Guards Club ♂ (1810–1826); Royal Thames Yacht Club ♂ (1857–60).
  50: Crockford's ♂ (1823–46); Military, Naval and County Service Club ♂ (1848-51); Devonshire Club ♂ (1874–1976).
  54: Verulam Club ♂ (1843–90).
  57–58: New University Club ♂ (1864–6; 1868–1938).
  Unnumbered, but between 60 and 61: Brooks's ♂ (1778–present).
  63: Royal Societies' Club ♂ (1894–1941).
  64: Weltje's ♂ (1781–99); Cocoa Tree Club ♂ (1799–1932).
  69: White's ♂ (1698–1733; 1736–78); Miles's ♂ (1785–1809); Arthur's ♂ (1827–1940); Carlton Club ♂⚥ (1943–present).
  74: Thatched House Club ♂ (1815–43); Conservative Club ♂ (1845–1950)†; Bath Club ⚥ (1950–9).
  85: Attwood's ♂ (1772–85); Albion Club ♂ (1811–42).
  86: Union Club ♂ (1817–20); Civil Service Club – *upstairs* ♂ (1865–9); Clarendon Club – *ground floor* ♂ (1866–70); Thatched House Club ♂ (1869–1949); Union Club ♂ (1951–64); Constitutional Club ♂ (1969–79).
  87: Graham's ♂ (1802–1904).
  88: White's ♂ (1773–6); Conservative Club ♂ (1840–5).

St John's Wood Road, NW8
  Unnumbered: Marylebone Cricket Club ♂⚥ (1814–present).

St Martin's Lane, WC2
    87: Wantage Club ♀ (1897–1903).
    112: Library ⚥ (2014–20).
St Martin's Place, WC2
    8: Alpine Club ♂⚥ (1858–95).
St Swithin's Lane, EC4
    24–27: City Carlton Club ♂ (1879–1940)††.
Salisbury Street, WC2 – *now demolished*
    12: Arundel Club ♂ (1865–83).
Sandell Street, SE1
    1: Union Jack Club ♂⚥ (1975–present).
Savile Row, W1
    1: New University Club ♂ (1866–8).
    2: Stafford Club ♂ (1860–75); St George's Club ♂ (1875–85); Royal London Yacht Club ⚥ (1885–1906); Northumberland and Northern Counties Club ♂ (1907–11); Kennel Club ♂ (1911–16).
    3: Almack's ⚥ (1929–39); Albany Club ♂ (1939–56).
    4: Scientific Club ♂ (1879–83).
    7: Regency Club ♂ (1881–2).
    12: Savile Club ♂ (1871–82).
    17: Burlington Fine Arts Club ♂ (1869–1952).
    22–23: Alpine Club ♂ (1895–1937).
Seymour Street, W2
    63–79, 'Connaught House': Connaught Club ♂ (1906–43)†; Victory Services Club ♂⚥ (1948–present).
Shaftesbury Avenue, W1
    21: Eccentric Club ♂ (1893–1914).
    61–63: Century ⚥ (2001–present).
Shoe Lane, EC4
    76, International Press Centre: Press Club ♂ (1973–86).
Soho Square, W1
    21: National Sporting Club ♂ (1930–8).
South Audley Street, W1
    2: University Women's Club ♀ (1921–present)†.

8: Bachelors' Club ♂ (1930–41); American Officers' Club ♂ (1942–5).
74: Alpine Club ♂ (1937–90).
76: Ladies' Automobile Club ♀ (1914–39).
Spring Gardens, SW1
    9: Medical Club ♂ (1866–75); Spring Gardens Club ♂ (1875–7); New Club ♂ (1878–81).
Stanley Gardens, W11
    24–29: Twentieth Century Club ♀ (1902–20).
Stephenson Way, NW1
    2: The Magic Circle ⚥ (1998–present).
Stockwell Avenue, SW9
    10: Upstairs at the Department Store ⚥ (2018–present).
Strand, WC2
    2 Bull Inn Court: Savage Club ♂ (1858).
    3 Clement's Inn: Polyglot Club ♂ (1906–12).
    5–6 Clement's Inn: Playgoers' Club ⚥ (1895–1912); Polyglot Club ♂ (1912–14).
    5 Beaufort Buildings: Yorick Club ♂ (1888–97).
    15: Colonial Club ♂ (1870–85).
    80–81: Scandinavian Club ♂ (1886–92).
    143–145: India Club ⚥ (1964–2011).
    162–165, Anderton's Hotel: Press Club ♂ (1884–7).
    180: Soho House – 180 Strand ⚥ (2020–present).
    229–230: Wig and Pen Club ♂ (1908–2003).
    354: Savage Club ♂ (1859–62).
    372, Haxell's Hotel: Savage Club ♂ (1876–9).
    447: Ladies' Chess Club ♀ (1895).
Stratford Place, W1
    11, 'Stratford House': Stratford Club ♂ (1816–25); Portland Club ♂ (1825–90); Oriental Club ♂⚥ (1962–present).

Index of Clubland Addresses

17–19: German Athenæum ♂ (1907–14).
Stratton Street, W1
    15: New Oxford and Cambridge Club ♂ (1921–33).
Suffolk Street, SW1
    1: United University Club ♂ (1826–1971).
    26: New Athenæum ♂ (1883–92).
Tottenham Court Road, WC1
    186: Ladies' Chess Club ♀ (1896–8).
Trafalgar Square, SW1
    Morley's Hotel: Old Colony Club ♂ (1920–1).
    Unnumbered, west side: Union Club ♂ (1827–1924).
Trinity Square, EC3
    10: Ten Trinity Square ⚥ (2017–present).
Tudor Street, EC4
    2–4: Irish Club ⚥ (2009–11).
Tufton Street, SW1
    11: Parliamentary Labour Club ⚥ (1924–7).
Upper Grosvenor Street, W1
    17: United Hunts Club ⚥ (1930–76).
    Unnumbered: International Sportsmen's Club ♂ (1929–66).
Upper Street, N1
    181: The Dally ⚥ (2024–present).
Upper Thames Street, EC4
    Bell Wharf Lane: Little Ship Club ⚥ (1962–present).
Vauxhall Bridge Road, SW1
    296: Denison Club ⚥ (1905–15).
Victoria Street, SW1
    102, 2 Albert Mansions: Kennel Club ♂ (1873–7).
    110: New Era Club ♀ (1901–7).
    145: Ladies' Victoria Club ♀ (1891–4); Victoria Club ♀ (1894–1918).
    155, 'The Mederies': Gentlewomen's Employment Club ♀ (1899–1914).
    Victoria Palace Hotel: National Liberal Club ♂ (1916–20).

Villiers Street, WC2
    The Arches: Players' Theatre Club ⚥ (1946–2002).
Walbrook, EC4
    37A: Walbrook Club ⚥ (2000–present).
    Unnumbered: City Liberal Club ♂ (1877–1921).
Warwick Street, W1
    1: 1 Warwick ⚥ (2023–present).
Waterloo Place, SW1
    6: Hogarth Club ♂ (1859–61).
    6A: Cigar Club ♂ (1880–99).
    7: Pall Mall Club ♂ (1876–1920).
    12: Travellers Club ♂ (1819–21); Athenæum ♂ (1824–30).
    Carlton Hotel: Carlton Club ♂ (1835–6).
Waterloo Road, SE1
    91: Union Jack Club ♂ (1907–71)†.
Wellington Street, WC2
    18: Victoria Club ♂ (1863–1960).
    25: The Other House, Covent Garden ⚥ (2025–present).
Wells Street, W1
    79: London Sketch Club ♂ (1903–14).
West Halkin Street, SW1
    11B: Mosimann's ⚥ (1988–present).
    11C: Grace ♀ (2016–19).
West Street, WC2
    9: Ivy Club ⚥ (2008–present).
White Horse Street, W1
    Unnumbered: Junior Travellers Club ♂ (1887–9).
Whitehall, SW1
    61, 'Gwydyr House': Reform Club ♂ (1838–41).
Whitehall Court, SW1
    2: Authors Club ♂ (1891–1966); Northumberland and Northern Counties Club ♂ (1893–1901); Farmers Club ♂ (1904–42); 1920 Club ♂ (1921–3); Chemical Club ♂ (1920–71).
    2A: Golfers' Club ♂ (1891–1968); St Andrews Club ♂ (1892–1939); Lady Golfers' Club ♀ (1911–62).

Whitehall Court, SW1 – *continued*
3: Farmers Club ♂⚧ (1942–present); Flyfishers' Club ♂ (1951–70).
4: Royal Automobile Club ♂ (1897–1902); Auxiliary Forces Club ♂ (1901–10); Municipal and County Club ♂ (1903–17); Westminster Club ♂ (1904–6); United Sports Club ♂ (1904–11); Welsh Club ♂ (1905–12); Junior Army and Navy Club ♂ (1910–70); West Indian Club ♂ (1912–71); Northumberland and Northern Counties Club ♂ (1911–19).

Whitehall Gardens, SW1 *(demolished in 1938 for redevelopment as the Ministry of Defence building)*
1: National Club ♂ (1852–1913).

Whitehall Place, SW1
1: National Liberal Club ♂⚧ (1887–1916; 1920–present)†.

Wilfred Street, SW1
4: 1920 Club ♂ (1920–1).

William IV Street, WC2
Toole's Theatre (originally Folly's Theatre in 1876–82): Beefsteak Club ♂ (1876–96).

Wood Lane, W12
101, 2 Television Centre: BBC Club ⚧ (1960–2013); Soho House – White City House ⚧ (2018–present).
Unnumbered: Gun Club ♂ (1891–6).

York Street, W1
3: Suffrage Club ♀ (1910–16).

RULES OF ENGAGEMENT

'But you haven't included the [insert name of club here]!', I hear you cry. And I am already resigned to all manner of whataboutery on this.

To make this guide remotely feasible, I have had to work with a strict definition of what is – and is not – a club. This has been necessary to stop the book from getting out of hand, listing every pub, scout hut and church hall that has ever hosted a meeting. But it has meant sticking to some rules, and any snubs of dearly beloved institutions are not intentional.

There is a method to my madness, dear reader. The 'rules of engagement' I have used to define a club have been as follows:

1. **It needs to have members, who pay for membership.** This rules out a loose gathering of regulars in a pub. It also rules out any number of luxury lounges in airports, restaurants and hotels. For instance, Langan's restaurant in Mayfair has opened 'Upstairs at Langan's', which is promoted as a club – yet as they say, 'We do not seek either a joining fee or a subscription', so it doesn't fall within my definition of a club, fine restaurant though it may be.
2. **It needs to have some sort of body which scrutinises applications for membership.** This may be an elected committee of members, or it may be a board maintained by the proprietors as a mere licensing convenience. But it means that organisations that offer club-like facilities to anyone paying a fee, large or small, do not qualify.
3. **It needs to have physical premises.** This recognises the

importance of a shared space where members may meet – a correspondence club, or a series of Zoom lectures, or a group of friends meeting in a rented room once a month, may well be a worthy undertaking, but they do not have the same dynamic of regulars popping in, asking for 'the usual'. This rules out venerable groups like the Roxburghe Club, a group limited to forty individuals who make up the oldest society of bibliophiles in the world, who publish rare and scholarly volumes; or the New Sheridan Club, a group of wry fops who have been meeting in the upstairs room of a Fitzrovia pub for a monthly talk and drinks since 2006, with regular outings – but have no permanent clubhouse. (The question of whether 'the funds' will stretch to any number of faded mansions is a running gag there.) It also rules out the many ward clubs in the City of London.

4. **At least part of the premises need to be private, for the use of members.** This rules out any number of cafés, bars, pubs and hotels fully open to the general public – no matter how opulent.

5. **It must primarily be recognised as a social club, and it cannot be an institution that first and foremost performs another function.** The sporting clubs stretch this definition to the limit – and the ones listed here tend to have widely recognised social aspects that can eclipse their sporting functions. Nevertheless, it is an important rule, or clubs would encompass all manner of professional bodies, learned societies, military regiments, inns of court, etc. This rules out a number of perfectly worthy and reputable establishments, like the London Library (a first-rate private library which spun out of the Travellers Club's library, but which is not in the business of serving as a social club), or the Honourable Artillery Company (which has premises with a club-like social ambience, but which is first and foremost a reserve regiment of the British Army), or the Royal Society of Medicine (which provides impressive club-like amenities, but is primarily a learned society). It also rules out institutions that started out as a club, but evolved over time to occupy a different

role: for instance, the Institute of Directors, which began as the 'Number 10 Club' for company directors (that had nothing to do with Downing Street, but was founded at 10 Belgrave Square in 1955), and now has its headquarters in the vast clubhouse of a defunct former club, the United Service Club on Pall Mall; or the Alpine Club, which was long considered a private members' club with successive clubhouses in Mayfair, but which now serves as Britain's foremost mountaineering society, its Shoreditch home since 1991 offering its members a bar, library and bunk beds.

6. **It cannot simply have the word 'Club' in it.** The term is overused, often by luxury brands; whereas many bona fide clubs do not even have 'club' in their name. For that reason, it does not include any number of hotel lounges, airport spaces, supermarket reward schemes, etc., which are all branded as a 'Club'.

7. **It cannot be a working men's club.** I'm a big fan of working men's clubs: as I showed in my last book, they consciously and deliberately sprang out of the Pall Mall clubs as an attempt to popularise 'clubbism' for the masses. They are often on the receiving end of unpleasant and uncalled-for snobbery, when they can be rather impressive, with extensive facilities, and the camaraderie which marks the most enjoyable clubs can be found in abundance. They are also under serious threat, with beloved institutions like the Bethnal Green Working Men's Club recently closing down. But because their aims and expectations are very different, and as there are some 1,200 of them across the British Isles, they are not included in the scope of this book, not least as the book would have to run to several volumes.

DECLARATIONS

The author is currently a member of two very different clubs in London – the Athenæum on Pall Mall, and the New Evaristo Club in Soho – and of the Northern Counties Club in Newcastle-upon-Tyne; and was formerly a member of the National Liberal Club in London for nineteen years. At some point over the last two decades, he has visited (and often accepted hospitality from) members in all but half a dozen of the London clubs included in this book; but he feels in no way obligated towards any of them. He strenuously resists any efforts to lobby or bribe him into endorsements, but he is always happy to talk about clubs; and all opinions expressed are his own.

ACKNOWLEDGEMENTS

I should firstly thank the London clubs themselves. This book was written entirely independently of them, without their knowledge or encouragement; but late in the process of writing, I supplied a draft of each club's entry in Section 1 to that club; and I was very grateful for how most of them came back to me, with a succession of club secretaries and/or chairs offering constructive comments and corrections. While their feedback in no way constituted an endorsement – and I suspect a few were a tad exasperated at my opinions – I found the overwhelming majority of the responses to be gracious and helpful. I should further thank those London clubs which kindly granted permission for directly quoting recipes, rules, songs and other documents, namely the Athenæum, Brooks's, Buck's, the Cavalry and Guards Club, the National Liberal Club, the Oriental Club, the Royal Automobile Club, the Savile Club, the Travellers Club, and White's, as well as the Leash Club of New York City with its impressive cocktail book. I would also like to thank, for permission to quote two long extracts, Sally Sampson on behalf of the Estate of Anthony Sampson, and the Estate of Sir Winston Churchill managed by Curtis Brown.

I should also like to thank the innumerable friends, well-wishers, fellow historians, hosts and co-conspirators across Clubland who have welcomed me over the years. In particular, I have always said that I am more interested in really good, stimulating questions, than in set answers. And so many people have come up with outstanding questions, which I have done my best to answer. While these are too many to mention, they include Yuri Aguilar, Mark R. Altherr, Rebecca Atkinson-Lord, Katherine Bavage, Janet Berridge, Marcus Binney CBE, John Bonham, Alex Borwick, Sarah Bowerman, Dr Linda Briggs, Dr Ted Bromund, Phillip Burgess, David Carruthers, Ioannes Chountis de Fabbri, Claire Christensen, Dr Peter Clark, Andrew Copson, the Revd Dr Alec Corio, Brian Curragh, Gina Decio, German Delgado, John Delikanakis, Annette Dittert, Nick Doherty, Matthew Dupee, Henry Dyer, Richard Feigen, Quinby Frey, Pip Fryers, Dr Laura Gazzoli, Charles Gillett, Sarah Green MP, Chris Hallworth MVO, Dr Jessica Hambly, John Harper, Andrew Harrison, David Harry, James Heale, Bill Hobbs, Peter Hogan, Mark Hollingsworth, the late Barbara Hosking CBE, Matthew Howard, Havard Hughes, Diana Ibáñez López, Jim Iorio, Dr Rachel Iredale, Naila Jassim, Charles Keates, Tom Kibasi, Dr Nick Kirby, Marie Le Conte, Alexander Learmonth KC, Gordon Lishman CBE, Dr Andrew Lownie, Alderman Tim McNally CC, Deborah McWilliams, Dr Laura-Jane Maher, Stephen Maher, Mahnaz Malik, Claire Mayne, Squadron Leader Kevin Mehmet MBE, Tiva Montalbano, Francis Ng, James North, Peter Oborne, Lord Parkinson of Whitley Bay, Daniel Paterson, Rowan Pelling, Paul Pettinger, Marcus Potter, Paul Powlesland, Professor Munro Price, Mark Prizeman, Dr Simon Radford, Karin Rehacek, Karen Revel-Chion, Dr Fern Riddell, John Martin Robinson, Tansy Robson, Prannoy Roy, Chris Schüler, James Scrymgeour, Charles Sebag-Montefiore CBE, Dr Keir Shiels, Edward L. Shugrue III, Professor Sunny Singh, Michael Smeeth, Lady Julia Smith, Naomi Smith, Nigel Smith, Arthur Snell, the late Graham Snell, Dorab R. Sopariwala, Leslie Stephenson, Veronique Thévoz, Gwawr Thomas, Dr Kit Toda, Dr Lew Toulmin, Dr Peter Urbach, Ian Vaculik, Anne Wallace, Ima von Wenden and Hannah Young.

My biggest thanks of all go to Philipp Hass, a fellow Anglophile with Swiss roots, who has been an enthusiastic sounding board through every stage of the book's development, and who read the manuscript in full, and it has hugely benefitted from his input. Genevieve Arblaster-Hulley,

Acknowledgements

Dr Melissa Chaplin, Suzanne Coles, Genevieve Jenner, Stephen Klimczuk-Massion and Ben Schott all read parts of the manuscript, and their insightful comments and feedback were utterly invaluable.

My agent Tom Cull has believed in this project from its inception, while my editor Tom Asker and the whole team at Hachette have been unwavering in their support, with invaluable inputs from David Andrassy, Sophie Ellis, Simon Pearsall, Felicity Price, Rebecca Sheppard and Howard Watson.

This is my third book on London Clubland (or fourth, if you include my PhD thesis). Each book has been a thoroughly enlightening journey, and an extremely different style of work from the last: one an academic monograph, one a 'popular' history for the general reader, and this one a modern-day guidebook. Nevertheless, they all built on extensive research undertaken for the previous book(s), and so I should repeat my thanks to the assorted archivists, librarians and club staff who assisted with those.

While every effort has been made to ensure accuracy, it is sadly inevitable that mistakes are almost guaranteed to creep into a book of this kind. And of course, all impressions and opinions (and at times, the book can be very opinionated) are my own. You may strongly disagree with them, and I'm happy to discuss things over a glass of port, to see if you can sway me. I'm also particularly nervous of inevitable omissions around the latest clubs: as you may gather from the length of the section covering modern clubs, new establishments are popping up all the time, and it is virtually certain that an extra club or two will have appeared between the manuscript being finished in August 2024, and publication of the book in May 2025 (and you will no doubt be reading the book some time after that). Indeed, at the time of writing, I was aware of plans for new clubs such as Lighthouse Social, based in the grounds of Fulham Football Club; or The Carrington, a new business-focused Mayfair club by Robin Birley in collaboration with Jamie Reuben, on the Reuben brothers' One Carrington mixed-use site behind Cambridge House; or a new club across three floors of Camden's town hall building; or the Surrenne wellbeing club dug into four basement floors of

Knightsbridge; or the new Six Senses Place, a wellbeing club embedded into a hotel, due to be opened in a converted Bayswater department store – but specific details were not forthcoming in time for publication. There have even been some clubs that have closed down while the book was being written; or planned new clubs which were announced, but then fell silent. Plus, there are clubs launched as temporary popups, like Colony Room Green (which has sought to recreate the old Colony Room Club), and Greys Club (launched by members of the defunct Black's Club).

If you should spot any factual errors, omissions or outright howlers, please do let me know – especially if there is the chance to correct subsequent editions. Similarly, all efforts have been made to contact rights holders for permission to quote, but again, if anything has inadvertently crept through, please do contact me. You can do so through my personal website, or my Clubland Substack (which are respectively – and imaginatively – located at www.sethalexanderthevoz.com and clubland.substack.com). As ever, all errors and omissions are my own.

Seth Alexander Thévoz
Muswell Hill, London
August 2024

INDEX

Academicians' Room, 125, 239, 244, 297, 302
Academy Club, 93, 94–5, 239, 293, 297
Admiralty Arch Club, 143–4, 297
Albemarle Club, 322
Albert's (Albert's at Beaufort House), 152
Alfred Club, 39, 322
All England Lawn Tennis and Croquet Club, 83–4, 240, 302
AllBright, 10
Almack, William, 219–20, 223
Almack's, 18, 219
Alpine Club, 322–3
American Club, 144
Annabel's, 99–100, 103, 162, 222, 238, 293, 297, 375
Apollo's Muse, 167–8, 297
Arboretum, 152–3, 239, 297
Arlington Club *see* Turf Club
Army and Navy Club (The Rag), 32–3, 286, 296, 302, 325, 328, 343
 architecture, 231
 foundation of, 227
 freehold status, 240
 gaming and, 274, 275
 mergers and acquisitions, 323
 motto, 242
 Naval Club, The, 32, 322–3, 324, 346
 Portland Club, The, 32, 274, 297, 324
 prime ministers and, 299
Arthur, John, 220
Arthur, Robert, 220
Arthur's club, 220, 274

Arts Club, 42–3, 44, 66, 286, 293, 296, 302, 322, 324
Aspinall, John, 121–2, 221, 222, 275
Aspinall's, 121–22, 293, 297
Association of London Clubs, 250
Athenæum, The, 25–6, 244, 251, 257, 293, 296, 302, 305, 343, 350
 architecture, 230–31
 foundation of, 225, 227
 gaming and, 274, 275
 listed status, 239
 mergers and acquisitions, 322
 prime ministers and, 298–301
 recipes, 384
Authors Club, The, 66, 242, 324

Babington House, 171, 174
Bachelors' Club, 322
BAFTA (British Academy of Film and Television Arts), 126, 297
Bangalore United Service Club, India, 298
Bath and Racquets Club, 100–101, 222, 293, 297, 302
Bath Club, 323, 324, 326
BBC Club, 95–6, 297
Bedford Square, 217
Beechwood Club, 148–9
Beefsteak Club, 55–6, 240, 286, 297, 300–301, 302, 372
 anniversaries, 293
 architecture, 233
 freehold status, 240

Beefsteak Club – *continued*
  gatecrashing at, 331
  motto, 242
Bianco, Elisabetta, 12, 221
Bianco, Francesco, 12, 221–22
Birley Group Clubs, 99–107, 138, 168, 222–3
Birley, Marcus (Mark), 99–100, 102–4, 222, 304, 375
Birley, Robin Marcus, 93, 99, 105–7, 145, 222–3
Black's, 66, 304, 324
Bombay Club, 322
Boodle, Edward, 223, 245
Boodle's, 17–18, 251, 286, 297, 302, 345, 350
  architecture of, 229, 230, 235
  club songs, 245–6
  dress code, 308–10
  foundation of, 219, 223
  gaming and, 274, 276
  gatecrashing at, 331
  listed status, 239
  prime ministers and, 298–300
  recipes, 376–7, 381–2
  sobriquets, 244
Boston Club, New Orleans, 363
Bretton Hall, 171–2
Brooks, William, 223
Brooks's, 18–20, 60, 147, 229, 286, 297, 302, 328, 331, 350
  architecture of, 230–31
  betting book, 269–73
  Club, The, 10, 19, 386–7
  dress codes, 310
  in film, 344
  foundation of, 220, 223
  freehold status, 240
  gaming and, 274
  listed status, 238
  mergers and acquisitions, 323
  prime ministers and, 298–300
  recipes, 362, 377
  Society of Dilettanti, 19
  St James's Club, The, 19, 147, 274, 293, 322–3
Bruton Club, 76, 322
Brydges Place Club, 126–7, 242, 293, 297, 302
Buck's, 20–21, 189, 285, 287, 293, 297, 302
  architecture of, 230, *234*
  prime ministers and, 300–301
  recipes, 363, 366
Byculla Club, Bombay, 382

Caledonian Club, 58, 242, 251, 293, 297, 301, 302, 326, 390
Callaghan, James, 300
Cambridge House, 144–5, 238, 297
Cameron, David, 301
Campbell-Bannerman, Henry, 300
Canning Club, 37, 324
Canning, George, 299
Carlton Club, 24, 29, 61–2, 251, 286, 293, 296, 302, 324
  architecture of, 231, 232, 235
  bomb damage, 326, 328
  in film, 343
  foundations of, 228
  gaming and, 274
  listed status of, 239
  mergers and acquisitions, 323
  National Club, 61, 297, 324
  prime ministers and, 299–301
  Thatched House Club, 61, 323
  wartime lodgings, 326
Carnegie Club, 148
Carrington, The, 145
Cavalry and Guards Club, 33–4, 189, 242, 251, 293, 296, 302
  Ascot tent, 17
  freehold status of, 240
  listed status of, 239
  mergers and acquisitions, 323
  motto, 242
  prime ministers and, 300
Cavalry Club, The, 34, 305, 323, 328, 361
Century, 127–8, 293, 297, 302, 322
CEO Club London, 153–4
CEO Club, Kyiv, 153–4
Cercle de l'Union Interalliée, Paris, 276
Chamberlain, Neville, 300
Chelsea Arts Club, 44, 286, 293, 296, 302
  architecture, 232, *236*
  listed status, 238
  gaming and, 275, 276

Index

Churchill, Winston, 6, 62–3, 85, 298, 300, 353–4, 375
City Carlton Club, The, 60
City Liberal Club, 60
City Livery Club, The, 72, 242, 324
City of London Club, 69, 240, 242, 293, 297, 299, 302
City University Club, 69–70, 72, 238, 293, 296, 302, 323
Civil Service Club, 73–4, 293, 297, 328
Clermont Club, 8, 100, 122, 221, 275
Cloud Twelve, 164, 297
Club at the Ivy *see* Ivy Club
Club for Acts and Actors, The, 44–5, 240, 296
Club Managers Association of Europe, 251
Clubhouse, The, 154–5, 297
Cocoa Tree Club, 322
Colony Club, 135
Colony Room Club, 94, 127
Columbia Club, 148–9
Commonwealth Club, 301
Concert Artistes' Association, 45
Conduit, The, 128–9, 239, 297, 301
Connaught House Club, 148–9
Conservative Club, The, 60, 274, 323
Constitutional Club, The, 60, 232, *236*, 300, 323, 324–5
Cosmopolitan Club, 322
Cosmos Club, Washington, DC, 276
Cowdray Club, 37, 323
Crockford, William, 224
Crockford's, 119–20, 224, 226, 299
Croker, John Wilson, 26, 224–5
Crown London Aspinall's *see* Aspinall's
Curtain Club, 297

Dally, The, 129–30, 297
Danish Club, 324
Dartmouth House, 145–6, 239
Den Norske Klub, 37, 293, 324
Derby, Edward Smith-Stanley, 14th Earl, 272, 299
Devonshire, William Cavendish, 4th Duke, 298
Devonshire Club, 10, 35 60, 300, 326
Dickens, Charles, 257
Disraeli, Benjamin, 61, 299
Distinguished Clubs, 250

Distinguished Clubs of the World, 250
Douglas-Home, Alec, 300
Durham, John Lambton, 1st Earl, 225
Dutch Club, 323

East India Club, 34–6, 262, 286, 293, 297, 302
  architecture, 231, 233
  Devonshire Club, 10, 35 60, 300, 326
  Eccentric Club, 35, 53, 141, 242, 244, 323
  freehold status, 240
  gaming and, 275, 276
  listed status, 239
  mergers and acquisitions, 322–3
  motto, 242
  Public Schools Club, 35–6, 323
  Sports Club, 35, 322
  wartime lodgings, 326
East India United Service Club, The, 36
Eccentric Club, 35, 53, 141, 242, 244, 323
Eden, Anthony, 300
Egerton Club, 322
Eight, 155–6, 293, 297
Electric House, 111–12, 239, 293
Emblehope and Burngrange Estate, 172–3
Empress and Royal Societies' Club, 323
Empress Club, 322–3
Estelle Manor, 160–61, 173
Europe House Club, 324

Farmers Club, 74–5, 189–90, 239, 293, 296, 301, 302
Female Coterie (Ladies' Boodle's), 220
Festival Club *see* Brydges Place Club
50 Pall Mall, 219, 223
5 Hertford Street, 1, 93, 105–6, 223, 239, 293, 297, 301
Flyfishers' Club, 52–3, 242, 297, 324, 326
40 Greek St, 109–10, 239, 286, 293
Fox Club, The, 10, 19, 386–7
Free French Officers' Club, 137
Free Trade Club, 36
Freemasons, 3
Fry, Stephen, 131, 287, 334, 343

431

Frontline Club, 130–31, 190, 293, 297, 302

Garrick Club, 11–13, 45–7, 251, 286, 301, 302, 324, 326
  anniversaries, 293
  architecture of, 231
  Ascot tent, 17
  Dickens–Thackeray feud, 257
  in film, 344
  freehold status, 240
  gaming and, 274, 276
  listed status, 239
  membership list leak (2024), 11–13
  motto, 242
  snooker at, 276
  wartime lodgings at, 326
  women, admission of, 297
General Military Club, 322
George, 101–2, 222, 293, 297, 304
Gerry's, 96–7, 239, 293, 297
Gladstone, William Ewart, 67, 299
Goat Club, 37, 323
Goderich, Frederick John Robinson, 1st Viscount, 299
Gold Alliance, 251
Golfers' Club, 322–3
Grafton, Augustus FitzRoy, 3rd Duke, 298
Graham's, 322
Grenville, George, 298
Grenville, William Wyndham, 1st Baron, 299
Grey, Charles, 2nd Earl, 225, 246, 299, 386–7
Grillion's, 299
Groucho Club, 92, 124, 131–2, 171–2, 286, 297, 302
  anniversaries, 293
  snooker at, 276
Guards Club, The, 34, 274, 300, 323, 324, 381
Guildhall Club, 70–71, 293, 296, 302

Half-Circle Club, 322
h-Club, 10
Ham Common Polo Club *see* Ham Polo Club
Ham Polo Club, 84
Harry's Bar, 102–3, 222, 293, 297, 362

Heath, Edward, 300
Helena Club, 149
High Road House, 112–13, 293
Hogarth Club, 322
Home Grown club, 37, 118–19, 297
Home House, 117–18, 293, 297, 341, 344
House of Commons, 63–4, 286, 296, 302, 304
  Sports and Social Club, 63
House of KOKO, The, 159–60, 297
House of Lords, 64–6, 251, 274, 286, 296, 302
Hurlingham Club, 85–6, 88, 89, 183, 190, 293, 296, 302, 304
  freehold status, 240
  gaming and, 274, 275
  listed status, 238
  prime ministers and, 300

In and Out Club *see* Naval and Military Club
Inter-Club Younger Members' Group, 251
International Associate Clubs, 252
Ivy Club, 135, 137–8, 168, 293, 297

Jockey Club, 364, 375
Johnson, Boris, 62, 105, 301
Junior Army and Navy Club, 37, 323
Junior Athenæum, 322
Junior Carlton Club, The, 25, 60–61, 274, 299–300, 323, 324–5
Junior Conservative Club, The, 60
Junior Constitutional Club, The, 60
Junior Naval and Military Club, 37, 322
Junior United Service Club, 255, 323

Keystone Crescent, 168–9, 297
Kit-Cat Club, 298

Ladies' Alpine Club, 323
Ladies' Carlton Club, 37, 60, 323
Ladies' Empire Club, 323
Ladies' Imperial Club, 322
Ladies' Town and Country Club, 148–9
Lady Golfers' Club, 323
Langham Sketch Club, 47–8, 297
Lansdowne Club, 66, 75–6, 262, 293, 297, 302, 322, 325
  architecture, 233, *237*

freehold status, 240
gaming and, 274, 275
listed status, 239
wartime lodgings at, 326
Le Beaujolais Club, 136–7, 239, 293, 297
Le Réunion des Gastronomes, 251
League of Club Chefs, 251
Leeds and County Liberal Club, 233
Les Ambassadeurs, 120–1
Library club, 153
Little House, Balham, 113
Little House, Mayfair, 113–14, 293
Little Houses, 164–5
Little Ship Club, 71–2, 324, 296, 302
    City Livery Club, The, 72, 242, 324
Liverpool, Robert Jenkinson, 2nd Earl, 299
Lloyd George, David, 62, 300, 353–4
Lloyds Club, 70, 323
Londonderry, Robert Stewart, 2nd Marquess, 224
London Sketch Club, 47–8, 232, 240, 293, 297, 302, 310
London's ladies' club, 77
Lyceum Club, 77, 226–7
Lyford Cay Club, Bahamas, 365

MacDonald, Ramsay, 300
Macmillan, Harold, 6, 300
Magic Circle, The, 48–9, 240, 242, 244, 296, 304
Maison Estelle, 160–61, 173, 238, 297
Major, John, 301
Manchester Reform Club, 233
Mark's Club, 103, 222, 293, 297, 301, 302
Marlborough Club, 323, 326
Marlborough-Windham Club, 323
Marylebone Cricket Club (MMC), 86–7, 183, 239, 240, 274, 275, 296, 300–301, 302
Maslow's Group Clubs, 122–4
Massingberd, Emily Langton, 225–6
Maxime's, New York, 223
May, Theresa, 301
Melbourne, William Lamb, 2nd Viscount, 299
Metropolitan Club, Washington, DC, 373
Minerva Club, 148–9

Ministry, The, 156–7, 297
Mortimer House, 123–4, 297
Mosimann's, 135, 138–9, 238, 293, 297

National Club, 61, 297, 324
National Labour Club, 60, 300, 322
National Liberal Club, 66–7, 190, 286, 290, 302, 322, 324–5, 341–2
    anniversaries, 293
    architecture of, 232
    Authors Club, The, 66, 242, 324
    dress code, 309
    in film, 344
    IRA bombings, 328
    listed status, 239
    song, 248–9
    gaming and, 275, 276
    listed status of, 239
    prime ministers and, 299–300
    snooker at, 276
    women, admission of, 296
National Sporting Club, 283–4
Naval and Military Club (In and Out Club), 36–8, 144, 286, 293, 296, 302, 348, 350
    architecture and, 230
    bomb damage, 328
    Canning Club, 37, 324
    Cowdray Club, 37, 323
    Den Norske Klub, 37, 293, 324
    freehold status of, 241
    gaming and, 274, 275
    Goat Club, 37, 323
    Junior Army and Navy Club, 37, 323
    Junior Naval and Military Club, 37, 322
    Ladies' Carlton Club, 37, 60, 323
    mergers and clubs within, 37, 322–3, 324–5
    motto, 242
    New Cavendish Club, 37, 119, 323
    Royal Cruising Club, 37, 323
    United Service Club, 25, 37, 230–31, 234, 299, 322–3, 324–5
Naval Club, The, 32, 322–3, 324, 346
Ned's Club, 114–15
New Cavendish Club, 37, 119, 323
New Evaristo Club, 97–98, 242 293, 297, 342
New Oxford and Cambridge Club, 322

New University Club, 27, 233, 322
Newcastle, William Cavendish, 1st Duke, 298
NEXUS Club, 165–6, 297
Nikita, 169–70
1920 Club, 300, 322
North, Frederick, Lord, 298

Ocean Racing Club *see* Royal Ocean Racing Club
Ognisko Polskie (The Polish Hearth), 59–60, 241, 297
ONDA, 252
1 Warwick, 122–3, 297
180 House, 111
Ootacamund Club, The, 276
Oriental Club, 35, 38–40, 189, 251, 293, 296, 302, 304, 322
    Alfred Club, 39, 322
    foundation of, 227
    freehold status, 241
    gaming and, 275, 276
    prime ministers and, 299
    recipes, 374, 379
Orleans Club, 170, 326
Orly's House, 165
Oswald's, 106–7, 223, 297, 302
Other House, The 146–7
Oxford and Cambridge Club, 26–8, 262, 286, 293, 296, 302
    architecture, 231
    gaming and, 274, 275, 276
    listed status, 239
    mergers and acquisitions, 323
    New University Club, 27, 233, 322
    prime ministers and, 299–300
    United University Club, 27, 233, 299–300, 322–3

Pall Mall
    50 Pall Mall, 219, 223
    67 Pall Mall, 135–6, 239, 297, 302
Palmerston, Henry John Temple, 3rd Viscount, 144, 299
Parliamentary Labour Club, 300, 322
Pasley Tyler, 157, 238, 297
Pathfinder Club, 323
Pavilion Club, 158
Peel, Robert, 299

Pegu Club, Rangoon, 365
Pelham, Henry 298
Perceval, Spencer, 299
Phoenix Arts Club (the Phoenix Artist Club), 98
Pioneer Club, 225–6, 322
Pitt the Elder, William, 298
Pitt the Younger, William, 24, 299
Playboy Enterprises, 120, 122, 221
Playgoers' Club, 45
Portland Club, The, 32, 274, 297, 324
Portland, William Cavendish-Bentinck, 3rd Duke, 299
Pratt, William Nathaniel, 56–7, 226, 233
Pratt's, 13, 56–7, 226, 233, 239, 241, 293, 297, 300–301, 302
Prince's Club, 88
Public Schools Club, 35–6, 323
Purple Dragon, 166–7, 293, 297
Putney Constitutional Club, 68

Queen's Club, 87–8, 190, 293, 302, 345
Queensberry, John Douglas, 9th Marquess, 283
Quent's, 8, 119–20
Quo Vadis, 135, 139–40, 239, 276, 293

Racquet and Tennis Club, New York, 101
Ranelagh Club, 89
Real Casino, Madrid, 276
Reform Club, 3, 28–9, 60, 286, 293, 296, 302, 305, 311, 326
    architecture of, 231, 237
    in film, 345, 346
    foundations of, 225
    gaming and, 274, 275, 276
    listed status of, 239
    prime ministers and, 299–300, 353
    recipes, 378, 383–4
    sobriquets, 244
    song, 246–8
Rehearsal Club, 45
Ritz Club, 120–21
RNVR Club *see* Naval Club
Rockingham, Charles Watson-Wentworth, 2nd Marquess, 298
Roehampton Club, 88–9, 190, 241, 274, 293, 297, 300, 302, 304, 341
Roof Gardens, The, 161–2, 297

Rosebery, Archibald Primrose, 5th Earl, 299
Royal Aero Club, 325
Royal Air Force Club (RAF), 76–7, 189, 233, 238, 262, 286, 293, 302
  freehold status, 241
  motto, 242
  women, admission of, 296
Royal Anglo-Belgian Club, 325
Royal Automobile Club (RAC), 78–9, 170, 175, 286, 289, 293, 302, 332, 341
  architecture of, 232, 233
  in film, 345
  gaming and, 274, 275, 276
  listed status of, 239
  prime ministers and, 300
  recipes, 365
  women, admission of, 296
Royal Cruising Club, 37, 323
Royal Kennel Club, 49–50, 172, 174, 240–41, 242, 293, 296
Royal Ocean Racing Club, 89–90, 241, 293, 297, 300
Royal Over-Seas League (ROSL), 79–80, 238, 241, 242, 293, 297, 302
Royal Societies' Club, 322
Royal Thames Yacht Club, 90–91, 189, 241, 297, 300, 302, 323, 325
Russell, John, 1st Earl, 246, 299, 386–7

Salisbury, Robert Gascoyne-Cecil, 3rd Marquess, 299
Salmagundi Club, New York, 298
Savage Club, 50–51, 238, 243, 244, 286, 293, 297, 302, 325, 326
Savile Club, 52–3, 189, 286, 293, 297, 302, 311, 324
  club motto, 243
  in film, 346
  Flyfishers Club, The, 52–3, 242, 297, 324, 326
  gaming and, 274, 276, 277–282
  prime ministers and, 300
  sobriquets, 244
Schuylkill Fishing Company, Andalusia, 364
Service Women's Club, 149
Sesame Club, 322–3
76 Dean Street, 110–11, 293

Shelburne, William Petty, 2nd Earl, 298
Shoreditch Arts Club, 132, 297
Shoreditch House, 115–16, 293
Siegi's Club, 103
67 Pall Mall, 135–6, 239, 297, 302
Sloane Club, 148–9, 293, 296, 302
Smedley, Anne Constance, 226–7
Snail Club, 135, 140–41, 238, 243, 297, 304
Society of Dilettanti, 19
Soho Farmhouse, 173–4
Soho House chain, 1, 93, 107–17, 138, 168, 170, 171, 173–4, 238, 252, 297
Soho Mews House, 116
Solly, Henry 227
Special Forces Club (SF Club), 40–41, 189, 243, 293, 297, 302
Sports and Social Club, 63
Sports Club, 35, 322
St Andrew's Club, 322
St James's Club, The, 19, 147, 274, 293, 322–3
St James's Hotel and Club, 147–8
St Stephen's Club, 299, 300–301, 322–3, 324
Starmer, Keir, 301
Stoneleigh Park, 174–5
Stratford Club, 39, 274
Sunak, Rishi, 129, 301
Surrenne, 342
Ten Trinity Square, 149–50, 239, 297
Thackeray, William Makepeace, 257
Thames Yacht Club *see* Royal Thames Yacht Club
Thatched House Club, 61, 323
Thatcher, Margaret, 21, 298, 301
Tramp, 162–3, 293
Travellers Club, 30–31, 251, 286, 297, 302, 305, 324–5, 350–51
  anniversaries, 293
  architecture, 229, 231
  in film, 346
  foundation of, 224
  gaming and, 275
  listed status, 239
  prime ministers and, 299–300
  recipes, 380
  reciprocation, 290
  sobriquets, 244
  wartime lodgings at, 326

435

Trisha's *see* New Evaristo Club
Truss, Liz, 105, 301
Turf Club, 22–3, 229, 274, 293, 297, 300, 302, 305, 331
12 Hay Hill, 151–2, 293, 297
Twentieth Century Club, 148–9
Twenty Two, The, 150, 239, 297
Twickenham country club, 170

UnHerd Club, 135, 141–2
Union Club, 133, 230–31, 238, 285, 293, 297, 299, 323
Union Jack Club, 80–81, 82, 262, 293, 328
United Clergy and Laity Club, 325
United Club and Hotel, 325
United Oxford and Cambridge Club, 323
United Service Club, 25, 37, 230–31, *234*, 299, 322–3, 324–5
United University Club, 27, 233, 299–300, 322–3
University Club for Ladies *see* University Women's Club
University Women's Club, 53–4, 230, 241, 293, 297, 302
Upstairs at the Department Store, 133–4, 297
Upstairs Club at L'Escargot *see* Snail Club

Veterans' Club *see* Victory Services Club
Victory Services Club, 81–2, 262, 293, 328, 341
Voluntary Aid Detachment Ladies' Club, 37, 119
Vout-O-Reenee's, 134–5, 293, 297

Walbrook Club, 99, 104, 156, 293, 297, 302
Walpole, Robert, 298
Wellington, Arthur Wellesley, 1st Duke, 6, 32, 39, 227–8, 299
Weltje's, 322
Westminster Reform Club, 299
White City House, 116–17, 239
White's, 12, 23–4, 60, 99, 180, 251, 286, 293, 297, 302, 331, 342
  architecture, 229
  betting book, 268–73
  foundation of, 220
  freehold status, 240
  gaming and, 274, 276, 285
  listed status, 238
  mergers and acquisitions, 322
  motto, 243
  prime ministers and, 298–301
  recipes, 377
Whitehall Club, 322
Wilmington, Spencer Compton, 1st Earl, 298
Wilson, Harold, 300
Winchester House Club, 67–8, 238, 243, 293
Windham Club, 325, 326
Woodcote Park, 175–6
Working Men's Club and Institute Union, 227

Yeoman Warders Club, 41–2, 239, 296, 342